ROYAL NAVY
HANDBOOK
1914–1918

ROYAL NAVY
HANDBOOK
1914–1918

DAVID WRAGG

SUTTON PUBLISHING

First published in the United Kingdom in 2006 by
Sutton Publishing Limited · Phoenix Mill
Thrupp · Stroud · Gloucestershire · GL5 2BU

British Library Cataloguing in Publication Data
A catalogue record for this book is available from the British Library.

ISBN 0-7509-4203-7

Typeset in 10/13pt New Baskerville.
Typesetting and origination by
Sutton Publishing Limited.
Printed and bound in England by
J.H. Haynes & Co. Ltd, Sparkford.

CONTENTS

INTRODUCTION

The Royal Navy in 1914 was the largest in the world, largely because of the many years in which British defence policy had had as its cornerstone the so-called 'two-power standard', meaning that the fleet had to be equal to the combined strength of any other two fleets in the world. This was partly the result of the United Kingdom's having created the greatest empire the world had ever seen, but it was also a reflection of the fact that the United States had still to discover sea power, while Germany was itself a new creation that had only just embarked on a major warship construction programme. Neither Germany nor Japan had a major shipbuilding industry at the turn of the century, although both were well on the way to creating one.

Despite the power inherent in such a fleet, here was much that was uneven about the service. It had benefited from the attentions of a dynamic First Sea Lord, Admiral of the Fleet Lord 'Jacky' Fisher, who had thrown out many ships that 'could neither fight nor run away', been responsible for the creation of the modern battleship, the dreadnought, and had recognised the importance of submarines and aviation. Yet, it had also suffered from almost a century without major fleet actions, and the initiative allowed to the commanders of warships, and especially smaller warships,

during Nelson's time had been lost in a service more concerned with fleet manoeuvres and evolutions. On many ships, polished brass had become more important than gunnery practice. The Admiralty still contained many who believed that experiment and innovation should be avoided. Worst of all, the Royal Navy had been neglected by the pre-war Liberal governments, allowing the United Kingdom's greatest rival in Europe, Germany, to begin to close the gap with an energetic programme of warship construction.

Even so, the fleet of 1914 compared well with the number of surface vessels available to the Royal Navy a quarter of a century later. The navy had also been one of the first to take aviation seriously, although this was not reflected throughout the fleet. That other new arrival, the submarine, was still regarded as being unsporting and un-British.

For many, the First World War at sea means Jutland, the great set-piece sea battle from which so much was expected. It was far more than Jutland. The Royal Navy was thrashed at Coronel; emerged victorious at the Falkland Islands; fought many inconclusive actions; was the first to lose a major warship, the armoured cruiser *Pathfinder*, to submarine attack; suffered the greatest naval disaster of the war when three armoured cruisers were sunk by a single U-boat within just one hour; used seaplanes offensively for the first time; was given responsibility for the air defence of the United Kingdom; and won the battle of Dogger Bank. Jutland was a tactical defeat, but conceivably a strategic victory, as the German High Seas Fleet remained in port afterwards. Much has been written about the disastrous Gallipoli or Dardanelles campaign, in which the Royal Navy played an important part, but there were also plans for an invasion of Germany's Baltic coast; both were plans to shorten the war. The Royal Navy was also slow to introduce a convoy system, and indeed argued against it until merchant shipping losses nearly brought the country to its knees.

The war cost the Royal Navy 2 dreadnoughts, 3 battlecruisers, 11 pre-dreadnought battleships, 25 cruisers, 54 submarines, 64 destroyers and 10 torpedo boats, and the lives of 34,642 men, almost a fifth of them in the great naval battle at Jutland, with another 4,510 wounded.

Complementing the author's *Royal Navy Handbook 1939–1945* and *Fleet Air Arm Handbook 1939–1945*, this book tells the story of how the Royal Navy adapted to the demands of war, beginning with a look at the service in 1914, and the way in which the Royal Navy's command structure worked. The chapters that follow show how the Royal Navy fared, with narrative covering the major wartime engagements, and look at the role of the still-young submarine service and of naval aviation. The appendices provide details of the main classes of warship, as well as the main naval bases and stations at home and abroad, details of ranks and insignia, medals and decorations and the training of both officers and men.

ACKNOWLEDGEMENTS

In researching and compiling a book such as this, an author is heavily dependent on the help and assistance of many others. In particular, like many other researchers, I am grateful to Jerry Shore, assistant curator and archivist of the Fleet Air Arm Museum, and his enthusiastic team; to the Photographic Archive team at the Imperial War Museum; to Stephen Courtney of the Royal Naval Museum, Portsmouth, and to Stephen Snelling, author of *VCs of the First World War – The Naval VCs*, for their assistance with photographic material.

No work on something as vast as our First World War Royal Navy can cover every inch of ground, and I would recommend those whose appetite is whetted by this book to consult the bibliography at the back. There you will find accounts of the war at sea from every perspective, including the all-important personal accounts, as well as volumes of sheer factual matter.

David Wragg
Edinburgh
Summer 2006

CHAPTER ONE

MORE THAN A CENTURY AFTER TRAFALGAR

The navy is an impenetrable mystery surrounded by seasickness.
AF Lord Fisher

The shadow of Nelson's great victory at Trafalgar in 1805 still reached out to the Royal Navy at the dawn of the twentieth century. The ships had changed, and so had the uniforms, but there had been no major fleet actions over the intervening years to test the readiness of the service for the new weapons and new means of propulsion that had arrived in the meantime. Naval officers of the day still harked back to this famous victory, although, of course, none of them had been there. Not that the Royal Navy had been completely out of touch with modern developments. It is all too often overlooked that Trafalgar was Nelson's third victory, after the Battle of the Nile, or Aboukir Bay, in 1798, and Copenhagen in 1801. In many ways, Copenhagen was a more daring and dashing victory, since finding that the Danes would not set sail, Nelson sent frigates into the port to ferret them out. Just a few years later, in 1807, the Royal Navy was back at Copenhagen, using artillery rockets for the first time in the West to bombard the city. Originally invented by the Chinese, artillery rockets had reached Europe via India, where they had been used by the Tipu Sultan's troops against the Duke

of Wellington's forces in 1799. Reinvented by Sir William Congreve, who test fired his rockets in 1805, the artillery rocket was effective over a longer range than cannon. The bombardment of Copenhagen on 2–4 September 1807 used incendiary rockets and had such an effect that, on 5 September, the Danes surrendered their fleet after suffering 200 naval and army personnel killed and another 350 wounded; as a foretaste of the shape of wars to come, 1,600 civilians were killed and another 1,000 wounded. Having lost the best of its fleet, Denmark was reduced to waging a 'gunboat war' against the Royal Navy.

The following year, eighteen 'rocket boats' bombarded Boulogne and set the town on fire.

A good idea of the might of the Royal Navy early in the nineteenth century can be gained from the fact that it possessed 120 ships of the line, against 40 for France, 30 for Spain and 20 for the Netherlands.

After France pressured Russia to join the 'Continental System' in 1807, the Russian fleet became another obstacle to be surmounted by the Royal Navy. As the Russian Mediterranean Fleet sailed home after fighting with Turkish forces in September 1808, it was blockaded in Lisbon by the Royal Navy and the crews were only allowed safe passage home after the ships had been surrendered.

As war with France and her allies and satellite states continued, British interference with neutral shipping so angered the United States that war between the two countries broke out in June 1812. US policy was to some extent coloured by the ambition to take Canada from the British. A number of mostly minor naval engagements followed, including actions on Lake Erie in 1813 and Lake Champlain the following year. Nevertheless, by 1816, a combined British, American and Dutch naval squadron was active in the Mediterranean against the Barbary pirates who had spread terror from their bases in North Africa. This was the first action that saw the United States involved across the Atlantic and in alliance with the British. British and Dutch ships also bombarded Algiers.

THE AGE OF STEAM AND ARMOUR

While steam made its appearance aboard shipping well before the first passenger-carrying railways, at first this was confined to merchant shipping, and especially canal and river craft. Even so, the last major naval battle to be fought completely under sail was during the Greek War of Independence, at Navarino in 1827, when a Turkish and Egyptian combined fleet was confronted by an Anglo-French–Russian fleet led by Vice Adm Sir Edward Codrington, RN.

The Turko-Egyptian fleet was heavily outnumbered by its opponents, with just seven ships of the line against four each from the UK, France and Russia. While both sides wanted action, Codrington was under orders to engage the enemy simply as a last

resort, and negotiations were put in hand when the two fleets met in Navarino Bay, on the south-west coast of the Peloponnese peninsula. Ships' boats shuttled between the ships of the two sides, and when one boat was fired on by mistake by Turkish troops who mistook it for a boarding party, one of the British ships fired a cannon shot, and soon everyone was firing. A battle then ensued, during which the Turks lost one ship of the line, twelve frigates out of fifteen, and twenty-two of their twenty-six corvettes. Turkish gunnery was poor, and even when fireships were used, they caused more damage to their own side than to their enemies.

By the time of the Crimean War in 1853, a number of warships were steam-powered, although it remained usual for a full set of sails to be retained. The reasons for warships retaining sail and for navies being reluctant at first to consider steam propulsion were practical rather than conservative. The early steamships were propelled by paddles that were not only vulnerable to cannon fire, but also took up so much space on the sides of ships that they reduced the number of cannon that could be carried. It was not until the advent of screw propulsion in 1829 that steam became a viable option as auxiliary power for frigates, but the first steam-powered ship of the line did not appear until 1848.

The changes in propulsion were accompanied by changes in armament. First, rifling of cannon improved accuracy, and then, in 1821, the Frenchman Henri-Joseph Paixhans invented the explosive shell, which was so devastating against wooden hulls that there was a rush to introduce armour plating, initially over the wooden hulls. By this time, despite its numerical strength, the Royal Navy was lagging behind in technology. The French were the first to introduce an all-armoured warship, the frigate

Gloire in 1859, but during the Crimean War they had used batteries towed by tugs.

British and French involvement in the Crimean War really dated from 1854, when steamships sped the movement of an Anglo-French expeditionary force of 60,000 men. In October, the bombardment of Sevastopol took place, with six screw-driven steamships involved, supported by another twenty-one sailing ships of the line, which had to be towed into position by steam tugs. Beginning at noon on 17 October, the operation should have had a crippling effect on the Russian defenders, but the opposite proved to be the case; there was little damage to the defences, while the attacking fleet received so much damage in six hours that many ships were badly damaged and 340 men were killed or wounded. The age of the wooden wall had ended and that of the armoured warship had begun.

These developments could not conceal the fact that the Royal Navy spent most of the nineteenth century on the sidelines, a massive instrument of power. It could be argued that the policy of maintaining a fleet that was the equal of any two others was the ultimate deterrent, and that the long Victorian era that was largely peaceful was the result of this policy. Other factors also need to be taken into consideration. Germany and Italy were only just becoming unified national entities, while the United States had still to recognise the potential of sea power, and was in any case preoccupied with the Americas. France took some time to recover from its Napoleonic defeats.

The American Civil War, 1861–5, did not affect the Royal Navy directly, but it did see much progress in naval warfare. Afloat, as well as ashore, this conflict saw the beginnings of modern warfare. As early as August 1861, Unionist forces used a captive balloon aboard a ship for artillery observation. Mines and submersibles made their appearance, and the famous battle between the armoured ships *Merrimack* and *Monitor* showed that armour could defeat explosive shells, at least of the kind then available. A primitive submarine sank a blockade ship using a 'spear' torpedo, just one of thirty-two ships that were sunk by the new underwater weapons of mine or torpedo during this conflict.

Other changes were also taking place that would influence the deployment of the Royal Navy during the following century. The opening of the Suez Canal in 1869 meant that the Mediterranean, which had become something of a backwater following the Battle of Lepanto in 1571, once again assumed strategic importance. Indeed, it became a vital thoroughfare, more important than at any time since the end of the crusades, or perhaps even the fall of the Roman Empire. Almost overnight, Gibraltar, Malta and Alexandria became important for the Royal Navy.

The 'spear' torpedo had its equivalent in the surface fleet with the advent of the ram, a forward projection on the bows of battleships, mainly beneath the waterline. While in the two world wars, warship commanders would, in desperation, ram an enemy submarine caught on the surface, as an instrument of warfare in its own right and in manoeuvres the ram was to prove not just an overrated weapon, but a hazard to one's own side. In fact, one of the most successful actions in which ramming played a vital part, the battle between Austria and Italy off Lissa on 20 July 1866, saw the Austrian warships 'ram' Italian ships even though none of their vessels had a proper ram, but simply a cutwater formed by the joint of the armour plating. The Italians lost two ships and 612 men, while the Austrians had one ship badly damaged and lost thirty-eight men. One outcome of this battle was the realisation that the ironclad was vulnerable because of the immense weight of its thick armour – as thick as 24in in one example – which made them difficult to handle, and top-heavy.

The ram was a weapon that belonged to an earlier age, one in which ships made physical contact, getting as close to the enemy as possible. It did not belong to an age in which gunnery ranges were opening up, with opposing fleets several miles away. Not only was the period of close contact, of getting alongside the enemy, past, but the rams could be a hazard to other ships when steaming in close proximity.

In 1893, the Mediterranean Fleet under the command of Vice Adm Sir George Tryon was steaming in two parallel divisions when Tryon ordered them to reverse course with each column turning inwards, a manoeuvre that required the ships to be some distance apart before it started. Aboard one of the leading ships, *Camperdown*, was Rear Adm Markham, who soon realised that the distance between his ship and the other leading ship, *Victoria*, with Tryon aboard, was less than their combined turning circles, meaning that a collision was inevitable unless the order was changed. The state of mind of even senior officers in the Royal Navy at the time was that no one dared say a word, even though the inevitability of disaster was soon apparent to many officers on the bridges of both ships. Tryon alone was oblivious to impending disaster. As a result, *Camperdown* cut through the side of *Victoria*, killing Tryon and 360 officers and men. Had the ships not had rams, the collision would have been far less disastrous.

Victoria was, incidentally, an example of much else that was wrong with the Royal Navy at the time. Her 16.25in guns were so heavy that their muzzles sagged under their own weight and they had never been fired with a full explosive charge.

MENACE BENEATH THE WAVES

Torpedo development continued apace as it became clear that, in most cases, warfare at sea would involve opposing fleets being further apart, and that close contact with the enemy would no longer be desirable, or indeed possible, as the range of naval artillery increased. The Austrian navy attempted the development of self-propelled torpedoes, but it took an Englishman working at Fiume, Robert Whitehead, to perfect this in 1869. The Whitehead torpedo used compressed air and could run submerged at 6kts for 300yd carrying an 18lb explosive in the nose. It was soon improved by the addition of a gyroscope to ensure that it remained on course. The following year, 1870, the Royal Navy was the first to purchase this weapon.

A variation on the Whitehead was the towed torpedo or Harvey, named after Cdr Harvey, RN, which was launched from the deck of a steamship and towed by wire, before diverging from the track of the towing vessel and heading off at an angle of 45 degrees. On reaching the target, it could be exploded by contact, although electric detonation was also possible. In fact, the Harvey never fulfilled its promise, and it fell to the rival Whitehead torpedo to score the first success.

Mine warfare also began to make an impact, the leading proponents being the Russians; they were the first to use the Whitehead torpedo in anger when, on 26 January 1878, Russian torpedo boats sank the Turkish warship *Intibah*. That was the same year that John P. Holland built his first submarine. It was in 1885 that the Swedish submarine *Nordenfelt I* entered service, not only carrying a Whitehead torpedo in an external bow casing, but also being the first submarine to carry a surface armament.

The world's navies had a fixation with the power of the torpedo during the early twentieth century. Extensive defensive measures were taken and, of course, every navy had to have torpedo boats, such as *TB116* shown here. Submarines were regarded with scorn. *(IWM Q 22011)*

At first, the Royal Navy had little success with breech-loading guns, and after some accidents returned to muzzle-loading. Meanwhile, debate continued over whether warships should have a central battery of guns, which had replaced the long lines of cannon on both sides of ships as steam had started to take over from sail, or use a turret system, as with the US *Monitor*. Capt Coles, one of the leading British advocates of the turret system, was allowed to design HMS *Captain*, a turret ship for the Royal Navy, but she proved to be top-heavy and capsised in the Atlantic on 7 September 1870. Nevertheless, the Admiralty's own design, HMS *Monarch*, proved to be more successful. Neither ship would have been a practical proposition, as the sail rig cluttered the deck and limited the radius of fire of the guns. It was not until HMS *Devastation* entered service in 1873 that the Royal Navy received its first major warship without sails and with turrets, and she served successfully with the fleet until the early twentieth century.

Even with turrets, forward firing of guns could be difficult with the rise of the forecastle towards the bow, especially as at this stage 'superfiring', that is having B turret higher than A turret, or X higher than Y, had still to appear.

A number of experimental designs entered service with the Royal Navy during the late nineteenth century, including HMS *Agamemnon* in 1883, one of the ugliest ships to see service with the fleet, which had turrets placed amidships on either side able to fire forward and aft. Spurred on by a new Italian warship with 17.7in guns and armour plating confined to protection of the machinery, magazines and turrets, the Royal Navy ordered what was the largest warship of its day, HMS *Inflexible*, 11,000 tons, with four 16in muzzle-loaded guns, and capable of 15kts. The new ship came with two 60ft torpedo boats, which for the first time had submerged tubes, anti-rolling tanks and electric light. This concept of having torpedo boats aboard a larger ship was to be resurrected during the Second World War, but never came to anything in practice.

The Royal Navy was not alone in testing different approaches to warship design at the time. One German admiral described the new Germany's navy as a collection of prototype designs. *Inflexible* saw action in 1882, when the Mediterranean Fleet bombarded Alexandria in Egypt after a number of Europeans had been massacred. Eight ironclads, including *Inflexible*, shelled the fortifications, a difficult target, against which traditionally ships had been at a disadvantage, as at Sevastopol less than twenty years earlier. Nevertheless, Adm Sir Frederick Seymour's force ensured that the forts were eventually surrendered, while at one of them the powder magazine blew up under shellfire from HMS *Superb*.

One further significant invention was to appear before the century closed. This was the steam turbine, which its inventor, Sir Charles Parsons, had used in the building of a small, fast craft, *Turbinia*, that gate-crashed the Naval Review of 1897, demonstrating beyond all doubt the turbine's superiority over the reciprocating engines then in use. Speed was not the sole advantage of the steam turbine. The new engine had a much lower profile than the reciprocating engines, which on a large ship rose up through the level of several decks. This meant that space existed above the engine for heavy deck armour plating, and the lower centre of gravity also allowed heavier armament to be carried. The massive superstructures that were to become a feature of battleships as the twentieth century progressed would not have been possible with tall, reciprocating engines.

USING THE NEW TECHNOLOGY

Commanding officer of *Inflexible* at the time of the bombardment of Alexandria was Capt John Fisher, a keen-eyed and outspoken naval officer. Fisher was quick to point out that, while the gunnery left much to be desired, it was also hampered by dud shells and poor fuses, with one shell landing amid 300 tons of gunpowder without inflicting any damage. The lack of big breech-loading guns by this time, when the French had already perfected the mechanisms, was a further handicap, leading to an agonisingly slow rate of fire. Fisher's ship had to depress her two twin 16in turrets so that reloading could take place.

Many older ships had survived into the twentieth century, and were given less demanding but important roles. This is the coast defence vessel *Glatton* in dry dock. Note the immense torpedo bulges. *(IWM SP 2003)*

One admiral told his men that everything they saw that was modern was thanks to Lord Fisher. As Second Sea Lord, he reformed many of the conditions for the men of the fleet, and as First Sea Lord was responsible for new ships and, above all, aircraft and submarines. This is Fisher as vice-admiral in 1897. Note the old-style smaller cap, still favoured by many officers during the war years. *(IWM Q 22155)*

Other changes were taking place at the same time. During the eighteenth and nineteenth centuries any ship that 'cruised', or patrolled, was described as a 'cruiser', while in effect most were frigates. But the frigate began to fall out of naval service, to be replaced by the forerunner of the cruiser of the twentieth century. Initially there were two types of cruiser developed: the protected cruiser and the armoured cruiser. The former lacked side armour but were built of steel of varying thickness, while protection was improved by locating the coal bunkers at the sides of the ship and ensuring sufficient watertight divisions of the hull. The first two were the *Iris* and *Mercury* of 1877, the first British ships constructed entirely of steel. Armoured cruisers had heavy armour plating and often heavy armament, but this affected speed and endurance, while placing in jeopardy one of the main duties of the cruiser: reconnaissance. The first cruiser action used the smaller protected cruiser and involved the French Navy in engaging Chinese forces on the Min River in French Indo-China in 1884. Nevertheless, British shipyards soon established a thriving business building cruisers for many of the world's navies.

A cruiser also featured in the outbreak of the Spanish–American War in 1898, when the USS *Maine* blew up at Santiago in Chile, most probably as a result of spontaneous combustion in either her coal bunkers or her magazine, but the Americans suspected Spanish treachery. Nevertheless, the war was unremarkable technically or strategically, but it did persuade the American body politic to take a closer interest in naval matters for the first time.

Fisher became Third Sea Lord and Controller of the Navy in 1892. This was a more than usually distinguished term of office, for he introduced the water tube boiler, thus improving the efficiency of warship propulsion, and also the destroyer, although these ships were far smaller and less heavily armed than those of sixty or seventy years later.

The first genuine major fleet action for the new warships came during the Russo-Japanese War of 1904–5, with the Battle of the Yellow Sea on 10/11 August 1904, which saw the Japanese win, even though they had four battleships against the Russians' six. This was partly a result of superior Japanese tactics and gunnery, but also because the Japanese had overwhelming superiority in destroyers and torpedo boats, which they used to harass the Russians after darkness fell, while their own major fleet units were rested. The war concluded with the major Russian defeat in the great naval battle of Tsushima on 27/8 May 1905. The stately progress of the Russian ships from the Baltic to the Far East had been marked by paranoia over Japanese torpedo boats, which led to an 'engagement' between the Russians and British fishing vessels in the North Sea, and by the necessity for repeated recoaling of the ships. The balance of power was on the side of the Russians, who had eight battleships against the four of the Japanese, although the latter had eight armoured cruisers against one armoured cruiser and three armoured coast defence ships. The Japanese had superiority in cruisers and destroyers, as well as many torpedo boats, which were to play a crucial role in the battle.

At Tsushima, the Russians lost all eight battleships sent to the Far East, with six sunk and two surrendered, while one coastal armoured ship was sunk and another two surrendered, three armoured cruisers were sunk, two cruisers were sunk and three interned, five destroyers were sunk, one interned and another captured, and four of the eight auxiliaries were also sunk. The

Russians lost 5,000 men dead, 500 wounded and 6,000 became prisoners of war, but only after they had broken into their ships' vodka stores and consumed the contents – doubtless starting captivity with a massive hangover.

By contrast, the Japanese lost three torpedo boats, while three battleships and two cruisers were badly damaged. Casualties were 600 dead and wounded.

FISHER

In October 1904, Adm Sir John Fisher became First Sea Lord. He was already well known at the Admiralty, having been Second Sea Lord, responsible for personnel, since 1902, and had already done much to improve conditions for the men of the fleet. He had, as already mentioned, earlier been Third Sea Lord. His elevation more or less

Fisher will always be associated with HMS *Dreadnought*, the first all-big-gun battleship, which made every other battleship obsolete. By the time war came, she had also been surpassed by the so-called 'super-dreadnoughts', such as the Queen Elizabeth class. Note the extensive provision along her sides for torpedo nets. *(IWM Q 21184)*

coincided with a proposal by an Italian engineer, Vittorio Cuniberti, that the ideal battleship for the Royal Navy would be around 17,000 tons displacement, carry an armament of twelve 12in guns capable of firing salvoes, have armour 12in thick over the machinery spaces and magazines, and be capable of 24kts. Such ideas were shared by Fisher, an aggressive, fighting admiral, who saw no point in low speeds or light-weight armaments. The end result of his thinking was HMS *Dreadnought*, the ship that made all other battleships obsolete; subsequently all such vessels would be divided into 'pre-dreadnoughts' and 'dreadnoughts'.

Dreadnought was built within a year at the Portsmouth Royal Dockyard. Turbine-powered, she displaced 17,900 tons, could steam at 21kts and had an armour belt that was 11in thick at its strongest point. Armament consisted of ten 12in guns, and, showing the importance attached to this particular weapon, she also had five submerged 18in torpedo tubes. The feeling of many at the Admiralty was that Fisher had introduced too many innovations in one go, but the nature of the Admiralty was one of ultra-conservatism. Fisher was a man in a hurry, and did not have the time or, just as important, the budgets to introduce innovation piecemeal.

A good example of Admiralty conservatism was to be found in the accommodation aboard warships; with that for officers still being aft, a reflection of the importance of their being near the steering and navigating positions on the quarterdeck of a sailing ship, but a long way from the command and control positions on a ship without sail. *Dreadnought* was the first to have the officers' accommodation forward, so that they could be at their posts within minutes.

The only real drawback with such a radical departure from the accepted standards for a battleship was that the Royal Navy found itself starting again from scratch, losing the advantage that it had previously held over every other navy. With the commissioning of *Dreadnought*, the rest of the British battle fleet was obsolete and would have to be rebuilt. The danger in this was that inherited fleets no longer mattered, and it was the availability of funding and the possession of a substantial shipbuilding industry that would provide the winner in the race to create the twentieth century's most powerful navy. The Imperial German Navy received its first dreadnought, the Nassau class, in 1907, and this proved to be the start of a desperate Anglo-German naval race.

The ideal of having an all-big-gun ship soon had to be compromised. Smaller-calibre, fast-firing guns were also necessary, initially to fend off attacks by torpedo boats; but such armament was also eventually to prove useful, indeed essential, for anti-aircraft warfare once the concept of high angle, HA, or combined high and low angle, HA/LA, weaponry was developed.

The next stage in the development of the twentieth-century fleet was the battlecruiser. The original intention was that this type of ship would have as radical an impact on cruiser design as the *Dreadnought* had had on the battleship, making all earlier vessels obsolete. First of these was *Invincible*, with eight 12in guns and a 6in armoured belt, but with a far higher speed, at 26kts. The intention was that she should be able to blow any enemy cruiser out of the water; but instead of replacing the cruiser, which continued its own development, the battlecruiser became what almost amounted to an intermediate type of vessel, falling between the cruiser and battleship, intended primarily for scouting and reconnaissance ahead of a battle fleet, and for commerce raiding. The weakness of a

HMS *Eden* differed from many other destroyers of the E or River class in having just two funnels, and steam turbines. *(IWM Q 21205)*

battlecruiser was apparent when it encountered an opposing battleship, a situation in which its lack of armour left it vulnerable. This was not to be a ship for fleet actions, but that is where it often found itself. It is debatable whether the battlecruiser ever fulfilled expectations.

Larger still were the Lion class of battlecruisers, with the leadship, *Lion*, launched in 1910, displacing 30,000 tons, heavily armed with 13.5in guns and capable of 28kts. Her sister ship was named *Tiger*, and the class was sometimes referred to as the 'big cats'.

Other changes were taking place. The fear of the torpedo boat had resulted in a countermeasure, the torpedo boat destroyer, and before the First World War broke out, this was already evolving into a larger category of escort vessel, the destroyer. The battle squadrons of the coming conflict were to be escorted by cruisers and destroyers, the former more capable of maintaining station with battleships in the open seas, but the latter having the manoeuvrability necessary for close-quarter actions in coastal and offshore waters. Both types of vessel carried torpedoes, intended for attacks on larger warships, but while this was sometimes the case with destroyer torpedo attacks, for the most part torpedoes fired by surface vessels were used to deliver the *coup de grâce* against enemy ships already crippled by heavy gunfire.

Even though the Admiralty was conservative, by 1900 the Royal Navy did have submarines, with five Holland-type boats in service. Nevertheless, much of the surface fleet was very old, and as late as 1890, the training cruiser was a sailing ship. Fisher incurred the wrath of many senior officers by bringing home from the various fleets, squadrons and overseas stations many older

British warships have always been renowned for their smartness. This is the crew cleaning a warship the hard way. *(IWM Q 22544)*

Warships of the period were far dirtier than later as many were coal-fired. Coal was dirty enough as a fuel, but coaling a ship was a filthy and exhausting exercise, which, on a battleship, might need to be done every eight or ten days. This is aboard the battleship *Australia*. *(IWM Q 18753)*

ships which, in his words, 'could neither fight nor run away'. Many of the ships in reserve were in a similar condition and were scrapped. The senior officers who had preceded him had confused sheer numbers with efficiency, an extreme case of quantity rather than quality. The problem was that there had been no major fleet action between Navarino in 1827 and Tsushima in 1905, and the Royal Navy was absent from the more recent and relevant of these battles.

EVOLUTIONS BEFORE EVOLUTION

Fisher inherited a service that had lost its edge since its victories a hundred years or so earlier. Initiative was stifled. In Nelson's day, the commanding officers of frigates did much of the work of any navy, and the old phrase about 'sending a gunboat' more usually meant sending a frigate, not unlike the role of destroyers and frigates in the latter half of the twentieth century. This responsibility and the limitations of communications at the time meant that initiative was necessary and that commanding officers carried a heavy burden of responsibility. The major ships of the line came together for the big set-piece fleet actions, in which case the role of the frigate was changed, acting both as despatch vessels and also sailing abeam of the battle fleet so that signals from the flagship could be repeated for the benefit of ships some miles astern.

The late-Victorian navy had become obsessed with appearance and with fleet manoeuvres, so that handling the ship successfully and maintaining its place in the formation, fleet evolutions, was more important than being able to fight the ship. Some commanding officers would have their ship repainted every six or seven weeks; with others it could be six months. It was common for the more zealous to augment the paint supplied by the dockyard by paying for additional supplies from their own means. When HMS *Victoria* was lost, her commanding officer, the future Lord Jellicoe and commander of the Grand Fleet, found that his friends had arranged a collection to compensate him for the paint bought before the ship sailed from Malta. The collection raised £75, equal to about £12,000 in today's values.

The present Sovereign has had just three Royal Fleet Reviews in more than fifty years on the throne, but before the First World War these were far more frequent, with Royal Reviews at Spithead in June 1911, another at Dublin and finally one at Weymouth in May 1912. The last was notable for the arrival of Charles Rumney Samson's aeroplane, which stole the show. The Royal Reviews of the Fleet were just the most important of the navy's relations with the community. Instead of being largely out of sight and out of mind, as today, the pre-First World War navy would send ships, sometimes squadrons of ships, into seaside resorts to the delight of the admiring holidaymakers. Before this, in 1891, the Royal Naval Exhibition had attracted 2.5 million visitors, in a country with a far smaller population than today.

The fact that warships were deployed as squadrons was significant. A 'squadron' of warships meant major warships, specifically battleships, battlecruisers or cruisers, or today it would mean aircraft carriers. Destroyers, and today frigates, would have been part of a flotilla, not a squadron. There was no preset number of ships in a squadron other than the fact that it had to be at least two, but in the Victorian and Edwardian navy, and later during the First World War, it more usually would mean four or five major warships. Flotillas could mean a dozen or more.

Aboard ships, spit and polish were far more highly regarded than fighting capability, so that aboard one battleship, the watertight doors had been polished to a degree of thinness that meant that they were useless. Gunnery practice was neglected because it made the ship dirty, and it was not unknown for practice munitions to be quietly dumped overboard.

The irony was that ships did become dirty whenever they had to recoal, a process that took some time, since a battleship or battlecruiser required some 3,000 to 3,500 tons of coal. Loading was largely by hand, apart from the simple hoist that lifted the coal out of the barge or collier; the entire ship's company performed the operation, working at the rate of some 300 tons per hour. Ships used less coal when steaming at a relatively high speed; consumption increased at slow speeds. Coaling was necessary every seven to ten days. As an example, *Dreadnought* could carry 2,900 tons of coal and was regarded as being very economical with a consumption of around 300 tons a day. Aboard destroyers, just four or five men would struggle to bring aboard fifty tons of coal, and the ship could be recoaling every three days if spending much time at sea.

The range and availability of ships improved considerably with the advent of oil firing. Refuelling with oil was cleaner than recoaling and should have been much quicker, but the Royal Navy was to lag behind the United States Navy in the development of under-way replenishment,

One of the super-dreadnoughts was HMS *Orion*. She was part of the Grand Fleet at Jutland. *(IWM Q 39777)*

British ships still using a slow system of transfer with the receiving ship trailing behind the oiler, as naval tankers are known. This situation persisted into the Second World War.

The USN developed the abeam method, which was faster and could also continue in fairly rough weather. The widespread adoption of oil as a fuel was delayed in the Royal Navy, not so much because of conservative attitudes but because of fears over the security of supplies during wartime; the country had scant natural oil resources of its own at this time, but coal was abundant. A sign of the future, however, was that the Queen Elizabeth class ships were oil-fired from the start.

As a side issue, it is worth noting that the contract for supplying oil to the Royal Navy was awarded to British Petroleum, BP, in return for the state's taking a half-share in the company.

CHAPTER TWO

THE ROYAL NAVY IN 1914

Strong nowhere, weak everywhere!
Lord Fisher, 1914

The Royal Navy in 1914 was still the world's largest navy, but was now expected to have to face the fast-growing might of the Imperial German Navy. The Germans had no great history of sea power and indeed, on the creation of the country, had only some fifteen coast defence vessels. This meant that the fleet had to be created from the most unpromising conditions, with no tradition or infrastructure. The service had been regarded as unfashionable and had nothing to offer the more ambitious and patriotic in its early days; for such as these, the only option was the army. The creation of the formidable fighting force that it became was due to Alfred von Tirpitz, the navy minister, backed by the Kaiser, who had long had an ambition to make Germany a great naval power to rival the United Kingdom.

The battlecruiser made the armoured cruiser obsolete. This is HMS *Good Hope* some years before the war. She is flying the flag of a rear admiral. *(IWM Q 21296)*

The advent of the Dreadnought class of battleships and the battlecruiser had given the Royal Navy a head start, but it was no more than that. By declaring all pre-dreadnought ships obsolescent, it had overnight consigned its own vast fleet, if not to the scrap yard, then at least to a poor second place, throwing away its great numerical advantage. The way was open for other navies to match the Royal Navy's pace of warship construction and so erode the two-power standard.

The problem for the Royal Navy in 1914 was much as it remained in 1939–41: while stronger than its opponents, it had so much more to do and was spread so much more thinly as a consequence. Even so, Prof Arthur Marder, the authority on Lord Fisher, has rightly pointed out that the Royal Navy, on the outbreak of war in 1914, lacked:

minelayers,
purpose-built minesweepers,
night gunnery systems,
anti-airship weapons,
anti-submarine equipment and tactics,
efficient torpedoes,
safe harbours.

It also had just eight ships fitted for direction firing, without which bringing a salvo down on an enemy would be difficult.

On the plus side of the equation, the Royal Navy did have a small but growing fleet of submarines and had come to recognise the value of the seaplane carrier. It had the world's largest fleet of dreadnought-type battleships and battle-cruisers, and its most up-to-date light cruisers were a match for anything in service elsewhere.

Yet, there were other problems. All was not well. While a major European war had been expected for some time, little had

Admiral His Serene Highness Prince Louis of Battenberg was First Sea Lord on the outbreak of war, but anti-German feeling was running high and he was forced to resign. *(IWM Q 72596)*

been done to prepare for it. Ships were being built, but the rate of construction was hampered by the reluctance of the Liberal government to pay for a strong navy. The Admiralty was run almost as a club. Working hours were short; civil servants and officers arrived at 10.00 and departed at 16.00, and that included a leisurely lunch. More important, it was not until 1911 that the Admiralty gained a naval staff and a war staff, and there was no staff college until 1912. The credit for these innovations is due to Winston Churchill as First Sea Lord. Despite his enthusiasm for the fleet and for technical innovation, and his recognition that naval warfare would in future be largely influenced by what was under the waves and in the air above them, Fisher failed to grasp strategy and the demands of running a complex fleet under wartime conditions.

While wireless telegraphy had transformed communications, there were severe limitations on what could be achieved. Distances over which W/T could be used effectively were still short, and many ships still had carrier pigeons. Ships without a high masthead, such as submarines, would attempt to raise their aerial to an operational height using kites, not always with success. Many merchant ships and trawlers still lacked any form of wireless at all, and skilled operators capable of tapping out the morse and interpreting the replies were in short supply.

There was much to be learnt about modern warfare. It was not until April 1915 that the first steps towards camouflage were introduced, when the order was given to paint false bow waves on all ships to help confuse U-boat commanders. Later, dapple camouflage schemes came into vogue. Concerned to confuse gunnery directors on enemy warships, canvas baffles were fitted to funnels and superstructure to soften the outline.

Mines could not distinguish between ships, and so in 1907 a Hague Convention had ruled that the open seas should be kept free of these weapons. Warring nations could lay mines only in hostile territorial waters, which at the time meant within three miles of the enemy coastline. This condition

The battleship HMS *Canada* was originally laid down for Chile, but requisitioned by the Admiralty on the outbreak of war. *(IWM SP 171)*

was to be disregarded by the Germans during the war years, tempted by the shallow waters of the North Sea that made it suitable for mines; a total of 25,000 mines were laid during the war years. On the first day of war with the United Kingdom, the converted packet steamer *Königen Luise* was caught by the British in the act of laying mines off the Suffolk coast.

The Royal Navy was completely unprepared for mine warfare, despite its having been used in the Russo-Japanese War of 1904–5. Regarding the mine as a cowardly weapon that no decent nation would use, the British had few mines, no strategy for using them or ships for deploying them, despite the fact that Fisher advocated their use. In October, a small defensive minefield was laid off the east coast to seal off the northern approach to the English Channel, but this was a failure. Not only was the minefield too small, the mines themselves were poorly designed and built, sometimes blowing up as they hit the water from the minelayer. Those that were laid often broke loose from their moorings and drifted away. All in all, they posed a greater risk to British ships than to those of the enemy. Just fourteen ancient destroyers had been converted as minesweepers before the war started, and the Grand Fleet was assigned just six of these.

AMPHIBIOUS OPERATIONS

Others have pointed out that the Royal Navy lacked the equipment and training for mounting amphibious operations. This was Fisher's fault, and it was to be all the more incredible that he, with Winston Churchill, the First Lord of the Admiralty, would press for ambitious amphibious operations, including not only the ill-starred Gallipoli campaign, but also another 'war shortening' scheme, an invasion of Pomerania in

Germany, followed by a rapid advance on Berlin. To be fair, the man who had effectively rebuilt the Royal Navy was no less wise than service chiefs elsewhere, and as late as the German invasion of Crete in 1941, troops were expected to be landed from barges, something that must cast doubt on the ability of the Germans to have invaded the UK. The modern landing craft did not appear until the middle years of the Second World War. What is open to question is whether or not Fisher was a great strategic thinker, with the imagination and genius to lead a fleet, let alone an entire navy, in war. He was clearly a man with a flair for recognising worthwhile technical advances, a good organiser capable of delivering value for money, and an enlightened and humanitarian commander with respect to the welfare of his men.

Fears of a German invasion, a constant theme during the first couple of years of the Second World War, were just as real in the ealier part of the century, once war in Europe seemed increasingly likely.

In July 1913, when Jellicoe was Second Sea Lord, a major exercise was mounted, with a 'Red' fleet representing an invading German force and a 'Blue' fleet, the Home Fleet commanded by Adm Sir George Callaghan. No less than 350 warships were involved, with a token force consisting of three battalions of infantry and one of marines. Jellicoe successfully avoided the defending Blues and landed his invasion force at the mouths of the Tyne and the Humber. His success forced the First Lord of the Admiralty to bring the exercise to an abrupt and premature end, for fear that the Germans might discover Jellicoe's success and the reasons for it.

Throughout the war, the British feared an invasion by up to 10,000 German troops, but at no time was such a possibility considered by the Germans.

Seen here as a vice-admiral, Adm Sir George Callaghan was replaced by Jellicoe as commander-in-chief of the Grand Fleet on the eve of war, much to the latter's embarrassment. *(IWM Q 22154)*

NAVAL BASES

Great Britain had spent much of its history fighting the French, with wars against the Dutch and the Spanish, and more recently the United States. Accordingly, the main naval bases were in the south, at Chatham, ideal for action against the Dutch, and Portsmouth and Plymouth. With the emerging threat from Germany, bases further north were needed. This was more difficult. The east coast of England and Scotland had few places ideally situated as naval bases, with the added disadvantage that the further north any base might be, the more difficult would be communications. The railway network thinned out dramatically north of Edinburgh, and became very thin indeed north of Aberdeen.

To resolve this problem, Rosyth was built as a major base and dockyard close to the likely threat to emerge in northern waters, but it was not universally liked. Indeed, on becoming First Sea Lord in 1904, Fisher demanded that not a penny be spent on Rosyth. The reasons for this were sound. Rosyth was too far from the open sea, while the Forth Railway Bridge meant that access could be denied if the bridge were to be felled by gunfire or sabotage or, as became possible within a very short time, aerial attack. Another problem that was to have an impact on the performance of the Grand Fleet in wartime was that there was nowhere close to Rosyth that was suitable for gunnery practice. The result was that little worthwhile was done at Rosyth between 1904 and 1910, much to the displeasure of other senior officers, including Jellicoe, and in 1912 Churchill, as First Sea Lord, had to tell the House of Commons that the two large dry docks would not be ready until 1916.

It was also decided that the battle fleet could be based further north on the Cromarty Firth, with Invergordon as the main shore base, while light forces could be based further north still, at Scapa Flow, off the south coast of the mainland of Orkney. Nevertheless, because of a shortage of funds, little was done to develop or ensure protection for either of these bases. Invergordon had the problem that access by railway from the south was slow and depended on a single-track line, while Scapa lacked railway access altogether, and fuel and all of the other necessary supplies needed by the fleet would have to come by sea. In 1912, the cost of a modest defence for Scapa Flow was estimated at £379,000, about 20 per cent of the cost of a new dreadnought battleship; the Admiralty decided against it. In 1913–14, £5,000 was earmarked for work at Scapa Flow, out of naval estimates of £46,409,300.

Scapa gave the impression of a sheltered anchorage in fine weather, but in winter storms, the many entrances open to the sea and the sheer size of the anchorage itself meant that it could be very exposed. Ships dragged their anchors and most put down two of them, but collisions did occur and in one winter storm, four seamen were washed off their ships and drowned.

At the Admiralty before the outbreak of war, one success for Adm Jellicoe was ensuring that a large floating dock was stationed on the Cromarty Firth, so that major units of the fleet did not have to make the long and, in wartime, hazardous voyage from Scapa Flow to Portsmouth or Plymouth, where the Royal Navy's main dockyard capacity was situated. Even so, while the construction of a new naval base and Royal Dockyard at Rosyth would also have helped, this still proceeded in fits and starts, not least because many senior naval officers, while appreciating the need for a new, purpose-built base further north, continued to be worried that the base could easily be blocked by an enemy.

PREPARING FOR WAR

The Royal Navy in 1914 was, on paper, the most powerful fleet the world had ever seen. Incredible as it might seem today, the doctrine was that the fleet should be equal to the size of the two largest fleets with which it might have to do battle. This was the 'two-power standard'. It was also before the emergence of the United States as a major naval power, and certainly before the even later development of significant Russian naval power, which really started under Khrushchev. In 1914, the Royal Navy had 69 capital ships (by which it meant the 20 modern dreadnought and 40 pre-dreadnought battleships and nine battle-cruisers), 46 cruisers and 62 of the modern light cruisers, 28 gunboats, 11 sloops, 215 torpedo-boat destroyers, 106 torpedo boats, 76 submarines, a seaplane carrier and 7 minelaying boats.

The statistics alone do not tell the whole story. The cruiser of the day could be either an obsolescent armoured cruiser that would be no match for a battlecruiser, or a light cruiser that was certainly larger than the destroyers of the Second World War, but still no match for the cruisers of the later conflict, and with a tonnage often less than that of a present-day destroyer or frigate. The destroyer had started to grow in size well before 1914, but many of them were still very small indeed, as indeed were many of the submarines. A quick look at the warships in Chapter 14 will soon show how small many ships were.

Needless to say, the aircraft-carrying ships were seaplane carriers, and a far cry from the fast fleet carriers that appeared from 1940 onwards. For conversion to a seaplane carrier, the ships that were most sought after were Channel and Irish Sea steam packets, with a fair turn of speed, accommodation and sufficient space to place a seaplane hangar. To put it succinctly, in 1914 command of an aircraft carrying ship was not a position to be sought by an ambitious naval officer; carriers were not capital ships.

Manpower in August 1914 totalled 147,667, but this increased dramatically with the mobilisation of reserves to just over 201,000 men, including 6,970 retired officers and pensioners, 27,395 men of the Royal Fleet Reserve, 13,510 of the Royal Naval Reserve, RNR, 2,345 in the Royal Naval Volunteer Reserve, RNVR, and 3,130 in the RNR's Trawler Section. (Sainsbury and Phillips, *Royal Navy Day by Day*) Later, manpower peaked at 450,000 in 1917, slightly more than half the Second World War peak, and remained at that level the following year, by which time it also included some 7,000 women of the Women's Royal Naval Service, the Wrens.

The years leading up to the war had not been ones of unlimited defence expenditure. The Liberal governments that held power from 1905 until 1915, when the coalition government took over, had been keen to reduce expenditure on defence. To a great extent, during his years as First Sea Lord, Fisher was popular with his political masters. His thorough scrapping of ships that were, in his words, 'unable to fight or run away' reduced costs. He brought ships home from foreign stations, and thoroughly reduced the dockyards' building capacity, effectively removing most of that abroad. The German navy was gaining ground, and the naval lobby in the UK was agitating for increased expenditure, even though manpower levels had increased from around 127,000 earlier in the century.

In 1914, the Royal Navy consisted of a Home Fleet with its ports at Plymouth, Portsmouth and Chatham, an Atlantic Fleet, based at Gibraltar, and a Mediterranean Fleet, based on Malta. The Home Fleet

The protected cruiser *Topaz*, probably at Malta. *(IWM SP 633)*

comprised a First Fleet with three battle squadrons of modern dreadnoughts manned by regular personnel; a Second Fleet, consisting of two pre-dreadnought battle squadrons which when needed would be manned largely by personnel from the naval schools; and a Third Fleet, manned by skeleton maintenance crews but dependent entirely on naval reservists for operations and having the oldest ships still in service. On its own, the First Fleet actually outnumbered the German navy.

The Mediterranean Fleet in 1914 consisted of three dreadnought battlecruisers, *Inflexible*, *Indomitable* and *Indefatigable*, of 18,000 tons each. These were already superseded by the more modern battlecruisers of the Home Fleet but bore eight 12in guns apiece, which made them among the most heavily armed ships in the area. There were also four armoured cruisers, *Defence*, *Duke of Edinburgh*, *Black Prince* and *Warrior* (which, while comparatively modern, were by this time outclassed by the new concept of the battlecruiser), four modern light cruisers and a flotilla of sixteen destroyers.

Further afield, there were three squadrons of ships east of Suez. One of these was the China Squadron, based at Hong Kong and consisting of a pre-dreadnought battleship, *Triumph*, the armoured cruisers *Minotaur* and *Hampshire* and two light cruisers, *Newcastle* and *Yarmouth*. On the outbreak of war, *Triumph* was in dockyard hands; she was quickly returned to service, although finding a ship's company proved difficult. Four Yangtze River gunboats were quickly decommissioned and their crews transferred, but efforts to recruit Chinese stokers proved fruitless and volunteers had to be

sought from the Duke of Cornwall's Light Infantry, which eventually provided 106 men and two officers. At Singapore, base for the East Indies Station, there was a sister of *Triumph*, the pre-dreadnought *Swiftsure*, as well as two light cruisers, while the French placed two armoured cruisers under the command of the flag officer, and the Russians followed, providing two elderly light cruisers. Strongest of the squadrons was the Australian squadron, based on Sydney, and consisting of the Indefatigable class dreadnought battlecruiser *Australia* and two modern light cruisers, *Sydney* and *Melbourne*, as well as two older light cruisers.

Closer to home, in the Atlantic, the North American and West Indies Station, based on Bermuda, was maintained at a

This photograph gives some idea of the vast size of the anchorage at Scapa Flow. The boat in the foreground is an admiral's barge. *(IWM Q 23338)*

reasonably high strength for fear that German commerce raiders might interfere with merchant shipping. The squadron consisted of four armoured cruisers, *Suffolk*, *Berwick*, *Essex* and *Lancaster*, and the modern light cruiser *Bristol*, but shortly after mobilisation a further four armoured cruisers were sent from the UK, *Carnarvon*, *Cornwall*, *Cumberland* and *Monmouth*, all brought out of reserve, as well as *Good Hope*, deployed from the Grand Fleet.

The problem with these dispositions was that, in Fisher's words, away from home waters, the fleet was: 'Strong nowhere, weak everywhere!' Fisher was referring to the chief of staff at the Admiralty, Vice Adm Sir Frederick Doveton Sturdee, whom he blamed for the loss of the Battle of Coronel: 'Never such rot as perpetrated by Sturdee in his world-wide dispersal of weak units!'

The need for economy saw the annual fleet manoeuvres for 1914 cancelled, and a face-saving mobilisation of the reserves was substituted instead. This meant that as the gathering crisis grew in the Balkans in July 1914, the fleet was effectively mobilised by coincidence, putting to sea on Monday 20 July under the command of Adm Sir George Callaghan, Commander-in-Chief of the First Fleet. The fleet was due to demobilise on Monday 27 July, but before this could happen, the Admiralty issued the order: 'Standfast the Fleet!'

Scapa Flow, the major anchorage on the south coast of the mainland of Orkney, began to move to a war footing on 2 August 1914, two days before the British ultimatum to Germany expired. The local territorial troops were mobilised to join marines from ships already stationed there to prepare harbour defences, while warning was given that navigational lights within the harbour might be extinguished. A small head-quarters was established ashore, and the seagoing repair ships *Cyclops* and *Assistance* were moored off the pier, with a telegraph cable running from *Cyclops* to Kirkwall and then on to the mainland of Scotland, down to the Admiralty in London.

In fact, a succession of commanders-in-chief of the Grand Fleet, including both Callaghan and his successor Jellicoe, expected attack by German destroyers and, later, once the great range of the U-boats became apparent, by these as well, on the ships at Scapa. Fortunately, such an attack did not materialise until after the defences had been put in hand, and it is generally believed that the reason that the Germans did not attack was that they could not believe that the main base for the Grand Fleet would be virtually undefended.

The defences put in place included placing two elderly battleships *Hannibal* and *Magnificent*, with their four 12in guns, at the two main entrances to Scapa Flow, while shore batteries of 4in and 6in guns were also provided. Elementary anti-submarine defences were installed, initially consisting of buoys across the channels with nets strung between them, but the nets soon proved too weak to withstand the winter weather and stronger nets, and then herring drifters with nets between them, were installed. Fifty trawlers armed with guns and towing explosive sweeps began to patrol the entrances, while contact mines were laid in defensive minefields. Yet, it was not until May 1915 that Scapa Flow could be said to be secure.

As ultimatums and declarations of war flashed around the European capitals, it was decided to move the First Fleet to the safety of Scapa Flow. This was done in consider-able secrecy, leaving Portland in Dorset on the morning of 29 July and timed to pass through the Straits of Dover under cover of darkness, showing no lights. With the Third Fleet mobilised already and the Second Fleet being quickly brought up to strength, and the whole augmented by the Atlantic Fleet, the combined fleet became the Grand Fleet. Even so, the hope remained at this stage that the United Kingdom need not become embroiled in a continental war; but the country was a guarantor of Belgian sovereignty and the crunch came when Germany demanded that 700,000 troops be allowed across Belgium to attack France. On Saturday 1 August the UK sought assurances from both France and Germany that Belgian neutrality would be respected, while the Admiralty mobilised the Royal Navy. Two days later, Germany declared war on France, and the Admiralty took up nine ocean liners to commission as armed merchant cruisers, although three of these were soon returned to trade as their fuel consumption was regarded as being too high.

At 2300 GMT on Tuesday 4 August, when a British ultimatum to Germany expired, the signal was flashed to all ships wherever they were: 'Commence hostilities against Germany.'

CHAPTER THREE

STANDFAST THE FLEET!

The fact is that in 1914 the Royal Navy was almost totally unprepared for war and remained in that condition for most of the period 1914–18.

Cdr Stephen King-Hall

While the Grand Fleet needed to be moved to a safer anchorage, priority had to be given to moving the British Expeditionary Force to France. Between 9 August and 22 August, 80,000 British infantrymen, and 12,000 cavalrymen with their horses, were moved to France, reaching ports from Le Havre north to Calais and Dunkirk. The busiest days were 15–17 August. During this period, a major German assault was expected, although no one knew whether it would be by U-boats, destroyers or the entire German High Seas Fleet. British submarines maintained a watch off the German coast in the Heligoland Bight, supported by destroyers, but the Germans remained in port and the BEF reached France without being challenged and without losing a single soldier or horse. It was not a moment too soon, for although the operation was completed three days earlier than expected, the first British contact with German forces in Belgium came late on 21 August, and by 24 August there was heavy fighting.

To Jellicoe's embarrassment, on the outbreak of war he was sent to take command of the Grand Fleet, replacing Adm Callaghan.

Promoted to the rank of full admiral, Jellicoe wasted little time. As early as October 1914, he established his strategy for a major fleet engagement. His aim, stated in a letter to the Admiralty on 30 October, was to confront the Germans in the northern North Sea rather than the southern end, because the latter would favour the Germans, who would be able to deploy minelayers and submarines. Even so, for fear of finding a chain of submarines waiting for his forces when in pursuit of a retreating German force, he might hesitate to follow in the desired direction. He wrote, 'The situation is a difficult one: it is quite possible that half our battle fleet might be disabled by underwater attack before the guns opened fire at all.' His plan was to move the battle fleet at high speed to a position on the enemy's flanks before engaging them.

Jellicoe saw his duty as retaining control of the seas and he placed this as a far higher priority than engaging the enemy. The loss of significant fleet units was a factor in this, as he needed to keep the Royal Navy's overwhelming dominance intact, but he also knew that being able to maintain the blockade of German ports was the key to winning the war on land as well as at sea.

In the North Sea, a stand-off developed. The German admirals had little idea of what they could do, while the Grand Fleet swept the coast of Norway looking for German ships, but found none. Nevertheless, one action that could be taken was to destroy German links with the world outside Europe. Just five hours after the UK and Germany found themselves at war, a British cable ship, the *Teleconia*, dropped grappling irons into the mud of the sea bed off the German port of Emden, and one by one broke five German overseas telegraph cables, running to Brest in France, Vigo in Spain, to Tangier in North Africa, and two running to New York.

That same day, 5 August, also saw the first German ship to be sunk, when the steamer *Königen Luise* was caught disguised as a Great Eastern Railway ferry, dropping mines near the Thames estuary. She was promptly sunk by gunfire from the light cruiser *Amphion*, which then rescued fifty-six from her crew of 130. Half the prisoners were cast into a compartment in the bows of the cruiser, so that if she hit a mine, they would be the first to go, and shortly afterwards, when she did, they were. There was just one survivor. An idea of how intensive the minelaying must have been can be judged from the ship's striking a second mine which exploded as she settled in the water. In the end, in addition to twenty-seven German prisoners, 132 members of *Amphion*'s ship's company were killed or seriously wounded.

THE SEARCH FOR A SECURE BASE

Whether it was paranoia over the threat from the U-boats, or simply common sense – the feeling that in wartime anything that can go wrong will go wrong, and planning for the worst – attack from under the waves was feared. There was good reason for this: none of the northern bases was truly secure, while at the outbreak of war there were no depth charges with which to attack submerged submarines, and so anti-submarine warfare consisted of a number of unlikely ideas, combined, as we will see later, with attempts to encourage the U-boat to surface. Worst of all, there was no means of detecting a submarine. Asdic had still to be invented.

The loss of the three cruisers off the Dutch coast, mentioned later in this chapter, only showed that the fears of the threat posed by submarines were well founded. At the Grand Fleet's anchorages, watches were strengthened in the desperate look-out for a tell-tale periscope or, even worse, torpedo tracks. Unfortunately, both Scapa Flow and the Cromarty Firth were frequently visited by seals and dolphins and, until positively identified, any disturbance in the water resulted in a false alarm.

On 26 October 1914, at around noon, the Grand Fleet was off Invergordon in the Cromarty Firth when a submarine was reported and the alarm raised. The harbour defences consisted of trawlers and destroyers, augmented by picket boats. These were madly patrolling, looking for submarines, while aboard Beatty's flagship, the battlecruiser HMS *Lion*, observers thought that they saw a disturbance in the water as if caused by a periscope travelling at 20kts – far too close inshore for a submarine, and far too fast for a submerged submarine at the time, and for several decades afterwards. *Lion*'s port 4in guns opened fire, hitting the supposed periscope, but also landing on several houses ashore in the small village of Jemimaville, starting a small fire in the village and another one in a wood nearby. The likely culprit seems to have been a whale or a dolphin.

Rather than admit that they were guilty of panic, some of the officers from the ship went ashore afterwards, 'to reassure the inhabitants that the submarine had been sunk'. This event became known as the 'Battle of Jemimaville'. Fortunately, the only casualty was a baby with a slight injury to a leg.

The vulnerability of the northern bases was brought home on 8 August 1914 by an unsuccessful U-boat torpedo attack, and again the next day when the light cruiser *Birmingham* rammed *U-15*. In mid-October, Jellicoe dispersed the Grand Fleet's battleships to Loch Ewe on the west of Scotland and to Lough Swilly on the north coast of Ireland, but this in itself was no guarantee of safety, as the events of 27 October were to show.

U-boats were not the only threat. The modern battleship *Audacious* was exercising off the coast of Ireland with the other ships of the 2nd Battle Squadron. At 0840 she struck a mine, although many aboard thought that it was simply the recoil of her own guns. The sea conditions were not good, and the other ships moved away believing that the damage had been done by a torpedo from a U-boat. The ship steamed to Lough Swilly at reduced speed, but eventually all power was lost as water continued to flood through the lower decks. Attempts by cruisers to put a tow aboard were hampered first by the ship being out of control in a rough sea, and then by one of the ships getting the towing line around a screw. As many of the crew as could be spared were sent away in the ship's boats, but at 1830 it was decided to abandon the *Audacious*, and the final fifty men were taken off as her decks were awash. She capsized and blew up at 2100, without any losses among her ship's company, although a seaman on the deck of the cruiser *Liverpool*, 800 yards away, was killed by a piece of armour plate.

The irony was that the mine was one of 200 laid by the *Berlin*, an armed former liner, which were not intended for the ships of the Grand Fleet, but had been laid along a major shipping lane and had actually accounted for a merchantman the day before.

The reasons for moving to Loch Ewe and Lough Swilly were sound in themselves, but they also increased the distance between the Grand Fleet and their German opponents, making the hoped-for naval battle less likely. On the other hand, this and other events showed that on both sides, their battle fleets were prized almost too much. The battleship may have been a sign of dominance and security, but it was also a liability, as it had to be protected, and both sides were scared of losing any of them. The massive effort of screening these ships with cruisers, and screening the cruisers with destroyers, meant that there were not sufficient ships for a convoy system, even if at the time the Admiralty had been of a mind to instigate such a system.

BLOCKADING

During the century that followed Trafalgar, the Admiralty prepared no plans for war. No consideration was given officially to the changed nature of warfare – that future naval engagements would be fought at some considerable range, rather than seeing a captain, in Nelson's words, putting his ship alongside that of the enemy. The objective was to find the enemy and bring him to battle; this was repeated by Vice Adm Sir Spencer Robinson in 1871, and again by the Admiralty in writing in 1908, when the Sea Lords instructed the Commander-in-Chief of the Channel Fleet that 'the principal object is to bring the main German fleet to decisive action and all other operations are subsidiary to this end'.

The policy depended on the Royal Navy's establishing a close inshore blockade of enemy ports, observing every move of the enemy fleet and being ready to give battle if and when it ventured out. At Copenhagen in 1801, when the Danish fleet refused to put to sea, Nelson had sent in frigates to force it out. Fisher was the first to recognise officially that such a plan was doomed to failure. The mine and the torpedo, especially if fired from a submarine, meant that it would be foolish to hazard battleships in such waters. Instead, a close blockade would be provided by destroyers and other light vessels patrolling offshore, keeping a watch on the enemy's movements, providing an early report of the German fleet sallying forth, before the close blockade itself fell back under the cover of the battleships and battlecruisers.

Even this amended policy was subject to limitations. Provided that he had enough food and water, an admiral in the days of sail could have spent some considerable time cruising off the enemy coast, careful only not to be driven ashore by adverse

HMS *Edgar* and her sisters, twenty years old at the outbreak of war, were employed on the initial blockade of Germany. The elderly protected cruisers were soon withdrawn as unfit for service. *(IWM SP 64)*

Maintaining the naval blockade of Germany was one of the most important tasks. This is the armed boarding steamer *Rowan*, clearly a former merchant vessel herself. *(IWM SP 95)*

weather conditions. The warships of the First World War period needed coal and oil, and for a destroyer, it would be necessary to return to port every four days to recoal, which with the time taken for the return voyage meant that a third of the force would always be away. To provide a satisfactory blockade would require twice the Royal Navy's total number of destroyers in 1914.

The solution was to close off the North Sea. The southern end, the Straits of Dover,

was easy to control, with minefields, the warships of the Dover Patrol, submarines and shore batteries. The northern end was more difficult, with a 200-mile gap between the north of Scotland and Norway, but here cruisers would patrol, with the Grand Fleet anchored at Scapa Flow, kept in readiness.

Blockading an enemy's ports could be highly successful, but it could also be highly controversial. Even in wartime, belligerent

Dazzle-painted, HMT *Olympic* was clearly a liner taken up from trade. She was a White Star vessel and a near relative of the *Titanic*. Early in the war, her boats helped to rescue survivors when the battleship *Audacious* hit a mine off the north coast of Ireland. *(IWM)*

nations would be supplied by neutral ships, and the question was what to do with them. In the blockade of German ports, inevitably some of the traffic stopped was bound for neutral ports, such as those in Denmark and Sweden, or even friendly ports, such as those in Russia. A conference held in London during the winter of 1908/9 involving Austria, France, German, Italy, Japan, the Netherlands, Russia, Spain and the United States, as well as the United Kingdom, laid

down some basic rules, known as the Declaration of London.

Blockading ships had first to determine the nationality of vessels entering or leaving port; if a vessel belonged to a belligerent nation, both ship and cargo could be seized. If it was neutral, the cargo and destination together determined its fate. War materials could be seized, defined as 'all materials useful to enemy armed forces'. Non-contraband included many types of raw materials and foodstuffs, especially if intended for neutrals. In between, there was a grey area of 'conditional contraband', consisting of goods suitable for military or civilian purposes, the most significant of which was, of course, fuel. Conditional contraband was escorted to a port in the blockading nation and the fate of the cargo was to be decided by a prize court. If caught in neutral waters, a blockading ship could be subject to internment for the duration of the war.

The new rules provoked an outcry in the UK, where many felt that the rights of neutral nations to trade in wartime had been given prominence over the rights of belligerent nations to enforce a blockade. The plans for a blockade of German commerce were drafted by Adm Sir Arthur Wilson, who was First Sea Lord between 1910 and 1912. The plan called for a close blockade, with strong naval forces taking the initiative deep inside the Heligoland Bight and stopping all German merchant shipping. This plan was amended when Winston Churchill became First Lord in 1912, as the new Board of Admiralty felt that it would involve heavy losses of ships to mines and torpedoes. German commerce would be controlled by a distant blockade, with the Grand Fleet held on the northern limits of the North Sea, preventing German warships from straying into the wider oceans and ready for a decisive naval engagement when the time came.

The German naval minister, Adm von Tirpitz, correctly guessed the British intentions. His plan was to use neutral ships sailing to neutral nations, such as the Netherlands and Denmark, where their cargoes could be unloaded and moved by railway and coastal shipping, or, in the case of cargo unloaded at Rotterdam, by barge. This scheme was so effective that in the first few months of war German imports from

the United States fell from US$32 million (£6.04 million, at the then exchange rate of $5 to £1 sterling) in December 1913 to just $2 million (£400,000) a year later, while over the same period imports from Sweden rose from $2.2 million to $17.7 million; from Denmark, from $3 million to $14.5 million; from the Netherlands, from $19 million to $27 million; and from Norway, from $3 million to $17.2 million.

The significance of the blockade was that Germany imported around a quarter of its food before the war, as well as half of its animal fodder, from Russia, a source that would be closed once the fighting began. While Germany was self-sufficient in some basic items, such as potatoes, the country's agriculture was also heavily dependent on fertilisers, half of which came across the Atlantic or from North Africa and were essential to get crops to grow in the sandy soil of northern Germany. The country was completely dependent on the United States for cotton, and for 60 per cent of her copper needs.

Although Germany is not today regarded as a maritime power, in 1914 the German merchant marine was significant, totalling 5.5 million tons, or 12 per cent of the world total. After 5 August 1914, the British moved quickly to seize German and Austrian merchant vessels, with 623 German and 101 Austrian ships seeking refuge in neutral harbours, while 675,000 tons of the Central Powers' shipping was seized and another 405,000 tons captured on the high seas. Within weeks, the usable German merchant fleet was down to just 2 million tons.

Anxious to avoid the use of neutral ports, on 20 August the War Cabinet changed the rules of blockade so that the ultimate destination became the determining factor – the doctrine of 'continuous voyage'. The problem was, of course, that cargo manifests might not tell the true story, so the Royal Navy was given power to interpret the evidence. In addition, the Declaration of London lists of contraband, conditional contraband and free goods were also amended, so that many items that could be used for civil or military purposes were interpreted as being for military use. There was a certain rough logic to this, as rubber and copper had obvious military applications, but even paper was included in the contraband list.

Blockades were enforced by dint of merchant ships' being requested to stop while a small boarding party from the blockading warship went across to inspect her papers. The boarding party usually included two officers. On boarding, the officers would endeavour to confirm the ship's identity using her papers and a copy of Lloyd's *Register of Ships*. They would then try to establish the nationality of the crew, which could be difficult as few British naval officers could speak any tongue fluently other than English. The enquiries were helped by an official list giving unusual nautical terms in every major European language, while there were drawings of familiar objects. Personal possessions might also be examined.

The next item on the boarding party agenda was the cargo manifest, which was examined closely, before members of the boarding party descended into the cargo holds to see if the manifest and the cargo tallied. Any apparent discrepancies would result in the ship's being sent to a nearby port, usually Kirkwall on the mainland of Orkney, for a closer examination, which could, even if the ship was cleared, mean a delay of several weeks.

That the work was important was clear, but it was far from glamorous and entailed spending weeks aboard elderly ships in seas that were seldom calm and in weather conditions that made the launch of the ship's whaler for the row across to the waiting merchantman a hazardous affair.

While the blockade was seen as vital, for the first four months the routine was handed over to twelve elderly cruisers, all of which would have been embarrassed on being confronted by a modern warship. To put this into perspective, the Royal Navy was short of suitable ships. The destroyer had started to outgrow its torpedo-boat destroyer origins, but none of the destroyers of the day would have matched those of the Royal Navy in the later twentieth century, and many were very small indeed, as Chapter 14 shows. The light cruiser of the day was, in tonnage and armament, more akin to the destroyer of the Second World War and later.

At the northern end of the North Sea, the eight ships of the Edgar class patrolled the 200 miles or so between Shetland and Norway, but as the need for frequent visits to recoal manifested itself, rarely were more than six on patrol, meaning that they often patrolled steaming as much as thirty miles apart. Given the prevailing weather conditions in such northern latitudes, the chances of a blockade runner slipping through the wide mesh of this net must have been fairly good. There was no radar and these ships could not carry aircraft. The four ships patrolling at the western end of the English Channel were matched by four French light cruisers.

The blockaders were easy prey for German forces. On 14 October, *Hawke* was torpedoed and sunk by a U-boat while on her northern patrol. Three more of these ships developed serious defects as the month passed by. The start of the severe winter weather hastened the demise of others. On 11 November, a gale saw *Edgar* ordered into port with engine trouble, while the flagship, *Crescent*, was so battered that the flag officer aboard reported that everyone aboard feared that she might sink. Two other ships had to heave to. Once the storm abated, half the ships were sent to the Clyde for repairs, where the report was so damning that on 20 November all seven remaining Edgar class cruisers were withdrawn from service.

It was fortunate that the United Kingdom at this time possessed the world's largest merchant navy and, since this was before the days of air travel, no fewer than 100 ocean liners were available on the outbreak of war. Naturally enough, they varied, with maximum speeds ranging from a mediocre 15kts to 25kts. The crews from the retired Edgar class ships were drafted to these ships and members of their peacetime crews were signed up as members of the Royal Naval Reserve. Armed with 6in and 4.7in guns, the conscripted vessels took over the Northern patrol line. There was a sense of urgency, which saw no fewer than eighteen ships in service by the end of December 1914, while in due course no less than twenty-four saw service. The liners had armament but no armour, but the elderly cruisers had had little of that in places. A strong plus-point was that the ex-liners had a better speed in the open sea, being larger, and could remain at sea for up to forty-two days in the case of *Alsatian*, 18,000 tons, which became the new flagship and which could manage 23kts, although a fuel-saving 13.5kts was more usual.

CHAPTER FOUR

THE DARDANELLES AND GALLIPOLI

And now the Cabinet have decided on taking the Dardanelles solely with the Navy . . .
We have a new plan every week!
Fisher to Jellicoe, January 1915

The wartime building programme was pressing ahead. Five battleships of the Royal Sovereign class were under construction when Fisher returned to the Admiralty, and he had these converted from coal-burning to oil. Two other battleships, *Repulse* and *Renown*, had been funded but were still to be laid down, delayed because too much time would be needed for their completion. Believing that the Battle of the Falkland Islands had vindicated the battlecruiser concept, Fisher had them reconfigured as battlecruisers so that less time would be needed in their construction. To save weight and ensure that they would have a design speed of 32kts so that they could catch the German *Lützow* with its maximum speed of 28kts, one 15in twin turret was sacrificed, along with deck armour, and the weight saved was devoted to more powerful machinery. When the keels were laid on 25 January 1915, Fisher's 74th birthday, he insisted that they be completed in fifteen months; but in fact *Repulse* needed nineteen months, and her sister twenty.

Fisher was also anxious to pursue a plan to shorten the war by an invasion of the Baltic coast of Germany through Pomerania, giving the shortest route to

Berlin. The idea was that Russian troops would be used. Quite how these ambitions could be attained with German mining of the approaches to the Baltic and with most of the High Seas Fleet likely to be in a position to intercept, has never been fully explained. Nevertheless, the idea gave birth to a new class of warships with a shallow draught and light construction, the Courageous class. (See Chapter 9 for more on the troubled evolution of these ships.)

The plans for invasion also led to the construction of monitors, ships of just 6,000–7,000 tons but carrying a single turret with 12in or 14in guns. These ships had no armour and were slow. There were also 200 steel-plated invasion barges, motorised with oil engines and each capable of carrying 500 infantrymen at 5kts – too late for the Gallipoli campaign, which would have been the only time they could have been usefully deployed. These were the forerunners of the landing craft of the Second World War.

Fisher had a free hand, probably no First Sea Lord before him and certainly none since wielded such power. His passion was shipbuilding and, freed from all restraints, he embarked on a programme such as had never been seen before or since. Finding

The Gallipoli landings included troops put ashore by the steamer SS *River Clyde*, which had doors cut in her side so that troops could disembark quickly and run over an improvised pontoon to the shore. Heavy fire from the beaches resulted in massive loss of life among those attempting to get ashore. *(IWM Q 50468)*

that the army had been recruiting in the shipyards, Fisher demanded that Lord Kitchener put a stop to it, otherwise he would resign his position that afternoon. Kitchener wrote the order there and then.

Nevertheless, it does seem that Fisher was no strategist. The problem was partly that the Royal Navy had not engaged in any major fleet action since Trafalgar (the second battle of Copenhagen and the Anglo-American naval war of 1812–15 having been relatively low-key affairs). Fisher wanted to trap the Germans in the Heligoland Bight using minefields, and then have the Grand Fleet force its way through the Skagerrak and Kattegat, then through the Danish Belts, past the islands and into the Baltic.

Churchill, as First Lord, never short of gung-ho spirit himself, nevertheless took a more cautious view, reluctantly coming to appreciate that the German navy would never allow such a challenge to pass and that the destruction of the High Seas Fleet was a necessary preliminary to the idea, cherished by both men, of invading Germany. Churchill wanted to capture an island close to the German coast, which would either force the High Seas Fleet to emerge and give battle, or alternatively enable the Germans to be blockaded.

Apart from Heligoland itself, sacrificed some years earlier in exchange for Zanzibar, the islands that seemed suitable were Borkum, just off the Ems river, and Sylt, off the coast of Schleswig-Holstein. These plans were opposed by most in the Admiralty, who saw the problem as one of holding on to an island once captured, and keeping it resupplied when it was such a short distance from enemy territory but so far from home. There was one senior officer in favour of the idea, Adm Sir Arthur Wilson, who advocated the seizure of Heligoland, ignoring the fact that it was just thirty miles from the High Seas Fleet's main base at Wilhelmshaven, surrounded by minefields and heavily defended by heavy artillery installations. To be fair, Churchill also advocated that the Kiel Canal should be disabled to prevent the High Seas Fleet moving between the North Sea and the Baltic. To Churchill, the opposition of professional naval officers to his scheme was 'palpable reluctance . . . manifested by lethargy'.

DEALING WITH TURKEY

The two major problems facing the British and French, the Entente powers, in the Mediterranean were those of Italy, and of Turkey and the Ottoman Empire.

Italy, Austro-Hungary and Germany had a pre-war Triple Alliance, and the original war plan was that the fleets of all three nations would assemble at Messina in Sicily, from where they could cut the Mediterranean in half, taking control away from France and the United Kingdom. Italy initially declared her neutrality, and then sided with the Allies, making it easier to keep the Austro-Hungarian fleet bottled up in the Adriatic, and thus solving one problem.

Turkey was a different matter. There was little doubt that Turkey posed a threat to the Suez Canal, to Britain and France's ally Russia, and to Greece. The Ottoman Empire had been in a state of contraction, and while it lacked the most up-to-date equipment, it possessed two invaluable

assets. The first of these was abundant manpower. The second was a crucial strategic position. Both sides wooed Turkey, but a number of blunders and some insensitivity on the part of the British, and some skilful diplomacy on the part of Germany, meant that the latter country gained the trust of the Turks.

While the United Kingdom had the luxury of being able to consider whether or not to go to war, and the question was eventually decided by the matter of guaranteeing Belgian independence, the French were simply waiting for the German attack to materialise. To face the German threat, the French priority was to gather as many experienced troops as possible in France, and especially the 80,000 men of the XIX Army Corps stationed in North Africa. The problem was that while they were in transit across the Mediterranean, these men and their equipment would be extremely vulnerable. Worse, the French Mediterranean Fleet had been reduced by the decision to send two of its most modern dreadnought battleships to escort the President of France on a state visit to Russia.

The German contribution to the naval strength of the pre-war Triple Alliance had been small, just two ships, the larger of which was the modern battlecruiser *Goeben*, 23,000 tons with ten 11in and twelve 5.9in guns, capable of 28kts, making her the fastest and most powerful warship in the Mediterranean. The smaller ship, essentially an escort for *Goeben*, was the modern light cruiser *Breslau*, 4,500 tons, with twelve 4.1in guns and capable of 27kts, making her also a significant fleet unit. A larger German fleet would have been hard to sustain, the country having no naval bases in the Mediterranean, and more significant commitments elsewhere, closer to home.

Goeben had been deployed in the Mediterranean as early as 1912, partially to

The ex-London & North Western Railway steamer *Cambria* became a hospital ship and then a troopship. *(IWM Q 22780)*

display German naval might and 'show the flag', but more specifically to obstruct any attempt by the French to move troops from North Africa. Unknown to many observers ashore, *Goeben* was no longer the significant threat imagined, as she was desperately overdue for a major refit, with her hull fouled and her boilers needing retubing. On the eve of war, the *Goeben* headed for the Austro-Hungarian naval base at Pola, at the head of the Adriatic, where new boiler tubes sent from Germany were waiting to be fitted. The work was still in progress, being handled by *Goeben*'s own engineers, when

the German commander, Rear Adm Wilhelm Souchon, heard that war was imminent.

Ideally, Souchon would have liked to take his ships into the western Mediterranean, wreak havoc among the French troop convoys, and then slip past Gibraltar for commerce raiding in the Atlantic, before heading back to Germany to join the scouting force of the High Seas Fleet. Instead, he took *Goeben* to Brindisi, where he rejoined *Breslau*, and was disappointed to find that neither at Brindisi nor at Taranto would the Italians provide coal, initially

Cdre Roger Keyes in conversation with an army officer during the Gallipoli campaign. As chief of staff to the admiral, he was an enthusiastic advocate of submarine warfare, but less successfully he also advocated forcing the Dardanelles with surface vessels. *(IWM Q 13722)*

claiming that the sea was too rough. Souchon correctly guessed that the Italians were intending to withdraw from the Triple Alliance. He moved on to Messina, where he could commandeer coal from German merchantmen. It was at Messina that he learned of Italian neutrality, and was refused coal once again. He requisitioned the German East Africa passenger liner *General* as a naval auxiliary, and seized the coal aboard other German ships in the harbour, gaining some 2,000 tons.

Leaving Messina on the night of 2/3 August, Souchon despatched *Breslau* to attack the French North African port of Bone, while he took *Goeben* to Philippeville, both in present day Algeria, and while on passage, he received the news that Germany was at war with France. The First Lord of the Admiralty made it clear to Adm Sir Archibald Berkeley Milne, commanding the Mediterranean Fleet, that his first priority was to safeguard the passage of the French XIX Corps, but if possible he should use the opportunity to engage *Goeben*. Milne was not to engage superior forces unless he could do so with French support. Indeed, it was also made clear that Milne should husband his resources at the outset, with the promise of reinforcements later. In fact, Milne then received a succession of signals, demanding that *Goeben* be tailed by two battlecruisers, and that a watch be kept on the southern end of the Adriatic.

On 4 August, the battlecruisers *Indomitable* and *Indefatigable* had *Goeben* in sight, but the damage had already been done. Souchon had arrived with *Goeben* at Philippeville on 4 August, flying a Russian flag, which was dropped immediately before the battlecruiser opened fire. Just fifteen shells were fired during a ten-minute bombardment, blowing up a magazine, damaging the lighthouse and the railway station, but leaving the troopships undamaged. The bombardment was so brief because Souchon was ignoring his orders to reverse course and head for Constantinople, where it was hoped that the presence of his two ships would encourage the Turks to move beyond a simple anti-Russian defensive alliance with Germany and declare war.

Once war broke out, an agreement had been concluded with France that they would have overall control of operations in the Mediterranean, but no arrangement was

made for communications between the two navies actually in the Mediterranean. When the French decided to delay the sailing of the troopships from North Africa for a few days because of the danger presented by the German ships, Milne was not told. Despite the bombardment, when the British battlecruisers passed *Goeben*, steaming in the opposite direction, at 1034 on the morning of 4 August, they could do nothing, as Britain and Germany were not yet at war; they could only turn and tail the German ship at a distance of some six miles. *Goeben* opened up to full speed and the distance between the pursued and pursuers increased, for like *Goeben*, the hulls of the British ships were also fouled and, in any case, they had never been as fast. Despite being joined in the chase by a modern light cruiser, *Dublin*, by 2100 the two German

One ruse resorted to during the war was to build 'dummy' ships to confuse the enemy about the location of major fleet units and the Royal Navy's strength in any one theatre of war. This is a dummy battlecruiser at Mudros. *(IWM Q 138410)*

ships had given their pursuers the slip. A little more than four hours later, the Mediterranean Fleet heard that it was at war.

Despite their earlier opposition to coaling the German ships, on Souchon's return to Messina the now officially neutral Italians allowed him twenty-four hours in which to coal. After some delay to the Italian colliers, during which more coal was taken from German merchantmen, some 400 German merchant seamen and civilians from these ships were enlisted to speed up the heavy work of coaling in the summer heat. Once again, he had to make do with less coal than he needed as men dropped from exhaustion, and a rest had to be ordered before he sailed at 1700 on 6 August, so that his men would be ready for battle. He need not have worried. The British ships had gone west to act as guardians for the French troopships. A single light cruiser, *Gloucester*, was sent to keep track of the Germans and report their position, while other ships were guarding the entrance to the Adriatic. Souchon encouraged those aboard *Gloucester* to believe that he was heading for the Adriatic, but then changed course towards the Aegean.

To the north of the direct route the Germans were taking to their destination lay Rear Adm Troubridge with his four armoured cruisers. While the superior armament of the German battlecruiser would leave these ships vulnerable, Troubridge decided to try to cross their path, hoping that the 9.2in guns of his ships would give them some chance before at least some of them were pounded to destruction. His ships would have to come within ten miles of the enemy before they had any chance of striking back. Troubridge was dissuaded from taking this action by his flag captain, a gunnery expert, while his

orders were in any case to avoid engaging a superior force, and it could be argued that *Goeben* was indeed that.

The one obstacle to the Germans was the light cruiser *Gloucester*, and when *Breslau* was turned back to try to discourage her, the British ship opened fire, and a brief gunnery duel ensued until *Goeben* herself turned and started to fire. At this point *Gloucester* reversed course, having already hit *Breslau* on the waterline, but without inflicting serious damage. When *Goeben* resumed her eastward dash, *Gloucester* resumed the chase until ordered by Milne not to go east of Cape Matapan, at the tip of the Peloponnese. Nevertheless, the voyage eastwards had not been without pain for the Germans, as the work on her boilers cut short by the outbreak of war soon began to tell, with tubes bursting and eventually four men scalded to death.

Although Milne eventually sent a strong force eastwards, after taking on coal at Piraeus, Souchon was able to enter the Dardanelles and head for his destination. The Turks were still undecided, to the extent that no one knew how they would react to two German ships arriving. The situation was resolved by the German ambassador, who suggested that the ships be 'sold' to Turkey, which appealed to the Turks, as the Royal Navy had requisitioned two battleships being built in British yards for Turkey. On 16 August, the ships were transferred to Turkey, but complete with German crews, even adopting the Turkish fez as headgear. *Goeben* became the *Sultan Selim* and *Breslau* became the *Midilli*.

THE COURSE TO GALLIPOLI

The failure to stop the *Goeben* and the *Breslau* from reaching Turkey was one of the earliest failures of the Royal Navy, and it was keenly felt. At the end of October 1914,

Souchon took his two ships, supported by Turkish vessels, and entered the Black Sea, where they bombarded Russian forts. On 31 October, the United Kingdom declared war on Turkey and, on orders from Churchill, the Royal Navy's Dardanelles Squadron, led by Vice Adm Sackville Carden, started off with a heavy bombardment of the forts on the Gallipoli coast, which produced results that were initially encouraging. However, the operation failed the acid test of strategic value, for it alerted the Turks and their German mentors to the importance of the area and the danger of Allied attack.

The narrow Dardanelles strait was easily defended by the Turks, being narrow and with many shallows as well as strong currents. It was to prove extremely difficult to penetrate, with surface vessels subjected to constant heavy bombardment and threatened by mines. It was no easy task for a submarine to penetrate the Dardanelles, especially since the currents ran at between 4 and 6kts, while for many the submerged speed was little more than 7kts, and that just for two hours before the battery needed to be recharged on the surface. Nevertheless, submarines did enter the Dardanelles and enjoyed spectacular success. The first of these ventures was by *B11*, on 13 December 1914, commanded by Lt Norman Holbrook, for which he received a Victoria Cross (his exploit is dealt with in Appendix III).

In the desperate search for a means of shortening the war and by-passing the stalemate on the Western Front, the Gallipoli campaign was conceived. Churchill was an enthusiastic supporter, and the War Cabinet was equally anxious to find such an alternative. There was also the advantage that an operation like this would show the Royal Navy in a good light, relieving the pressure on the army. It was also believed that attacking Turkey would do much to relieve the pressure on Imperial Russia on the Eastern Front. Like Stalin just over a quarter of a century later, Tsar Nicholas II sought Allied help, in this case through Grand Duke Nicholas, commander-in-chief of the Russian army. Unlike Stalin's, this request was couched in diplomatic terms, and in contrast to Stalin's case, the Allies felt that they already owed the Russians a debt for their efforts on the Eastern Front from the outset of the war.

The need to tackle Turkey went beyond the desire to aid an ally. Turkey also posed a threat to the Suez Canal, which for the First World War remained in use as a vital link with the Middle East and India, and for Australia and New Zealand. On 3 February 1915, the Royal Navy repulsed a Turkish attack on the canal with help from the French navy and the Royal Indian Marine.

Many in the Admiralty doubted that such an operation could be mounted, still less successfully. Fisher took the view that it could succeed if it were to be a powerful joint naval and military operation, adding that it would have to be immediate and that he knew it would be neither. In fact, Fisher became increasingly hostile to the idea of action in the Dardanelles and ashore on Gallipoli, partly because it risked denuding the Grand Fleet of major warships, and partly because he could see the hazards.

Optimism and naivety were the hallmarks of the campaign among planners ashore and afloat. The Minister for War, Lord Kitchener, even assured the general commanding the invasion force, General Sir Ian Hamilton, that the Turkish defences could be brought to a state of collapse with a single British submarine in the Sea of Marmara, even saying that: 'Supposing one submarine pops up opposite the town of Gallipoli and waves a Union Jack three times, the whole Turkish garrison on the peninsula will take to their heels and make a bee line for Bulair.' This ignored the fact that a British submarine had already sunk a Turkish battleship.

The Gallipoli peninsula divided the Aegean Sea from the Dardanelles, the approach to the Sea of Marmara on which the then Turkish capital, Constantinople (now Istanbul) stood; further on lay the Bosporus, and beyond that the Black Sea and the ally of Britain and France in this war, tsarist Russia. A successful campaign in this area would at one and the same time relieve the pressure on the Western Front by forcing the Germans and Austro-Hungarians to release forces to the area, and similarly reduce the pressure on Russia. It would also end any German or Turkish threat to Egypt and to the Suez Canal, while hastening the departure of Turkish forces from those parts of the Arab world which were still part of the Ottoman Empire.

The irony was that shortly after war with Germany had broken out, Greece had offered Britain her armed forces on 20 August, but the offer had been rejected for fear of damaging relations with Turkey. The Greeks had planned to land 90,000 troops to neutralise the Gallipoli peninsula, and give the Allies control of the Dardanelles. Despite provocation by the Turks, whose troops had attacked British forces and whose fleet had attacked the Russian ports of Odessa and Sebastopol, it was not until 31 October that Britain declared war on Turkey. Still no attempt was made to invade, or even to neutralise Turkey, whose defences were out of date, with many gaps and insufficient trained troops to man them all. The Turkish fleet, including its new German additions, could have been squeezed between the British Mediterranean Fleet and the Russian Black Sea Fleet, and Turkey's two munitions factories, on the Bosporus near Constantinople, could have been blown to pieces by naval gunfire. Decisive action so

soon could have eased the pressure on both Egypt and Russia.

In Malta, the new commander-in-chief of the Mediterranean Fleet, Adm Limpus, had argued that instead of shelling the forts, an army should be landed instead.

Even the one decisive and convincing British action at this early stage, that of the British submarine, *B11*, which sank the battleship *Messudieh*, was not part of a sustained campaign that could have done much to undermine Turkish resistance. As an isolated incident, it again alerted the Turks to the Allied threat.

FORCING THE DARDANELLES

In late 1914, the idea of a naval campaign in the Dardanelles gained increasing favour, especially with Winston Churchill. From the outset, it was also conceived as a joint operation with land forces, who would occupy the forts overlooking the Dardanelles to allow the warships an unrestricted passage. The problem was that there were no less than fourteen forts, and of these, six dominated the Narrows, a nautical bottleneck less than a mile wide. The guns in the forts varied between 4in and 14in calibre, and while many were old, they were still capable of inflicting severe damage on any passing warship, as even in the widest part of the Dardanelles, the channel would never be more than three miles from the shore. Between the forts, batteries of howitzers had been established, which could make survival difficult for the minesweepers that would have to accompany any forcing of the Dardanelles.

The Royal Navy was likely to be faced with the difficult situation that its battleships would not be able to get close enough to the forts to be able to destroy them until the minefields in the Dardanelles had been cleared, while the minesweepers would not be able to clear the mines until the guns in the forts and the howitzers in between had been silenced. Even so, trawlers were requisitioned for minesweeping duties. Given the strong currents, these ships would struggle to move as fast as three knots, making them easy targets for the howitzers. The civilian crews eventually turned their ships round and returned to port, only to be replaced by naval crews.

Vice Adm Carden, commander of the Dardanelles Squadron, planned to force the Dardanelles by destroying the outer forts using gunfire and, if necessary, by landing demolition parties. The minesweepers would then sweep the minefields, allowing the battleships to move within range of the forts guarding the narrows, which would then be destroyed, allowing the combined British and French squadrons to enter the Sea of Marmara, anchor off Constantinople and, under the threat of their heavy guns, the Turks would surrender.

At first, all seemed to go to plan. On 19 February 1915, the pre-dreadnought battle-ships *Agamemnon*, *Cornwallis*, *Triumph* and *Vengeance*, with the battlecruiser *Inflexible*, the cruiser *Amethyst*, destroyers and the French battleships *Bouvet*, *Gaulois* and *Suffren*, started a heavy bombardment of the forts at Sedd-el-Bahr and Kum Kale at the lower end of the Dardanelles. While the bombardment had relatively little impact on the heavily built forts, a second bom-bardment on 25 February was more successful as it was followed up by the landing of marines and seamen the next day to spike any guns that had survived the bombardment; in the event, the landing force found little opposition once ashore. Nevertheless, the warships had taken damage and suffered casualties in an exchange of fire with the forts.

The seaplane carrier *Ark Royal* had arrived at Lemnos with her six aircraft. These were to be used to provide reconnaissance and also to report back to the squadron on the fall of shot, provided that the aircraft could get airborne, which required good weather. This early attempt to provide what amounted to an aerial observation post for the surface fleet was largely a failure, simply because of frequent equipment failures and also the complete inexperience of the observers in the aircraft and the gunnery direction officers aboard the ships in working together. It was also later to be discovered that an aircraft providing observation for more than one ship could often have difficulty in knowing which ship was firing, so reducing the value of its reports considerably. Rather more successfully, these aircraft also took a number of the submarine commanders on reconnaissance flights over the Dardanelles, not only helping them to find targets, but also showing them the danger spots from minefields and shore batteries.

Starting on 1 March, the forts were bombarded on most days, while the squadron was reinforced by the arrival of the battleship *Swiftsure*. The heavy naval bombardment sometimes succeeded in silencing the guns at a particular fort, but within weeks these were functioning again. Further landings suffered heavier casualties, but the troops involved were always taken off again and no attempt was made to establish a foothold. In fact, the operation was more of an irritant factor for the Turks, rather than providing any strategic benefit, and instead had exactly the opposite effect, alerting the Turks to their own weakness in the area and the threat from the Allies.

Even when the minesweepers were able to advance under heavy covering fire from the battleships, which now included the new *Queen Elizabeth*, the best the Royal Navy could provide, and which was sorely needed by the Grand Fleet, they were forced back by heavy howitzer fire. Morale was sagging and Carden, on the point of a breakdown, was recalled home, command passing to his deputy, Vice Adm John De Robeck.

On 18 March, a major effort was made to force the straits with eight British and four French capital ships, advancing in three lines. The first line consisted of the British *Queen Elizabeth*, with De Robeck aboard, the pre-dreadnoughts *Agamemnon* and *Lord Nelson*, and the battlecruiser *Inflexible*; the second line, commanded by the French Adm Guepratte, comprised the pre-dreadnoughts

Charlemagne, Bouvet, Gaulois and *Suffren*; the pre-dreadnoughts *Albion, Irresistible, Ocean* and *Vengeance* made up the third line. On the flanks were the pre-dreadnoughts *Majestic* and *Prince George* on the European or Gallipoli shore, and *Triumph* and *Swiftsure* on the Asiatic shore. The three light cruisers *Amethyst, Dartmouth* and *Dublin* accompanied the force, with the inevitable destroyers and trawler minesweepers. A pattern emerged of first four British battleships and then four French battleships taking four-hour turns at inflicting a heavy bombardment on selected forts.

The pre-dreadnought battleship *Ocean* was one of the ships lost in attempting to force the Dardanelles, after hitting a mine. *(IWM Q 39769)*

While the operation seemed to go well, with direct hits on many of the forts, several of the ships were hit by accurate fire from them, with the *Gaulois* damaged beneath the waterline and having to be beached on Rabbit Island, near Kum Kale. The continuous fire from the fleet nevertheless soon began to take its toll of the Turkish positions, with some knocked out and others running low on ammunition. At 1400, De Robeck ordered the French squadron to retire so that his ships could cover the advance of the minesweepers. Just as the French turned at high speed, the *Bouvet* was either struck by a 14in shell and the flash penetrated into her magazine, or she hit a mine, but eye-witness accounts tell of a terrific explosion and the ship beginning to list heavily to starboard. She went on to her beam ends and then bottom-up in less than three minutes, so that just thirty-five survived out of her ship's company of 674.

Inflexible was next to suffer, striking a mine that forced her to withdraw. Then, at 1610, *Irresistible* struck a mine and, as she lost way, the Turkish guns turned on her. *Ocean* went to tow the stricken *Irresistible* as most of her crew were taken off by a destroyer, leaving just enough men aboard to handle the tow. At 1730, *Ocean* struck a mine and her engines were stopped as water and Turkish shells poured into her. The order to abandon ship was given, and three destroyers went alongside, but one of these was also hit by Turkish shells. Both *Irresistible* and her would-be rescuer were sunk.

De Robeck ordered the remaining ships to withdraw.

A SECOND ATTEMPT

That night, Cdre Roger Keyes, who had been transferred from command of the Harwich submarines to become De Robeck's chief of staff, went in the destroyer *Jed* to see if either of the two British pre-dreadnoughts could be saved. He found nothing, as both ships had sunk. Nevertheless, in the silence he felt that the

HMS *Cornwall* is engaging Turkish shore batteries in the Dardanelles. After early success in bombarding forts before the landings, this became a fruitless task in which the warships were more likely to be damaged than the forts. *(RNM)*

Turkish forts had been beaten, and that a further push through was bound to succeed. He went back aboard *Queen Elizabeth* and tried to press De Robeck into trying again, but his flag officer refused. In fact, Keyes was wrong. Just four out of 176 guns in the Turkish defences had been destroyed and only one out of ten lines of mines had been swept, while the Allies had lost three pre-dreadnoughts and had another three badly

damaged; some 700 men had lost their lives.

By the time of the Allied landings on Gallipoli, aerial observation was becoming much better. The RNAS put as many as six aircraft a day into the air on these duties, and one of the veteran naval airmen, Charles Rumney Samson, even paid great credit to the battleship *Prince George*, which 'used to do exactly what we told her . . . One day with her, the shells were getting too

Aircraft at the Dardanelles included the Short Admiralty Type 166 seaplanes, shown here still with a Union flag painted on the side, although there are roundels on the mainplane. In the background (right) is a seaplane carrier, probably *Pegasus*. (FAAM Short 234)

One of the pioneering naval aviators was Sqn Cdr Charles Rumney Samson, seen here about to get into his aircraft, probably at Lemnos, during the Dardanelles campaign. Samson and the other pilots often took submarine commanders who were about to go through the Dardanelles on an orientation flight to see the situation for themselves. *(IWM Q 13542)*

close to the Turks . . . we could see them running away . . . We signalled, "Salvoes, 100 yards more range", and to our delight, within 20 seconds, two beautiful bursts were right among them.'

The campaign saw the first attempt by an aircraft to bomb a battleship; the bombs had little effect on the *Hairedin Barbarossa*, but she was not to survive for much longer. Rather more successful was the torpedo attack by Flt Cdr Charles Edmonds on 12 August, when he sank a 5,000-ton Turkish supply ship, dropping down to 14ft and releasing his torpedo at 300yd. Five days later, he sank three tugs. A comrade, Flt Lt D'Acre, suffered from engine trouble and landed his Short seaplane; he then taxied

towards a large steam tug, firing his torpedo to sink the vessel. Freed of the torpedo, his aircraft managed to take off again and return to the seaplane tender *Ben-my-Chree*.

Meanwhile, Keyes was continuing to press for a second attempt to force the Dardanelles, even while consideration was being given for an evacuation of Allied troops from Gallipoli. He took his case in person to the Admiralty, and on 4 November, it looked as if Keyes had won his case. Four pre-dreadnoughts, *Albemarle*, *Hibernia*, *Russell* and *Zealandia*, were ordered to the Dardanelles with four destroyers and no less than twenty-four minesweeping trawlers. It was tactfully suggested to De Robeck that he was doubtless tired and should return home.

Yet, only hours later, the War Cabinet decided that any attempt solely by naval vessels would not get through unless timed to coincide with a major offensive by the army. The army had no troops to spare, as Salonika was by this time a more pressing priority, so it was decided that a naval operation on its own would be pointless.

Keyes returned to the Dardanelles, where Rear Adm Sir Rosslyn Wester Wemyss had taken command of the fleet. Wemyss was persuaded by Keyes that a further attempt should be made to force the Dardanelles. His plan involved eight elderly battleships, four light cruisers and ten destroyers entering the Dardanelles at nightfall, followed by a further four battleships as supply vessels, all fitted with mine bumpers. They would be hidden from the searchlights by smokescreens and move at high speed through the minefields and past the forts guarding the Narrows, which they would then bombard. At daybreak, six more up-to-date battleships would follow, but stop short of the Narrows and attack the forts from the other side.

Ashore, the new commander of ground forces, Lt Gen Sir Charles Monro, objected to any further attempt to force the straits. Promoted to acting vice-admiral early in December, Wemyss continued to press his case. His arguments were rejected, and instead he was ordered to prepare for the evacuation of Gallipoli.

THE GALLIPOLI CAMPAIGN

To prepare for the campaign, the Royal Navy turned the port of Mudros, on the Greek island of Lemnos, into a harbour. Jetties and pontoons also had to be assembled, but the effort did not compare with the Mulberry Harbour assembled for the Normandy landings in 1944.

Floating piers for use in the landings, designed by an enterprising army officer, were supposed to be delivered to the beaches by the Royal Navy, but the job was

Ashore at Gallipoli, this is an RNAS armoured car in its protective dugout. *(FAAM CAM 290)*

subcontracted to merchant shipping and, of the eight, seven were abandoned in the Mediterranean, and the one that reached Mudros was abandoned there. Gen Hamilton, meanwhile, had assembled 75,000 men, many of them Australians and New Zealanders, who were to prove to be among his best troops.

The landings came on the morning of 25 April 1915. The first were made by 1,500 men of the Australian 1st Division, starting at 0130, when they disembarked from the battleships into small boats, which were towed by small steam pinnaces towards the beach. First light came at 0405 and the pinnaces cast off their tows at 0425, leaving the boats to be rowed towards the shore by sailors. It was at this moment that the first fire came from the defenders, initially badly aimed, it became increasingly accurate as the light improved and the boats closed on the coast. Even so, most of the first wave reached the beaches safely, but those who were wounded in the boats had to remain in them during subsequent trips between the beaches and the destroyers bringing the next wave of men. Those ashore soon discovered that they had been landed too far north, and as they attempted to leave the beaches and advance inland, they were faced with steep cliffs, rather than low and gently rising sandhills. This mistake meant that the 8,000 men of the initial landing were unable to achieve their objective of overrunning the Turkish outposts and taking Gun Ridge, which dominated Chanuk Bair, before the Turks had time to respond.

Meanwhile, at Cape Helles, just a thousand Turkish troops watched the landings by the 29th Division. At Y Beach and S Beach, the men also went safely ashore without encountering opposition. Two parts of the main landing force at Cape Helles met opposition. That at X Beach only occurred once they were safely ashore and

had advanced half-a-mile inland, but this left the beach safe for the main body to follow. At W Beach, as the naval bombardment ceased, the surviving Turks held their fire, watching the British troops being rowed towards barbed wire, much of it out of sight under the water. As the boats grounded, they opened fire on the men of the Lancashire Fusiliers. Their commander, Brig Hare, found a safer landing for as many of his men as possible, and then they started a magnificent fight, advancing slowly on to higher ground to outflank the Turks, forcing them to withdraw. At this stage, a vital point, Hill 138, was open to the advance, but Hare had been wounded and his replacement was shot dead after a few minutes. Effectively leaderless for the moment, the men concentrated on helping their wounded and missed the opportunity. More than half the 950 men landed were casualties.

At V Beach, an old ship, the *River Clyde*, had been converted, with doors cut in the sides of the hull so that a large number of troops could land quickly, running across a bridge of lighters. The lighters were towed into place by a tug, and almost immediately began to break away in the strong currents, only being held together by the prompt action of Cdr Unwin and AB Williams, who dived into the water and held the lashings secure. Unwin shouted and the first of 2,000 men of the Munster Fusiliers and the Hampshire Regiment ran through the doors, and immediately they were cut down by a well-planned and well-aimed burst of Turkish fire. About half of the men were caught on the pontoon bridge, with half remaining inside the ship, where they used their machine guns mounted in the bows to stop the Turks from advancing on to the beaches. Meanwhile, men of the Royal Dublin Fusiliers had been caught in the same defensive fire while still in open boats.

Despite hearing the firing, Gen Hunter-

An artist's impression of steam picket boats towing boats full of troops in the Dardanelles. This was the only way of conducting an assault until landing craft became available. *(RNM)*

Weston on board the command ship *Euryalus* failed to take any action. At 0830, the order was given for the main force to land in the face of the fire, led by Brig Napier, who ignored the warnings from the officers trapped aboard the *River Clyde*; within minutes Napier and his staff were dead. Help did not come until Hamilton, aboard the new battleship HMS *Queen Elizabeth*, ordered heavy supporting fire, but while this moved the Turks from their firing positions, they were soon back once it stopped. Hamilton wanted to divert the troops to Y Beach, but Hunter-Weston rejected this as interfering with the planned arrangements.

Meanwhile, the Turkish prisoners at Gaba Tepe, where the nearby beach had been given the name Anzac (Australian and New Zealand Army Corps) by the invaders, had revealed that they had just two regiments south of this location. Despite this valuable information being passed on to Hamilton at 1240, and again at 1700 and 2230, no action was taken – officially because the information was not believed. It was later found to be accurate, but too late. At the same time, at Y Beach the troops had advanced a short distance inland, and waited in vain for fresh orders from Hunter-Weston. By the evening, Turkish reinforcements had arrived and the two sides had dug trenches and settled into a stalemate, the inevitable outcome of not making the most of the initial advance, which, in Hamilton's view, could have 'cut off the enemy troops on the toe of the peninsula'.

At Anzac Cove, the Australians and New Zealanders had remained close to their narrow beach, and were by evening facing determined and repeated counter-attacks by large Turkish forces, whose positions were favoured by the terrain. In the brutal hand-to-hand fighting which followed, seven battalions were severely mauled. Evacuation was considered, but rejected out of hand by the Royal Navy as administratively impossible. Instead, those ashore were told to hang on, and were supposed to be comforted by the news that the submarine *AE2* had passed through the Dardanelles to sink an enemy ship. *AE2's* career was to be brief, as she was scuttled on 30 April 1915 in the Sea of Marmara after being attacked by the Turkish torpedo boat *Sultan Hissar* and shelled by shore batteries.

From here on, the situation deteriorated into a crude resemblance of the trench warfare of the Western Front, but with three differences. One was the lack of water, the second the proximity of the opposing front lines, which highlighted the third, the lack of grenades, which were so needed that home-made bombs were improvised out of tins. A further difference was that the summers were hotter and drier, and the winters were colder. When air support was provided, under the command of none other than the courageous and colourful Cdr Charles Rumney Samson of the Royal Naval Air Service, their reconnaissance reports were ignored or not passed on, and they were restricted to a hundred 100lb bombs per month – a supply which they could happily have used within a single day!

There was, nevertheless, another aspect to the campaign that those on the Western Front had not had to contend with: a simultaneous naval campaign. While the Royal Navy had been showing exceptional skill and courage in getting its submarines into the Sea of Marmara, the Germans finally managed to get one of theirs off Gallipoli. On 13 May, the pre-dreadnought *Goliath* was torpedoed and sunk in a courageous attack by the Turkish destroyer *Muavenet-i-Millet* while off the Gallipoli shore. The senior naval officer, Admiral De Robeck, heard on 17 May that a German submarine had been sighted passing through the Straits of Gibraltar. On 25 May, off Anzac Beach, the pre-dreadnought battleship *Triumph* was torpedoed by *U-21*, at one and the same time giving a boost to the morale of the Turks and reducing that of the Australians and New Zealanders, who could also see the great ship roll over, float upside-down for about twenty minutes and then sink.

With the sudden realisation that the warships off the shore were vulnerable, the fleet moved away. The next day, 26 May, the Royal Navy's oldest battleship, *Majestic*, returned and anchored, spread her torpedo nets and awaited her orders to commence a bombardment of enemy positions ashore. On 27 May, at 0640, a seaman spotted the conning tower and periscope of a submarine, and almost immediately saw a torpedo heading towards the ship. Once again, there was an explosion and the ship rolled over, but this time the keel could be seen sticking out of the water for months.

Another pre-dreadnought, *Lord Nelson*, at Mudros. The ships deployed to the Dardanelles and off Gallipoli were for the most part obsolete, apart from the E class submarines, and while this says much about attitudes to the campaign, it was also probably just as well, given the losses suffered. *(IWM SP 257)*

DISASTER AT SUVLA BAY

Hamilton called for a third assault to break the deadlock. The idea was that 22,000 men would be landed at Suvla Bay, where Turkish opposition was expected to be minimal, followed by a rapid advance inland to occupy a semi-circular range of hills. From here they could join the Anzacs and make a surprise attack on a major Turkish strong-

point, a hill at Sari Bair. Surprise was essential, speed at least as much so if the objectives were to be gained before the Turks, aided by superb German commanders in the field, were not to be able to react and redeploy their forces.

The landings started on 7 August and were completed by 15 August, with the innovation that on this occasion fourteen motorised landing craft, each capable of carrying 500 men and with bow ramps, were available. They were nicknamed 'beetles', because the raised landing ramps looked like antennae.

The landings were led by Lt Gen Frederick Stopford, an officer who had never undertaken such a command before, and one who was, moreover, suffering from poor health. Despite the fact that just 1,500 Turkish troops stood between IX Corps and their objectives, a fact soon verified by junior officers on the ground, Stopford regarded the landing itself as a great achievement, and decided that the men should rest for a day before advancing inland. He also demanded an artillery barrage before they could seize their objectives, despite the lack of any suitable targets.

Not hearing from Stopford, but aware from aerial reconnaissance that there were no Turks in the hills, Hamilton sent two senior officers to find out what was going on. What was in fact going on amounted to what has been described as 'August Bank Holiday in England' with soldiers bathing in the peaceful bay. Stopford himself was resting, happy with the progress made, and blissfully unaware that the sort of military opportunity commanders can only dream about was slipping through his hands. Even as the two officers urged him to make progress, news arrived of a major Turkish advance, but without artillery support Stopford, supported by his two almost equally inactive divisional commanders, would not order an advance. Hamilton himself arrived to find out what was happening, and received the same complacent response.

When Hamilton sent Maj Gen Hammersley ashore to order an advance himself, he instructed the troops who had occupied Scimitar Hill, one of the initial key objectives, to return to the beaches, where they were ordered to form up before advancing a short distance inland to prepare trenches. While this was going on, the now unoccupied vantage point was

Christmas dinner ashore at Mudros during the Gallipoli campaign, 1915. The menu included biscuits and bully beef (corned beef). *(FAAM)*

occupied by Turkish forces. The next day, when Stopford finally went ashore, a force of 800 Turkish troops was allowed to hold up 6,000 British troops; indeed, in one sector a junior officer complained that they were not allowed to advance against three Turkish soldiers, said to be 'one little man with a white beard, one man in a blue coat and one boy in shirt sleeves'.

After nine days, Stopford was sacked, but the damage was done. The British assault on the major strongpoint of Oglue Tepe, unoccupied at the time of the Suvla Bay landing, cost 8,000 casualties, and cost the Allies any chance of making a success of the Gallipoli campaign. Eventually, with stalemate ashore and ships being lost at sea, the Royal Navy had to consider the unthinkable and arrange an evacuation. If the campaign had been a disaster, the evacuation was a quiet triumph, literally.

The desire to continue with the campaign remained strong with Churchill, still First Lord of the Admiralty, but by early October the opinion within the War Cabinet, while still divided, was swinging steadily in favour of evacuation. Bulgaria's delayed entry into the war on the side of the Central Powers meant that a direct railway link between Germany and Turkey had become available, with the prospect of German troops and artillery being moved rapidly to the battlefield. A change of commander had been necessary; Hamilton was recalled and a successor, Gen Sir Charles Monro, sent out in his place with an open brief. Monro recommended evacuation. Opposition to this course from Churchill was so strong that Kitchener, the Minister for War, was dispatched to the area, basically to undertake the task just completed by Monro; he returned with the same recommendation. It was not until 23 November 1915 that the War Cabinet finally voted for evacuation. There was little opposition: Churchill had resigned on 18 November, and on 1 January 1916 took command of the 6th Battalion the Royal Scots Fusiliers on the Western Front.

The decision was not in time to spare those ashore at Gallipoli from further misery and loss. After the baking heat of summer came the cold of winter. On 26 November, torrential rain that drowned men in the trenches as it flowed down the hillsides was followed by a two-day blizzard, and 200 men froze to death. No less than 16,000 Allied troops suffered from frostbite. It was small consolation that they soon found that the bodies of drowned and frozen Turks had also been swept down the hillsides.

THE EVACUATION

The one outstanding success of the entire Gallipoli and Dardanelles campaign was the evacuation. The Royal Navy had to take 118,000 men, 7,000 horses and mules and 300 artillery pieces from Anzac Cove, Cape Helles and Suvla. The operation needed to be conducted in complete secrecy for fear of a Turkish assault on a weakening front. During the hours of darkness, men would be moved quietly from their positions, leaving rifles, preset by candles burning through strings or water dripping into a tin, to fire at the enemy lines for up to half an hour after the troops had departed. Time-fused bombs blew up munitions dumps.

The first night of the evacuation from Anzac and Suvla was 12 December 1915, and by 18 December half the men had been embarked. On just one night, 18/19 December, 20,000 men were taken off, and in dense fog the following night, the remainder quietly departed. Throughout the entire operation, not one life was lost.

The 35,000 men ashore at Cape Helles had to wait until January 1916; again they moved at night. By 7 January, just 19,000 men were left. Having experienced the quiet retreat from Anzac and Suvla, the Germans realised that the same was happening at Cape Helles, and started an artillery bombardment during the afternoon of 7 January. The bombardment lasted for four hours, after which Turkish troops were ordered to attack, but to everyone's surprise, refused to do so. The British were leaving and there was no need to attack. The nights of 7/8 and 8/9 January saw the remaining British troops evacuated from Cape Helles. Again, time-fused bombs blew up munitions dumps, and one of these caused the sole casualty of the entire exercise: a rating was killed when a large piece of debris from an explosion fell on his head as his boat was pulling away from the shore.

The Royal Navy did not leave the area completely. Mudros continued to be a base, and from there on 14 April 1916 two aircraft bombed Constantinople, probably doing little damage, but the exploit boosted morale and earned both the pilots the DSO. More successfully on 26 July 1916, the Turkish destroyer *Yadighiar-i-Milet* was badly damaged by bombing by RNAS aircraft in the eastern Mediterranean. Again, on 9 July 1917, RNAS aircraft from Mudros bombed the *Sultan Selim* (ex-*Goeben*) and the *Midilli* (ex-*Breslau*) at Constantinople.

CHAPTER FIVE

TRAGEDY AND TRIUMPH IN THE SOUTHERN HEMISPHERE

The map of the world in the Admiralty War Room . . . on this map the head of a pin represented the full view to be obtained from the masts of a ship on a clear day.
Winston Churchill, 1923

After successfully landing the BEF in France, the Admiralty dispatched its older warships to British bases around the globe, the logic being that these were to watch for German surface raiders. The German armoured cruisers presented a major threat, but light cruisers were also a force to be reckoned with and there were seven of these, as well as two armoured cruisers and the two ships that had already 'joined' the Turkish navy, soon to be a belligerent. Ideally, the Admiralty should have sent its new light cruisers to counter the threat, being able to outgun their German opponents and having a higher speed and lower fuel consumption than the many pre-dreadnought battleships that were despatched. Older British armoured cruisers were saved from the scrapyard and sent to sea, while twenty-four ocean liners were taken up and armed as armed merchant cruisers.

With the BEF safely installed in France, troops were then gathered from the Empire. In September 1914, the Royal Navy had to escort 50,000 men from India to the UK, with some 25,000 transported across the Atlantic in October, and then in November, 26,000 Australian and New Zealand troops. Fearful of German intervention following widespread Canadian press reporting of the troop movements, additional protection was afforded the Canadian troops, and after a U-boat was reported off the Isle of Wight, their landfall was changed from Portsmouth and Southampton, close to the British army's bases at Aldershot and on Salisbury Plain, to Plymouth.

FIGHTING THE COMMERCE RAIDERS

The German commerce raiders *Emden* and *Karlsruhe* between them sank thirty-nine merchant ships, accounting for 176,000 tons of merchant shipping. *Emden* was disguised as a four-funnelled British light cruiser, but had gained a certain public regard for the way in which the crews of its victims were allowed to leave their ships before they were sunk. Nevertheless, on 9 November 1914, *Emden*'s luck ran out. Personnel at a telegraph station on the Cocos Islands spotted the ship and their signal was picked up by the Australian light cruiser *Sydney*, faster, heavier and better armed than the German ship, which left the Australian troop convoy it was escorting to the Red Sea and headed to intercept the *Emden*. A gunnery duel resulted, and after two and a half hours, *Emden* was driven on to a reef, already a burning wreck.

Karlsruhe, intended to be another thorn in the British flesh, never had the chance to display her full potential, sinking in the Caribbean on 4 November 1914 following an internal explosion.

CORONEL

While *Emden* had used subterfuge to score her successes against the Royal Navy, a German battle squadron was on the loose in the Pacific. This was the East Asia Squadron, based on Tsingtao, commanded by Admiral von Spee, with the two armoured cruisers *Scharnhorst* and *Gneisenau*, and the light

HMS *Cornwall*, an armoured cruiser. One of her sisters, *Monmouth*, was lost at Coronel in 1914. (IWM Q 38548)

cruisers *Leipzig* and *Nürnberg*, although a third, *Emden*, was, as already mentioned, to lead a freebooting existence as a solitary commerce raider. This was a powerful force, but in total, the British and Allied force was far stronger, while certain of the British ships outclassed their German rivals. This was especially true of *Australia*, but also of *Minotaur*, which was superior to either of the German armoured cruisers; moreover *Newcastle* and *Yarmouth* outmatched the German light cruisers too. The Germans, on the outbreak of war, also pressed into service the armed merchant cruiser, *Prinz Eitel Friedrich*.

Despite a reluctance to introduce convoys elsewhere, and a shortage of destroyers with which to provide escorts, with German merchant raiders loose it was essential that troops from India, Australia and New Zealand were brought to Europe in well protected convoys, and this rapidly became a duty for the squadrons in the east. There were other priorities as Australia and New Zealand moved to seize German possessions in the Pacific, for which they needed naval support.

Von Spee spent some time cruising the Pacific, uncertain as to which course to take. His squadron made the most of the limited facilities allowed to belligerent warships by neutral nations. His initial plan was to rendezvous with the cruisers of the German American Station, but on his way down the coast of South America he encountered Rear Adm Sir Christopher Cradock, who had taken part of his squadron round Cape Horn seeking the German East Asia Squadron. Cradock had just the armoured cruisers *Good Hope* and *Monmouth* (the former being his best ship, although already obsolescent and undergunned for her 14,100-ton displacement), as well as the new light cruiser *Glasgow* and the armed merchant cruiser *Otranto*, an Orient Line

ship intended to hunt down German merchantmen rather than engage warships. *Monmouth* had been due to be scrapped. Although the balance of naval power in the southern oceans was in Britain's favour, when it came to battle the situation was reversed. Lacking aerial, let alone satellite, reconnaissance, and with limited communications, searching for enemy forces was akin to seeking a needle in a haystack, if not even more difficult.

The opposing forces met off the Chilean coast near Coronel in bad weather with high seas on 1 November. Only the armoured cruisers were able to use their guns effectively because of the sea state, but the two elderly British armoured cruisers were silenced quickly by their more modern German opponents, the flagship *Good Hope* sinking after an hour, with Cradock becoming the first of four British admirals to lose his life in battle during the war. *Monmouth* was then sunk by a torpedo from a German cruiser and went down with no survivors. This sacrifice did at least enable *Glasgow* and *Otranto* to escape.

FALKLAND ISLANDS

War is sometimes like a pendulum, swinging from one side to the other. It was not to be long before the disaster that was the Battle of Coronel for the British would be avenged. The bad news from Coronel took three days to reach the Admiralty, and when it did, it came mainly from German sources, anxious to boast of their victory.

For Churchill and Fisher, the immediate question was what would Spee do next? Would he attempt to intercept ships carrying food from the Argentine and Uruguay to the United Kingdom? Rear Adm Stoddart was already in the area with the South Atlantic Squadron, including the armoured cruiser *Defence*. Alternatively,

Vice-Adm Doveton Sturdee was the victor at the Battle of the Falkland Islands, but he was sent there by Fisher to get him away from the Admiralty, where he was blamed for not concentrating the Royal Navy's resources, instead spreading them too thinly. *(IWM Q 18062)*

Spee could use the Panama Canal, and engage and defeat the West Indies Squadron before heading up the east coast of the United States to free the German armed merchant liners in New York to sail. A third option was that he could cross the South Atlantic and do his best to hinder the campaign being fought by South African forces for the German colony of South-West Africa (now Namibia). Finally, he could go to the Cameroons and disrupt shipping supporting the Anglo-French invasion. To discourage any interference with the seizure of the German colonies in Africa, cruisers were deployed south. The battlecruiser *Princess Royal* was sent to the

West Indies to reinforce the squadron there.

Further weakening Beatty's battlecruiser squadron, Fisher and Churchill then ordered the battlecruisers *Invincible* and *Inflexible* to Devonport to prepare for service overseas. Fisher overruled the management at Devonport who maintained that *Invincible* needed work that would take until 13 November, and demanded that both ships sailed on 11 November, if necessary with the dockyard workers still aboard. He also ordered the elderly pre-dreadnought battleship *Canopus* to ground herself in the mud on the approaches to Port Stanley to act as a fort. This became the first time in the war that modern, powerful British warships had been deployed away from home waters.

Fisher used the opportunity to get rid of Vice Adm Sturdee, who had been Chief of Staff at the Admiralty and whom Fisher blamed for the poor disposition of ships and, as a result, the disaster at Coronel. Sturdee became Commander-in-Chief South Atlantic and Pacific. Sturdee and Stoddart were to rendezvous off the coast of Brazil and then hunt down Spee, with the Falklands as their coaling base. It took Sturdee twenty-six days to reach Port Stanley, not helped by taking two days out for gunnery practice, with each ship towing a target for the other to fire at. One delay of twelve hours was caused by *Invincible* fouling a towing cable on one of her screws. Another delay was caused after coaling at St Vincent Island, when a member of *Inflexible*'s crew was killed, and both ships stopped for the burial at sea. The combined force reached Port Stanley on the Falkland Islands on 7 December 1914, and would have been later had not one of Stoddart's commanding officers pressed him to make haste as he knew that the governor of the Falklands was worried that Spee might

attempt to land.

On arrival, most of the ships started coaling, although the battlecruisers waited until morning to take their turn, so that at any one time, some ships would be ready for sea. Aboard the battlecruisers, coaling started at 0530, and at first no one seemed too worried about a four-funnelled warship which appeared on the horizon at 0800. It was not until 0900, when two ships approached the outer harbour at Port William, to the north of Port Stanley, and *Canopus* fired on them that anyone realised what was going on. Coaling stopped immediately and the order was given to raise steam for the main engines, with oil sprayed on to the coal to obtain a higher temperature. At 1000, Sturdee's force was leaving the harbour.

The two ships had been the armoured cruiser *Gneisenau* and the light cruiser *Nürnberg*, which by this time were racing back to rejoin Spee, who was aboard *Scharnhorst*. Had Spee instead come forward to join them, the two battlecruisers could have prevented the reinforced South Atlantic Squadron from leaving the Falklands and could even have caused considerable damage. Spee had been unaware of the presence of the two British battlecruisers, despite the news being known in Germany; a signal forwarded to him did not reach him, as by the time it was transmitted, he was out of range of the Chilean radio station.

The Germans were hoping that nightfall would give them an opportunity to escape, but at 1300 the first shells started to fall around *Leipzig*, a light cruiser. At this point, Spee divided his forces, hoping that the sacrifice of his ship and the *Gneisenau* would give the light cruisers a chance to escape. *Scharnhorst* and *Gneisenau* faced the advancing British ships. The Germans were heavily outgunned, facing the 12in guns of the Royal Navy with 8in guns, so that for thirty minutes, while the Germans were within range of the British ships, they could not retaliate. Sturdee made frequent changes of course to put off the German gunners, but his own men had difficulty because of the amount of smoke that obscured their vision. At 1615, *Scharnhorst* went down with all hands aboard, followed by *Gneisenau* at 1800.

Meanwhile, Sturdee had also divided his forces, sending his light cruisers after their German counterparts. *Cornwall* and *Glasgow* headed after *Leipzig*, while *Kent* chased after *Nürnberg*, which outgunned her. Nevertheless, *Kent* persisted, and although at one stage those aboard thought the *Nürnberg* was about to surrender, before long the German ship was ablaze and sinking. Meanwhile, *Glasgow* and *Cornwall* had been engaging the *Leipzig*, although the exchange of fire started with an hour of shooting beyond range by both sides, and then an hour and a half of striking at each other. At one stage, *Leipzig* fired three torpedoes at the British ships, but none found a target. At 1815, *Cornwall* changed to firing lyddite and began to score more hits, which also had the advantage of putting *Leipzig*'s gunners off aim. She, too, was soon on fire and sinking, finally disappearing between 2023 and 2035.

Gunnery was to be a major problem for the Royal Navy during the First World War. Eventually, a standard of 5 per cent of shells being fired hitting their target came to be accepted as reasonable, and this was achieved at the Battle of the Falkland Islands in 1915. At the time, however, 5 per cent was seen as being very poor. The reason for this was that peacetime exercises had not been thorough in simulating actual battle conditions, with a ship moving at high speed having to hit another ship also moving at high speed. Not only the motion

of the sea had to be taken into account, but the vibration from the machinery in a fast-moving ship also blurred the gun layers' and trainers' telescopes, while smoke (for on both sides ships were still largely coal-fired) also not only hid the target, but in certain conditions it was not uncommon for a warship's own smoke to get in the way of accurate gunnery direction or gun-laying.

Some of those present had expected *Glasgow* to chase after *Dresden*, but she escaped, only to be found three months later 600 miles to the west of Chile hiding in Cumberland Bay at Robinson Crusoe Island in the Juan Fernandez Islands. These were the territorial waters of neutral Chile. When *Kent* and *Glasgow* approached and opened fire at just over three miles range, her commanding officer ordered her to be scuttled as she had run out of coal, due in no small part to British jamming of her radio signals so that her colliers could not meet her.

RUFIJI RIVER

The victory at the Falklands had all but removed the threat by German surface raiders to British trade, while the U-boat campaign had yet to start. Between the outbreak of war and January 1915, the surface raiders had accounted for just under 2 per cent of British-flagged merchant ships. The surface raiders had had a short life and their work could not compare with the British naval blockade of Germany.

The one surviving surface raider by early 1915 was the light cruiser *Königsberg*. German East Africa, or Tanzania as it is now known, provided a base for this ship, which could not be caught by the obsolete cruisers of the Royal Navy's Cape Squadron. Her base was in the Rufiji river delta, an extensive area of around 1,500 square miles with many channels running through and

The monitor HMS *Severn* was originally laid down for Brazil, but taken over by the Admiralty, and she ended up on the other side of the world, in East Africa, helping to destroy the *Königsberg*. Here, she has tree branches on her main mast to help conceal her from the air. *(IWM SP 978)*

around the swamps, sandbanks and islands. Mangroves helped to keep her hidden, while the channels were a mystery to the Royal Navy and could in any case only be navigated with safety at high tide.

While the *Königsberg* was the last of the surface raiders to be caught, she was also the least effective. The one overriding weakness was her need for coal, and once the Royal Navy caught and stopped her collier leaving Dar es Salaam, and then followed this up by buying up the stocks of coal in Portuguese East Africa, now Mozambique, the ship's potential was severely compromised.

From time to time, the *Königsberg* would venture out, sometimes using channels unknown to the Royal Navy, and find coal from colliers that had escaped British attentions, but she was in no state to pose a serious threat. Despite this, she did take the British light cruiser *Pegasus* by surprise, sinking her while she was repairing her machinery off Zanzibar. There was a certain irony in this, as the *Königsberg* herself was suffering from engine problems, and at one time her boilers had to be transported by land to Dar es Salaam to be repaired. Her prime target, merchantmen, largely escaped, as she managed to sink only one. Later, before the Royal Navy had a chance to reach the *Königsberg* herself, her life was made even more difficult when the cruiser *Hyacinth* sank the German *Kronburg* off East Africa, stopping supplies reaching the beleaguered cruiser.

The real theatre of operations for the *Königsberg* was the Indian Ocean, rather than the coast of East Africa. The mass of shipping from the Persian Gulf, from India and Malaya, and, of course, from Australia, heading towards the Suez Canal would have suffered terribly had she had the fuel and the endurance to be let loose in the open sea. As it was, the great Anzac convoy

was assembling to take Empire troops to Egypt.

The *Königsberg* was discovered by the Royal Navy on 30 October 1914. The pre-dreadnought battleship *Goliath* was sent to keep her bottled up, but could not reach the *Königsberg* herself. A steam picket boat was despatched with orders to torpedo the German ship, but failed and then sank a collier in the river. Those aboard the British ships now believed that they had *Königsberg* well and truly bottled up, but there were far too many channels for this to be the case, and in any event, the cruiser was also hindering the Royal Navy's ability to support the British campaign to seize German East Africa. Meanwhile, ashore, the German authorities were doing their best to arrange for supplies, especially coal and ammunition, to be taken overland from Portuguese territory. Even while Spee was still a threat in the Pacific, the Royal Navy was forced to station twenty-five ships off East Africa to counter the perceived threat from the *Königsberg*.

It was clear that the ship could not be allowed to dominate the strategic position in this way, but the Germans then moved her further upriver and ensured that she was placed in a more concealed position, while new gun batteries were installed on both banks of the river. The RNAS attempted to bomb the ship but, in marked contrast to her namesake in the Second World War, failed to hit her.

Fortunately, at the outbreak of war, two monitors had been under construction for the Brazilian navy in British yards, and these ships had been taken over by the Admiralty. They were intended for river use, with a shallow draught, while their armament consisted of two 6in guns and two 4.7in howitzers each, the latter being especially useful in the prevailing situation, as they could fire shells over trees and high ground.

Instead of attempting to bomb the ship, which was unlikely to succeed, given the small size of bomb that could be carried, the RNAS would spot for the monitors, just as it was to do in the Dardanelles. Named *Mersey* and *Severn*, the two monitors arrived off the Kikunja mouth of the Rufiji delta at daybreak on 6 July 1915.

At this time, *Königsberg* was lying at anchor behind Kikunja Island, just half an hour's steaming from where the two monitors had arrived. The two monitors were met by fire from the shore batteries as they steamed through the entrance at around 0600, returning the German fire. An attempt to torpedo one of the British ships was foiled when *Severn* sank a small boat carrying the torpedo. Past the shore batteries, small arms fire was directed at both ships. At 0630, both ships anchored out of sight of the *Königsberg*, with a couple of islands in between the opposing forces. The two sides opened fire, with many of the German shells falling short amid the trees on an island, but by 0700 the *Königsberg*'s gunners were getting closer, while the gunners aboard the monitors still had no indication from the air as to how close their shells were getting to the German ship.

Despite having been out of action for some time, the *Königsberg* was able to fire some thirty rounds a minute, helped by spotters hiding in trees overlooking the British ships and in telephone contact with the cruiser. At around 0710, a shell hit a 6in gun aboard the *Mersey*, killing four gunners and wounding three more. The shell also ignited a charge being loaded into the gun so that a flash shot down into the magazine, burning a petty officer. Fortunately there were no charges lying around, otherwise the *Mersey* could have been blown up by her own magazine exploding. The ship's commanding officer, Cdr Wilson, slipped

the stern anchor and pulled up the bow anchor, ordering his ship full steam ahead, only just being missed by the next salvo. It was not until 0800 that an aircraft signalled that a shell from *Severn* had struck the *Königsberg*, while the *Mersey*, anchored in a fresh spot, also scored a hit afterwards with her stern 6in gun. *Severn* was also forced to move as shells from the *Königsberg* edged closer. Shells from the British ships were aimed among the artillery spotters in the trees, and after this, the standard of gunnery from the *Königsberg* started to falter.

By mid-afternoon, without further reports from the aircraft acting as an aerial observation post and with a stretch of forest between the British and German ships, it was decided that the two monitors were simply wasting time and ammunition, and they withdrew. By this time, the *Königsberg* was firing with just one gun and the rate of fire had fallen off considerably. The two British ships returned down the river, finding that most of the shore batteries remained silent except for one near the mouth. By 2000 they were back with the fleet, transferring their wounded to another ship (although two died later) and burying their dead.

A second attempt to sink the *Königsberg* followed on 12 July, when, with the assistance of tugs to get their shallow-draught vessels to the mouth of the river, the two monitors entered the delta at 1120. The gun near the mouth once again opened fire and caused damage and three casualties aboard the *Mersey*. As before, both ships fired at the shore batteries, which did not seem to have been expecting a return visit, and there was the same constant hail of small arms fire from Germans hiding in the trees on either side.

As the two monitors approached the *Königsberg*, *Mersey* turned broadside on and opened fire, herself drawing the German fire to allow *Severn* to get closer. *Severn* anchored and *Mersey* stopped firing, so as not to confuse the spotting, which it was felt had been difficult during the first visit with two ships firing. *Königsberg* turned her attention to *Severn* and scored many near misses, so that almost fifty large pieces of shrapnel were picked up from the ship's decks after the engagement.

At about 1235, *Severn* had got the range of the German ship and scored her first hit, followed by several more. At this stage, a distress signal was received from the aircraft, saying that she was hit and asking for a boat to rescue them, but almost immediately afterwards, with the engine out of action, the observer sent a further signal saying that all of *Severn*'s shells were hitting the cruiser forward. The engine of the aircraft had taken a direct shell hit, but the pilot managed to glide down close to the *Mersey* while his observer continued to spot the fall of shot. The landplane overturned on hitting the water, but both the pilot, Flt Lt John Cull, and observer managed to escape and were picked up by a boat from the monitor. The airmen were aboard the *Mersey* for around three minutes when a large explosion was heard aboard the *Königsberg* and her guns stopped firing altogether.

The two monitors started to move closer to the German ship, but they lacked accurate charts and had been so disappointed by the performance of the river pilot on their previous trip that they had decided not to bring him. *Mersey* ran into an 8ft bank stretching across the river, denting her bow, and decided to anchor. A fresh spotter aircraft was by this time in the air and, resuming firing, *Mersey* scored a hit with her third shot. Firing continued until 1445, when *Königsberg* was ablaze from stem to stern. The monitors also opened fire on a motor launch hiding under low hanging branches and with a torpedo, obviously waiting to attack the British ships.

Not wishing to be caught in the river on an ebb tide, the two monitors then withdrew, to find that an elderly light cruiser was providing covering fire against the German shore batteries. Over the two days the whole engagement had accounted for a total of 943 rounds of 6in, 389 rounds of 4.7in, 1,860 rounds from the 3pdrs, and no less than 16,000 rounds from the Maxim and machine guns aboard the two British ships.

The menace of the *Königsberg* had been ended. Nevertheless, some of her armament was salvaged and taken ashore, while at least some of her officers and men fought ashore with the German troops, in a campaign that lasted until after the Armistice, with Gen von Lettow-Vorbeck not surrendering until 25 November 1918.

Chapter Six

GUARDING THE NORTH SEA

We are still wandering about the face of the ocean . . . in the hands of . . . the Germans as to when they will come out and be whacked.
Vice Adm Sir David Beatty, 1914

The First World War was remarkable for the enthusiasm that was so widespread in the beginning. Far too few seemed to realise the significance of war, and of the technological changes that had taken place since the United Kingdom had last been involved in a major conflict. For everyone at the Admiralty who saw the danger of the torpedo, the mine, the airship or the aeroplane, hundreds if not thousands of others saw themselves as members of a great imperial power and subscribed to the view that it would all be over by Christmas.

The problem was, of course, that after 1815, Britain had largely fought colonial wars. The only exceptions were the Greek War of Independence and the Crimean War, but even these were, by the standards of the day, far away, and certainly not conflicts that required a major naval campaign. The one major naval battle involving the Royal Navy was that of Navarino in 1827, but the Allies fighting the Turks faced a fleet that was so incompetently led and badly trained that their gunnery missed and even the fire-ships caused more damage to their own side than to the Allies. As the last great battle of the age of sail, it hardly offered any clues to tactics in the age of steam.

In the belief that invasion was a serious danger, patrol flotillas were created using

One of the guardians of the North Sea was Cdre Reginald Tyrwhitt, who commanded the destroyers. Here, he is seen in a warmer climate. *(IWM Q 115159)*

the older destroyers. These were based on the Forth, Tyne and Humber, and at Dover, and were commanded by an Admiral of Patrols, although this was soon changed to Rear Admiral Commanding the East Coast of England. The Dover Patrol was separated from the rest and placed under the command of Rear Adm the Honourable Horace Hood – the "Onourable 'Orace' to the lower deck.

While the Dover Patrol and the major estuarial patrols were intended to counter any attempt at an invasion, attacks on the major naval ports themselves were to be countered by local defence flotillas at the Nore, Portsmouth, Devonport, Pembroke in Wales and Queenstown in the south of Ireland. These had to patrol off these ports using the oldest destroyers, torpedo boats and submarines. A Channel Fleet was created and, with the 12th Cruiser Squadron, came under the direct control of the Admiralty. At Harwich, a destroyer flotilla was created with more than twenty destroyers and a small number of light cruisers under Cdre Tyrwhitt, while Cdre Roger Keyes became Cdre (S) with a Harwich-based submarine flotilla.

Other measures were put in place, although there were problems with the barrage created between Folkestone and Cap Gris Nez. Consisting of nets between drifters, the barrage proved to be too long and the tides too strong to be completely effective. On 15 February 1918, the barrage, or the ships between which it was strung, were attacked by German destroyers. Some eight ships were sunk, while many more were damaged.

EARLY LOSSES

On 8 August, the dreadnought *Monarch* was attacked by a submarine, *U-13*, although the torpedo missed her and her two sisters *Ajax*

and *Audacious* as they steamed off Fair Isle, between Orkney and Shetland. Next day, the light cruiser *Birmingham* found a submarine sitting on the surface, from which her crew could hear hammering inside. The cruiser immediately opened fire, and the submarine started to move forwards, but so slowly that *Birmingham* was able to turn and speed towards her and then ram her, slicing the submarine, *U-15*, in half. This was the Royal Navy's first U-boat success of the war. This victory delighted the Admiralty as much as it alarmed the Grand Fleet, who had not expected to find a submarine so far north.

So far, the British and the Germans had been lucky and unlucky in equal measure, but grim reality was not long in coming. On 22 September 1914, three elderly British armoured cruisers, *Aboukir*, *Cressy* and *Hogue*, were on patrol when they were spotted by Otto Weddigen, commander of *U-9*. Weddigen fired his first torpedo at the middle ship of the three, *Aboukir*, at 0620, at a distance of 550yd, before taking his submarine down to 50ft. Exactly thirty-one seconds later, he and his crew heard an explosion and a crashing sound. The torpedo had penetrated the cruiser amidships on her starboard side, below the waterline; water started to flood into the engine and boiler rooms and she began to take on a list. No one had seen the submarine's periscope or the torpedo, so aboard the assumption was that she had struck a mine. Her commanding officer hoisted a mine warning and called for the other two ships to come alongside so that the wounded could be transferred.

Attempts were made to save the stricken ship by flooding compartments to correct the list, but it soon became clear that she was sinking. Only one lifeboat was available; the others had been destroyed by the explosion or could not be swung out as

Hogue was one of three elderly cruisers all torpedoed within an hour off the Dutch coast – an early blow to British morale. The funnel markings are to identify the ship, a more complicated system than pennant numbers. *(IWM Q 21355)*

there was insufficient steam to power the derricks.

It was aboard *Hogue* that it was first realised that there was a submarine in the area, and her commanding officer signalled *Cressy* to look out for a periscope. At 0655, as *Aboukir* rolled over and slid beneath the waves, leaving the sea dotted with the heads of the members of her ship's company, *Hogue* was struck by two torpedoes, about five seconds apart. Despite closing all watertight doors immediately, within five minutes the quarterdeck was awash. There was an explosion from below, and the order

was given to abandon ship. At 0715, *Hogue*, too, rolled over and sank.

By this time, *U-9*'s batteries were running low, but Weddigen still had one torpedo left for his bow tubes, and two more in his stern tubes. Immediately after *Hogue* had been hit, *Cressy*'s commanding officer heard that a periscope had been spotted and ordered his engines to full speed intending to ram, but he saw nothing and decided to return to pick up survivors. *Cressy* was stopped in the water, picking up survivors from her two sister ships when, at 0720, *U-9* fired both stern torpedoes, and those aboard heard one explosion. The cruiser was struck on the starboard side, quickly heeled over to starboard and then briefly righted herself. The other torpedo had passed under the ship without doing any damage. At 0730, a further torpedo struck the ship on her port side, rupturing the tanks in the boiler room and scalding the men on watch below. *Cressy* followed her sisters, rolling over, but then remained afloat upside down for twenty minutes before, at 0755, she finally sank.

For the ship's company of *Cressy*, the awful truth was that all of her boats were away rescuing those from the other two ships when she went down. They had to make do with whatever came to hand.

Dutch trawlers nearby were reluctant to approach, having seen three large ships sunk in less than ninety minutes. It was not until 0830 that the first trawler approached and eventually picked up 286 exhausted men from the water. Another small Dutch vessel rescued 147 men. British trawlers then began to help, followed later by Tyrwhitt's destroyers from Harwich. Just 837 men were disembarked at Harwich, shoeless, and many had also lost their clothes and were wrapped in blankets, while sixty-two officers and 1,397 men had been lost.

Meanwhile, those ashore at the Admiralty were casting around for culprits. Fisher, in

Another armoured cruiser, this time one of the Cressy class. *(IWM Q 38577)*

A coastal airship keeps watch over a convoy. *(IWM HU 67885)*

retirement, criticised the decision to send the ships on patrol so close to waters in which the Germans were likely to be present. It was clear that the southern North Sea was no place for large warships.

Further north, the Grand Fleet had meanwhile led a charmed existence. As early as the morning of 24 November 1914, *U-18*, finding the Pentland Skerries navigation light lit the previous night, entered Hoxa Sound. The submarine's periscope was noticed by an armed trawler which rammed it, and while the submarine was able to crawl away, eventually it had to be scuttled, leaving the ship's company to be rescued by British destroyers. At this stage, anti-submarine warfare technology was non-existent, but later hydrophones

became available that could pick up the sound of passing ships, while cables laid on the seabed registered the magnetic field of any passing vessel on a galvanometer. These defensive measures proved their worth on 28 October 1918, when *UB-116* was detected and the minefield remotely activated. When *UB-116* raised her periscope shortly after 2330, heading for the boom entrance, the mines were remotely detonated, crushing the submarine and leaving a tell-tale oil slick on the surface, but no survivors.

THE RAIDS ON THE EAST COAST

During the First World War, at no time did the Germans consider an invasion of the United Kingdom, despite British fears.

Nevertheless, the towns of Britain's east coast were at risk. The estuary patrols between the Forth and the Humber, the flotillas based at Harwich, and the defences of the Nore and the Dover Patrol, impressive though they might sound, did leave a number of weak points in the defence of an island nation. To suggest that there were areas left undefended would be wrong, but the strength of defences has always been, and will always be, relative. In both world wars, the Royal Navy decided early on that its major fleet units would be too vulnerable in the southern North Sea because of the danger from mines and torpedoes, to which could be added air attack in the later conflict.

Great Yarmouth in Norfolk, had as the town's protection during 1914, six elderly destroyers and a small gunboat that was additionally equipped for minesweeping, although three submarines were also in port. On 3 November 1914, the mine-sweeping gunboat and two of the destroyers had put to sea, when the gunboat and then one of the destroyers found themselves confronted by the battlecruiser squadron of the German High Seas Fleet, commanded by Rear Adm Franz von Hipper with the three German battlecruisers *Seydlitz*, *Moltke* and *Von der Tann*, the armoured cruiser *Blücher*, and the four light cruisers *Graudenz*, *Kolberg*, *Stralsund* and *Strassburg*. After a short gunnery engagement, during which the gunboat *Halcyon* suffered some damage until protected by the destroyer *Lively*'s smokescreen, Hipper broke off the engagement for fear of being drawn into a minefield further south, and at 0740 turned his ships to bombard the town. The light cruisers were with the battlecruisers both as a protective screen and also to lay mines off Great Yarmouth and Lowestoft.

Halcyon had started to send wireless signals as soon as she had spotted the German ships, and despite her damage continued to do so. In the harbour at Great Yarmouth, the four destroyers began to raise steam while the three submarines put to sea. Only one of them, *D5*, got close to the Germans, but she struck a mine, killing everyone on board except two officers and two men in the conning tower.

The Admiralty had known since 0700 that major German fleet units were at sea that morning, but normal procedures had been disrupted as news of the disaster at Coronel had been coming through. Jellicoe, commander-in-chief of the Grand Fleet was away from his ships, returning north to Scotland from a meeting at the Admiralty, but had he been with his ships, there would still have been little that he could have done, given the distance between the anchorage at Lough Swilly and Norfolk. Even when *Halcyon* returned to harbour at 0830 to confirm that there were eight German ships offshore, the Admiralty did nothing, and it was not until 0955 that Beatty was ordered to give pursuit with his battlecruisers, by which time the Germans were on their way back to Wilhelmshaven.

The Admiralty had by this time obtained no less than three copies of the German codebook and could decipher the signals sent by and to the High Seas Fleet. The copies had been obtained by various means, and indeed it took some time before the importance of the first, from a steamer seized off Australia, was fully appreciated and sent to London. The second had come from a sunken light cruiser and had been found by the Russians, who had been prompt in recognising its value and handing it over to the British. The third had been found by sheer chance. On 17 October, British warships had sunk four German destroyers laying mines off the Netherlands, and although the commanding officer of one of the destroyers had dropped his ship's papers overboard in a sealed chest, this had been dragged up in the net of a British trawler.

On this occasion, the exercise had been of limited strategic benefit to the Germans. Their newly laid minefield had accounted for a submarine and three trawlers, but their shells had simply landed in the sea or on a deserted beach. They had, by chance, lost another of their armoured cruisers as she attempted to enter Wilhelmshaven in fog and hit a mine in the protective minefield, sinking with the loss of more than 200 of her ship's company.

It was not to be long before the Germans were back. The knowledge that at least two of Beatty's battlecruisers had been deployed to the Falklands encouraged them to consider a hit-and-run raid. The operation was also considered useful to repair German morale after the defeat in the South Atlantic.

Hipper led his ships to sea at 0300 on 15 December 1914, flying his flag in the battlecruiser *Seydlitz*, and accompanied by the *Derfflinger*, *Moltke* and *Von der Tann*, as well as the armoured cruiser *Blücher*, and four light cruisers, including one, *Kolberg*, carrying a hundred mines. There was also a screen of eighteen destroyers. Twelve hours later, the High Seas Fleet followed Hipper's force to sea, in theory ready to provide cover if the British should attempt to cut off Hipper's force on its way back, but never close enough to risk an engagement.

In the darkness of the night of 15/16 December, steaming without lights, the Germans were nearly discovered at sea when the destroyer *S-33* sent a wireless message to the light cruiser *Strassburg*, requesting a course, and received the curt reply 'Stop wireless'. Unable to obtain a course, the commander of the destroyer reversed course and, near the Dogger Bank, found four British destroyers. Outnumbered, the German commanding officer decided to join the British ships in the hope that they would take him for one of their own, and steamed just 200yd from the nearest British ship for twenty minutes, before calmly making a course adjustment and slipping away.

Stormy winter weather contributed to the difficulties the Germans faced that night. The light cruisers complained that it was too rough for gunnery, while further down the scale, the destroyers' decks were awash; it would be impossible to load torpedoes into the deck tubes, and many of them had lost their masts. Hipper considered cancelling the operation, but was loath to do so. Instead, he ordered his light cruisers and destroyers back to the protection of the High Seas Fleet, which he believed to be much closer to him than was in fact the case, with the exception of the minelaying cruiser *Kolberg*. He then divided his force into two, with *Derfflinger*, *Von der Tann* and *Kolberg* sent to Scarborough, where *Kolberg* would leave the other ships to lay mines off Flamborough Head. Hipper himself went with *Seydlitz*, *Moltke* and *Blücher* to Hartlepool.

On the misty morning of 16 December 1914 at 0800, the inhabitants of Scarborough, a holiday resort on the Yorkshire coast, were shaken by the sound of gunfire at sea, followed by shells crashing, not into the beach, but into the centre of the town. Shells hit the old castle, while others hit the Grand Hotel, exposed on its cliff top. All in all, by the time the guns stopped firing at 0830, seventeen of the inhabitants were dead and another ninety-nine wounded.

Further north, but still on the Yorkshire coast, the fishing town of Whitby was the next target, with the aiming point being the coastguard station on the cliff tops near the old abbey on the south side of the town. The first shell hit the cliffs just below the coast-guard station and a splinter decapitated one of the coastguards who had just stepped outside. This bombardment was even briefer than that at Scarborough, lasting for just ten minutes. Two people were killed and another two wounded.

Much further north, about forty miles from Whitby, the shipbuilding town of Hartlepool was defended by a territorial company of the Durham Light Infantry, as well as three old coast artillery 6in guns, and two old light cruisers, four elderly destroyers and a submarine. Here the War Office had sent a message instructing the local commander that a 'special lookout be kept all along the east coast at dawn'. No one warned the warships, but they were doubtless expected always to be ready. In the event, the rear admiral commanding the coastal patrols had told his subordinate commanders to send ships to sea only when specifically ordered to do so because the weather had been so bad. It would seem that an invasion was expected, rather than a bombardment, as the men of the DLI numbered less than 200, and the 250 rounds of ammunition with which they were each issued shortly after being woken at 0430 would have been completely useless against warships.

In fact, the four old destroyers, *Doon*, *Moy*, *Test* and *Waveney*, were at sea and at 0745 the watch on the bridge of *Doon* became aware of three large warships approaching, but could not make out their identity. At 0746, the army commander was warned that warships had been sighted a few miles away at the mouth of the River Tees, and then a few minutes later he was advised that three large warships were approaching at high speed. The destroyers increased speed and headed towards the warships to investigate, to be greeted by heavy fire, and although the shells burst in the water, they were close enough to send splinters flying into the destroyers. Still beyond torpedo range, three of the destroyers turned back, but *Doon*, the leader, headed towards the gunfire and launched a single torpedo at a range of three miles before turning away. Aboard, she had one man dead and another eleven wounded. The torpedo missed.

The shells started falling on Hartlepool at 0810, with one of the first striking the larger of the two artillery positions, killing seven men outright and wounding another eleven. The two guns returned the fire, as did the single gun near the lighthouse. The coastal batteries were saved by the fact that the range was too short for the fuses on the German shells to work. The shells that did explode were those sent over the batteries and into the town behind.

The local naval commander aboard his ship, the light cruiser *Patrol*, immediately tried to put to sea, while the other light cruiser's engineers desperately tried to raise steam. As *Patrol* cleared the harbour, she was hit by two 8.2in shells, killing four men and wounding seven, while her commanding officer, Capt Alan Bruce, had to run her aground to save her. Her guns were no match for the 11in, 8.2in and even the 5.9in of the German ships.

The submarine *C9* also tried to make it to the open sea, but as shells exploded around her she submerged in just 18ft of water and immediately grounded. Had she not done so, or had she been at sea, the German armoured cruiser, which was stationary in the middle of the bay, would have made an ideal target, although she would have needed luck for her torpedoes to have made any impact on the three battlecruisers steaming backwards and forwards, even if they had hit the target. Afterwards, the commanding officer was on the receiving end of Roger Keyes's displeasure, as the submarine had been based at Hartlepool for just such an eventuality as the arrival of a German raiding force.

Fisher, too, had anticipated just such a raid. At this time, with three of Beatty's battlecruisers away, four of Jellicoe's battleships refitting after the strain of constantly being on the move – a penalty of not having a secure base – and the loss of *Audacious* off Ireland, the Grand Fleet was at its weakest and the imbalance between it and the High Seas Fleet less than it would be at any time. By now, the Admiralty's Room 40 monitoring and deciphering unit was fully operational and had some idea of German fleet movements, making the lack of any definite instruction to the force at Hartlepool all the more difficult to understand.

The bombardment ended at 0852, with 1,150 shells having been pumped into the town and the shipyards and factories. Damage was severe. In one shipyard, seven men were killed and two ships being built collapsed on to the slipways. Five hotels, more than 300 houses, seven churches and ten other large buildings had all been hit, accounting for the lives of eighty-six civilians and no less than 424 wounded, as well as the men on one of the coastal batteries and aboard *Doon*.

Jellicoe had been ordered by the Admiralty to send his battlecruisers and the 2nd Battle Squadron, supported by light cruisers, to intercept Hipper, much to his dismay, as he knew that though the force would be more than enough to engage Hipper, it was not strong enough if the entire High Seas Fleet came out and isolated his ships. His own strategy revolved around the maximum concentration of force, and the 2nd Battle Squadron was also weakened by the loss of *Audacious* and the refitting of another, even though it still had the six most modern and powerful battleships in the world. When Jellicoe protested, the Admiralty, while still forbidding him to send the entire Grand Fleet, allowed him to

strengthen his force with the addition of the four armoured cruisers of the 3rd Cruiser Squadron based on Rosyth.

At Harwich, both Tyrwhitt with his destroyers and Keyes with his submarines, were also ordered to sea. At this time, wireless communications were sufficiently difficult for submarines to have a controlling destroyer with them during a flotilla action, and so two destroyers were sent with the eight submarines ordered eastwards. Tyrwhitt sent no less than two light cruisers and forty-two destroyers to sea.

Jellicoe sent his ships to a point twenty-five miles south-east of the Dogger Bank, which he regarded as the best position to block Hipper's homeward passage. At no time had the Admiralty or Jellicoe considered intervening to catch the German ships before the bombardments started. Undoubtedly, time was not on their side, but the main reason was that they did not at this early stage want to lose their one advantage over the Germans, prior knowledge of the High Seas Fleet's movements, by arousing suspicions that could have resulted in the German naval codes being changed. There was another complication. The Admiralty knew that the Germans were at sea, but did not know their objective, leaving the Grand Fleet to suspect it to be Harwich or the Humber, with even the latter being too far south, while Tyrwhitt was ordered to be off Great Yarmouth.

As the battlecruiser force headed south, the destroyer *Lynx*, leading Beatty's destroyer screen, encountered an unidentified ship at 0515 on 16 December. The ship gave the wrong reply to a challenge, and turned away with seven British destroyers following. A brief gunnery exchange ensued between the British ships and *V-155*, which was part of the High Seas Fleet's advance screen. *Lynx* was hit twice and forced to turn away at 0541, with the rest of the destroyers following, not realising what had happened. This exposed the destroyer *Ambuscade* to further fire from *V-155*, which scored a hit below the waterline and left the British ship with 5ft of water on her mess deck, so that at 0550 she too turned back.

This was the start of a battle between a handful of British destroyers and the light cruisers and destroyers providing the advance screen of the High Seas Fleet. At 0553, two British destroyers, *Lynx* and *Shark*, stumbled on the German light cruiser *Hamburg* at around 700yd. The German ship wasted no time, switching on her searchlights as soon as the British ships were spotted and opening fire, and within minutes *Hardy* was on fire, with her steering gear out of action and the engine room telegraph cut. Despite this, *Hardy* continued to return the cruiser's fire and launched a torpedo, which missed but caused the *Hamburg* to turn away. Back in line, the remaining British destroyers sighted German destroyers at 0603 and turned towards them, but the German ships turned away.

The destroyer engagement might have seen the Royal Navy come off worse, but it convinced Adm Friedrich von Ingenohl, in command of the High Seas Fleet, that he had exposed his ships by coming too far west, and at 0530 he reversed course and headed east. His action was prompted partly by the Kaiser's orders not to hazard the High Seas Fleet, and partly by fear of a night torpedo attack by the British ships.

The engagement was not completely over, however, as a further destroyer action followed between the remaining British destroyers and German ships. This turned into a game of cat and mouse when the British recognised first one and then three German light cruisers, who jammed the British radio signals. It was not until 0725

that the message about the German light cruisers eventually reached the British battle squadron, but it did not reach Beatty's battlecruisers for another thirty minutes as a result of failings on the part of the signals staff aboard the battlecruiser *New Zealand*, which was acting as a signals station for the destroyers. The battlecruisers, *New Zealand* in the van, were chasing the German light cruiser *Roon* and gaining on her when they heard the news about the attack on Hartlepool, and then the Admiralty signal about the attack on Scarborough, and abruptly changed course for the Yorkshire resort. It was at this time that the Admiralty decided that Jellicoe should take the rest of the Grand Fleet south, but while the ships had steam up, they were many miles to the north at Scapa Flow.

The British were now desperately trying to cut the Germans off as they returned to their base. At 1125, the light cruiser *Southampton* sighted enemy ships and prepared to engage, although by this time the weather had changed from the calm of early morning, as the British ships found the same storm that had battered Hipper's light cruisers and destroyers the night before. Confusion then reigned as visibility fell to as little as a mile at times, and when other light cruisers started to leave the battlecruiser screen, leaving Beatty without a scouting force or protection against German destroyer attack, he ordered a recall, which was taken to mean all of the light cruisers, including *Southampton*, which broke off her battle with the German ships. It was only at this stage that Beatty realised that *Southampton* was fighting not one but several German ships, and that they could be the advance screen of Hipper's raiding force.

Worse was to follow. The German light cruisers then nearly ran into the British battle squadron and its armoured cruisers, but the order to fire was not given quickly enough, giving them time to turn, chased by the armoured cruisers, who were soon left behind by the faster light cruisers. Misunderstanding a signal from the battle squadron, Beatty decided that he had to head in their direction to stop the fast German battlecruisers slipping past the slower battleships, and in so doing, he missed the Germans completely.

DOGGER BANK

It was not to be until the following January that the two navies were to clash again. On 24 January 1915, Hipper was again at sea, on this occasion looking to attack British trawlers and light forces off the major fishing ground of the Dogger Bank. The trawlers were important because many German naval officers suspected that they acted as an early warning for the Royal Navy, although in fact few, if any, of them had wireless.

Alerted by the Admiralty that the Germans were at sea, once again Beatty took his battlecruisers south hoping to surprise the enemy. By this time, Beatty had a stronger force of ships than his opponent, with five battlecruisers against Hipper's three battlecruisers and the armoured cruiser *Blücher*, while Beatty also outnumbered Hipper in cruisers, at seven to four, and destroyers, at thirty-three to eighteen.

At 1000, Beatty's ships opened fire at a range of just over ten miles, and before long *Blücher*, in the rear of the German battle line, was hit and began to fall astern. The *Seydlitz* lost her two aft turrets to a direct hit from Beatty's flagship *Lion*, while other German ships also took heavy punishment, including *Derfflinger* and the light cruiser *Kolberg*. Then it was *Lion*'s turn to take a beating as she was hit by three shells,

including one below the waterline, and began to fall astern. As she lost way with water flooding in, *Lion* took further hits from the German ships, which then turned their attention to *Tiger*. Command passed to Rear Adm Arthur Moore in *New Zealand*, although Beatty never formally transferred command because *Lion* was without electricity and could not send a wireless signal. Moreover, his signal halyards were partially shot away, which, with smoke from the fires on board, made sending signals difficult. Misunderstanding the signals that were sent ordering the battlecruisers to 'attack the rear of enemy', instead of chasing after the rest of the German force and finishing *Seydlitz* off, Moore had the British ships concentrate their fire on the *Blücher*.

The Germans, meanwhile, with just one ship capable of fighting – the battlecruiser *Moltke* – withdrew, believing that they had sunk the *Tiger*, which had burned fiercely for some fifteen minutes and whose damage had also been confirmed by the Zeppelin *L-5*.

The British battlecruisers were soon joined by Cdre Tyrwhitt, who arrived in the light cruiser *Arethusa* with four destroyers, which fired torpedoes into the stricken *Blücher*; *Arethusa* herself also fired two. Then, with her fires under control, *Tiger* rejoined the battlecruisers and all four started to pump shells into the *Blücher*, circling her, even though by this time such efforts were wasted as she was beyond saving. At 1145 Moore ordered a cease-fire and, shortly after midday, *Blücher* rolled over, floated briefly bottom up with many of her crew scrambling over the upturned hull, and then sank. The Harwich destroyers closed to pick up survivors, but of 1,200 men aboard, just 234 were saved. Many of those who were lost had suffered in the cold winter water, but many others were killed as the Zeppelin *L-5* and a seaplane appeared and the seaplane's observer started to drop 20lb bombs out of the cockpit, believing that the British vessels were picking up British sailors. The British ships then withdrew, leaving many of *Blücher*'s crew behind.

The Germans were not finished with the towns of the east coast. These were among the targets for the Zeppelin bombing raids, starting on 1 April 1916, although there was some consolation that day when the first airship to be brought down by AA fire, the *L-15*, crash-landed in the Thames estuary and its crew surrendered to a patrol vessel. Later in the war, on 25 January 1917, German destroyers raided Southwold and Wangford in Suffolk, and a month later they attacked Margate and Westgate in Kent, with an attack on Ramsgate and Broadstairs on 18 March. Ramsgate was attacked again on 27 April. This attack was followed almost nine months later, on 14 January 1918, by a raid on Great Yarmouth.

The major set-piece naval battle at Jutland in 1916 is covered separately, as it deserves its own chapter. Throughout the war, the North Sea continued to be a crucial theatre of operations for the two navies, but at the same time it remained one that offered more promise of action than it fulfilled. Probably the most exciting events were the attacks on the German-held harbours at Zeebrugge and Ostend in 1918, with a second attack proving necessary at Ostend after the first attempt went wrong. These actions earned well-deserved Victoria Cross awards for a number of those involved, and so are dealt with more fully in Appendix III.

CHAPTER SEVEN

JUTLAND

There seems to be something wrong with our bloody ships today.
Vice Adm Sir David Beatty to Capt Ernle Chatfield, 31 May 1916

Jutland is probably second only to the great battle of Trafalgar in the general public's awareness of naval history, albeit for vastly differing reasons. Trafalgar was a victory and fixed for all time the reputation of the British commander. On paper and in terms of losses, Jutland was a defeat and did little for the reputation of the British commander, or some might say commanders, and there has been debate ever since over where the blame for missing what should have been a great victory should lie.

The battle was the major fleet engagement that the Royal Navy had been preparing for and which the British public had been expecting. The first two years of war had seen the Grand Fleet frustrated at their inability to bring the German High Seas Fleet out into the North Sea and to action. German delay had been due largely to two factors. The first was the Kaiser's wish to avoid losing any of his precious dreadnought battleships. The second was the desire to reduce the advantage in numbers of these vessels that the Grand Fleet held over the Germans. The importance of what might be described as the 'numbers' game should not be underestimated. The perceived need to maintain the strongest fleet possible ready to repulse any German foray into the North Sea was behind the decision to concentrate as much as possible of the dreadnought force, both battleships and battlecruisers, in home waters, leaving the rest of the world with pre-dreadnought warships, obsolescent at best, given the technical advances brought by HMS *Dreadnought* and her peers.

For their part, having failed to reduce the Royal Navy's major fleet units sufficiently in the early part of the war, the Germans planned that any major fleet action would be preceded by the British ships having first to cross a line of U-boats which, it was confidently expected, would inflict heavy losses on the Grand Fleet's dreadnoughts.

THE FLEETS

Submarines and aircraft apart, the two opposing fleets were as near mirror images of one another as the disparity in numbers would allow. Both main battle fleets were led by battlecruiser forces, led respectively by Vice Adm David Beatty and Vice Adm Franz von Hipper, although at this time Beatty had a battleship squadron attached to his force while one of his own squadrons was away for gunnery practice. For his part, the commander of the Grand Fleet,

Two of Beatty's battlecruisers: his flagship *Lion*, with *Tiger* following. *(IWM SP 1393)*

Adm Sir John Jellicoe, expected Beatty's battlecruisers to lure the High Seas Fleet, commanded by Vice Adm Reinhard Scheer, to within range of its guns. This was the first time that dreadnought battleships and battlecruisers confronted each other in such numbers, and also the last.

Beatty's battlecruiser force included his flagship *Lion*, with *Tiger*, *Princess Royal*, *Queen Mary*, *New Zealand* and *Indefatigable*, as well as four of the fine new Queen Elizabeth-class battleships, *Barham*, *Malaya*, *Valiant* and *Warspite*. He also had a seaplane carrier, *Engadine*, fourteen light cruisers and twenty-seven destroyers.

The main battle fleet, commanded by Jellicoe, consisted of no less than twenty-four dreadnought battleships. In addition to the flagship *Iron Duke*, these were *Agincourt*, *Ajax*, *Benbow*, *Bellerophon*, *Canada*, *Centurion*, *Collingwood*, *Colossus*, *Conqueror*, *Erin*, *Hercules*, *King George V*, *Marlborough*, *Monarch*, *Neptune*, *Orion*, *Revenge*, *Royal Oak*, *St Vincent*, *Superb*, *Temeraire*, *Thunderer* and *Vanguard*, supported by three of Beatty's battlecruisers, *Invincible*, *Inflexible* and *Indomitable*. There were also six armoured cruisers, twelve light cruisers and fifty destroyers, as well as a solitary minelayer.

The German Scouting Force under Vice Adm Franz von Hipper in the battlecruiser *Lützow*, also included *Derfflinger*, *Moltke*, *Seydlitz* and *Von der Tann*, supported by five light cruisers and thirty destroyers.

The main force of the High Seas Fleet, with Vice Adm Reinhard Scheer in his flagship *Friedrich der Grosse*, included *Grosser Kurfurst, Helgoland, Kaiser, Kaiserin, König, Kronprinz, Markgraf, Nassau, Oldenburg, Ostfriesland, Posen, Prinzregent Luitpold, Rheinland, Thüringen* and *Westfalen*, plus six pre-dreadnoughts, *Deutschland, Hannover, Hessen, Pommern, Schlesien* and *Schleswig-Holstein*. This force was augmented by six light cruisers and thirty-one destroyers.

THE COMMANDERS

Once described by the First Lord of the Admiralty, Winston Churchill, as 'the only man on either side who could lose the war in an afternoon', Adm Sir John Jellicoe, commander of the Grand Fleet, had been one of a number of younger naval officers identified by Fisher as showing potential. Jellicoe was at the gunnery school, HMS *Excellent*, at Portsmouth in 1884 when Fisher was the school's commanding officer. He became a member of the select group known as the 'Fishpond'. Needless to say, Jellicoe followed Fisher's beliefs in reform, efficiency and readiness, believing in technological change, personnel management and the future importance of gunnery, and big guns especially.

Being a member of the 'Fishpond' did not mean that Jellicoe's career was based on his following Fisher through the service, although Fisher kept track of the rising star, whom he described as one of the 'five best

brains in the Royal Navy'. The two reunited after Fisher became First Sea Lord in 1904, when Jellicoe was called to the Admiralty to help design HMS *Dreadnought*. Later, Jellicoe occupied a number of other posts, including Director of Naval Ordnance, second in command of the Atlantic Fleet, and then Third Sea Lord and Controller, responsible for design, construction, fitting out and repair of all warships. It was at this stage that Jellicoe realised that the Germans were building far better warships, with better damage protection. He also pressed for armour-piercing shells with longer range to be developed but, after he moved on, this project was allowed to drop, as was his demand for wider docks so that ships with a broader beam, which had the advantage of providing a better gunnery platform, could

The battleship *Warspite* was rebuilt between the wars and her two funnels were combined into one, partly to stop gases making life difficult for those on the bridge and the gunnery direction platform. Here she is seen with canvas baffles on her funnels, to confuse enemy gunnery directors by softening her outline. *(IWM SP 1049)*

be built and maintained. Despite Fisher's support, Jellicoe frequently crossed swords with the then Chancellor of the Exchequer, David Lloyd George, who opposed defence spending. Lloyd George was deaf to Jellicoe's warnings that the Germans were improving their production of gun mountings.

Jellicoe was far less flamboyant than his subordinate David Beatty. Photographs show him wearing a small naval officer's cap of a style that was by the day already old-fashioned. He had a strong sense of duty and commitment to the men under his command, and events were to prove that, apart from standing up to politicians, he had the rare quality of moral courage that meant that he could take the difficult decisions with the longer term in mind.

By contrast, Vice Adm David Beatty, at the time the Royal Navy's youngest admiral since Nelson, portrayed an impression of flair, charisma and élan, all of which might be supposed to be excellent qualities for a man leading the battlecruisers, whose role was meant to include scouting for the fleet. An exhibitionist, Beatty not only wore the new style of larger naval cap, but also went against regulations and had just six buttons on his uniform jacket, rather than the standard eight.

Beatty had come to notice while still a young lieutenant commanding a river gunboat on the Nile, supporting Kitchener's reconquest of the Sudan. While his vessel was under fire, a shell had come to rest by his feet without exploding; he picked it up and threw it overboard. Later, after the victory at Omdurman on 2 September 1898, it was Beatty's gunboat which took the general further upstream, some 400 miles to Fashoda. He was awarded the DSO for his part in the operation and was promoted to commander (there was no rank of lieutenant-commander at the time) over the heads of some 400 lieutenants senior to him. Later, ashore at Tientsin in China, he served with such distinction that he was promoted to captain at the age of 29, when the average age for such promotion was 42. As a young rear admiral, he had refused the much sought-after seagoing post of second in command of the Atlantic Fleet because it was based at Gibraltar and he wanted the Home Fleet, partly because it was more likely to be involved in any war with Germany, and partly because he wanted to be close to his wife, a wealthy heiress. This action led to considerable anger at the Admiralty.

THE BATTLE

The German battlecruisers had left harbour at 0100 on 31 May 1916. They were followed at 0220 by the main battle fleet. The original plan had been that the main battle fleet would provide cover for the battle-cruisers making another raid on the English north-east coast, in this case the port and shipbuilding centre of Sunderland. Poor weather meant that the planned Zeppelin reconnaissance could not be mounted, so instead Hipper was sent with his battle-cruisers to patrol the Skagerrak, as if threatening British warships and merchant shipping off Norway. This revised plan had the advantage that it left the German forces closer to home, and if the Grand Fleet did come out, Scheer could more easily return his ships to their bases.

Twelve hours after the High Seas Fleet left the Jade, the light cruiser *Galatea*, on the port wing of an advance cruiser screen, spotted a Swedish merchantman and turned to investigate, just as a German light cruiser on the port wing of their advance cruiser screen did the same. The two warships spotted one another and soon both fleets were alerted to the presence of the enemy,

One of the ships to blow up at Jutland when her magazines were ignited by flash was the battlecruiser *Queen Mary*. *(IWM Q 21661A)*

HMS *Iron Duke*, flagship of the Grand Fleet, in 1916, the year of Jutland. This photograph was probably taken at Scapa Flow, the large anchorage in Orkney. *(IWM SP 1903)*

but neither realised the other's strength. The seaplane carrier *Engadine* flew off a reconnaissance aircraft at 1510, the first time that this happened in any naval engagement.

The fact that the German flagship *Friedrich der Grosse* was at sea was known to the Admiralty's Room 40, which undertook decrypts of German radio signals. Capt Thomas Jackson, the Director of Operations at the Admiralty, had visited Room 40 shortly before noon and asked the location of the call-sign 'DK', Scheer's harbour call-sign. He was assured that it was still located on Wilhelmshaven, but didn't realise that Scheer used a different call-sign when at sea, transferring 'DK' to another ship in the harbour so that anyone intercepting his transmissions would believe that he was still in port. Had Jackson asked the simpler and more direct question about Scheer's position, he would have been told that he

was at sea. This massive failure of intelligence meant that Jellicoe continued south at leisure, economising on fuel, while many of his ships wasted time searching neutral ships.

At 1530, a game now began in which Hipper's battlecruisers steering south-east attempted to entice those of his opponent to within range of the guns of the battleships of the High Seas Fleet. Beatty, of course, hoped to do the same. Soon the two forces were steering a parallel course, with the Royal Navy to the west.

At 1548, the German scouting force flagship *Lützow* opened fire, and three minutes later the first shot was fired by Beatty's ships. Battle had been joined between five German battlecruisers and six British battlecruisers. At 1605, *Indefatigable* was sunk by accurate German gunfire from the *Von der Tann*. Shortly afterwards, Beatty's four battleships, which had been left behind

The seaplane carrier *Engadine* with a Fairey seaplane on her stern, aft of the hangar. *(IWM SP 413)*

Adm Sir John Jellicoe aboard his flagship *Iron Duke*. In command at Jutland, he was let down by the Admiralty and his subordinate Beatty, neither of whom communicated effectively. He realised that his priority was to keep the Grand Fleet intact rather than gamble with it. *(IWM Q 55499)*

The Battle of Jutland, fought in poor visibility and not helped by intelligence failings at the Admiralty. While on paper a German victory, it enabled the Royal Navy to maintain control of the high seas. *(IWM Q 20439)*

by the faster battlecruisers, caught up and opened fire from the north of the opposing scouting forces. At 1625, under fire from *Derfflinger* and *Seydlitz*, the *Queen Mary* blew up as flash from exploding shells penetrated her magazines. Meanwhile, a few minutes before, each force sent its destroyers into action, using torpedoes against the enemy units. In this action, *Seydlitz* was hit by a torpedo, but remained in the battle.

With the Royal Navy having taken unexpectedly heavy losses, at 1646 the main body of the German High Seas Fleet appeared and it became Beatty's turn to try to lure Scheer to within range of the guns of the Grand Fleet. He turned north, followed by both Hipper and Scheer, neither of whom realised that the Grand Fleet was at sea. Beatty at this stage

outflanked the Germans on an easterly course, but thick mist settled and prevented a continuous engagement.

At 1755, the advance battlecruisers, light cruisers and destroyers of the Grand Fleet entered the battle. Caught between the forces, the German light cruiser *Wiesbaden* lay a burning wreck, and sinking. At 1810, 80 miles west of Jutland, the main fleets clashed. The *Wiesbaden* was soon followed by the British armoured cruiser *Defence*, which blew up at 1820, while another armoured cruiser, *Warrior*, was battered by shell fire and would sink the following day. The *Warrior* had been saved from immediate destruction because, at 1830, one of the newest ships in the battle, the battleship *Warspite* suffered problems with her steering gear and, with her rudder jammed, left the battle line steering in circles at high speed, being hit several times until steering control could be regained.

Invincible had been firing well, showing that her diversion north from Rosyth for gunnery practice with the Grand Fleet had been worthwhile. She scored several hits on both *Derfflinger* and *Lützow*, but at 1833 *Invincible* blew up under German gunfire. Nevertheless, in the gunnery duel, one of her opponents, *Lützow*, was so badly damaged that she left the German battle line at 1845 and sank the next day.

Jellicoe turned his fleet into the classic line of battle, crossing the German fleet's 'T' and cutting off the line of retreat. During this manoeuvre, the British battleship *Marlborough* was struck by a torpedo, the only British capital ship to be hit in this way during the battle. Mystery surrounds the identity of the ship that fired the torpedo, but most believe that it came from the sinking *Wiesbaden* as the battleship passed by at the then considerable range of more than five miles. Realising that his best chance of escape was to wait until nightfall to slip away in the darkness, taking into account that the British were poor at night gunnery, Scheer put his fleet into a battle

At Jutland, the modern battlecruiser *Invincible*, one of the victors at the Falklands, was one of the victims. *(IWM Q 39279)*

turnabout while his destroyers laid a smokescreen. Realising the dangers of torpedo attack through the smokescreen, Jellicoe declined to chase through after the German ships. Nevertheless, at 1915 a German destroyer attack also forced the British away. A further gunnery exchange followed at 2015, after which the engagement between the two battle fleets ended.

Jellicoe's plan at this stage was to renew the battle the following morning off the Danish coast, near the Horn Reefs. As a defence against German attack, he placed his destroyers as a rear screen. Shortly afterwards, at 2110, Scheer sent his destroyers to make a night attack on the Grand Fleet, but in the darkness they steamed too far to the north and missed the British ships. Scheer himself took his battleships through the British cruisers and their destroyer screen in the dark, although the light cruiser *Frauenlob* was hit by shells and torpedoes from British light cruisers and sank at 2223.

The battle continued after dark, and 1 June began with continuous British destroyer attacks from 0130 onwards. At a cost of five British destroyers, the light cruiser *Elbing* was rammed by a German battleship as she took evasive action and sank two hours later, while at 0210, another light cruiser, *Rostock*, was torpedoed and sank at 0430. At 0410, during the last torpedo attack of the battle, the predreadnought *Pommern* was torpedoed and exploded. The night-time losses were not exclusively German, for at 0220 the British armoured cruiser *Black Prince* sank under heavy German fire.

At 0500, unable to find the Germans, Jellicoe turned his fleet north to search for damaged ships and survivors. By the end of the day, the Grand Fleet was back in its ports. The Germans were back in theirs by noon.

In all, the Royal Navy lost three battlecruisers, three armoured cruisers and eight destroyers, with the lives of 6,090 men. The Germans lost one battlecruiser and an obsolete pre-dreadnought battleship, four light cruisers and five destroyers, taking with them 2,550 men. Jellicoe and Scheer were both criticised for their conduct, and in fact only Hipper came out of the engagement with his reputation undiminished. The Admiralty failed to give Jellicoe the information that they held, and Beatty was also guilty of neglecting the needs of his superior. On paper, it was a German victory, but Jellicoe's caution had stopped it becoming a complete disaster for the Royal Navy. In practice, because the High Seas Fleet only ever ventured out again twice (the second time was to surrender), Jellicoe had retained British control of the seas. This had been his objective from the early months of the war. Hazarding his precious fleet to ensure further destruction of the High Seas Fleet would have been extremely risky and unnecessary. Nevertheless, in the uproar that followed over the heavy losses suffered by the Grand Fleet, Jellicoe's reputation suffered.

Jutland was the first major naval battle between large forces of opposing dreadnought battleships and cruisers, but it was also to be the last. The battle variously known as Punto Stilo or Calabria, in 1940, saw just three battleships on the British side and two on the Italian. The United States Navy came close to a battleship engagement in the closing stages of the battle for Guadalcanal, but one of the two US battleships suffered an electrical failure and could not fire her guns. The Imperial Japanese Navy also sought to finally make use of its battleships in the Battle of Leyte Gulf, but failed as carrier-borne aircraft took over. The two major battles of the Russo-Japanese War of 1904–5 were, of course, fought between pre-dreadnoughts.

A repeat of the Jutland engagement, possibly even one that would have given Jellicoe all that he, and the British public and media, were waiting for, nearly came some eleven weeks later. On the night of 18/19 August, Scheer took the High Seas Fleet to sea again, but this time the weather enabled him to enjoy the benefit of reconnaissance by a force of eight Zeppelins. Room 40 at the Admiralty warned both Jellicoe at Scapa Flow and Tyrwhitt at Harwich that the High Seas Fleet was at sea. Meanwhile submarine *E23* torpedoed the German battleship *Westfalen* 60 miles north of Terschelling, forcing her to return to port.

Ironically, the Zeppelins proved to be more of a hindrance than assistance, as the commander of *L-13*, not a naval man, spotted Tyrwhitt's five light cruisers and twenty destroyers and mistook them for the Grand Fleet. On learning that the Grand Fleet was approaching from the south, Scheer set off, hoping to engage them, until he received a message that the Grand Fleet was to the north and reversed course. Tyrwhitt gave chase, but realised that he could not get into position for a torpedo attack until after the moon was up, and that his forces would stand no chance at all without the cover of darkness. Believing that the High Seas Fleet was too far south to be caught, and in any event the southern North Sea was by this time regarded as too dangerous for large warships, Jellicoe returned to base. Unfortunately, in doing so he crossed the U-boat line, and the light cruiser *Falmouth* was torpedoed by *U-66*. Although taken in tow she was finished off by *U-63* on 20 August.

Once again, the ambitions of the two most senior admirals at sea with the belligerent navies were spoiled, as the two fleets missed each other completely.

CHAPTER EIGHT

THE U-BOAT WAR

The question that really troubles me is not whether our *submarines could render the enemy's position intolerable, but whether* their *submarines could render our position intolerable.*
Arthur Balfour to Lord Fisher, May 1913

Following Jutland, the Royal Navy's main preoccupation became the battle against the German U-boats. The war against submarines in the Atlantic, the Mediterranean and home waters was vital to the British war effort. The U-boat proved to be the most successful weapon in the German naval armoury, all the more so because the number actually deployed at any one time was often small. The news that Germany was considering a submarine blockade of the British Isles surfaced in an interview between the navy minister, Tirpitz, and an American journalist, published in Germany on 21 December 1914. The interview had by-passed censorship because the journalist did not submit his copy for consideration, and then arranged for it to appear first in a Dutch newspaper, thus forcing the Germans to allow their newspapers to run the story. This was despite the Kaiser's objections to submarine warfare. Nevertheless, it was not until February 1915 that the Kaiser signed the order declaring the waters surrounding the British Isles, including the entire English Channel, to be a 'military area'. From 18 February onwards, all enemy merchant ships in the area would be

destroyed regardless of the risk to passengers and crew. The threat extended to neutral shipping, because of the use of neutral flags authorised by the British government at the end of January.

Shortly before the outbreak of war, the German naval staff had calculated that an operational force of at least 222 U-boats would be needed to maintain effective standing patrols off the British Isles. Fortunately, Germany had neglected U-boats before the war and, in February 1915, the country had just thirty U-boats, of which only twenty were suitable for longer-range work. Initial hopes that half the submarines would be at sea at all times were soon dashed as it came to be appreciated that, with time spent moving between their home ports and their patrol areas, and the need for effective maintenance, at best only a third of the total number could be in position at any one time. Between March and September 1915, the average daily number of U-boats enforcing the blockade was never more than seven or eight.

Despite Balfour's well-founded misgivings before the war, on 15 February 1915 Churchill assured the House of Commons that, while losses would no doubt be incurred, no vital injury would be done if ships put to sea regularly. This was, of course, the antithesis of the convoy system. The view was that convoys interrupted normal traffic while ships waited for the convoy to form, and then overloaded port facilities once the convoy arrived. They were also thought to attract enemy warships. Finally, the Royal Navy lacked sufficient escort vessels, and many of the destroyers in service could not have escorted a convoy across the Atlantic.

The submarines had had their first victories long before the official U-boat campaign started. On 20 October 1914, the cargo ship *Glitra*, 866 tons, was stopped by *U-17* in international waters off the Norwegian coast, boarded, had her cargo of coal, oil and sheet-iron inspected and, while the crew lowered the boats, the boarding party opened the seacocks to scuttle her. The whole affair seems to have been gentlemanly, with the submarine towing the ship's boats to within easy rowing distance of the Norwegian coast. Far less so was the torpedoing of the French *Amiral Ganteaume* off Cap Gris Nez on 27 October, after the commanding officer of *U-24*, viewing the ship through his periscope, mistook figures crowding the decks for soldiers rather than Belgian civilian refugees. Most of the 2,500 refugees on board were taken off by a British merchantman, but forty died in the chaos that took over after the attack. The *Amiral Ganteaume* survived to be towed to port.

There were further successful sinkings of British ships in November, and on 30 January 1915, three were sunk off Liverpool in a single afternoon. On 1 February, the hospital ship *Asturias* was genuinely mistaken for a troopship and attacked off Le Havre, but escaped. All in all, by the end of January 1915, ten British and French

merchant vessels had been sunk, mainly by scuttling or by shell-fire rather than by torpedoes.

THE U-BOAT CAMPAIGN

This soon changed. The policy was that British and French ships were to be sunk on sight; neutrals were stopped while a boarding party inspected the ship's papers. Those carrying contraband had to take to the lifeboats while the ship was sunk, usually using explosive charges or by gunfire, while the ship's papers were sent to a German prize court that could grant compensation to the owners if it thought this justified. The sinkings started on 22 February and, between then and 28 March, U-boats accounted for 25 merchantmen, of which 16 were torpedoed without warning, killing 52 crewmen, 38 of them in a single attack when a ship carrying fertiliser blew up. At first it seemed that even with the increased scale of losses, the Admiralty had been right, as 4,000 vessels a month entered and left British ports. In fact, to put matters into perspective, the number of neutral ships stopped by the Royal Navy whose cargoes were either seized or retained with compensation paid to the owners – 743 during the U-boat campaign – was three times the number sunk by U-boats.

The first full year of war, 1915, saw the tonnages of food and raw materials imported by the United Kingdom exceed those of the last full year of peace, 1913. This was helped, no doubt, by the massive tonnage of ships taken from the Central Powers in the first month or so of war, which had given the British merchant fleet a huge boost, despite the fact that 20 per cent of the pre-war fleet had been either taken up from trade by the Royal Navy or diverted to move men and supplies to the battlefronts. Nevertheless, there were some ominous signs as the country moved to a war economy. New merchantmen launched in the last three months of 1914 totalled 416,000 tons, but dropped sharply in the first quarter of 1915, almost halving, and by the final quarter of that year the new tonnage was just 146,000 tons. There were two reasons. The first was that so many skilled men had enlisted in the army, although Fisher was soon to demand that these be returned. The second was the massive new warship-building programme initiated by Fisher.

It also helped that at the outset the battle was far from one-sided. The Germans lost three of their scarce U-boats in January

In two world wars, the German U-boats were the greatest threat to the United Kingdom, but it took some time before depth charges were available. This is an early depth charge exploding. They were in short supply at first, and the two in the foreground are almost certainly that ship's entire supply. *(IWM Q 18853)*

1915, although one was sunk by a torpedo from another U-boat. In March, *U-8* was caught in the nets at Dover and sunk by the destroyer HMS *Ghurka*. On 10 March, another destroyer, *Ariel*, found *U-12* on the surface and rammed her. A new U-boat, *U-29*, commanded by Otto Weddigen, the ace who had sunk the three cruisers *Aboukir*, *Hogue* and *Cressy* as they steamed in formation, and later sank *Hawke*, was rammed by *Dreadnought*, also on 10 March, off Scapa Flow. Encountering the Grand Fleet's battle squadrons in the Pentland Firth, which separates Orkney from the Scottish mainland, Weddigen had fired a torpedo at the battleship *Neptune*, but missed. Concentrating on the target, he failed to realise that *Dreadnought* had spotted his periscope.

In the absence of Asdic or depth charges, anti-submarine measures lagged far behind the growing menace. Admiralty advice to wear neutral colours once in the war zone backfired when the neutral nations protested, obviously concerned that such a measure increased the risk to their own ships.

Countermeasures did not simply border on the farcical, they often went beyond that. Yachts and motor launches were sent to patrol harbour mouths, yet most of these were armed with nothing heavier than a rifle with which to fire at the submarine periscope. Worse still, a number carried swimmers, the intention being that the launch would get as close to the periscope as possible, so that one swimmer could attempt to place a black bag over the periscope; if this failed, the other would attempt to smash the lens with a hammer. Of one plan to teach seagulls to perch on periscopes and defecate, nothing more needs to be said. Possibly slightly more practical was the use of seals in anti-submarine experiments in the Gare Loch, in

the west of Scotland, during January 1917.

On sighting a periscope, larger vessels could ram it, hoping that the submarine itself would not be too far below. Minefields were laid, but anti-submarine mines, moored deeply to catch submerged submarines without affecting surface vessels, were in their infancy. Even so, more than 7,000 mines were laid in twenty-two minefields east of the Straits of Dover during the first winter of war. The effort was wasted, as British mines of the period were extremely poor in quality; more than 4,000 either sank or floated away. Others exploded prematurely (especially when being laid, when they were more of a hazard to the minelayer than to the enemy) or failed to explode at all.

In desperation, a plan was hatched to create the defence boom of all defence booms, from Folkestone to Cap Gris-Nez, but the tides were too strong for the mooring cables.

Even so, no less than forty-nine U-boats were sunk between the outbreak of war and the end of 1916, when at last depth charges were available and *UB-29* was sunk by this new weapon in the English Channel.

Meanwhile, the introduction of a convoy system was hampered by a shortage of destroyers, not least because the major fleet units of the Grand Fleet expected a strong cruiser screen with a destroyer screen for their cruisers. Some have also estimated that the volume of steel used to build airship sheds would have been better used in providing a further dozen destroyers.

ANTI-SUBMARINE MEASURES

Convoys on their own would not have been enough to protect ships from the U-boats as long as they remained undetectable while submerged, except in very clear water. Moreover, no device existed that would destroy a U-boat while it stayed underwater. Asdic (or strictly 'ASDIC' since the initials stand for Allied Submarine Detection Investigation Committee) did not get to sea – aboard the armed trawler *Ebro II* – until 16 November 1918, five days after the Armistice. It was simply fortunate that this device was persisted with, so that by the time the world was at war again, Britain led the way in both Asdic and radar technology.

In the meantime, a submarine-detection device was developed and ready for use in 1915. This was the hydrophone, and the early versions could, in good conditions, pick up the tell-tale sounds of a submarine propeller up to 2 miles away. On 4 February 1915, the new device was fitted to the drifter *Tarlair*.

Hydrophones were laid in the approaches to Scapa Flow, where they were to be successful in detecting a U-boat; but aboard a moving vessel, they failed to work, as the sounds of the ship's own machinery and the noise made by the rush of water along the hull drowned out any sound from a distant U-boat. For a ship on anti-submarine duties, stopping to listen for a U-boat was hardly an option, as it then became a sitting duck. Nevertheless, hydrophone development continued, since at first it was the only means available of detecting a submerged U-boat.

The following year, 1916, the first depth charges became available. These consisted of a metal barrel containing 300lb of TNT and fitted with a pressure fuse that could be adjusted to explode at a specific depth. Rolled off the stern of a fast-moving destroyer, this was the long-awaited anti-submarine weapon, and a thousand of these devices, known as the Type D, were ordered in August 1916. Production of depth charges was slow, with so much else demanded of the ordnance factories, so starved of skilled labour that it has been calculated that as many as a third of all

shells sent to the Western Front for the British Army failed to explode. In 1917, anti-submarine warships were rationed to two depth charges apiece, and it was not until 1918 that this was increased to a more useful thirty-five to forty, so that in the last ten months of the war, nineteen U-boats were sunk by depth charges.

On 4 December 1916, the first depth charge to destroy a U-boat was dropped by the L-class destroyer *Llewellyn* off Dover, sinking *UC-19*. Even those on the surface were appalled by the power of the new weapon. Its explosion created a massive column of water, followed, if the depth charge exploded near the submarine, by a muffled secondary explosion as the submarine imploded. As the air inside the stricken vessel escaped there would be what one observer described as 'an enormous volcano of water and all kinds of debris' welling up from the sea.

The only consolation in such circumstances was that the crew of the U-boat did not suffer and that their fate was no worse than that of the crew of a surface vessel when its magazines exploded, or of that of a ship loaded with ammunition. It was not unknown for a depth charge to cause severe damage but not to destroy a U-boat. This was far worse. Those on the surface could hear the repeated attempts to move the submarine as it moved a few yards along the sea bed. If they could, they would drop further depth charges to put the submarine, or in truth its crew, out of its misery, since escape techniques from crippled submarines were simply unknown at the time. In one especially traumatic end, the surface vessels had used all of their depth charges and yet there was still life aboard the downed submarine. In this case, using the hydrophones, those on the surface could hear a night of frantic attempts to move the submarine or bring it to the surface, with the noise growing fainter as the hours passed and the atmosphere became more fetid. In the following afternoon, they heard a sharp, piercing noise, the crack of a revolver. They then heard a further twenty-four such shots, followed by silence as the U-boat commander had performed one last act of mercy for his crew.

The simple pinging of an Asdic set was to be infinitely preferable.

UNRESTRICTED WARFARE

At first, the Germans played by the so-called prize rules. This meant that merchant vessels were not attacked without prior warning, allowing time for their crew, and any passengers, to take to the ship's life-boats, leaving the submarine, or U-boat, either to capture the merchantman or sink it by gunfire or torpedoes. Nevertheless, by the start of 1915, within British territorial waters, an unrestricted U-boat campaign was initiated, the excuse for this being that it was a counter to the Royal Navy's blockade of German ports, and especially the approaches to the Baltic.

This early campaign ended in September 1915, largely because U-boat losses in British coastal waters were too high for the results, with about one U-boat lost for every twenty merchant ships sunk, and these were often fairly small coasting vessels. There had also been international opprobrium following the sinking of the liner *Lusitania* in May 1915, with many Americans among the casualties, effectively starting the process that brought the United States into the war.

The U-boat campaign did not stop, but for the rest of 1915 and throughout 1916, once again U-boat commanders were under orders to apply the prize rules. The best that could be achieved in this way was a loss of some 300,000 tons of Allied shipping per month. This was not enough to hamper the

Allied, and in particular the British, war effort. As the stalemate in France continued, and the number of operational U-boats rose to more than a hundred, pressure for an unrestricted campaign increased. The argument went that, with the United States now in the war and starting to send troops to Europe, there was nothing now to be lost by offending international goodwill. The U-boat fleet also had a strong tactical advantage, with twenty-three submarines based in Flanders, comfortably close to the English Channel supply routes on which the British armies in France depended. The Germans calculated that monthly losses of 600,000 tons of merchant shipping would cripple the British war effort and, at least to some extent, also hamper that of the French.

The impact of the new rules was dramatic. Starting on 1 February 1917, merchant shipping losses rose sharply to 520,000 tons in March 1917, and eventually reached a high of 860,000 the following month. In terms of the number of ships lost, the Germans sank 250 in February, 330 in March and 430 in April, and all for the loss of four U-boats in February, five the following month, and just three in April. The chance of Britain being starved to death was suddenly very real and, as the reduction in supplies rose to around 20 per cent, the priority that was given to supporting the armed forces abroad meant that the full impact of the losses was felt by British civilians.

The German strategy was twofold. German naval planners sought to reduce the size of the British merchant fleet, with losses outstripping shipbuilding. At the same time, they also wished to frighten off neutral vessels from carrying essential supplies to the United Kingdom. In fact, while neutral vessels did stop voyaging to British ports at first, the financial incentives to do so soon brought them back.

Q SHIPS

In the absence of the means of detecting or of destroying U-boats while submerged, it was eventually decided that the only way of dealing with the menace was to lure the U-boats to the surface. A variety of ships were taken up from trade and converted, with guns hidden under false deck housings or cargo hatches. These ships were known by several different names, such as 'mystery ships', or 'special service ships', but the title that has found favour is 'Q ships'.

The concept was that U-boats would surface and order these 'merchant ships' to stop. At this point the U-boats would be vulnerable and, as they closed on their supposed prey, the Q ship's guns would appear and open fire on the unsuspecting U-boat. A refinement was that part of the crew of the Q ship would provide a 'panic party' that would be running for the lifeboats, so that any suspicions on the part of U-boat commanders would be allayed. Some took the panic party role so seriously that in at least one case the personal belongings included a stuffed parrot in a cage to make it appear that the 'master' of a ship was taking his favoured pet with him.

Lt Ronald Niel Stuart, a Canadian reservist, was chosen by the crew of *Pargust* to receive a VC. *(Canadian Pacific)*

In the absence of sonar or depth charges, the only means of combating the U-boats was to lure them to the surface with seemingly innocent-looking merchantmen, the decoy Q ships. This is *Lothbury*. (IWM SP 2861)

Some Q ships wore neutral flags, but as the guns were revealed, these would be run down and the white ensign run up. Even so, as the Q ship campaign progressed and the number of U-boat casualties escalated, many submariners became suspicious. Instead of obeying the rules, U-boat commanders would put a torpedo into a ship and ask questions afterwards. As will be seen from Appendix III on the Victoria Cross, many Q ships were torpedoed. The panic parties then did their little act and, when the U-boat surfaced, ready to deliver the *coup de grâce*, those left aboard the Q ship would open fire. As the war progressed, sailing ships were pressed into service as Q ships in the belief that U-boat commanders would be less suspicious of sailing ships than of steam. A number of warship types were also built to look like merchantmen.

The early Q ships were introduced during the first winter of war, no doubt because the

idea of using guile and trickery to defeat the submarine menace appealed to the then First Lord of the Admiralty, Winston Churchill. Unfortunately, these early Q ships enjoyed no success at all. One of them never saw a submarine, and it probably was not the last to suffer such a disappointment. Another actually did see a submarine, just once, but the U-boat simply dived and was not seen again. No doubt the real reason for such a poor result was not the failure of the Q ship concept, but the very small number of submarines then available to the Germans.

In May 1915, a variation on the Q ship theme was attempted, an idea originating with Cdr Frank Spickernell, Beatty's secretary. This entailed a trawler steaming slowly across the sea with two lines draped from its stern. One of the lines was a tow cable with a submerged submarine at the other end, while the other was a telephone line to the submarine. The idea was that once a U-boat appeared, its position would be given to the submarine commander, who would then release the tow and move into position to torpedo the U-boat. Surprisingly, it worked. On 23 June 1915, the submarine *C24* was being towed by the trawler *Taranaki* when *U-40* surfaced off Aberdeen. There were just three German survivors, including the commanding officer, who, on being rescued, complained bitterly about the 'dirty trick' played by the British. The trawler–submarine combination scored a further success just a month later, when *C27* and the trawler *Princess Louise* sank *U-23*.

As soon as the U-boat was close enough, guns would appear from false hatch covers and deck houses. This is what *Lothbury* had in store for the U-boats – a hidden gun. *(IWM SP 2865)*

The first Q ship success was in July 1915, when the *Prince Charles*, commanded by Lt Mark Wardlow, sank *U-36*. A month later, *Baralong*, commanded by Lt-Cdr Herbert, sank *U-27*.

Despite these successes, the work of the Q ships was one of seemingly unrelenting boredom, interspersed with moments of intense activity. Patience was required, as many U-boat commanders took their time before coming close enough to be attacked. It was important that the Q ship's cover should not be blown too soon, and that the U-boat was within comfortable range so that it could be disposed of quickly and before it could transmit a signal to warn its head-quarters. Several of the Royal Navy's Victoria Cross awards were won by the officers and men serving in the Q ships, of which more in Appendix III; the awards to Lt Gordon Campbell and A/Lt William Edward Sanders, RNR, among others, include stories of successive acts of heroism in several cases. The gazetting of the awards to these men was kept deliberately vague, which must have intrigued any German agents coming into possession of the *London Gazette*. Chapter 13 also includes further details of the Q ships.

Service in the Q ships must have been frustrating. The number of vessels converted has never been accurately detailed, but it seems that many of them maintained their monotonous patrols without ever seeing a U-boat, let alone being attacked. Part of the problem in writing about the Q ships is that almost invariably when a ship was taken up from trade to act as a Q ship, the name was changed. A successful Q ship might then expect its name to be changed yet again, so that the chance of the enemy recognising a particular name as belonging to a Q ship was much reduced.

Some of the Q ships survived incredible damage, but others were not so fortunate. One of these was *Q6, Zylpha*, which was torpedoed by *U-82* off the west of Ireland on 11 June 1917, and sank four days later.

The real problem was, of course, that eventually the Q ships' secret was out, described by the German press as 'barbarous' and 'contrary to the rules of civilised warfare', and this gave the U-boat commanders the freedom to treat every Allied merchant vessel as a possible Q ship. The losers were the ships' companies of the many merchantmen simply plying their trade. It must have been small consolation to them that the Germans were being forced to expend precious torpedoes rather than sinking ships either by shellfire or by boarding and placing explosive charges.

THE CONVOYS

Yet, at first, the British Admiralty resisted suggestions that it should instigate a convoy system. There was nothing new about the concept of the convoy; it had been invented by the Romans, and was employed much later by the Spanish, to protect shipping from pirates in the Mediterranean and the Caribbean respectively. One of the main reasons for the existence of the Royal Navy was, and always has been, the protection of merchant shipping. Britain had the world's largest navy; it also had the world's largest merchant fleet.

The reasons for not instigating a convoy system included the pressures on the fleet, especially in maintaining the blockade of the German fleet in the Baltic and the Turkish fleet in the eastern Mediterranean, all of which was valid. The Admiralty also maintained that putting merchant shipping into convoys would only encourage the U-boats to concentrate on the convoys rather than having to seek individual merchant ships. Convoys, by their very nature, would also have to proceed at the speed of the slowest vessel. Again, these arguments were true, but only up to a point. The problem was that seeking a submarine in the open sea was akin to searching for the proverbial needle in a haystack. If submarines were drawn to convoys, then at least their likely position was known and countermeasures could be taken. The problem of proceeding at the speed of the slowest could be eased to some extent by having faster and slower convoys.

This is not to suggest that a convoy system did not have disadvantages. Supplies were likely to be held up as ships waited for a convoy to form, and, at the receiving end, ports were likely to be working at peak pressure as a convoy arrived, and idle in between. Warehousing was also placed under pressure as convoys arrived. Some argued that U-boats looking for solitary merchant vessels had a succession of targets, against a single chance against a convoy, but if a U-boat managed to evade the escorts and get among a convoy, it did have a large number of targets to choose from, and might have more than one success before being forced to evade the escort vessels.

It was not until May 1917 that the British finally introduced a convoy system. The first, which sailed from Gibraltar to the UK on 10 May, was almost in the nature of an experiment, and was escorted by two Q ships. On 24 May, the first North Atlantic convoy sailed from Newport News, escorted by the armoured cruiser *Roxburgh*, while from the other side of the Atlantic, the USN had begun to station destroyers at Queenstown in the south of Ireland. Meanwhile, the German U-boats continued their attacks and losses mounted, while the number of U-boats in service continued to rise to a total of 120. Even after the convoys were introduced, losses continued for some time. Nevertheless, by the second half of the year, U-boat losses reached forty-six, while new construction provided just forty-two replacements. The tide had started to turn. Other measures helped, with a new and much improved form of mine being laid at the southern end of the North Sea, so that U-boats at what had been their forward bases in Belgium could no longer slip through the Straits of Dover, but had instead to take the lengthy route around the north of Scotland.

The result of these measures was that during 1918, a total of 1,133 Allied merchant vessels were sunk, a much reduced rate. Just 134 of these were sailing in convoy; the remainder, the majority, were individual sailings. In May, thirty-six convoys crossed the patrol line maintained by eight U-boats off the west coast of Ireland, but only five were intercepted, with the loss of a total of just three merchant ships.

The Admiralty had been slow to react, and had even defended its decision not to form convoys. Given that it took time for the convoys to work properly, the losses continued beyond the initial formation, with an inevitable delay in achieving the benefits. Losses would have been much less had a convoy system been in place, with seamen – both naval and civilian – accomplished in convoy procedures.

In the end, the German surrender was brought about by the combined effect of the convoy system and the blockade of German ports, plus FM Haig's successful final hundred days of war in France. It might not have been so. The German forces in France were refreshed by the collapse of the Russian armies on the Eastern Front, simultaneously reducing the demands on the German armed forces and giving the country access to food and raw materials. The significance of this was such that the Germany navy was planning to increase submarine production to new heights in 1919 and 1920.

CHAPTER NINE

THE ROYAL NAVAL AIR SERVICE

Britannia (in holiday mood): 'What are the wild waves saying?'
Mr Punch: 'Well, if you ask me, ma'am, they are saying that if you want to go on ruling 'em,
you've got to rule the air too.'
Punch – 14 June 1922

The Royal Flying Corps had been created in 1912 with both Naval and Military Wings. A Central Flying School at Upavon opened on 19 June 1912, and by April 1913 the first ten naval officers had qualified as pilots. Volunteers, who had to be at least the rank of lieutenant in the RN, or, in the RM, captain or lieutenant with two years' or more service in the rank, were called for, subject to the approval of their commanding officer. The courses were also open to RNR or RNVR officers, with preference given to those who had undergone a period of training in a warship or naval establishment. Anyone who had obtained their pilot's qualification privately – in practice this meant the Certificate of the Royal Aero Club – was awarded the sum of £75, liable to be repaid if he left the service within four years; subject to prior approval, he would receive full pay with lodging and other allowances. Once qualified, naval airmen were liable to be allocated to airships or aeroplanes as required and had no choice in the matter.

The Committee for Imperial Defence, CID, set up an Air Committee as early as April 1912.

The creation of a distinct naval aviation service was largely at the instigation of Capt Murray Sueter, first Inspecting Captain of Naval Aviation and at the time Director Air Department, Admiralty, who wrote a paper dated 24 February 1914.

Interestingly, it was first proposed that officers were to have one year's seagoing experience in a commissioned rank, and not be away from the fleet for more than four years. Ratings were also expected to have seagoing experience early in their service and certainly before attaining the rank of petty officer. In practice, many of these requirements were later dropped, so that on its formation civilians could join.

By July 1914, Admiralty documents were discussing a Royal Naval Air Service, but this remained part of the RFC until after Churchill had left the Admiralty in 1915.

The RNAS consisted of:

the Air Department, Admiralty,
the Central Air Office,
the Royal Naval Flying School,
Royal Naval air stations,
aircraft and airships, seaplane ships, balloons and kites.

While the Germans used their rigid Zeppelins for offensive purposes, the semi-rigid airships of the RNAS were better suited to convoy protection. This is a North Sea class airship, one of the first to have a proper cabin rather than a modified aeroplane fuselage. The distinctive shape is given by having three internal air bags. Ground handling was very labour-intensive. *(IWM Q 27433)*

Whenever a naval air station was established at a point where there was already a coastguard station, its duties would include those of the coastguard station.

The Central Air Office was the heart of the RNAS, and in August 1914 it was headed by Wg Cdr Francis Scarlett, who was the Inspecting Captain of Aircraft.

By July 1914, there were six naval air stations, at Dundee, Calshot on Southampton Water, the Isle of Grain, Felixstowe, Fort George and Great Yarmouth, while there was also a naval flying school at Eastchurch on the Isle of Sheppey. There was an airship section at Farnborough, doubtless shared with the RFC until the RNAS assumed responsibility for all airships,

and an active station at Kingsnorth on the River Medway. The practice adopted later of giving all naval air stations ship names so that they had dual designation, as with, for example, RNAS Lee-on-Solent, HMS *Daedalus*, had yet to be adopted, but for all administrative purposes these units and their personnel were on the books of HMS *Pembroke* at Chatham.

In May 1914, it had been proposed that further air stations be prepared at Scapa Flow, Peterhead, on the Humber and near Newcastle, while plans were laid for an airship shed at Cromer. Squadrons of fighting aeroplanes were also proposed for a number of air stations, including Eastchurch, for which ten aircraft were proposed, although elsewhere squadrons initially consisted of eight aircraft in two flights. At the time, the Naval Wing consisted of 55 seaplanes and 40 landplanes, of which 35 were biplanes. Another 45 seaplanes were on order, along with 4 biplanes. Airships were in service and one Parseval and one French Astra Torres were on order, while the Military Wing's airships were being transferred to the Naval Wing, which was to assume development of all lighter-than-air craft. Seven non-rigid airships were in service and another seven on order, as was a single rigid airship. Eight squadrons were earmarked for expeditionary service.

The war saw the RNAS blossom, although rivalry with the RFC soon took hold, and became a storm in 1916, giving encouragement to those already pressing for a single integrated air service, including Sueter, despite his position at the Admiralty. The RNAS sent its No. 3 Wing to Gallipoli, and a Royal Air Service was proposed.

AA DEFENCE

The Admiralty assumed control of Britain's AA defences in September 1914, establishing the Royal Naval Volunteer Reserve Anti-Aircraft Corps. Prior to the declaration of war, no measures had been put in hand for AA defences, although on 8 August, the Royal Garrison Artillery had mounted three 1pdr pom-poms in Whitehall to protect the Admiralty and the War Office. The Admiralty had made provision for the defence of ships from air attack, but its armaments were needed for the protection of the ships. On 3 September, the Cabinet decided that the Royal Navy would undertake the aerial defence of the UK, since the army had neither the guns nor the personnel for this work; however, nor had the navy. The RN

itself had been so starved of funds before the war that it lacked the necessary personnel, but resolved the problem by raising part-time reservist forces, at first in London where the RNVR AA Corps came into existence on 9 October 1914. It was not demobilised until 15 February 1919. At one stage, in 1916, members of the RNVR AAC were sent to Ireland. Initially, the RNVR AAC was under the control of the Admiralty Air Department, but on 16 February 1916, when the army finally became responsible for air defences, its units were put under army control, and a number of them were later disbanded as army units took their place.

The RNVR AAC had an unhappy existence. In some cases, the members had been special constables. To begin with, they were committed to four hours every other night; then the Admiralty increased this to six hours, losing many men who could not meet the increased commitment. Eventually, many units were worked twenty-four hours on, twenty-four hours off, receiving standard naval pay if working full time, and half-pay if working half time. In some cases, twelve-hour shifts were worked. The service seems to have been the victim of much confusion, of constant change and reorganisation, with the constant doubt over whether kit would stay with the navy or be transferred to the army. Meanwhile, many members were no longer serving ashore but had gone to sea with the fleet.

There was a constant shortage of equipment, and one training exercise at Shoeburyness saw those men with previous firing experience not permitted to fire, and those with none allowed to fire a single round on an obsolete Nordenfelt gun. The more modern Hotchkiss machine guns had mountings so badly designed that they could not be loaded above an angle of 55 degrees; moreover, they could not be fired

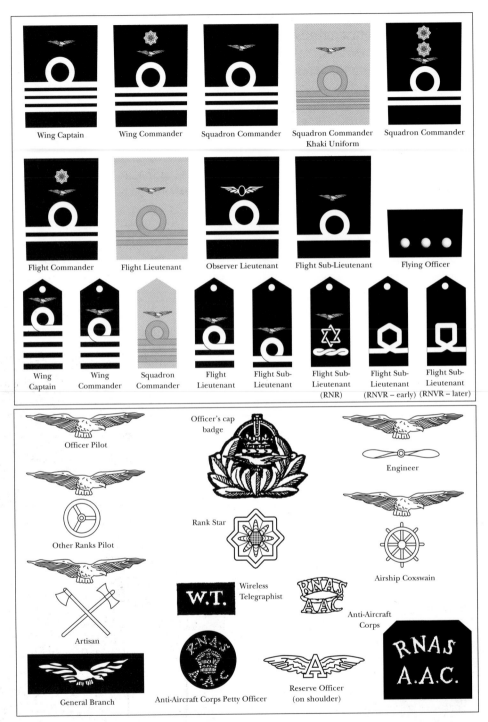

Rank badges and insignia of the Royal Naval Air Service differed from those later used by the Fleet Air Arm. Cap badges also changed, lacking the anchor. The use of khaki was more widespread than during the Second World War, with many units based ashore covering the Western Front or the Gallipoli campaign; and of course, until 1916, AA defences came under the RNAS. (Sources: various)

at an angle of more than 70 degrees, or less than 43 degrees – so much for air defence.

MARITIME RECONNAISSANCE

Initially, what would today be described as maritime reconnaissance was conducted by captive ballons, which were confined to the observation role and known as 'kite-balloons', and by airships, mainly of the semi-rigid variety, of which more detail can be found in Chapter 16.

The kite-balloon ships *Monica* and *Hector* were deployed to the Dardanelles for naval gunnery and spotting, but suffered from some problems with the launching and recovery of the balloons, which were difficult to handle until at least 200ft above

the water because of the tail fouling the superstructure of the ships. The balloons could not be launched in high winds, and suffered acute problems in the summer heat, when seams and patches started to come unstuck. The ships' gas production plants also caused difficulties and were a hazard to the vessel when they were under fire.

Unlike the Germans, the RNAS did not use its airships for offensive purposes. There was good reason for this, as the airships themselves were far more vulnerable than the robust German Zeppelin to both aerial attack and anti-aircraft fire. It was not to be until after the war that more suitable British designs became available. Compared to the German airships, the British types with their

An RNAS observer prepares to drop a bomb from an airship. The bombs of the day were small and primitive at first, and aircraft and British airships could not lift a significant warload. *(IWM Q 67695)*

slightly squashed shape were less manoeuvrable and access to their engines was often difficult. Warload tended to be limited by comparison with their German counterparts, as did endurance, while accommodation consisted of modified aircraft fuselages. One wartime naval aviator described the craft as 'a botched up job of half an aeroplane and half an airship'. If an engine began to overheat, water would have to be taken by hand from the water ballast, with the mechanic making his way along rope ladder walkways to the engine, where he would take off the radiator cap and pour in whatever water had not been spilt on his journey.

Nevertheless, the role that did show these craft in a worthwhile light was that of reconnaissance and convoy protection, with airships patrolling above convoys to give advance warning of U-boats and minefields. Initially, such duties were undertaken by the C class or 'coastal' airships and the SS class, with the C class having an endurance of up to twelve hours. The later NS or North Sea class had an endurance of up to twenty hours, and much more comfortable accommodation for the crew, who were divided into two watches.

Anti-submarine operations were based on Felixstowe in Suffolk, and were augmented in 1917 by the arrival of the first large Felixstowe flying boats and by the sizeable Curtiss America flying boats, such as the H12. Initially these aircraft enjoyed considerable success against German submarines, as they took U-boat commanders by surprise. Nevertheless, their score of successes was soon hampered by two factors. First, the Germans developed 'altiscopes', upward-looking periscopes that enabled them to search the sky for approaching aircraft before surfacing. The second problem was a lack of development, as the First World War aircraft and airships

did not carry any suitable anti-submarine weapon. Nevertheless, the U-boats were compelled to keep much further offshore, as much as fifty miles, thus making the coastal convoys safer, and it soon became clear that convoys with protection from the air were seldom attacked. Unfortunately, the flying boats still lacked the endurance to provide the cover needed; moreover, air cover still tended to be, if not completely a fair-weather affair, then one that was nevertheless affected by bad weather. Operations at night were also difficult, so this became the favoured hunting time for the U-boats.

Flying boats were more manoeuvrable than airships and could cope more easily with adverse winds. They were generally more economical with manpower, having a crew of four: a pilot, who was usually the captain, an observer, a wireless telegraphy operator and an engineer. Those of the RNAS were joined by USN flying boats towards the end of the war.

British involvement with the flying boat had dated from before the outbreak of war, when Lt Cdr J.C. Porte had cooperated with the American Glenn Curtiss in the design of the Curtiss America large flying boat. Curtiss had flown the first practical flying boat in 1912. On the outbreak of war, the Curtiss America was purchased by the RNAS. During the war years, the Curtiss H12, H16 and HS1 flying boats were operated by both the RNAS and the USN, and a factory was established at Felixstowe to produce the famous Felixstowe series of flying boats. On 20 May 1917, *UC-36* was sunk by an RNAS flying boat in the North Sea, the first U-boat to be accounted for by the RNAS.

By 1 April 1918, the RNAS resources devoted to anti-submarine or maritime reconnaissance operations totalled 291 flying boats and seaplanes, 23 landplanes

A Felixstowe F2A in flight, with dazzle finish. *(FAAM Felixstowe 52)*

A flight of six Felixstowe F2As on the slipway, possibly for an inspection. *(FAAM Felixstowe 51)*

and 100 airships. Unfortunately, Admiralty hopes of increasing this force in the final six months of the war were dashed as the former RNAS units were scoured for aircraft and aircrew for the RAF's newly formed Independent Air Force for bomber operations over Germany. While controversy resurfaced during the Second World War over whether heavy bomber aircraft were of greater use on maritime reconnaissance or strategic bombing, there can be little doubt that during the First World War, given the capabilities of the aircraft of the day and the numbers available, strategic bombing was a waste of time and had nothing other than symbolic value.

THE CUXHAVEN RAID

The best means of countering the Zeppelin threat was to attack their bases, the nearest of which was the Nordholz airship station, 8 miles south of Cuxhaven. The plan was prepared by the then Cdre Roger Keyes, and the force was commanded by Cdre Reginald Tyrwhitt – the two Harwich commodores. Originally, the raid was scheduled for 25 October 1914, but while the raiding force, including two seaplane carriers and their escorts, sailed from Harwich in a flat calm on 24 October, by dawn the next day, when the six seaplanes were hoisted over the sides of the ships, heavy rain prevented four of the frail aircraft from taking off. Of the two that did become airborne, one had to turn back after flying just 12 miles because the engine had stopped twice as a result of the heavy rain. The sixth aircraft went a little further, flying 20 miles before poor visibility forced it back.

Nordholz had become the headquarters for the German Naval Airship Division during October 1914. The base consisted of a single large shed accommodating two 518ft-long Zeppelins. The term 'shed' was itself a misnomer, as it weighed 4,000 tons and was mounted on a large turntable that could turn into the prevailing wind, so that the Zeppelins inside were not trapped by wind blowing across the door of the shed. The two Zeppelins represented exactly half the naval airship fleet suitable for operations over the North Sea, the other two being based at Hamburg. On 23 November, a further attempt was due to be made, and Jellicoe even went so far as to move the Grand Fleet into the North Sea to support the operation. Even before an aircraft was lowered over the side of a seaplane carrier, the Admiralty cancelled the operation. Accounts differ over the reasons. Churchill held that the weather was too bad, while Jellicoe maintained that the Germans had a superior force of ships at sea that would threaten the seaplane carriers and their escorts.

While the raid on Cuxhaven was still awaited, the Germans had made their raid on Scarborough, not with Zeppelins but with battlecruisers on 16 December.

Finally, the long-postponed raid was back on, again. With good weather forecast for the Christmas period, on 23 December the Admiralty ordered that the operation take place on Christmas Day. This time, three seaplane carriers, *Engadine*, *Riviera* and *Empress*, were used, escorted by three light cruisers, *Arethusa*, *Aurora* and *Undaunted*, and eight destroyers, again under the command of Tyrwhitt, who believed that a small force had a better chance of remaining undiscovered while in the Heligoland Bight. Keyes sent eleven submarines, mainly to keep watch in case German ships should emerge, in which case they were also to attempt to attack them. Some of the submarines were positioned at the launch and recovery points to protect the seaplane carriers, and also to rescue the crews of any aircraft that might have difficulty in taking

Rather more effective against ships was the torpedo, provided that the aircraft could get close enough to the target without being shot down. This aircraft is a Short 184. *(FAAM Short 229)*

off or in returning to their ships. To aid recognition, especially in poor visibility, red and white checkerboard stripes were painted around the submarines' conning towers, making the exercise exceptionally hazardous for any submarine caught on the surface. Despite Tyrwhitt's belief in small forces, the Grand Fleet was once again to be brought south, just in case.

Tyrwhitt sailed from Harwich at 0500 on Christmas Eve, without warning and reputedly leaving behind on the quaysides a number of stewards landed to obtain extras for Christmas Day. Entering the Heligoland Bight at 0430 the following day, they came across four German patrol vessels, and *Aurora* picked up German wireless transmissions soon afterwards. At this point,

Tyrwhitt, aboard *Arethusa*, considered abandoning the operation, fearful that the seaplane carriers might be sunk while waiting for their aircraft to return, but after two previous attempts had come to nothing, he was reluctant to turn back.

Just before daybreak, *Engadine*, *Riviera* and *Empress* stopped engines and each put three seaplanes on to a calm sea, with a light breeze and no sign of fog. The seaplanes were to take a total of twenty-seven small bombs, with about 3lb of explosives each, to bomb the airship sheds at Cuxhaven, before flying over the Cuxhaven and Wilhelmshaven anchorages, taking note of the German warships present. They would then proceed along the coast to Norderney island and turn north to rejoin the carriers. The aircraft each had enough fuel for three hours.

At 0630, the aircraft were in the water while their wings were unfolded and engines started and run up to their normal operating temperatures. Tyrwhitt signalled take-off at 0659. Nine aircraft started, but two soon suffered engine failure and were hoisted back aboard the seaplane carriers. The other seven, in the light breeze, had to make an extended take-off run.

It took an hour for the aircraft to reach land, by which time fog had come down covering the land. However, as it drifted and thinned before coming down again, it allowed the Zeppelin *L-6* to take off on patrol. In desperation, the seven pilots tried to find their target. One thought he saw the airship shed and dropped three bombs, one of which hit a fish-drying shed. Another discovered the airship shed but in the fog failed to recognise it for what it was, and instead attacked some anti-aircraft guns. One managed to miss the airship station and instead find the Jade estuary, only to be fired at by a battlecruiser, seven light cruisers and many destroyers. One of the observers in the aircraft was none other than Lt Erskine Childers, who before the war had written *The Riddle of the Sands*, predicting a future war with Germany; they found seven battleships and three battle-cruisers in Schillig Roads. Such targets were immune to anything a First World War aeroplane could do to them, but the pilot, who tried to attack the light cruisers *Graudenz* and *Strasland,* only managed to get one of his bombs 200yd from *Graudenz*.

The operation was over by 0930, and by 1000 the fog had thickened, encouraging the Germans not to hazard sending their ships to attack Tyrwhitt's force, which in any case they believed was probably only the vanguard of a far more powerful force. *L-6* had already located Tyrwhitt's ships little more than an hour after the seaplanes had taken off. At 0900, two German seaplanes attacked the seaplane carrier *Empress* with 10lb and 22lb bombs, some of which fell within 20 to 40ft of the ship, which was by this time suffering from boiler problems and trailing behind the rest of the force. *Empress* was then attacked by *L-6*, although her commanding officer, Capt Frederick Bowhill, quickly discovered that it was much easier to outmanoeuvre a Zeppelin than an aeroplane, which was just as well, as *L-6* dropped three 110lb bombs.

Around 1000, two seaplanes landed close to *Riviera* off Norderney, cut their engines and, after their wings were folded, were hoisted safely aboard. A third landed close to the destroyer *Lurcher* seeking directions, but as the aircraft had little fuel left, Keyes, who was directing his submarines from the destroyer, took the pilot on board and the aircraft in tow.

Tyrwhitt's ship, *Arethusa*, was attacked by two German seaplanes at 1030, although again their bombs missed. By this time, Tyrwhitt realised that his four remaining seaplanes must have run out of fuel, if they

A Short 184 seaplane sets off on patrol. The massive derricks in the background are for coaling warships. *(FAAM)*

had managed to survive the attack, and turned his force back to Harwich.

In fact, three of the four were already down near Norderney and had been picked up by the submarine *E11*, commanded by Lt Cdr Martin Nasmith, who had spotted the landing of a seaplane through his periscope and had immediately surfaced. He had agreed to give the aircraft a tow to the nearest seaplane carrier when he spotted the Zeppelin *L-5*. Then, seeing a submarine on the surface and believing it to be German, he prepared to dive. The other submarine also dived, because it saw the Zeppelin, and this confirmed its intentions in Nasmith's

view; however, he could not dive because two more seaplanes splashed down beside him. He quickly drove his submarine so close to one of them that its crew did not get their feet wet as they stepped out of the aircraft and on to the deck casing; the two crew members of the third seaplane were less fortunate and had to swim to the submarine. Quickly instructing a seaman to destroy the three seaplanes with machine-gun fire, Nasmith then crash-dived with *L-5* directly overhead. His submarine was shaken by the bombs, but undamaged.

Meanwhile, the other submarine was in fact *D6*, another British submarine that had been approaching to offer help to the seaplane crew. Its commanding officer decided to surface, only to find *L-5* overhead and machine-gunning his conning tower, forcing him to crash-dive again.

The seventh seaplane had a more mundane recovery. Its crew were picked up by a Dutch trawler and spent some time aboard while it completed its fishing trip before returning to the Netherlands. Rather than being interned for the duration in this neutral country, they were repatriated as shipwrecked mariners.

On its way back to Scapa Flow, the Grand Fleet encountered heavy weather. On 26 December, four men were washed overboard from their ships and lost, including one from a light cruiser, while three destroyers were so badly damaged that they had to be sent to dry dock. The following day, as the fleet approached Orkney, the battleship *Monarch* suddenly changed course to avoid a patrolling armed trawler, and was

hit by her sister ship *Caroline* following astern, with none of the ships showing lights. Both ships were extensively damaged and needed to be sent away for repairs.

The frail early seaplane and the difficulty of operating from seaplane carriers meant that successful sorties were difficult to achieve. Later in the war, on 25 March 1916, five seaplanes were sent from seaplane carrier *Vindex*, from a point 40 miles off the enemy coast, in an unsuccessful attempt to bomb the airship shed at Hoyer on the coast of Schleswig-Holstein. Operating in bad weather with snow and gale-force winds, three aircraft developed engine trouble, and had to land in German territory, so that their crews were captured. One pilot found that there was in fact no Zeppelin shed at Hoyer and bombed what he believed to be a factory instead. The fifth aircraft flew on to Tondern and actually found a Zeppelin shed, but when he dived down to bomb it, his bomb release cable jammed.

Flying boats were better able to handle bad weather than airships, and were also more manoeuvrable, but they lacked the endurance. This is an FBA flying boat. *(IWM Q 33761)*

A Felixstowe F2A flying boat is towed while aboard a lighter. This was probably safer than towing the aircraft directly, given the aircraft of the day, although during the Second World War, flying boats and amphibians could be towed. The main danger is that the lightly built aircraft could be picked up by a high sea and swept into or on to the towing vessel. *(IWM MH 2865)*

The cost of mounting these operations continued to be enormous. The fact that *Vindex* lacked the speed of an aircraft carrier and had to stop to hoist seaplanes over the side for take-off, and then do the same to recover any returning aircraft, meant that exceptional measures needed to be taken to protect her. On this occasion, Tyrwhitt's Harwich force provided an escort of five cruisers and eighteen destroyers. While the aircraft were away, German destroyers arrived, and in the resulting engagement, the destroyer *Laverock* rammed *Medusa*, an M class destroyer, which was so badly damaged that she had to be abandoned. The only success of the day was that Tyrwhitt's flagship, the light cruiser *Cleopatra*, rammed the German destroyer *G-194* and cut her in half, only to be herself rammed by another light cruiser, *Undaunted*. Unknown to Tyrwhitt at the time, Scheer was at sea with the High Seas Fleet, but fortunately the weather was so bad that he turned back; had he intervened, the British force would have been annihilated.

The first airship to be destroyed on the ground was the Zeppelin *LZ-38*, found in her shed by shore-based RNAS aircraft on 7 June 1915. A little more than a year later, *L-48* was shot down and yielded that most precious of gifts, the German naval signals book. Before this, however, the German submarine *U-21* had made a daring sortie into the Irish Sea and on 29 January 1915, shelled the airship shed at Walney Island, close to Barrow-in-Furness.

AIR DEFENCE

Even before the outbreak of war, the threat of air attack on the United Kingdom was beginning to be appreciated. Concern had been aroused when, on 13 and 14 October 1912, the Zeppelin *L-1* made a record thousand-mile flight, taking more than thirty-one hours from its base at Friedrichshafen to land eventually at Johannisthal, near Berlin, the following day. There were claims that the airship had been heard over Sheerness during the night, which caused considerable public concern and forced von Zeppelin to issue a statement maintaining that he had at no time approached the English coast.

The difficulty of tackling the Zeppelin menace meant that the RNAS insisted that it needed landplanes as well as hydro-aeroplanes. Nevertheless, it was not over the UK but over Belgium that the first Zeppelin was shot down by an aircraft. On patrol over Ostend in his Morane-Saulnier parasol monoplane on 7 June 1915, Flt Sub Lt Reginald Warneford spotted the *LZ-37* on a reconnaissance flight. With some difficulty, he managed to climb above the airship's gas bag before opening fire with his machine gun, raking its entire length with bullets. The *LZ-37* caught fire and then broke up, scattering debris over a wide area near Ghent – mainly farmland, but including a convent. Without parachutes, the crew of the Zeppelin were faced with the uninviting alternatives of being burnt alive or plunging to their deaths. The only survivor was the helmsman, who fell out of the gondola and through the roof of the convent onto a presumably unoccupied bed. Less happily, two nuns and two orphaned children in the convent were killed. Warneford received the Victoria Cross for his exploits, and there is more about this action in Appendix III.

The acclaim that followed Warneford's action was largely the result of the feeling of public helplessness over what had become the Zeppelin menace. As early as 19 January 1915, two of these airships had bombed Great Yarmouth, King's Lynn and Cromer on the East Anglian coastline. In Chapter 16, some of the measures adopted to cope with the ability of the Zeppelins to outclimb the aircraft of the day are covered.

THE SEARCH FOR AIR POWER AT SEA

The seaplane carriers in service early in the war were far from satisfactory, and although they were conversions from Irish Sea and cross-Channel packets, which were faster than most small or medium-sized merchantmen of the day, they were still too slow to keep up with the fleet. Worse still, they had to stop to place their aircraft in the water, as they lacked catapults, and then stop again to recover them.

The limitations of the seaplane carriers were as nothing to the shortcomings of the aircraft themselves. Naval aircraft at the time did not have to be floatplanes, even before the outbreak of war the RNAS knew that it needed landplanes as well, especially for fighter defence ashore and, later, for bombing missions. However, those that accompanied the fleet to sea did have to be hydro-aeroplanes, that is seaplanes (they were known initially as 'floatplanes', but Churchill is given the credit for the more usual term) or flying boats. It soon became clear that as fighters, the seaplanes were hampered by the drag of their floats and could not climb quickly; they were completely outclassed by the ability of a Zeppelin to climb at up to 2,000ft a minute simply by dumping its water ballast. Getting in a position above a Zeppelin to attack took

Getting a seaplane away from a carrier, or retrieving it after a sortie, was a slow business. Here is a Short Type 166 being steam-winched aboard HMS *Ark Royal* in the Aegean in 1916. Fortunately, the sea appears calm. *(FAAM Short/41)*

The long process of evolution that resulted in the aircraft carrier was by way of the seaplane carrier *Campania*, a converted liner, shown here in dazzle-finish camouflage, but the take-off ramp down which seaplanes trundled on trolleys can be seen. This shows her after the fore-funnel was divided to allow a longer platform. *(IWM SP 2190)*

time and skill. Attempting to attack from below was simply asking for trouble, as Zeppelins had considerable machine-gun defences, as indeed did many of their British counterparts, some of which even had a machine gun mounted on top of the envelope. The situation was little better when seaplanes were employed as bombers: they struggled to get a worthwhile warload off the water.

There were other problems with the seaplane as well. If the water was too rough, operations became hazardous or simply impossible. Dead-flat calm was little better, as seaplanes and flying boats tend to 'stick' to the surface of the water in a calm, and need at least some small waves to help them 'unstick'.

There were attempts to improve the seaplane carrier as the war progressed. The Cunard liner *Campania*, 18,000 tons, was requisitioned and joined the fleet in 1915 with a 200ft wooden deck built over the ship's forecastle. Fairey's new Campania seaplane could take off from the wooden deck using wheeled trolleys placed under the floats, so that at least the ship did not have to stop to launch the aircraft. The following year, the ship's fore-funnel was divided so that the take-off platform could be lengthened. Despite her pedigree, the ship was still too slow to keep up with the fleet. Performance of the Fairey Campania was far from what was needed, as cruising speed was a sedate 80mph and the operational ceiling was 2,000ft, but the three-hour endurance would have been useful for reconnaissance and observation.

During April 1916, the submarine *E22* conducted 'float-off' trials with two Sopwith Schneider seaplanes, with the intention of discovering whether these aircraft could intercept Zeppelins over the North Sea. The tiny seaplanes were, of course, still burdened with the drag of their floats, and the trials

were not a success. Had such been available, an aircraft carrier operating landplanes might have had a chance to catch the Zeppelins before they could reach the east coast, albeit at a heavy cost in protection for itself; but a seaplane stood very little chance at all.

Reconnaissance and observation duties were to become an important part of the duties of the RNAS. After some initial difficulty, aircraft were used for spotting the fall of shot during the Gallipoli campaign, and were also used by some of the submarine commanders for what almost amounted to an aerial orientation, and there is more about their efforts in Chapter 10. Aerial spotting was also a factor in the destruction of the German light cruiser *Königsberg* in mid-1915, with Lt John Cull and his observer continuing to spot even after a shell had destroyed the water jacket of their aircraft engine and they were gliding back to the relative safety of one of their own ships.

Many other solutions were tried. One of the most promising was to launch aircraft from lighters towed behind destroyers at high speed; this got landplane fighters into the air over the fleet or any escorted merchant vessels, but risked sacrificing the aircraft, as the pilot had to ditch when the sortie ended. A number of experiments followed, ending on 31 July 1918, during which it was discovered that the lighters could be towed at up to 30kts without throwing up spray, but that men needed to sit on the bows to keep the lighters level. On 18 August Flt Lt S.D. Culley took off from a lighter flying a Sopwith Camel to destroy the Zeppelin *L-53*. Afterwards, he landed alongside his towing destroyer, HMS *Redoubtable*, which actually managed to pick up his landplane using a special derrick, in the hope of salvaging it.

Meanwhile, a more practical solution had been achieved, with each major ship in the

Trials with a Sopwith Camel aboard a lighter, showing just how difficult it was to keep the lighter stable and the aircraft from blowing off. *(FAAM CAM 20)*

Grand Fleet carrying two aircraft. These were an anti-Zeppelin air defence fighter that could be launched from a platform on one of the after turrets, and another two-seat aircraft for reconnaissance that could be launched from a platform on one of the forward turrets. The aircraft were still likely to be lost at the end of their mission, but the ships did not have to stop to launch them, and indeed could rotate the turret into the wind to avoid the need to change course. These landplanes had a better performance than the seaplanes. Picking up the pilot, and possibly salvaging the aircraft as well at the end of a sortie, could be handled by a destroyer that could then transfer the pilot, or pilot and observer in the case of a reconnaissance machine, to the battleship or battlecruiser. Such aircraft even flew off cruisers, as on 21 August 1917,

when a Sopwith Pup was flown off from a cruiser to shoot down the Zeppelin *L-23*, the first time that a landplane flying from a cruiser managed this feat, which would have been beyond a seaplane.

Just as it seemed that the Royal Navy was never to be offered ships that were large enough and fast enough to match the aspirations of the naval airmen, and meet the objectives of naval aviation, the situation changed with what was virtually the gift of a major warship. The battlecruiser HMS *Furious* was the last of three ships of what had became known in naval circles as the 'Outrageous' class. The First Sea Lord, Admiral of the Fleet Lord Fisher, recalled from retirement to make the British fleet ready for war with Germany and her allies, pressed ahead with an ambitious plan to land British and Russian forces in

The other way to get a landplane to sea was aboard a lighter being towed by a destroyer. Here is Flt Lt Culley taking off in August 1918. One can just make out the ratings hugging the deck of the lighter – their weight was necessary to maintain the stability of the craft at speed. *(IWM Q 27511)*

Landplanes had a far superior performance to that of seaplanes, as they lacked the weight and drag of floats, but how to employ these to provide air cover for the fleet was a major problem. One solution was to put take-off platforms over the turrets of battleships and battlecruisers, and here a Sopwith Pup fighter takes off. *(IWM Q 71274)*

Pomerania, on Germany's Baltic coastline, as close as possible to Berlin, and then advance inland. Central to this plan were three battlecruisers with a heavy armament and a shallow draught, making them ideal for operations off the coast. Two of the ships, *Glorious* and *Courageous*, had four 15in guns in two turrets, but *Furious* had two massive 18in guns. The direct attack on Germany was a non-starter. The British element of the invasion would have been an easy target on sailing through the narrow straits between Denmark and the rest of Scandinavia, and could so easily have been bottled up in the Baltic. And it was soon clear that the Russian army, ill-equipped and infiltrated by revolutionary activists, was going nowhere other than home.

The three battlecruisers had received an unhappy reception from the rest of the Fleet. To the wits on the lower deck, *Courageous* was known as 'Outrageous', *Glorious* as 'Uproarious'; or alternatively, the three ships were 'Helpless', 'Hopeless' and 'Useless'. These unfortunate nicknames soon proved well deserved when, on the night of 8 January 1917, in the undemanding weather conditions of a sea state 4 – barely choppy water – *Courageous*, her stem lifting by 3ft, broke her back.

An embarrassed Admiralty was faced with making the best of a bad job, not wishing to scrap a major warship in the midst of hostilities. Certainly, no one wished to admit that they had got it wrong. Seeking a worthwhile role for the new ships, it was decided to convert *Furious*, still on the slipway, to launch aircraft. The fleet's misfortune was to be good fortune for the naval aviators. Her forward turret was

The real problem was to land aboard a warship, and here is Sqn Cdr E.H. Dunning making the first such landing aboard *Furious* on 2 August 1917 in a Sopwith Pup biplane. *(FAAM Sopwith Pup/101)*

The development of the aircraft carrier and of carrier-borne operations was far from painless. This is Sqn Cdr Dunning's fatal accident as his aircraft goes over the side of *Furious* in August 1917. *(IWM Q 80597)*

replaced by an aircraft hangar, with the flight deck running from the roof of the hangar to the bows, although the after turret was initially retained. This soon proved useless, as one of her officers later recorded that when the massive 18in gun fired, her lightly built hull rippled and rivets flew out of the plates across his cabin.

Landplane operation required that aircraft could land on the ship, and on 2 August 1917, Sqn Cdr (the RNAS equivalent of lieutenant-commander) E.H. Dunning flew a Sopwith Camel fighter past the superstructure of the ship to land safely on the forward deck, just 228ft long. He was helped by his fellow officers, who dragged the aircraft down on to the deck by grabbing hold of the toggles placed under the lower-wing trailing edges. This was risky, since the deck really was only suitable for taking off. So it happened a few days later that a second attempt by Dunning resulted

in his frail aircraft being blown over the side of the ship; the unfortunate pilot drowned before he could escape from the cockpit.

The following year, *Furious* emerged from a further rebuild having lost her aft turret and gained a separate platform, 300ft long, for 'landing on', as naval terminology describes a deck landing. Aircraft could be manhandled on decking running on either side of the funnel and superstructure, connecting the landing and take-off platforms. In this form, she could carry up to twenty aircraft, and had the high maximum speed of 32.5kts. Landing was helped by arrester wires, running fore and aft, catching hooks under the undercarriage spreader bar, with a net to catch any aircraft missing the hooks. Alternatively, the landing platform could carry an airship.

Furious was the only aircraft carrier or 'aerodrome ship' to see operational service before the war ended, but even before the

Tondern raid, another aircraft carrier had entered service. The *Argus* was converted on the slipway from the Italian liner *Conte Rosso*, and her design was a complete contrast to that of *Furious*: she lacked any superstructure at all, being the first ship to have a through deck. Admiralty hesitation to select this as the shape of all future carriers was understandable, however, as the boiler room smoke escaped through two large ducts at the stern, making an approach uncomfortable and affecting visibility with smoke and heat haze. Two other ships were also at an advanced stage:

another conversion, *Eagle*, originally laid down as the *Almirante Cochrane*, a battleship for Chile, and the first purpose-built aircraft carrier, *Hermes*. The urgency for these two ships having gone with the Armistice, their completion was delayed while the ideal layout for deck and superstructure was fully considered. The fact that most, although by no means all, aircraft carriers built over the next eighty or more years followed the eventual layout is evidence that the time spent in solving these problems and finalising the design was indeed well spent.

A Short seaplane being refuelled, although whether from a ship or off a wharf is not clear. Nevertheless, it looks as if 4gal petrol cans and hard labour are the order of the day. *(IWM HU 66642)*

The next stage in the development of the aircraft carrier was the ability to carry landplanes. This is *Furious* in 1918 after the second stage of her conversion, which saw her gain a separate landing deck and hangars with the first lifts. Unfortunately, the superstructure still got in the way. *(IWM Q 19557)*

Before the war ended, *Argus* underwent deck landing trials with eighteen Sopwith Cuckoo fighter biplanes in the Firth of Forth in October 1918.

TONDERN

On 1 April 1918, the Royal Naval Air Service and the Royal Flying Corps were merged into the world's first unified and truly autonomous air service, the Royal Air Force. From the RNAS, the new service received 55,000 men and 2,500 aircraft. Despite the fact that this was undoubtedly no longer the RNAS, it is worth noting the successful operation in July 1918 against the German airship sheds at Tondern, the first to be flown from an aircraft carrier, HMS *Furious*.

Furious in March 1918 had had the second stage of her long conversion from battlecruiser to aircraft carrier. She now had a separate landing deck aft, but turbulence from her superstructure and the fact that an aircraft could, and did, run out of space from the central superstructure meant that landing on was still hazardous. During trials, all but three of the attempted landings had been failures, ending in crashes. On either side of the superstructure, narrow decks enabled aircraft to be moved from the after deck to the forward taking-off deck.

Known in the terminology of the day not as an aircraft carrier but as an 'aerodrome ship', *Furious* was the flagship of Rear Adm Sir Richard Phillimore, Admiral Commanding Aircraft.

On 19 July 1918, seven Sopwith Camel landplanes were flown off *Furious* to bomb the Zeppelin sheds at Tondern in northern Germany. On the way to the target, one Camel was forced down with engine trouble. The remaining six aircraft reached the target, where one shed was completely destroyed, and with it Zeppelins *L-54* and *L-60*. On the way back, three of the Camels had to divert and land in Denmark, where aircraft and airmen were interned until the end of the war. Two aircraft managed to return to *Furious*, but were unable to land on, so the aircraft were ditched and the aircrew rescued by a destroyer.

CHAPTER TEN

THE SUBMARINE SERVICE

Go and run amuck in the Marmara.
Cdre Roger Keyes to Lt Cdr Martin Nasmith, 1915

In 1904, the Royal Navy had just five or six small submarines, the 'Holland' series, commanded by Capt Reginald Bacon, described by Fisher as 'the cleverest officer in the Royal Navy'. During the fleet manoeuvres in March, they hit the battleships so many times that the umpires had reluctantly to judge two of the battleships 'sunk', doubtless to the chagrin of Adm Sir Arthur Wilson, an opponent of the submarine. The day was spoiled for the submariners, however, when a passing merchantman rammed and sank the submarine *A1*. The lesson learnt was that in future, battle fleets would need to be screened by a substantial force of destroyers. The submarine force grew rapidly, however, so that in 1910 there were sixty-one boats, twelve of them A class, by this time obsolete; there was one D class in service, with another eight under construction. This was the year that Roger Keyes, a destroyer officer, was appointed Captain (S). Keyes upset many by looking abroad for better craft and better equipment, especially periscopes. It was also the year that Fisher retired, but he continued to advocate building submarines, and larger ones at that.

On the outbreak of war, the priority was to get the British Expeditionary Force to France and Belgium as quickly as possible and with as few losses as possible. British submarines maintained a watch off the German coast in the Heligoland Bight, supported by destroyers, but the Germans remained in port and the BEF reached France without being challenged and without losing a single soldier or horse.

At the same time, the submarines of the D class and the new E class were assigned to take the war into German waters. The submarines were based at Harwich under the command of Keyes, by this time Commodore Submarines, or Cdre (S), and under the direct control of the Admiralty, rather than the Grand Fleet.

Much had to be learnt about tactics. On 10 September, *D8* encountered *U-28* on the surface and fired a torpedo, which was spotted by the Germans, who then dived. What happened over the next hour and a quarter was that the two opposing boats alternately dived and surfaced, neither quite knowing what to do about the other, until at last the German boat withdrew. First blood, nevertheless, was to fall to the Germans when, on 18 October, *E3* was stalked and then torpedoed by a German U-boat.

While much time and effort was devoted to using submarines as the preferred U-boat

Submarines berthed alongside a depot ship. Often, four or more might be moored on each side.
(IWM Q 18630)

countermeasure, experience began to show that this was not appropriate. Equally, the Royal Navy spent much time developing so-called 'fleet submarines' that could operate with the fleet, both as an anti-submarine defence and to attack enemy surface vessels. The real problem at the outset was that the warheads on British torpedoes were too heavy, with the result that the weapons used to run too deep and thus often missed their target. Adequate testing and exercising before the war could have shown up this fault.

Surface ships, rather than other sub-marines, were the more usual victims of submarine attack. On 13 September, Lt Cdr Max Horton, later to become an admiral, was in command of *E9* when she surfaced 6 miles south of Heligoland, finding the German light cruiser *Hela* 2 miles away. Moving to some 600yd, *E9* sent two torpedoes towards the enemy ship before

This is one of the submarine depot ships, HMS *Maidstone*. Her merchant ship origins are clear to see, and would have made her ideally suited for the task. *(IWM Q 21476A)*

diving. As the submarine dived, an explosion was heard. Surfacing, Horton found that his prey had stopped, but gunfire forced him to dive again, and to stay down for an hour. Surfacing again, he found nothing other than trawlers searching for survivors. Horton's next success came on 6 October while patrolling off the Ems, when he torpedoed and sank the destroyer *S-126*.

In two world wars, the greatest successes of the German navy were those of its submarines, the U-boats, but in both world wars, British submariners also had their successes. During the First World War, the greatest achievements of this still young and unfashionable arm of the Royal Navy lay in the Baltic and the Dardanelles. Neither of these seemed to be promising territory, but both were accessible to submarines when surface vessels simply could not be used.

THE BALTIC

At the outset of the war, the idea of sending a fleet into the Baltic to support a largely Russian invasion of Germany through Pomerania had seemed a possibility to some, while the menace of submarine warfare was so real that the Grand Fleet had moved to Loch Ewe and Lough Swilly, in the hope of avoiding German submarines. That even Ireland was not beyond the range of the U-boats was brought home by a succession of sinkings of merchantmen off her coast.

Later in the war, the endurance of the latest German U-boats was brought home with a vengeance on 7 October 1916, when *U-53*, with four of her ballast tanks altered to carry fuel, anchored in the harbour at Newport, Rhode Island. Her commander, Hans Rose, went ashore in full dress uniform and followed protocol in paying his respects to the US admiral in the port, who also followed protocol by paying a courtesy visit to the submarine. Rose went ashore, posted a letter to the German ambassador in Washington and bought the daily newspapers, which, as was the custom at the time, had details of the sailings of major merchant vessels. *U-53* sailed that evening at 1730, obeying the convention that limited the time a warship belonging to a belligerent nation could stay in a neutral port. The next day found *U-53* on the surface in international waters, where she stopped, searched and sank five British and two neutral merchant vessels, one Dutch and one Norwegian. Rose nearly rammed one American destroyer and asked another to move so that she could deliver the *coup de grâce* to the Dutch vessel. *U-53* returned to Germany without refuelling.

Nevertheless, it was decided to take the offensive, and the best means of doing this was seen as sending British submarines to the Baltic, where they could in turn wreak havoc on German shipping, in effect giving the enemy a taste of his own medicine. Cdre (S) Roger Keyes subsequently claimed the credit for the idea. It certainly seems to have his hallmark of daring and flamboyancy.

Other ideas being floated at the time included taking the island of Sylt, off the Danish coast, or the island of Heligoland, ceded to the Germans some years earlier by

the UK in exchange for territory in Africa. The entire objective was to take the war to an enemy that had swept through almost all of Belgium and much of France. The landings in Germany itself were the most extreme of these ideas and, compared to any of them, simply sending a flotilla of submarines into the Baltic to operate against German shipping from Russian ports seemed eminently practical, almost matter-of-course.

The idea had first been proposed at a conference with Jellicoe aboard the *Iron Duke* on 17 September 1914. By the time implementation was in hand, the flotilla had become just three boats, *E11*, *E9* and *E1*, with three hand-picked commanders, Lt Cdr Martin Nasmith, Lt Cdr Max Horton and Lt Cdr Noel Laurence respectively. Laurence was the senior officer.

Submarines were the only warships that could hope to enter the Baltic unobserved, at least in theory. Examination of the charts showed that there was not enough depth for submarines to submerge in the Kattegat, between Denmark and Sweden, while intelligence reports indicated that there were strong German destroyer patrols in the Baltic, ready to catch anything attempting to force its way through. Horton suggested that the way to enter the Baltic was to run on the surface, but with the submarine trimmed down as low as possible in the water in the hope that at night the small conning tower of these early craft might not be noticed. His two fellow commanders supported the idea.

E1 and *E9* left Gorleston just after nightfall on 15 October, leaving behind *E11*, whose engines had refused to start. The date had been chosen for maximum darkness with no moon, and it was not clear just how long *E11* would take to be repaired. The engines of the day were still far from reliable, and had already been much abused on war service, so it was far from surprising that as they crossed the North Sea on 16 October, *E9* also developed engine problems. Although these were far less serious than those of Nasmith's boat, she fell behind during the couple of hours needed for repairs to a broken shaft.

On reaching the Skagerrak during the afternoon, Laurence continued on the surface but dived each time a surface vessel approached. *E1* nevertheless managed to get through the Skagerrak without incident and settled down on the seabed to await nightfall before attempting the passage through the Kattegat. After dark, Laurence brought his submarine to the surface, where with the conning tower just above the water line, he moved slowly through the Kattegat, ever mindful that on both sides there would

be German agents, keeping a watch for just such an operation. Despite the dangers, *E1* was through and in the Baltic around midnight, when it was time for the submariners' main meal of the day.

Horton meanwhile had done his best to catch up in *E9*, but his chances of doing so had been spoilt by a succession of surface ships in the Skagerrak that had kept *E9* more or less continuously submerged. The boat arrived at the entrance to the Kattegat too late to get through during the remaining hours of darkness, so dawn on 17 October found the two boats resting on the sea bed at either end of the Kattegat.

After recharging his batteries overnight, Laurence started his first patrol in the Baltic on 18 October, believing that Horton had managed to catch up and was already safely

The cramped interior of an E class submarine. In contrast with many such photographs, the scruffiness of the uniforms suggest that this was not posed. *(IWM Q 18651)*

in the area. He took *E1* to periscope depth and spotted the German cruiser *Viktoria Luise*. The first torpedo was fired, but ran too deep because it was nose-heavy, and while Laurence fired a second torpedo, the first had been spotted so that the cruiser was turning to allow it to run harmlessly past the bows.

The damage had been done. The presence of a submarine or submarines in the Baltic was known to the Germans, and widely known as the cruiser sent a message to her headquarters. Patrols were reinforced in the Baltic, but especially in the Kattegat as the Germans immediately assumed that the submarine was British and sought to close the entrance to the Baltic. These same patrols were ready and waiting as Horton brought *E9* through. He only narrowly missed being seen and rammed by a destroyer in the darkness as he tried to dive in just 14ft of water. He eventually managed to slip past at very slow speed with just 4ft of water under his keel. Later, after a period running submerged, he surfaced to recharge his batteries and get some fresh air, only to find another destroyer heading towards *E9*. They dived, and once again escaped.

After a disappointing sortie into the harbour at Danzig, Laurence headed for Libau (now Liepaja in Latvia) where he was due to regroup with his two fellow commanders. He arrived to be greeted by a Russian pilot with the news that he had just sailed through a German minefield. Less happily, the pace of the German advance on the Eastern Front was such that the base was about to be evacuated and the three submarines would have to move to Lapvik. Laurence could not follow the Russians immediately as he had no means of telling the others of the change. On 22 October, Horton arrived with *E9*, but there was still no sign of *E11*. Increasingly concerned that

E11 had been sunk, they patrolled and waited for seven days, without finding Nasmith, and reluctantly followed the Russians to Lapvik on the Gulf of Finland.

Nasmith had been delayed for two days by *E11*'s engine problems. An experienced submariner, he knew that the Germans would be aware that submarines were infiltrating into the Baltic and that they would be waiting for him. So it turned out. The Kattegat was busy with destroyers and there was no question of running half-submerged.

There is a difference between courage and foolhardiness in war, and Nasmith recognised that if he continued, he would lose his boat and probably his men as well, with absolutely no chance of inflicting damage on the enemy. He decided to turn back. Once clear of the Kattegat, he had a change of heart and decided to try again, so he reversed course, and after recharging his batteries made a second attempt. This time he thought that he might account for at least one enemy vessel as he saw a conning tower ahead and, as he approached, he saw 'U-3' painted on the side. He fired a torpedo, and missed, which was just as well since *U-3* was a neutral Danish submarine. On 22 October, Nasmith gave up and headed back to Gorleston.

Fortunately, having a superior officer like Keyes who understood such matters and appreciated just how much the decision would have cost Nasmith, all was well. In fact, Keyes later wrote that Nasmith had shown moral courage that was 'as admirable as the bravery and enterprise which won him the Victoria Cross in the Marmara later'.

Meanwhile, the other two submarines were in danger of being frozen into their new base. Horton managed to obtain the services of an ice-breaker to get *E9* out into the Gulf of Finland, but once in the open sea she started to ice up, so that frozen slush clogged vents, and valves froze solid. Spray froze on the rigging wires and the torpedo-tube caps, and the periscope also froze. Horton was determined to discover whether or not *E9* could still dive and, to everyone's surprise, once she submerged the warmer water soon melted the ice and the submarine was able to operate normally.

Determined to make a mark in the Baltic, Horton took *E9* to Kiel Bay, where he spotted a destroyer, *S-120*, and fired a torpedo at her, but once again the torpedo ran deep. At first he thought that it had struck the ship when there was a tremendous explosion, but the torpedo had hit a sandbank and, although the ship was shaken by the explosion, she was un-damaged. The Germans now decided that the British had indeed sent a flotilla into the Baltic and that there must be a depot ship hidden in a remote bay. This did produce one benefit for the hard-pressed Russians, as major warships that had been giving gunnery support for the German armies were withdrawn to the safety of their harbours.

Spring 1915 saw the two British submarines back at sea again, and now they started to make an impact on German shipping in the Baltic. The prize rules were followed; ships were boarded and the crew allowed to take to the lifeboats before the ships were sunk. A German cruiser that had run aground had a narrow escape, as she was towed free just before Horton arrived to sink this particular sitting duck. Libau had fallen by mid-May, and Horton was sent to attack enemy transports returning to Danzig. He found three transports escorted by cruisers and destroyers. He missed the first cruiser he tried to attack, and a second torpedo ran too deep, but a third torpedo fired from *E9*'s stern tube hit a transport amidships. This was all done in a flat calm, and every time the periscope was raised, it gave his position away and led to German destroyers and cruisers firing at this small target. The Germans also lacked depth charges, but they used a primitive explosive sweep dragged by the destroyers, which was to prove effective in confined and relatively shallow waters. As *E9* was shaken by an explosion, Horton prepared to make a last effort, as his crew had just reloaded the torpedo tubes. He brought *E9* round as the destroyers moved away and then went back to finish off the stricken transport.

E1 had fractured one of her motors and was being repaired at their new base of Reval (now Tallin). Horton was left on his own with *E9*. After a brush with a U-boat – the two boats alternately surfacing and submerging together as neither knew what to do – the engagement was broken off. The next opportunity came when a cruiser appeared, leading four destroyers and a collier. Unbelievably, the collier and two of the destroyers stopped to recoal, despite German fears that British submarines were running amok in the Baltic, while the cruiser started to sweep around in a wide circle to protect them. Horton fired three torpedoes, aiming at the collier and the cruiser; he missed the cruiser but sank the collier and one of the destroyers alongside her.

There was little further action for some time as German shipping movements in the Baltic were curtailed by the threat posed by the imaginary submarine flotilla. Horton's next opportunity came on 2 July, after several days of fog, when he saw two large warships ahead escorted by a number of smaller vessels. He got ahead of the small group and fired two torpedoes, and was gratified to hear two large explosions. Unfortunately, the firing of two torpedoes at once had upset *E9*'s delicate trim and she shot to the surface; Horton dived her for safety but she then hit the seabed. The torpedoes had struck the cruiser *Prinz Adalbert*, putting her out of action for four months; the 18in torpedoes carried by the submarine did not have the power to sink a large ship.

REINFORCING THE BALTIC

It was decided to follow up the successes enjoyed by the two submarines in the Baltic by sending another eight vessels. Four of these were E class submarines, *E8*, *E13*, *E18* and *E19*, which had to enter the Baltic the hard way, through the Kattegat. The other four were the smaller and older C class submarines, *C26*, *C27*, *C32* and *C35*, which were towed to Archangel and sent overland to Petrograd. This was a daunting task, so to lighten the submarines, they had their batteries and torpedoes removed. The submarines reached Petrograd safely along canals and rivers and with a lot of manual labour by Russian workers, only to find that the ship carrying the torpedoes and batteries had been sunk. The submarines had to lie idle for months awaiting new batteries.

The E class boats went in two batches. First *E8* and *E13* were sent from Harwich on 14 August 1915, to meet *E9* off Dagerort in the Gulf of Finland. *E8*, commanded by Lt Cdr Goodhart, was forced to submerge by a small convoy as he entered the Kattegat, and then kept down by another ship. When he finally surfaced, he found that thick fog had come down, and so set off on the surface running on diesels, only to find that the fog started to lift, forcing him to submerge yet again, waiting for darkness. Running in the darkness with only the conning tower above the water, they were spotted by a German destroyer, which attempted to ram *E8*, but she dived first, hit the bottom and managed to bounce along in the shallow water. Surfacing, she slipped

past a German torpedo boat without being noticed, only to be spotted by a second boat, and forced to dive again in the shallow water, ripping off the blades of her starboard propeller. Despite her batteries being almost flat and the difficulty of controlling the boat with just one propeller, *E8* managed to make the rendezvous with *E9* and reach Reval, where a new propeller blade was fitted within twenty-four hours.

E13, commanded by Lt Cdr Layton, suffered a compass failure as she ran from the Kattegat towards the Baltic, swinging off course in the darkness and running aground on the Saltholm Flat, inside Danish territorial waters. Realising that if they remained for longer than twenty-four hours, they would be interned, the crew struggled to free their boat, but on 18 August the future looked bleak as time was running out. Despite the presence of a Danish destroyer, two German torpedo boats appeared and the first fired a torpedo, ignoring Danish neutrality, which hit the mudbank and exploded, but did not damage the submarine. The torpedo boats then opened fire at a range of 300yd, and within minutes several of *E13*'s crew were dead and the submarine was a blazing wreck. To avoid further loss of life, Layton gave the order to abandon ship, but the Germans fired into the men in the water, fifteen men being shot or drowned. The rest were saved by the action of the commander of the Danish destroyer in putting his ship between the men in the water and the attacking Germans. Layton and just fifteen survivors were picked up and sent to an internment camp, although they were repatriated before the end of the war as shipwrecked mariners.

On 19 August, *E1* was at sea in the Gulf of Riga when Laurence saw four German battlecruisers moving at high speed with a destroyer screen. He sent off two 18in torpedoes and dived to avoid detection, when he heard an explosion. One of the torpedoes had hit the battlecruiser *Moltke*, causing some damage but an even greater impact on German morale, with Adm von Hipper reversing his course rather than face further submarine attack.

While the loss of *E13* was unfortunate, the other two E class boats had managed to enter the Baltic and team up with Laurence. Their main objective was to disrupt the supplies of Swedish ore passing across the Baltic for German industry.

E8 scored her first success on 5 October, boarding a steamer and, after her crew had taken to the boats, sinking her with gunfire. She then went on patrol, but there was little further activity until the morning of 22 October, when Lt Cdr Goodhart spotted a cruiser and two destroyers approaching. Goodhart manoeuvred into position and, once one of the destroyers had passed, had the cruiser in his sights. He fired a single torpedo and, despite its small size, there was a terrific explosion; when he came back to periscope depth some eight minutes later, the cruiser had disappeared. This was the *Prinz Adalbert* again, and this time the torpedo had penetrated her forward magazine.

Before this, *E19* under Lt Cdr Cromie had sunk the ore-carrier *Walter Leonhardt*, boarded shortly after 0940 on 11 October, with her crew transferred to a passing Swedish ship. He then chased the ore-carrier *Germania*, which refused to stop and in her haste ran aground. The crew quickly abandoned ship, leaving her sinking. At 1400, *E19* stopped and boarded the *Gutrane*, another ore-carrier. A Swedish ship was stopped and inspected, before being allowed to continue on her way, but later, the *Direktor Rippenhagen*, also laden with ore, was stopped and sunk, her crew put aboard another ship. A fifth and final ship on this one day was the *Nicomedia*, which needed a shot across the bows before she would stop. She was also boarded and her crew placed in lifeboats before she followed the other ships to the bottom of the Baltic.

The activities of the submarines were successful in stopping the iron ore trade for a while, although hampered by Russian refusal to convene prize courts for neutral ships stopped with cargo suspected of belonging to Germany.

On 18 and 19 October, Horton sank four large merchantmen, after following the rules to the letter.

Nevertheless, all good things come to an end, and in December the Admiralty recalled Horton and Laurence, despite Russian objections. In an attempt to compromise, the Russians suggested that Horton become the Senior Naval Officer Baltic, but the Second Sea Lord turned this down on the grounds that Horton was 'something of a pirate'. Old attitudes were indeed dying hard.

After suspending operations during the winter of 1915/16, the submarines sallied forth again when spring returned, only to find that the Germans had established a convoy system, well before the Admiralty in London, and had no fewer than seventy torpedo boats and armed trawlers as escorts. Nevertheless, by this time the C class boats were operational. One of these sank an enemy transport, while another blew the bows off a German destroyer, although her crew managed to save her. Despite German efforts, only two of the submarines were lost while in the Baltic. *C32* was the victim of an accident, while *E13* disappeared and may have come to grief in a minefield.

The real end to the operations of the British submarines owed little to the Germans and more to the Russians, as the 1917 revolution was preceded by rumblings of discontent among the men of the Baltic

Fleet. By this time, too, the Baltic with its shallow waters was becoming difficult for the submarines as the Germans had discovered the depth charge, although none of the British boats was attacked successfully. Nevertheless, as the Germans advanced, the flotilla, by this time based on Helsingfors (now Helsinki), was faced with the prospect of surrender after the Russian Revolution. However, Cdr Cromie, by this time in charge, took the flotilla out, following a Russian ice-breaker, and with preset charges scuttled the surviving seven submarines, which went down with White Ensigns flying. While the ships' companies were all returned to the UK, Cromie himself remained and became Naval Attaché at the British Embassy in Petrograd, where he died

defending the building single-handed as it was stormed by a Bolshevik mob.

SEA OF MARMARA

Between May 1915 and the following January, no less than thirty passages of the Dardanelles were either made or attempted by nine British and one Australian submarine, *AE2*. Between them, they sank two battleships, a destroyer, two gunboats, seven troop transports and another 197 ships of all kinds. The price of this campaign was the loss of the Australian submarine and three British submarines. The passage of the Dardanelles, with its minefields, sandbanks and strong currents, often only slightly less than the submerged speed of a submarine

The one great success story of the Gallipoli and Dardanelles campaign was that of the submarine service. This is *E11* being welcomed back after one of her ventures in the Sea of Marmara, the landlocked sea between the Dardanelles and the Bosporus. *(IWM Q 13272A)*

of the day, was no easy task. In addition to these hazards, the water in the narrow stretch of water varied in density, often being diluted by fresh river water flowing into the straits, so that submarines porpoised and needed to have their trim constantly adjusted. The limited range of the submarines on batteries meant that as much of the passage as possible had to be on the surface.

Despite the problems, submarine operations in the Dardanelles were something that could not be ignored by the Royal Navy. There was a pressing need to ease the pressure Turkish forces were having on the Russians, while further Turkish troops had also tried to strike westward towards the Suez Canal. The Gallipoli campaign was seen as a means of shortening the war and reducing Turkish pressure on Russia and Egypt, but the difficult terrain, lack of good roads and absence of railways combined with the awkward geographical position of the Gallipoli peninsula meant that coastal shipping was vital to the Turkish defence of the area. The Commodore Submarines of the Harwich force, Roger Keyes, had by this time been transferred to become Chief of Staff to Rear Adm de Robeck, in command of the warships off the Dardanelles.

The first venture into the Dardanelles by a British submarine was by the obsolete *B11*, which left Tenedos before dawn on the most inauspicious date of Friday 13 December 1914. After encountering considerable difficulties in the passage of the Dardanelles, Lt Cdr Norman Holbrook, her commanding officer, found the 10,000-ton battleship *Messudieh* at anchor in Sari Sighlar Bay on the Asiatic side of the Dardanelles. He ordered *B11*'s starboard torpedo to be fired, hitting the battleship, which began to sink stern-first, before capsizing, all in just ten minutes. The return passage was no easier than the inward one,

with the submarine grounding at one stage and also under fire from Turkish forces. An indication of just how grim conditions must have been inside the submerged submarine was that when it eventually surfaced after nine hours, her engine could not be started because of the lack of oxygen in the air. For his leadership and bravery, Holbrook was the first submariner to be awarded the Victoria Cross, and a more complete account of his action is in Appendix III.

One result of Holbrook's bravery was that the Turks moved their larger warships out of the Dardanelles to Constantinople, and also sowed more mines in the Dardanelles in the hope that this would make the straits truly impenetrable. Another result was that four of the new E class boats, a considerable improvement on the B class, were sent to the Aegean, arriving on 5 April 1915. These craft would be able to reach Constantinople, unlike the earlier B class boats.

On 17 April, *E15* left Imbros to make the passage through the Dardanelles, with a diversionary air raid by the RNAS air squadron based on the airfield at Tenedos to enable the submarine to pass through the Narrows. The RNAS's efforts, led by Wg Cdr Charles Samson were in vain, as the strong currents swept *E15* ashore at Kephez Point. The crew escaped from the boat to be taken prisoner, leaving the RNAS with the task of trying to destroy her before she fell into enemy hands. Their bombs missed, but for a time succeeded in warding off a tug alongside *E15*, but Samson noted with satisfaction that his bombs were slightly less inaccurate than the shell-fire from one of the ships in the Dardanelles Squadron.

An attempt by the Australian-manned *AE2* to run through the Dardenelles was also unsuccessful, but she did at least return. What happened next fully justified the Admiralty's optimism in sending its most modern submarines to the area.

On 27 April 1915, one of the Royal Navy's most experienced submariners, Lt Cdr Edward Boyle, took *E14* towards the Sea of Marmara. The passage of the Dardanelles took seventeen hours, sixteen of them submerged. The Turks became aware of *E14*'s presence when Boyle found and sank the torpedo gunboat *Paykisevki*, a 700-ton ex-German vessel, sinking her with his second torpedo. Thence forward, the submarine patrols were intensified and Boyle faced problems in finding the opportunities to surface to recharge *E14*'s batteries. Even so, by 1 May the threat posed by Boyle had forced the Turks to reroute their troop movements over land, while he sank a second gunboat that same day. Lacking any heavier armament than a rifle, the following week Boyle went into the harbour at Rodosto, surfaced and exchanged rifle fire with troops. Then on 10 May, he sank the ex-White Star liner *Guj Djemal*, 5,000 tons, carrying no less than 6,000 troops and an artillery battery to Gallipoli. On 13 May, with only one torpedo left, and that defective, he forced a small steamer to run aground, using only rifle fire. Despite having nothing with which to attack the Turks, *E14* remained on station until 18 May, her presence stopping all shipping movements in the Sea of Marmara, and then returned through the Dardanelles. *E14* was to make two more successful offensive patrols between June and August.

On his return from his first patrol, Boyle briefed Lt Cdr Martin Nasmith, commander of *E11*. Already one of the most successful submarine commanders, Nasmith had been ordered by Cdre Roger Keyes to 'Go and run amuck in the Marmara.'

Nasmith needed no second bidding and left on 19 May. He had taken the then unusual step of flying over the Dardanelles and the Marmara in a Farman biplane on a personal aerial reconnaissance, and the havoc he created was even worse than that of *E14*. The result was that the Turks were convinced that, instead of a single submarine, a large Allied flotilla had penetrated the Dardanelles and was approaching the Bosporus. This was not surprising, for *E11* sank a large gunboat, an ammunition ship, three store ships and two transports, as well as four minor vessels, including a large troop-carrying barge encountered on one of two trips into the harbour at Constantinople. On this sortie, Nasmith took the first known photographs through a submarine periscope. On one occasion, while chasing a paddle steamer aground, he was engaged by Turkish cavalry and, after returning their rifle fire, finally decided to leave once holes started to appear in his conning tower.

Nasmith's actions were beyond the wildest yarns spun by the authors of stories in boys' comics. When a gunboat shot a hole in his periscope, he made emergency repairs and signalled for a replacement to be flown out, something few would have considered in 1915. On another occasion, he lashed his submarine to a sailing ship to keep it hidden. Rather than waste a torpedo, he sent his first lieutenant to place charges to blow up another sailing ship, cheerfully assuring the master that there were eleven British submarines in the vicinity. Earlier, Nasmith had given an interview to an American journalist he found while in Turkish waters. Nasmith modified his torpedoes so that they would surface if they missed the target rather than sinking to the bottom; they then had their firing pistols disabled and were manhandled back into a flooded torpedo tube.

Nasmith had expected to find a battleship in the Dardanelles on his homeward passage, but she had been moved. He turned *E11* round in the strong current to return up the Dardanelles, finding a

Turkish troop transport and sinking her with the two torpedoes. *E11* nearly met her end when she became entangled in the mooring cable of a mine on her homeward passage, but towed the mine for 11 miles, before finally putting *E11* to full astern and surfacing, on which the mine floated free.

Like Boyle, Nasmith went back into the Sea of Marmara twice, and on his next patrol, he finally achieved his ambition of sinking a battleship, the *Hairedin Barbarossa*, a gunboat, six transports, one steamship and twenty-three sailing vessels. In a further patrol lasting forty-seven days in November and December, he sank a destroyer, the *Yar Hissar*, as well as eight sailing vessels, five of them large.

Both Boyle and Nasmith received the VC and their exploits are given in greater detail in Appendix III.

E7 left Mudros on 30 June 1915, with both her CO, Lt Cdr Archibald Cochrane, and her navigating officer suffering diarrhoea, but with a somewhat bumpy passage through the Dardanelles, hitting the bottom on one occasion, and resting there on another, the submarine eventually made it into the Sea of Marmara. This was one of the first of the E class to have a deck gun fitted, in this case a 6pdr. On 2 July, they met *E14* with Boyle on board, and were warned that worthwhile targets were few on this trip. Nevertheless, on 3 July they came across two brigantines and a small steamer and, deciding that none of these was worth a torpedo, they prepared a charge for one of the brigantines and opted simply to use petrol to set the steamer on fire. The other brigantine was sunk by gunfire. The following day, they disposed of another brigantine, on this occasion using paraffin for greater safety.

The first lieutenant and another member of the crew had been burnt when the petrol was ignited aboard the steamer, and for the next three weeks suffered agonies from their burns while the patrol continued.

The patrol saw another sailing vessel destroyed by gunfire. They then torpedoed a sizeable steamer that had tried to protect itself by have two sailing ships moored alongside, but they did not stop her breaking in two when the torpedo exploded. An attempt to torpedo the pre-dreadnought *Muin-i-Zaffer* was foiled by poor helmsmanship, but a subsequent attempt saw a gunboat sunk. They also missed sinking a destroyer towing a German U-boat. Later, *E7* fired at some merchant vessels at Constantinople, where they found the water to be so greasy that the periscope had to be repeatedly dipped to clear the grease from the lens. Having had a number of steamers driven ashore by submarines, the Turks had by this time placed guns in the hills around the Sea of Marmara to discourage such activity. However, short of worthwhile targets, *E7* turned to attacking railway lines and destroyed two troop trains before shelling the embankment, which collapsed, blocking the line. All in all, *E7*'s patrol had accounted for a gunboat, seventeen large sailing ships and five steamers, and wrecked two trains.

Towards the end of *E7*'s patrol, there was another rendezvous with *E14*, which had been back to base while they were away. *E14* had been sent for two reasons: to warn them that a French submarine was on its way, so as to avoid the danger of their attacking it by mistake, and that an aerial reconnaissance flight had spotted the Turks laying nets across the Dardanelles. Nevertheless, *E7* returned safely. There were no more VCs, however, as someone, somewhere, clearly felt that the submariners were getting more than their fair share. Lt Guy D'Oyly-Hughes, first lieutenant on *E11*, went ashore to help sabotage a railway line. On his return passage through the

Dardanelles, he stood in the conning tower of the partially submerged submarine to obtain first-hand information on the net defences at Nagara, originally spotted from the air, discovering that the net was less forbidding than had been supposed, as 'it parted on impact'. For all this, despite a recommendation that he receive a VC, he had to be content with a Distinguished Service Order.

There were later patrols by some of the submarines, but by January 1916, when Lt Cdr Stock brought *E2* safely back to the Aegean through the Dardanelles, having sunk two large steamers and a transport, and joined *E11* in bombarding a railway line, strategic priorities had changed, with the defence of Greece more important and the Gallipoli campaign abandoned.

THE FLEET SUBMARINE

One weakness in the British approach to submarines was that they were seen as the best means of countering other submarines, something which made sense with the advent of the nuclear submarine, but which was beyond the technology of the day. The First World War submarine could, and did, sink U-boats, if it managed to find one sitting on the surface, as happened on 5 April 1917, when *C7* sank *UC-68* in the North Sea. The fact that it was viewed as an anti-submarine measure meant that the submarine was also seen as part of the screen for the fleet, and hence the concept of the fleet submarine was born. The problem was, of course, that the submarine of the day was far too slow, even on the surface, to keep pace with the fleet. Nuclear technology has solved this problem, but at the time even the diesel propulsion that was available could not offer sufficient speed. Steam propulsion offered the only answer, and thus came the K class.

The first of the K-class boats was commissioned in 1916 and, in all, seventeen were built during 1916 and 1918; an improved K class was ordered after the war, but only one was actually completed and the remaining five were cancelled. Recognition of these boats was easy, for they each had three collapsible smokestacks. These were large boats, with a displacement of 1,883 tons on the surface and 2,565 tons submerged, and a length of 338ft. Their geared steam turbines delivered 10,500hp through two screws, giving them a maximum surface speed of 25kts, sufficient to keep up with the battleships of the day. As with all submarines, once submerged, the best speed for a limited endurance was 9kts. Apart from the difficulty of diving quickly, the use of steam propulsion meant that the boats were unpleasantly hot once they were battened down. One critic said that the problems with the K class were that they had the speed of a destroyer, which was something of an exaggeration, combined with the turning circle of a battleship and the bridge facilities of a motor boat. Another said that the only good thing about them was that they never engaged the enemy.

For the time, the K class had a heavy armament, with eight 18in torpedo tubes, four in the bow and four on the beam, one or two 4in guns and a single 3in.

Trials of the first to be commissioned, *K3*, soon showed major problems. Even with the engine room hatches open, temperatures in the engine rooms were too high for comfort, and the hatches could not be left open in rough waters. Handling seems to have been bad, whether on the surface or under it. When *K3* arrived at Scapa Flow, her commanding officer earned the disapproval of Beatty, by this time a full admiral in command of the Grand Fleet, as, instead of dipping his ensign as he passed the flagship, he dipped his funnels. Less funny, in a storm a wave splashed down her funnels and extinguished the fires, leaving her helpless until a small auxiliary diesel engine could be started.

Having started badly, these ungainly craft continued with the loss of *K13* in the Gare Loch during trials. As she dived, the boiler room ventilators had not shut properly and soon the boiler room was flooded. The commander immediately ordered all tanks to be blown so that the submarine would surface, but she continued to dive. He could not use the voice tubes as water shot out of them, and then a short circuit caused a fire in the main switchboard. There were more men aboard because she was carrying a number of workers and managers from the builders at the time, so the normal complement of sixty was raised to eighty. When a roll call was taken by the commander, just forty-nine men answered.

The submarine's non-appearance alerted those on the surface to the fact that she must be in trouble, but the rescue attempt was bungled. Eventually, Lt Cdr Goodhart, the commanding officer of *K14*, who was aboard to gain experience, and *K13*'s commander, Lt Cdr Herbert, worked out a scheme to get a message to those on the surface by entering the conning tower, flooding it, and blowing Goodhart out as the air pressure built up. Herbert was to be in the conning tower to close the hatch, having decided that he should stay behind with his men. Air pressure in the conning tower was so great that when the hatch opened, both men were blown out. It was just as well, as Goodhart never reached the surface. Air tubes were connected to the submarine with difficulty, as ice blocked the pipes, but just in time to save the lives of the surviving crew. Rescue proved difficult as water had got between the inner and outer hulls, and eventually after an attempt to lift the submarine failed, she was partially lifted and a hole cut in her to allow those inside to escape, after fifty-seven hours submerged. She was refloated and renamed *K22*.

Worse was to come. On 31 January 1918, during a fleet exercise off the Isle of May in the Firth of Forth, both *K4* and *K17* were lost. The poor turning circle must have been a factor in the events of that day. *K4* was rammed by her sister, *K6*, then *K17* was rammed and sunk by HMS *Fearless*, while *K14* was rammed by *K22*, which in turn was rammed by the battlecruiser *Inflexible*. The last two were not sunk, but very badly damaged.

CHAPTER ELEVEN

THE ROYAL NAVAL DIVISION

Handymen to Fight on Land & Sea
Advertisement for RN Division recruits

The Royal Navy had sent men and guns ashore to assist the army during the Boer war. In 1914, as the Royal Navy was mobilised, the Admiralty suddenly realised that it had some 20,000 to 30,000 more men than it needed to man its ships. This was enough to form two Royal Naval brigades and one Royal Marine brigade. The move was far from popular with those concerned. A substantial number of the ratings were stokers from the Royal Fleet Reserve, meaning that they were ex-naval regulars who had returned to the fleet, and expected to be sent to sea. Their numbers were soon inflated by the addition of many volunteer reservists.

The RM brigade was moved to Ostend on 27 August 1914, but was brought back just four days later.

The German army was by this time making rapid gains through Belgium, but had by-passed the port of Antwerp. To Churchill, this seemed too good an opportunity, and when the Belgians seemed

With too many men for the available ships, the Royal Naval Division was formed. It saw action on the Western Front and here, at Gallipoli, in 1915. *(RNM)*

likely to surrender the port, he immediately sent the Royal Marine Brigade to augment the Belgian garrison, arriving on 4 October 1914. The next day, Churchill followed this up by sending the First and Second Naval Brigades, making a force of 10,000 men in total in what became the Royal Naval Division, although the men of the two naval brigades were, as soldiers, partially trained and inexperienced reservists. The Royal Naval Division was formed into eight battalions along army lines and wearing army uniform, albeit with naval badges for rank and trades. Rather than being given army-style titles, however, the eight battalions were each named after famous admirals, becoming Drake, Benbow, Hawke, Collingwood, Hood, Anson, Nelson and

Men of the Royal Naval Division at Gallipoli, which soon settled down into trench warfare, even though this was the one thing that Allied commanders wished to avoid. This is Hood Battalion, after taking the objective known as 'White House'. *(IWM Q 61127)*

A member of the Royal Naval Division at Gallipoli, acting as a motorcycle dispatch rider, drives through the trenches. *(IWM Q 61079)*

Howe. Each battalion was formed into companies, but in army style, as 'A Company', 'B Company', etc.

Churchill, in Antwerp himself, then offered the War Cabinet his resignation as First Lord and announced his intention of staying in command of the troops. Most of the War Cabinet were incredulous, except for Kitchener, who was ready to give his colleague a wartime commission as a lieutenant-general.

Antwerp capitulated on 10 October, while 1,500 men from the Royal Naval Division who retreated into the neutral Netherlands rather than becoming German prisoners of war, found themselves interned. In just five days from 5 October 1914, the division had suffered heavy casualties, and when it was withdrawn before the fall of Antwerp, Collingwood Battalion had just twenty-two men left.

The Admiralty did not have ships for its surplus manpower, but neither did it have the equipment to fit them out as soldiers. It is estimated that as many as 80 per cent lacked the most basic equipment when they were sent to Belgium, many of them not even having the khaki uniform at first, or mess tins, packs or water bottles. Just three days before they embarked, they were issued with ancient rifles. This was a purely infantry organisation, lacking artillery or any of the supporting units that would normally be expected.

On their return, the Royal Naval Division was given a depot of its own at Blandford Camp on Salisbury Plain, where Nelson Battalion was first to arrive in November 1914. Even so far from the sea, they still went 'ashore' when they left the camp, following one of the great naval traditions.

The next major wartime commitment for the Royal Naval Division was to be sent to the eastern Mediterranean, initially to Egypt before joining the Gallipoli campaign. Five of the battalions – Drake, Hood, Anson, Nelson and Howe – were marched out of the camp at 1915 on 27 February 1915, in pouring rain but wearing pith helmets. Marching overnight, by 0330 the following morning they were aboard the train for the docks at Avonmouth, as indeed were their mules, which would provide transport once they arrived. Meanwhile, they took passage aboard the Union Castle liner *Grantully Castle*.

Their ultimate destination was Gallipoli, the gallant effort to by-pass the impasse on the Western Front and shorten the war, while also easing pressure on the Russians. The problem was that the operation was hindered by poor leadership and a lack of commitment by many senior officers in London and in Egypt. The landings were on 25 April 1915, and among those units aboard the *River Clyde* when she carried the initial assault force ashore was a platoon from the Hood Battalion. Within days, the division was broken up and its units sent to wherever they were needed to replace the many casualties suffered in the initial landings. Hood lost its commanding officer, Lt Col Quilter, among ten officers and 343 men killed in the fighting. By 27 May, Gallipoli had fallen into the same frustrating static warfare that had become the curse of the Western Front. The units of the Royal Naval Division were withdrawn by the night of 7/8 January 1916, after suffering 7,530 officers and men, killed, wounded or missing.

Hoping to return to the UK, the remnants were told that they would be given ten days leave in Malta instead, and this was so badly received that when their officers called for three cheers to an inspecting general, he was given a loud raspberry instead. The leave in Malta was cancelled and all ranks were confined to barracks for five days.

The division was then reinforced, with many new recruits arriving in February, and during May 1916, the division's battalions were landing in France ready for service on the Western Front. In July of that year, the Royal Naval Division was incorporated as part of the British army, becoming the 63rd (Royal Naval) Division, marking the transfer of responsibility from the Admiralty to the War Office. As part of the British army in France, its units were to be present at many of the major battles that marked the final two years or so of the war, including the Somme, Arras, Ypres and Cambrai, and by the time it was finally demobilised in April 1919, it had suffered almost 48,000 casualties.

CHAPTER TWELVE

RECRUITMENT AND TRAINING

*My examination to enter the Navy was very simple, but it was adequate. I wrote out the
Lord's prayer and the doctor made me jump over a chair naked, and I was given a glass of
sherry on being in the Navy.*
AF Lord Fisher

With the above quotation, Fisher was being
what we would now describe as 'economical
with the truth', for he had already passed an
examination involving taking dictation of
some thirty lines of English, copied a
number of sentences from a morning
newspaper and taken a paper in arithmetic.
An earlier medical examination had been
more thorough, giving him a certificate to
show that he was free from any physical
defects. This, however, was June 1854, and
he was just 13 years of age. Fisher had also
been nominated, not by the Admiralty as was
the standard practice, but by Commander-
in-Chief Plymouth, Adm Sir William Parker,
a neighbour of Fisher's godmother.

This was one aspect of naval life that did
not change as much as one might have
expected over the intervening years. While
nepotism was steadily removed from the
service of the Crown during the Victorian
period, very senior officers did still manage
to ensure that their staffs contained a fair
number of people who were either family or
friends.

Fisher would have learnt his trade at sea
as a midshipman, but by the time of the First
World War the Royal Navy had become far

more technical. The move from sail to steam
had affected more than just the ships; it had
influenced not only the skills that were
necessary, but the way in which people were
treated. To attract bright and technically
minded young men as engine room
artificers, the navy's skilled tradesmen, and
keep them in the service, they had to be
treated as a breed apart. This meant putting
them into separate messes from the seamen
and, at a time when petty officers still wore
'square rig', giving them a uniform with a
collar and tie, and a peaked cap. The days of
the press gang were long gone. Even in the
early twentieth century, when life ashore was
harsher and less secure than it is today, the
Royal Navy had been forced to think of
attracting the right kind of manpower. The
solution for the lower deck – as the ratings,
as non-commissioned personnel are known
in the Royal Navy – was far easier to come by
than that for the upper deck, the officers.

OFFICERS IN A POST-REFORM NAVY

During his term as First Sea Lord between
1904 and 1910, the then Adm Sir John
'Jacky' Fisher had been one of the great

naval reformers, possibly even greater than Nelson, but in fact his work had started even earlier, when he was Second Sea Lord, then, as now, responsible for personnel. The Fisher-Selbourne Scheme of 1903, named after Fisher and the First Lord of the Admiralty, Lord Selbourne, was designed to remedy many of the defects appearing in a mechanised navy, where officers imbued with the traditions of sail saw engineers as a distinctly inferior species. The Fisher-Selbourne solution was that officers and seamen, engineers and marines, should all be of one company, joining, being educated and training together, after which, engineering would be treated as a specialisation, just as navigation, gunnery and torpedoes had become. The intention was that engineering officers, initially lieutenants (E), would, like lieutenants (N), lieutenants (G) and lieutenants (T), be able to rise to the upper reaches of the service.

That same year was also notable for the creation of the Royal Naval Volunteer Reserve, RNVR, to augment the Royal Naval Reserve, RNR.

Even for gunnery and navigation students there were problems to be resolved. Many, including Fisher himself, had to be convinced that the traditional means of training entirely at sea was no longer suitable. Fisher initially rejected plans for converting the main officers' training school, the Britannia Royal Naval College at Dartmouth, into a public school, but the difficulty facing him was that, while training was best done at sea, teaching was better done ashore.

The Britannia Royal Naval College had been based in hulks, including the old HMS *Britannia* herself, on the tidal reaches of the River Dart at Dartmouth, but by the end of the nineteenth century these old ships had outlived their usefulness. Sanitation was poor, and in the prevailing conditions

discipline was difficult to enforce. The new shore-based college, offering a four-year public-school-type education, was opened in 1905, but the need to move young cadets away from the hulks was so pressing that from September 1903 cadets went to a junior college at Queen Victoria's former residence at Osborne on the Isle of Wight, staying there for two years and then moving up to Britannia.

Thus it happened that cadets spent two years each at Osborne and Dartmouth, followed by six months in a training cruiser, before joining the fleet as midshipmen. Midshipmen – 'snotties' to the rest of the Royal Navy – had an officer's cap badge but were not officers, and occupied a no man's land between ratings and commissioned personnel. They were still under training, learning much of the practical side of their craft, and had no equivalent in the army or, for that matter, once it came into existence, the Royal Air Force.

Midshipmen's duties consisted mainly of assisting the officers of a ship, but there were some particularly of their own. One of these was commanding the picket boat, which provided a shuttle service between ship and shore, and for many a young man presented a challenge, not just in navigating safely in an often exposed and choppy anchorage or a busy harbour, but of dealing with drunken sailors often old enough to be his father. Picket boat duty was onerous, and some complained that it gave them no time to eat, for as soon as they settled down, there would be a call for the picket boat. As an aside, showing the naivety of senior officers, one officer considering naval airships thought that they could be handled with ease by anyone capable of handling a picket boat.

The Fisher-Selbourne solution was originally intended to take lieutenants at the age of 22 years and train them as

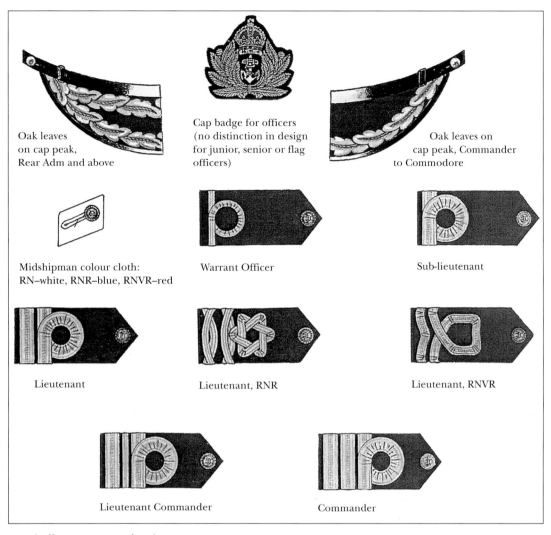

Oak leaves
on cap peak,
Rear Adm and above

Cap badge for officers
(no distinction in design
for junior, senior or flag
officers)

Oak leaves on
cap peak, Commander
to Commodore

Midshipman colour cloth:
RN–white, RNR–blue, RNVR–red

Warrant Officer

Sub-lieutenant

Lieutenant

Lieutenant, RNR

Lieutenant, RNVR

Lieutenant Commander

Commander

Naval officers' insignia of rank.

engineers at the Royal Naval Engineering College at Keyham. Nevertheless, intention and practice differed, with only one midshipman in twenty volunteering for engineering, largely, many suspected, because of pressures put on the youngsters by snobbish parents. The attitude of the parents was understandable. Anyone with a naval connection knew that navigation and gunnery were the only worthwhile arts and that naval officers in general looked down upon engineers, who were never quite regarded as being gentlemen. It was soon clear that a different approach was needed, but it was not until after the war that midshipmen were selected for engineering and sent on the long four-year engineering course at Keyham.

In the Victorian navy, it had been virtually impossible for ratings to become officers. In theory, warrant officers could be promoted to the rank of lieutenant for gallantry in action, but it was not until the golden jubilee honours of Queen Victoria in 1887 that two warrant officers received this promotion. The result was that warrant officers could spend as much as thirty years in the rank and pressure for reform built up in the service. This eventually took the form of the monthly *Naval Warrant Officers' Journal*, to press their case.

An opportunity seemed to arise in 1890 when the then First Lord, Lord George Hamilton, announced that the Royal Navy was short of 100 lieutenants, causing the warrant officers to issue 'An Earnest Appeal for Promotion from the Ranks, Royal Navy', pointing out that many were already performing the duties of sub-lieutenants and lieutenants. Despite strong public support, the government opposed their ambitions and the extra 100 officers were all RNR officers transferred from the Merchant Navy. Another warrant officer, Thomas Lyne, was commissioned for gallantry during the Boer War in 1902, and eventually became a rear admiral, the first from the lower deck since John Kingcome in 1818. Nevertheless, from 1903 onwards, warrant officers could expect to be promoted to lieutenant. In 1912, Churchill resolved the issue further by introducing the Mate Scheme, under which petty officers and above could attain commissioned status, and this option was extended to engineers in 1914. The rank of 'mate' equated to lieutenant.

It was not until 1914 that the rank of lieutenant-commander was introduced. The rank had existed in the United States Navy for some decades, and it was not completely new to the Royal Navy, as the extra 'half-ring' had been awarded to lieutenants with at least eight years' seniority in the late nineteenth century.

While engineer officers carried executive titles such as lieutenant or commander, they did not have the curl on their rings until 1915, but did have purple cloth between the rings. Surgeons', paymasters' and instructors' rings also bore no curl and had coloured inners (red, white and blue respectively); however, unlike engineers, these officers had no exective title, instead holding ranks such as assistant paymaster or surgeon. Paymasters were general administrators, since secretaries were members of the paymaster branch.

Another of the reforms introduced by Winston Churchill when First Sea Lord in 1913 was a special entry scheme under which cadets from other public schools joined the Royal Navy at the age of 18 years, spent two cruises in HMS *Highflyer* to absorb some seamanship skills, and then became midshipmen across the fleet. When war came, most of the new breed of engineer officers were not from Dartmouth but from the special entry scheme.

RATINGS

Given the high profile of the Royal Navy during the early years of the twentieth century, the service came fairly high on the limited list of career options available to young men from the working classes. The service might have been harsh, but life even for civilians was harsh, with long working hours and the understanding of occupational health minimal. It was in peacetime much safer than life at sea on the fishing fleets, and more secure than life in the Merchant Navy. It was more interesting than the army with its long spells of monotonous garrison life. Certainly the sailor of the day spent considerable periods of time away from home, but not as much as his soldiering counterpart, whose lengthy spells abroad were seldom accompanied by wife and children. A sailor saw the world, rather than the grim and gritty interior of a filthy factory or, even worse, a coal mine.

1. Gunner's Mate.
2. Gunlayer, 1st class.
3. Gunlayer, 2nd class.
4. Captain of the gun, 1st class.
5. Seaman gunner.
6. Rangetaker, 1st class.
7. Rangetaker, 2nd class.
8. Rangetaker, 3rd class.
9. Torpedo gunner's mate.
10. Torpedo coxswain.
11. Leading torpedoman.
12. Seaman torpedoman.
13. Diver.
14. Chief yeoman of signals.
15. Leading signalman and signalman.
16. Petty officer telegraphist.
17. Leading telegraphist.
18. Leading telegraphist.
19. Telegraphist.
20. Physical and recreational training instructor, 1st class.
21. Physical and recreational training instructor, 2nd class.
22. Good shooting badge.
23. Mechanician.
24. Chief Stoker and Stoker Petty Officer.
25. Leading stoker and stoker, 1st class.
26. Chief armourer.
27. Chief shipwright.
28. Chief petty officer artisan.
29. Shipwrights and artisans.
30. Master-at-arms.
31. Regulating petty officer.
32. Sick berth rating.
33. Writer.
34. Supply rating.
35. Cook.
36. Officer's steward.
37. Officer's cook.
38. Bugler.
39. Leading seaman.
40. Petty officer.
41. Chief petty officer cap badge.

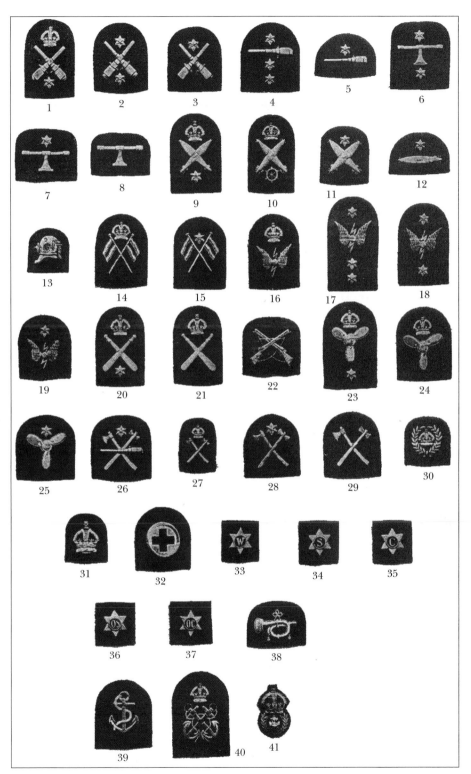

A selection of naval ratings' badges.

Uniforms differed from those of the Second World War. For example, this is PO James Cox in 'square rig', which was not replaced by jackets and peaked caps until the 1920s. *(IWM SR 85)*

The fact was that the Royal Navy in 1914 had been able to pick and choose its ratings. It had had to compromise and meet those whom it wanted for its technical branches halfway, but for the most part the life of a sailor was sought after.

As with officers, ratings joined the Royal Navy at a much earlier age than would be the case today, although instead of the 13 years or so of the Osborne cadet, the rating would join at 15 or 16. Most of the main naval ports had training establishments

Because of their growing importance, and to boost recruitment, engine room artificers, or ERAs, had better messing facilities and were allowed peaked caps and jackets. This is ERA Gilbert Adshead. *(IWM SR 27)*

nearby, although HMS *Ganges*, later transferred to a shore base near Ipswich, was based in Suffolk, away from the main naval bases. *Ganges* at this time was still a hulk, an old ship of the line that had been commissioned in 1821 and still retained her rigging. In a period when personal hygiene was more difficult to maintain, the Royal Navy took no chances with the new recruits, who were given a hot bath with strong disinfectant, followed by what many regarded as being a good hot supper – a large chunk of corned beef and some cheese, and a large bowl of cocoa.

Initial training meant six weeks of lessons in seamanship and ordinary schooling, before moving on to more specialised training. The brightest were sought after as boy signalmen, a demanding role as they had to be able to handle morse, semaphore and signal flags or bunting (the reason that signalmen in the Royal Navy were known as 'bunting tossers'), and have a good standard of English. Other intelligent cadets would find themselves selected for gunnery training, in which good mathematics was important.

Discipline was severe, and for simply hesitating when answering a question a boy could have the instructor's hand about his ear. For more serious offences, six strokes of the cane were usual. Insubordination or attempting to strike an officer meant twelve strokes of the cane and fourteen days in cells; for a man it would have meant two years in a naval prison. The punishment in cells centred around picking oakum, taking two days to unpick a foot of rope until it was soft. Food was also short.

Other training ships included *Warspite*, a hulk on the Thames that normally produced seamen for the Merchant Navy, but some of its intake found their way into the Royal Navy. Not so much running away to sea, but being sent to sea seemed to be the fate of many youngsters. On the Thames, *Arethusa* and *Exmouth* would train boys who were orphans, while *Cornwall* was for boys who were judged in need of correction, a type of nautical borstal. More advanced training was held aboard the training ship *Impregnable* at Devonport, and here the training included such subjects as algebra, electrics, wireless, gunnery and torpedoes.

For the engine room artificers, ERAs, training took place aboard HMS *Tenedos* until she was replaced by *Indus*. These ships had workshops aboard. Days were spent learning the technical aspects of their craft in the workshops, and after their evening meal they continued their schooling.

Weekend leave did not start until noon on a Saturday, and everyone had to be back by 0800 on Monday morning.

On completion of training, ratings were assigned to one of the manning ports, becoming part of a port division. These ports had their nicknames in the fleet, with Chatham being known as 'Chats', Devonport as 'Guzz' and Portsmouth as 'Pompey'. From these ports, they would be assigned to the ships of the fleet, returning to barracks in the port once their time aboard a ship was over and while they awaited their next posting. Ideally, of course, the rating would hope to pass from one ship to the next.

CHAPTER THIRTEEN

PERSONAL AND PERSONNEL

. . . and infuses into both that liberal obedience, without which your army would be a base rabble and your navy nothing but rotten timber.

Edmund Burke

Life for the Royal Navy during the First World War had its compensations, but naval discipline also imposed restrictions. Only officers were allowed spirits other than the traditional daily issue of 'grog', watered-down rum, while aboard ship, which, of course, included air stations and barracks ashore. Midshipmen were not allowed spirits and did not share the wardroom, but instead inhabited the gunroom mess.

UNIFORMS

Alone among the armed forces of all the belligerent powers during the First World War, even ratings in the Royal Navy had to pay for their own uniforms. This was one reason for desertion by men who either could not afford the full naval kit or who resented being disciplined for minor breaches of the uniform regulations. The uniforms for ratings were made from navy-blue serge, while those for officers were the double-breasted navy-blue barathea jacket, of a style and cut copied by many navies, and by the British Merchant Navy. The jacket had four pairs of gilt buttons, although Sir David Beatty, in command of the battlecruisers as a vice-admiral at

Jutland and later successor to Jellicoe as commander-in-chief of the Grand Fleet in the rank of admiral, ignored the regulations and had his tailor produce jackets with just three pairs of buttons.

The simplification of male dress, which was noticeable as the Victorian period advanced, gained pace early in the twentieth century, and was to be given a further stimulus by the utilitarian measures forced upon the service by two world wars.

For a start, naval surgeons found their black and gold sash replaced by aiguillettes after King Edward VII ascended to the throne in 1901. Further measures included the 1902 instruction that flag officers should wear a full dress belt with a frockcoat, and in 1912, this instruction was extended to all officers. The blue evening waistcoat lost its gold lace in 1903.

In 1913, the rank of mate was introduced for officers promoted from the lower deck, while the following year, the rank of lieutenant-commander was brought in, and eventually commanders became not the equivalent of a major in the army but of a lieutenant-colonel. In 1915, engineer officers were ordered to wear the curl on their rings.

Once war arrived, officers based ashore outside the UK were allowed to wear army uniforms with stripes of khaki braid instead of gold braid on blue, and the embroidered naval cap badge could be replaced by a brass version when likely to come under fire. A watch coat based on the British army officers' standard 'British warm' also became permissible under wartime conditions.

For ratings, frocks were abolished in 1906, their place to be taken by blue serge jumpers. Of these, the No. 1 had gold trade badges, an inside pocket on the left breast and two buttons to fasten each cuff, while the No. 2 lacked the cuffs and had red trade badges. The practice started of the No. 1 jumper being downgraded when it became scruffy and thus providing a 'new' No. 2, with the gold badges replaced by red. Instead of cloth trousers, blue serge uniform trousers were provided. For dirty work such as coaling and other manual labour, a blue denim combination suit or a canvas overall suit was provided, while engine room artificers wore blue overalls for work.

Naval officers could ask their tailor for a uniform in fine serge, which was lighter in weight than barathea, but this was frowned upon by many senior officers if worn on

Opposite, top: Accommodation aboard warships for senior officers was often palatial. This is Fisher in his day cabin aboard the battleship *Renown* as a vice-admiral in the late nineteenth century. *(IWM Q 22156)*

Bottom: By contrast, messing facilities for the lower deck were cramped and ratings had to eat, sleep and spend much of their off-duty time in the same space. Meals were collected from the galley and men ate them sitting eight to a table. *(IWM Q 18676)*

parade. Nevertheless, uniforms were in a state of change at this time. The officers' cap was becoming larger and many were wearing the style with which succeeding generations have become familiar; but others, including the commander-in-chief of the Grand Fleet, Adm Sir John Jellicoe, wore the older-style smaller cap, as can be seen from his photograph on p. 89. Shirt collar styles varied far more considerably than would be the case today, with winged collars and those clipped in still permissible.

One naval officer who did not wear a uniform was the padre or chaplain. Anxious that an officer's uniform shouldn't cause difficulties when exercising their pastoral duties on the lower deck, that is among the ratings, chaplains, while still members of the wardroom, were not uniformed. Under wartime conditions, this caused some embarrassment to many, especially when younger members of the chaplaincy department were off duty ashore; hence, many increasingly tended to order suits that had some resemblance to a uniform. It was not until 1918 that the Admiralty finally produced a gold lapel badge reading 'Chaplain Royal Navy', and it was some years later before chaplains wore the uniform of an officer. Some traditions remain, however, and to this day naval chaplains do not wear the insignia of rank, in contrast to their army and RAF counterparts, who bear commissioned ranks.

The standard naval uniform gave a clear indication of the trade of the rating wearing it, as well as his rank and his length of good conduct. For wartime, the rank, good conduct and trade badges were always red on the standard blue uniform, and blue on white tropical uniforms. Trade badges were worn on the right arm of all ratings with the exception of CPOs, who wore two identical badges on the collars of their blue uniform, or on the right cuff of tropical white

Clearly King George V is presenting a medal to a rating aboard his ship. Looking on is Sir David Beatty, possibly by this time a full admiral, but wearing a non-regulation jacket with just six buttons instead of eight. To Beatty's right is a midshipman, while behind the King is an RNVR lieutenant-commander. *(IWM Q 19802)*

uniform, or the right sleeve if a short-sleeved shirt was worn. The rank of a rating, whether ordinary seaman, able bodied seaman, leading airman, leading hand or petty officer, was worn on the left arm, above any good conduct stripes for regular personnel, and good service stripes for reservists. One good conduct stripe was awarded for the first three years of good conduct, or good service in the reserves, two for eight years and three for thirteen years. Good conduct was often referred to as 'undetected crime' by the more experienced, and cynical, naval people. This meant that an experienced man with good conduct would eventually be, for example, a 'three badge' leading hand; that is, he would have three stripes and confuse the

uninitiated, who might think that he was a sergeant. CPOs did not wear good conduct badges; their badge of rank was the row of brass buttons around the cuffs of the jacket. Young junior ratings were always wary of a 'three badge PO', who would be by definition an old salt, wise in the ways of the world and, more important, those of the Royal Navy.

The penalties for bad conduct varied, but anyone discharged from the service on the grounds of poor conduct would find that the top right corner of the first page of their service record had been cut off. There could be no fooling a future employer.

The cut of the uniform varied with rank. Below the rank of chief petty officer, ratings wore the traditional 'square rig', a serge jumper with collar and vest, and serge bell-bottom trousers. It was not until after the war that the uniform for a petty officer was changed to a pea jacket and peaked cap, although engine room artificers, the Royal Navy's skilled tradesmen, did wear a jacket and tie to denote their important status, while their cap badge was red. The vest was usually white, but in northern conditions would be navy blue. The blue collar that hung over the shoulders of the jumper was bordered by three white stripes, reputedly for each of Nelson's great victories at the Nile, Copenhagen and Trafalgar, while there was also a black ribbon, in mourning for Nelson, although this was swapped for white on the rating's wedding day. On parade and for walking out, a rope lanyard would be added. On his head, the rating wore the standard naval cap without a peak, known as a 'lid', which on major surface vessels would carry the name of his ship on a ribbon known as a 'tally'. When marching or on guard duty, ratings wore khaki webbing and gaiters. CPOs had double-breasted jackets and wore peaked caps with gold badges.

In tropical kit, which was usually white, the standard issue for junior ratings consisted of white shorts, while the white vest would be worn without the jacket. Stewards, petty officers and chief petty officers wore open-necked tropical white shirts. Ratings up to and including petty officers wore navy-blue knee socks and black shoes; chief petty officers had white knee socks and white shoes. White cap covers were only issued in summer or with tropical kit.

Occasionally, usually for those deployed ashore in the desert or the jungle, often in support of the army, khaki uniforms were issued. Except for badges of rank, etc., this was similar to the uniform issued to personnel in the other services.

Warrant officers wore a thin version of the traditional sub-lieutenant's ring and loop, with an officer's cap badge. Midshipmen wore buttons on their cuffs, with two pieces of cloth and brass buttons on their collars; the cloth was white for regulars, blue for the RNR and red for the RNVR. Regular officers wore straight rings and loops, RNR officers had a complex double ring, and RNVR ('Wavy Navy') officers were identifiable by their simple single wavy ring.

In the Royal Naval Air Service, pilots and observers did not wear 'wings', which were introduced after the war, but instead had an eagle, worn above the curl, although a form of wings was introduced for observers in 1917. With tropical kit or battledress, the eagle was worn on the left breast above any medals. RNAS ranks differed somewhat from those of the rest of the Royal Navy; sub-lieutenant became 'flying sub-lieutenant', while ranks up to and including wing captain paved the way for the future ranks of the Royal Air Force. Uniforms for the RNAS were almost identical to those of the rest of the navy, but for aircrew officers who had an eagle above the curl on the left sleeve and on the shoulder strap of the greatcoat and white tropical uniforms. All RNAS officers, including non-flying RNAS officers, had an eagle in place of the anchor on the cap badge and buttons. Realising that the uniform would not be practical for flying, grey shirts and collars were allowed, and instead of trousers, breeches could be worn with puttees, leggings or field boots.

The cap badge for warrant officers, midshipmen and officers was more elaborate than that for chief petty officers, with a single line of oak leaves on the peak for commanders, captains and commodores and two rows for rear-admiral and above.

In tropical kit, officers usually wore a white shirt and shorts, with white knee socks, shoes and cap cover, although in some cases khaki uniform was worn, with matching knee socks and cap cover, and black shoes. Markings of rank were worn on shoulder epaulettes when wearing tropical kit.

The Royal Marines wore blue uniform if they were gunners, or red for members of the Royal Marine Light Infantry, with a jacket that buttoned up to the neck for non-commissioned men. It was not until after the war that the 'blue' and 'red' marines were amalgamated. Wings were worn on the left breast. Officers wore their badges of rank, similar to those of the army, on their shoulder epaulettes. Tropical uniform was khaki, except for ceremonial, which was white.

THE WRENS

Faced with a massive manpower shortage, the Royal Navy eventually allowed the creation of a Women's Royal Naval Service,

WRNS, in 1917. The first director was Dame Katherine Furse, who had been in charge of the British Red Cross, and was, happily for the Admiralty, available, as she had some differences with her previous employer. Her salary was £200 p.a. Soon known as 'Wrens', members of the WRNS did not serve aboard warships.

Wren uniforms for officers were basically feminine versions of the officers' navy blue uniform, a jacket with collar, a shirt and tie and a skirt. For officers there was a tricorn hat of black velour. The cap badge was also a variant of that worn by the RN, but with the letters 'WRNS' inserted between the crown and the anchor, and blue instead of gold embroidered badges. The jacket buttoned right over left, reflecting the custom. Cuff stripes were pale blue with a diamond replacing the curl for the six grades of director (director, deputy director, assistant director, deputy assistant director, divisional director and deputy divisional director), but principals, deputy principals and assistant principals had rings without a diamond. Skirts were plain and just above ankle length. Blue braid and cap badges were used to economise on gold as wartime austerity began to bite.

The officers' uniform has been described as incongruous, but the ratings' uniform was far worse, with a sack-like serge frock buttoned almost to the throat, and a broad serge belt. The high neck was unpopular and no doubt uncomfortable, and was soon modified to have a deeper neck with a white flannel front and a square collar, initially without the white lines. Worst of all was the

Dame Katherine Furse was the first Commandant of the Woman's Royal Naval Service when it was formed in 1917. She celebrated her appointment by having a half-bottle of Chianti with her lunch. *(RNM)*

Right: One of the early tasks given to Wrens was that of running the telephone switchboard. The uniform collars were not issued at first. *(RNM)*

Below: A Wren writer, with her trade badge showing clearly on her right sleeve. *(RNM)*

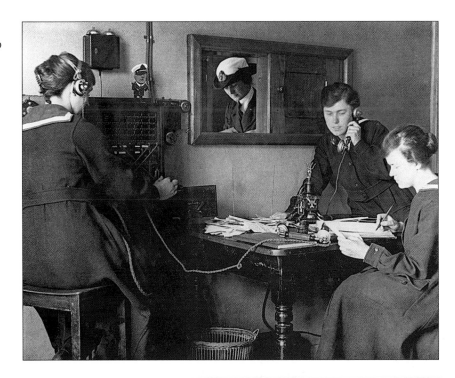

hat, made of gabardine and worn with a white cover in summer; it was shapeless and floppy, despite rows of stitching to give the brim some stiffness.

All ranks wore black stockings and shoes. Pay for the Wrens was notably lower than for their male counterparts. Compared with their counterparts in the Second World War, hemlines were considerably lower, reflecting the prevailing fashion in civilian life or 'civvy street'.

Officer ranks in the WRNS were as follows:

One thick and one standard ring with
   diamond – Director
One thick ring with diamond – Deputy
   Director
Four standard rings with diamond –
   Assistant Director
Three standard rings with diamond –
   Deputy Assistant Director
Three standard rings without diamond –
   Principal

Not all of the jobs were clean and office-bound, as these Wrens working in a store for ships' lamps show.
(IWM Q 19733)

WOMEN'S ROYAL NAVAL SERVICE
APPLY TO THE NEAREST EMPLOYMENT EXCHANGE

Above: For Mrs Gladys Barnes, handling a ship's boat in the company of her dog must have been a liberating experience in 1917. *(IWM Q 19727) Right:* A Wren recruitment poster, but, in contrast to the campaign in the Second World War, in which they were urged to 'free a man to go to sea', there was no definite mention of their role. *(RNM)*

Two standard rings, with half-width ring between, with diamond – Divisional Director

Two standard rings with diamond – Deputy Divisional Director

Two standard rings without diamond – Deputy Principal

One standard ring without diamond – Assistant Principal

One half-width ring above three buttons – Quarters Supervisor

PAY

Pay started at £9 2*s* 6*d* p.a. for a boy second class, rising to £22 16*s* 3*d* for an ordinary seaman. A petty officer received £54 15*s* on appointment, rising to £57 15*s* 10*d* after three years, and to £60 16*s* 8*d* after six years. A sailmaker was classed as the same rank as a PO, but was paid less, at £50 3*s* 9*d* on appointment. Possibly as a reflection of the changing priorities, a petty officer stoker was paid more, at £57 15s 10d on appointment. Engine room artificers were rated as chief petty officers, but received £100 7s 6d as fourth class and £118 12s 6d as first class, providing that they had re-engaged for a further ten years. This was compared to a CPO's pay of £66 18s 4d on appointment and £79 1s 8d after six years.

Flying pay for officers was 8s per day in addition to ordinary pay, the same as submarine pay; for ratings and warrant officers it was 2s or 4s a day.

Midshipmen received £31 18s 9d p.a., more than doubling to £63 17s 6d as an acting sub-lieutenant. Lieutenants received between 10s and 16s a day, depending on the number of years in the rank, plus a shilling a day if in command of a ship, plus extra sums for seagoing commands of up to £68 8s 9d per year.

A commission in the Royal Navy during the early years of the twentieth century was not for those from poor homes. The Admiralty had no hesitation in recommending that parents should top up their midshipman sons' salaries with an allowance of £50 per year. This did not stop until the early years of the First World War, reputedly because a father wrote to the Admiralty saying that he appreciated that his son might lose his life for his country, but he did not understand why he should be expected to pay for the privilege.

Mates were of equivalent rank to commissioned officers, but having been promoted from the lower deck they were paid around 8s a day, falling between sub-lieutenant's and lieutenant's pay.

FOOD AND ACCOMMODATION

Wartime conditions in the Royal Navy varied. There was the obvious discomfort in being in confined conditions aboard a ship, where even officer accommodation was cramped by the standards of those living ashore, and this situation was worsened by the increased complement of ships in wartime. The exception to this was in the accommodation for senior officers, which was almost palatial, especially for flag officers aboard their battleships and battle-cruisers. There was strict segregation between the lower deck – the ratings – and the upper deck – the officers. For the ratings, there were hammocks, often in large mess decks; for the officers, there were cabins, but it was not unusual for these to be shared by two or three officers, sometimes more.

Mealtimes for ratings were breakfast at 0800, lunch at noon, afternoon tea at 1600 and supper at 1900. The exception was the mealtimes for those serving aboard a submarine, where the main meal of the day was at midnight, known to many as 'big eats', with supper at 0600 and breakfast at 1900.

Ratings lived in 'messes', with a ship's company divided into separate messes for stokers, seamen, boys and Royal Marines. Seamen were divided into divisions – forecastlemen, quarterdeckmen, maintopmen and foretopmen – reflecting the old days of sail. Each of these divisions had its own mess deck, where the men would sleep, eat and spend their off-duty time.

The messing arrangements for ratings were either broadside or general messing, or canteen messing. General messing meant that the paymaster or his deputy would draw up a menu for all the lower deck, and each mess sent a duty 'cook', chosen by roster, to collect the meals for the agreed number of men in the mess. The meals would be served and eaten on the mess deck at a wooden table, with the men sitting on wooden stools or benches; at night the mess became the sleeping accommodation for the men. Each table, slung from the deckhead or ceiling by ropes, was usually for sixteen men and constituted a separate mess. Canteen messing was a misnomer, as it was anything but, and was basically a variation of general messing. Supplies were drawn for each mess using a book of chits, including a ration of meat, potatoes and any other vegetables from the ship's provision store and prepared in the mess, again by a duty 'cook', and then taken to the galley to be cooked. Once the meals were cooked, they would be collected and served as in general messing.

The food had improved under Fisher's spell as Second Sea Lord. The Admiralty's daily allowance per man was half a pound of meat, including any bone, fat or gristle, a pound of potatoes, an ounce of milk and the same of tea, with small amounts of salt and sugar. Tinned rabbit or salmon were standard ration issues. Extras included soup powder and vegetables, cheese, fish paste or bacon, and when the duty cook ordered these items they would be charged to the mess chit book using the allowance of 4d a day to each mess for this purpose. If a mess spent in excess of the allowance, it had to go on short rations until such time as the deficit was paid off.

The standard of catering varied, not made any easier by the absence of refrigeration on older and smaller ships. Storage was a problem, and even on large ships they soon ran out of potatoes. At a time when the civilian population had very conventional meals with little sign of today's international cuisine, rice was a staple part of the naval diet.

People had their favourites, made even more glamorous by naval slang. A 'cackle-berry' was an egg, a 'Spithead pheasant' a kipper, and a 'train smash' tinned herring in tomato source. Typical lunchtime dishes included a 'schooner on the rocks', which meant a shin of beef on potatoes, or a

✳ SAUCE ?

'three-decker', which was three layers of beef alternated with three of dough.

Breakfast could consist of a basin of very thick cocoa, with a quarter of a loaf of bread weighing half a pound in weight, usually served with either pork fat, treacle or jam, but no choice of which. Lunch would be meat, usually mutton that might be roasted or stewed, and when potatoes were served they would have their skins on, suggesting that there was no naval equivalent of the army's 'spud bashing'. The lunch menu would be boosted on Thursdays and Saturdays with a slice of plum pudding. Afternoon tea was often just that, a mug or bowl of tea. The evening meal, usually referred to as supper on the lower deck, was usually bread, jam and tea, but when canteen messing was in force, some duty cooks would provide a hot dish using leftovers from lunch, or even make fishcakes using canned fish. The navy would supply tins of salmon or rabbit as part of the ration, but not everyone seems to have used these, and so there was all the more for those who did.

When coaling was under way, until the work was completed the men received only lime juice if they were in the tropics or oatmeal in northern waters. By 'completed', the navy meant that not only had the coal to have been safely loaded into the bunkers, which could take eight to ten hours on a large ship, but then the ship had to be washed down completely to get rid of the coal dust, and the men themselves had to change out of their dirty clothing and take a bath, before getting back into their uniforms.

The rum ration was normally served at lunch. Ratings were not supposed to store their rum, but many found that giving their tot to a shipmate would earn favours, such as having ironing or some other chore done for them. Rum was also the source of a strictly unofficial treat that resulted from cheating on some ships. Men ashore, even for the day, would not be eligible for the rum ration, and the coxswain would be responsible for noting just how many men were ashore and reducing the rum issued accordingly. On smaller ships, such as destroyers, it was not unknown for the coxswain, or his stand-in if he was ashore, to cut the number of men ashore by half, and the rum for the other half would augment that for the warrant officers' mess and sometimes that for the chief petty officers as well.

To ease life aboard ship, some of the more enterprising started informal businesses tending to the needs of their shipmates. Typical of these were cutting hair or shaving other members of the crew.

Fresh water was another problem, as ships soon ran out of this for washing, shaving or bathing. Salt water had to be used for these functions, and special salt water soap was issued, which took a long time to lather. Experienced sailors soon adjusted and habitually became very careful in their use of water.

The shortage of water apart, for officers it was different. Meals were served in the wardroom, and on the larger ships this usually had an ante-room with a bar. Wardroom meals were served by stewards, and officers would also have a steward to look after their other needs, such as laundry, although usually it would be a case of one steward to two or three officers in the same cabin. The gunroom mess was also comfortable, a bit like a prefects' common room. On submarines and the smaller ships, however, the wardroom could be cramped, little more than a small dining room, while on submarines the officers' bunk space could also intrude.

On most ships, the wardroom had a hierarchy. Many senior officers would have a distinct corner of their own, and so too would the Royal Marines if there were a substantial number aboard. On all but the smaller warships, the commanding officer was not a member of the wardroom, and would only appear when invited by the wardroom president, usually his second in command.

Accounts differ over whether wardroom life was 'boozy' or not. Nevertheless, wardroom life was certainly sociable. Little money changed hands in the wardroom. Officers had an account, which had to be settled monthly. Senior officers kept an eye on this, and if anyone appeared to be drinking heavily, there would be a quiet word, and if notice was not taken, the account could be restricted or even closed altogether. A popular feature of wardroom life was the sing-songs around the piano. This was a time when most well-educated young men could play the piano, and when ships had many of the comforts of the wardroom stripped away and sent ashore when action seemed likely, one of the few exceptions made would be the piano.

While the engine room artificers did not have formal stewards, it was usual for a couple of stokers to keep their mess tidy. It was also less crowded than that for the seamen and marines.

ACTION STATIONS

When the ship went to action stations, the watertight doors throughout the ship would be closed to ensure that the ship became a series of watertight compartments, increasing the amount of damage it could take without sinking. Normal meal service was suspended and the only people allowed to move about the ship were the officers and the damage control and repair parties. Such was the pre-war navy's obsession with spit and polish, and the paintwork of the ships, that even as ships were trying to force the Dardanelles, the executive officer, that is the second in command, of one ship attempted to have men paint the side of the ship on which the guns were not firing, and which was not being fired upon. It nearly caused a mutiny and the order was rescinded.

Hoses would be run out and sea water would be poured on to the decks, often making the mess areas very wet indeed, to reduce the risk of fire. Before closing themselves in their gun turrets, the gun crews would ensure that they had buckets of water to drink and water for fire-fighting, as well as empty buckets in which to relieve themselves. Supplies of biscuit would be kept close to hand so that they could eat.

In contrast to the Second World War, anti-flash gear was not available, and even without being hit, gunners could sometimes suffer serious burns. Ear protection was limited compared with that of later years, and after the operation in the Rufiji river, one of the officers commented that the heavy firing had left them unable to hear properly for some time.

For those on deck and on the bridge, always open at this time, foul weather was to be dreaded. On a ship steaming at 25kts, waterproofs were anything but waterproof.

DUTIES

Unlike the Royal Navy a quarter of a century later, the First World War service still had most of its ships powered by coal. This was not a case of extreme conservatism at the Admiralty. The new Queen Elizabeth class battleships were oil burners. The fear was that oil supplies, most of which at the time were imported from the USA, were vulnerable, but the UK had ample reserves of coal. This was long before the discovery of North Sea oil, and while some oil-bearing shale existed around Edinburgh, such sources were limited.

In contrast to the practice in some navies, in the Royal Navy officers and men took part in the filthy business of coaling. The constant watch for the German High Seas Fleet emerging from its well-defended ports, and the sense of insecurity that prevailed at the Royal Navy's forward bases at Scapa Flow and Rosyth (still unfinished on the outbreak of war) meant that warships spent a considerable amount of time at sea. As a result of so much sea time, fuel consumption was high, as was the rate of wear and tear on machinery, and men also became fatigued; but senior officers felt more secure at sea than in port.

The steady move to oil-fired propulsion not only meant that refuelling became quicker and far less messy and labour-intensive; it also increased the range of warships. In battle, the heavy smoke produced by coal was a nuisance that seriously affected the accuracy of gunnery, and so for yet another reason, oil had to be the fuel of the future.

CHAPTER FOURTEEN

WARSHIPS

Those far distant, storm-beaten ships, upon which the Grand Army never looked, stood between it and the dominion of the world.
Alfred Mahan, on the influence of sea power, 1892

Warship design has been a continual process of evolution, but the pace of change accelerated in the second half of the nineteenth century. The advent of, first, steam propulsion and then turret gunnery in place of the old broadside were the most obvious changes. Even so, there was resistance to breech-loading at first as satisfactory breeches seemed to be difficult to find. However, muzzle-loading was clearly unacceptable as the size of projectiles increased, and a serious explosion aboard HMS *Thunderer* in 1879 while guns were being double-charged for a heavy muzzle-loaded projectile settled the debate once and for all.

Ships that incorporated all of the new features, such as steam propulsion and turret gunnery, were the official pre-dreadnoughts, and the first of these is generally taken in the case of the Royal Navy as being the Admiral class of 1887–9, although in this particular case, the differences between the ships of the class were far more extensive than has generally been the case in recent years. Armament varied, and to save weight as gun sizes increased, some ships of the class did not have turrets, but instead the guns were

mounted on turntables and enclosed in armoured barbettes. It was the Majestic class of 1895–8 that saw twin 12in guns mounted in turrets as standard. With one exception, the Majestic class ships were the oldest battleships to serve in the First World War. The exception was *Revenge*, one of the seven ships of the Royal Sovereign class of 1892–4, which was renamed *Redoubtable*, fitted with torpedo bulges and put to work as a monitor. The range of her 12in guns was increased to 16,000yd by flooding the bulges on one side to heel the ship over. In fact, she was by this time very much a ship that had been somewhat bodged up, as her original 13.5in guns, in barbettes, had been relined to become 12in, suggesting that they were no long considered safe.

Ships of the nineteenth century had been far more decorative in appearance than is the case today, or has been indeed for the past hundred years. The Victorian Royal Navy had black hulls with white lining and red boot-topping, white upperworks with yellow-ochre smokestacks, masts and ventilators, looking more like a vessel of a smart merchant shipping line than a warship. In 1903, this changed, and a uniform grey colour scheme, or lack-of-

The battleship *King Edward VII* after hitting a mine. *(IWM SP 438)*

colour scheme, was introduced. In 1909, the use of funnel bands so that ships of the same class could be distinguished from one another was standardised and a system introduced throughout the fleet that enabled identities to be deduced alphabetically. Only minor warships, and at the time that included submarines, used pennant numbers.

One point that may become apparent as one looks through the lists of ships that follow are the number lost through internal explosions. Much had still to be done to improve the handling of modern munitions, but it was also the case that many ships were still coal-fired and this had hazards of its own. An accumulation of coal dust could result in an explosion. Large bunkers of coal could also start to smoulder, increasing the risk of an explosion from other causes. Oil was not only cleaner to handle, it was also safer, as heavy marine oil was not explosive. The fact that a number of ships were 'lost' before the war should also not be too surprising. Apart from the coal problems already mentioned, in the absence of radar and, in many cases modern compasses, navigation was far more hazardous than in more recent times.

There are also a significant number of ships requisitioned by the Admiralty but originally intended for foreign navies. This was the result of a clause in shipbuilding contracts for foreign navies, giving the Admiralty the right to take over the ship if war threatened. It also reflected the importance of the United Kingdom as the world's leading shipbuilding nation at the time.

The 1918 Armistice precluded a number of interesting developments, with the Admiralty planning in 1917 to build two 'ocean' aircraft carriers and four North Sea or Mediterranean aircraft carriers. The latter may have had a bearing on the design of HMS *Hermes*, but the shape of the larger ships is something of a mystery.

PRE-DREADNOUGHT BATTLESHIPS

Majestic class
1895–8.
LOA: 413ft. Beam: 75ft. Displacement: 14,900 tons.
Triple-expansion steam engines delivering 12,000hp through two screws. Maximum speed: 17.5 knots.
Armour varied between 6in and 14in thickness. Complement: 757.
Armament: 4×12in; 12×6in; 16×12pdr, plus smaller weapons. 5×18in torpedo tubes.
Majestic, Magnificent, Prince George, Hannibal, Victorious, Jupiter, Mars, Caesar, Illustrious.
Majestic torpedoed by *U-21* in the Dardanelles, 1915, after which hulked and guns used in eight monitors.

Canopus, Formidable, London, Duncan and Queen classes
1900–4.
LOA: 430ft. Beam: 74–75.5ft. Displacement: 12,950–15,000 tons.
Triple-expansion steam engines delivering 13,500–18,000hp through two screws. Maximum speed: 18–19 knots.
Armour varied between 6in and 12in thickness. Complement: 750–810.

Armament: 4×12in; 12×6in; 12–16×12pdr, plus smaller weapons; 4×18in torpedo tubes.
Canopus*, Goliath, Ocean, Glory, Vengeance, Albion, Formidable*, Irresistible, Implacable, London*, Bulwark, Venerable, Duncan*, Russell, Exmouth, Albemarle, Cornwallis, Queen*, Prince of Wales.
* Lead ship of class.

Goliath torpedoed at the Dardanelles, 1915.
Ocean sunk by mine and gunfire at the Dardanelles, 1915.
Formidable sunk by *U-24* in English Channel, 1915.
Irresistible sunk by mine and gunfire at the Dardanelles, 1915.
Bulwark sunk by internal explosion, 1914.
Russell sunk by mine off Malta, 1916.
Cornwallis sunk by *U-32* in the Mediterranean, 1917.

Swiftsure and Triumph
1904.
LOA: 470ft. Beam: 71ft. Displacement: 11,800 tons.
Triple-expansion steam engines delivering 14,000hp through two screws. Maximum speed: 20 knots.
Armour varied between 6in and 10in thickness. Complement: 700.
Armament: 4×10in; 14×7.5in; 14×14pdr, plus smaller weapons; 2×18in torpedo tubes.
Swiftsure became depot ship 1916.
Triumph sunk by U-boat in Dardanelles, 1915.

King Edward class
1905–6. Originally known as the 'wobbly eight', they together formed the Grand Fleet's 3rd Battle Squadron.
LOA: 454ft. Beam: 78ft. Displacement: 17,500 tons.
Triple-expansion steam engines delivering 8,000hp through two screws. Maximum speed: 19 knots.

Armour varied between 6in and 12in thickness. Complement: 777.

Armament: 4×12in; 4×9.2in; 10×6in; 12×12 pdr, plus smaller weapons; 5×18in torpedo tubes.

King Edward VII, Commonwealth, Dominion, Hindustan, Zealandia*, Africa, Britannia, Hibernia.

* Originally named *New Zealand.*

King Edward VII sunk by mine off Cape Wrath, 1916.

Britannia sunk by *UB-50* off Cape Trafalgar, 1918.

Hibernia fitted with seaplane runways for first take-off from a British warship in 1911.

Lord Nelson **and** Agamemnon

1907 and 1908.

LOA: 445ft. Beam: 79.5ft. Displacement: 16,500 tons.

Triple-expansion steam engines delivering 16,750hp through two screws. Maximum speed: 18.5 knots.

Armour varied between 6in and 14in thickness. Complement: 865.

Armament: 4×12in; 10×9.2in; 15×12pdr, plus smaller weapons; 5×18in torpedo tubes.

DREADNOUGHT BATTLESHIPS

Dreadnought

1906.

LOA: 526ft. Beam: 82ft. Displacement: 17,900–20,700 tons.

Steam turbines delivering 23,000hp through four screws. Maximum speed: 22 knots.

Armour: belt 11in, turrets 8in. Complement: 862.

Armament: 10×12in; 24×12pdr but later altered; 5 (later 4)×18in torpedo tubes.

Bellerophon class

1909.

LOA: 526ft. Beam: 82ft. Displacement: 17,900–20,700 tons.

Steam turbines delivering 23,000hp through four screws. Maximum speed: 22 knots.

Armour: belt 11in, turrets 8in. Complement: 862.

Armament: 10×12in; 24×12pdr but later altered; 5 (later 4)×18in torpedo tubes.

Bellerophon, Temeraire, Superb.

St Vincent class

LOA: 536ft. Beam: 84ft. Displacement: 19,250–22,900 tons.

Steam turbines delivering 24,500hp through four screws. Maximum speed: 22 knots.

Armour: belt 10in, turrets 11in. Complement: 850.

Armament: 10×12in; 18×4in but later altered; 3 (later 2)×18in torpedo tubes.

St Vincent, Collingwood, Vanguard.

Vanguard destroyed by internal explosion, 1917.

Neptune

1911. An unusual ship with the wing turrets in echelon. For the first time on a British ship the after turrets were superimposed to enable superfiring, that is allowing X turret to fire over Y turret.

LOA: 546ft. Beam: 85ft. Displacement: 19,900–22,000 tons.

Steam turbines delivering 25,000hp through four screws. Maximum speed: 22 knots.

Armour belt 10in, turrets 11in. Complement: 900.

Armament: 10×12in; 16×4in but later altered; 3 (later 2)×21in torpedo tubes.

Colossus class

1911. Similar in layout to *Neptune.*

LOA: 546ft. Beam: 86ft. Displacement: 20,000–22,250 tons.

Steam turbines delivering 25,000hp through four screws. Maximum speed: 22 knots.

Armour: belt 11in, turrets 11in. Complement: 900.

Armament: 10×12in; 16×4in, but later

altered; 3 (later 2)×21in torpedo tubes. *Colossus*, *Hercules*.

Agincourt

1914. Ordered as the *Rio de Janeiro* for Brazil, then transferred to Turkey, but taken over by the Royal Navy on the outbreak of war.

LOA: 671.5ft. Beam: 89ft. Displacement: 30,250 tons.

Steam turbines delivering 34,000hp through four screws. Maximum speed: 22 knots.

Armour: belt 9in, turrets 12in. Complement: 1,267.

Armament: 14×12in; 20×6in; 8×3in; 2×3in AA; 2×21in torpedo tubes.

SUPER-DREADNOUGHT BATTLESHIPS

These ships had five turrets apiece, all superimposed, and guns of larger than 12in calibre, although the name 'super-dreadnoughts' was not an official term.

Orion class

1912.

LOA: 584ft. Beam: 85ft. Displacement: 22,500–25,000 tons.

Steam turbines delivering 33,000hp through four screws. Maximum speed: 22 knots.

Armour: belt 12in, turrets 11in. Complement: 900.

Armament: 10×13.5in; 16×4in, but later

In wartime, the Admiralty retained the right to take over ships being built in Britain for foreign navies. This is the dreadnought battleship *Agincourt*, originally intended for Turkey. *(IWM SP 1748)*

altered; 3 (later 2)×21in torpedo tubes.
Orion, Monarch, Thunderer, Conqueror.

King George V class
1912–13.
LOA: 598ft. Beam: 89ft. Displacement: 23,000–25,000 tons.
Steam turbines delivering 31,000hp through four screws. Maximum speed: 22 knots.
Armour: belt 12in, turrets 11in. Complement: 900.
Armament: 10×13.5in; 16×4in, but later altered; 3 (later 2)×21in torpedo tubes.
King George V, Centurion, Ajax, Audacious.
Audacious mined and then sunk by internal explosion off Lough Swilly, 1914.

Iron Duke class
1914.
LOA: 620ft. Beam: 89.5ft. Displacement: 26,400–30,380 tons.
Steam turbines delivering 30,000hp through four screws. Maximum speed: 22 knots.
Armour: belt 12in, turrets 11in. Complement: 1,022.
Armament: 10×13.5in; 12×6in; 2×3in AA; 4×21in torpedo tubes.
Iron Duke, Marlborough, Benbow, Emperor of India.
Marlborough torpedoed at Jutland, but she survived and returned under her own power.

The modern battleship *King George V* with a tethered observation kite-balloon in the background.
(IWM SP 365)

Erin

1914.

Ordered for Turkey as the *Reshadieh*, but taken over by the Royal Navy on the outbreak of war.

LOA: 560ft. Beam: 92ft. Displacement: 25,250 tons.

Steam turbines delivering 26,500hp through four screws. Maximum speed: 21 knots.

Armour: belt 12in, turrets 11in. Complement: 1,130.

Armament: 10×13.5in; 16×6in; 2×3in AA; 4×21in torpedo tubes.

Canada

1915.

Ordered for Chile as the *Almirante Latorre* and taken over by the Royal Navy on the outbreak of war but, unusually, transferred to Chile after the war, possibly because of the non-standard calibre of her main armament.

LOA: 661ft. Beam: 92.5ft. Displacement: 32,000 tons.

Steam turbines delivering 37,000hp through four screws. Maximum speed: 24 knots.

Armour: belt 9in, turrets 10in. Complement: 1,176.

Armament: 10×14in; 12×6in; 2×3in AA; 4×21in torpedo tubes.

Queen Elizabeth class

1915–16. Regarded as the finest battleships of their day, they introduced 15in guns, oil-fired propulsion and geared turbines for economical cruising.

LOA: 640ft. Beam: 90.5ft. Displacement: 31,000–33,000 tons.

Steam turbines delivering 75,000hp through four screws. Maximum speed: 25 knots.

Armour: belt 13in, turrets 11in. Complement: 1,016.

Armament: 8×15in; 12×6in; 2×3in AA; 4×21in torpedo tubes.

Queen Elizabeth, Warspite, Barham, Malaya, Valiant.

Royal Sovereign class

1916–17. Originally intended to be seven ships, but two redesigned as battlecruisers.

LOA: 624ft. Beam: 88.5ft. Displacement: 31,250–33,500 tons.

Steam turbines delivering 40,000hp through four screws. Maximum speed: 23 knots.

Armour: belt 13in, turrets 13in. Complement: 997.

Armament: 8×15in; 14×6in; 2×3in AA; 4×21in torpedo tubes.

Revenge, Royal Sovereign, Royal Oak, Resolution, Ramillies.

BATTLECRUISERS

The concept of the battlecruiser differed between the main naval powers. For the Royal Navy, this was a category of ship that placed the emphasis on speed and armament, but at the expense of armour. These ships were expected to deal with inferior ships, keeping out of range while using their superior armament to destroy them, and also to act as a scouting force. By contrast, the German ships were intended to act as the vanguard in a fleet action, and sacrificed speed for better armour protection.

Invincible class

1908.

LOA: 567ft. Beam: 79ft. Displacement: 17,250–20,000 tons.

Steam turbines delivering 41,000hp through four screws. Maximum speed: 26 knots.

Armour: belt 6in, turrets 7in. Complement: 837.

Armament: 8×12in; 16×4in (later altered); 4 (later 3)×18in torpedo tubes.

Invincible, Indomitable, Inflexible.

Invincible sunk at Jutland, 1916.

Inflexible mined in the Dardanelles but survived.

This is *Warspite* in 1916, when she had a 6in secondary armament, which was later removed. *(IWM SP 1029)*

Indefatigable class

1911–13.

LOA: 590ft. Beam: 80ft. Displacement: 18,750–20,000 tons.

Steam turbines delivering 44,000hp through four screws. Maximum speed: 27 knots.

Armour: belt 6in, turrets 7in. Complement: 860.

Armament: 8×12in; 16×4in (later amended); 3 (later 2)×18in torpedo tubes.

Indefatigable, New Zealand, Australia.

Indefatigable sunk at Jutland, 1916.

Lion class

1912–14.

LOA: 700ft. Beam: 88.5ft. Displacement: 29,700 tons.

Steam turbines delivering 80,000hp through four screws. Maximum speed: 32 knots.

Armour: belt 9in, turrets 9in. Complement: 1,056.

Armament: 8×13.5in; 16×4in; 2×3-in AA added later; 2×21in torpedo tubes.

Lion, Princess Royal, Queen Mary (slightly larger), *Tiger* (larger still at 35,000 tons). *Queen Mary* sunk at Jutland, 1916.

Renown class

1916.

LOA: 794ft. Beam: 90ft. Displacement: 32,700 tons.

Steam turbines delivering 120,000hp through four screws. Maximum speed: 33 knots.

Armour: belt 6in, turrets 11in. Complement: 1,250.

Armament: 6×15in; 17×4in; 2×3in AA; 2×21in torpedo tubes.

Repulse, Renown.

LIGHT BATTLECRUISERS

Courageous class

1916–17. Intended to take the war to the Baltic with an invasion by British and Russian forces on the coast of Pomerania.

The so-called light battlecruisers *Courageous* and *Glorious* at sea, with a destroyer between them. Intended to support an Anglo-Russian invasion of Germany's Baltic coast, these ships were of little use in the First World War, and between the two wars were converted to aircraft carriers. *(IWM SP 727)*

LOA: 786ft. Beam: 81ft. Displacement: 22,700 tons.

Steam turbines delivering 90,000hp through four screws. Maximum speed: 33 knots.

Armour: belt 3in, turrets 9in. Complement: 842.

Armament: 4×15in; 18×4in; 2×3in AA; 14×21in torpedo tubes (*Glorious* and *Courageous*).

Armament: 2×18in; 10×5.5in; 4×3in AA; 18×21in torpedo tubes (*Furious*).

The 18in gun proved too heavy for such a lightly built ship, so first the forward gun and then the aft gun were removed, and *Furious* became an 'aerodrome' ship.

ARMOURED CRUISERS

Armoured cruisers were effectively rendered obsolete by the advent of the dreadnought-style battlecruiser, and none were introduced after 1908.

Cressy class
1901–3.

LOA: 472ft. Beam: 69.5ft. Displacement: 12,000 tons.

Triple-expansion steam engines delivering 21,000hp through two screws. Maximum speed: 21 knots.

Armour: belt 6in, deck 3in. Complement: 760.

Armament: 2×9.2in; 12×6in, 13×12 pdr, plus smaller weapons. 2×18in torpedo tubes.

Cressy, Aboukir, Bacchante, Hogue, Sutlej, Euryalus.

Aboukir, Cressy and *Hogue* all torpedoed within an hour by *U-9*, North Sea, 1914.

Drake class
1902–3.

LOA: 535ft. Beam: 71ft. Displacement: 14,100 tons.

Triple-expansion steam engines delivering 30,000hp through two screws. Maximum

speed: 24 knots.

Armour: belt 6in, deck 2–3in. Complement: 900.

Armament: 2×9.2in; 16×6in; 12×12pdr, plus smaller weapons; 2×18in torpedo tubes.

Drake, Good Hope, King Alfred, Leviathan.

Good Hope sunk during Battle of Coronel, 1914.

Drake torpedoed off northern coast of Ireland, 1917.

Monmouth class
1903–4. Originally a class of ten ships, but *Bedford* wrecked, 1910.

LOA: 460ft. Beam: 66ft. Displacement: 9,800 tons.

Triple-expansion steam engines delivering 22,000hp through two screws. Maximum speed: 23 knots.

Armour: belt 4in, deck 2in. Complement: 720.

Armament: 14×6in; 13×12pdr, plus smaller weapons; 2×18in torpedo tubes.

Monmouth, Berwick, Donegal, Essex, Kent, Cornwall, Cumberland, Lancaster, Suffolk.

Monmouth was sunk at Coronel, 1914.

Devonshire class
1904–5.

LOA: 475ft. Beam: 68.5ft. Displacement: 10,850 tons.

Triple-expansion steam engines delivering 21,000hp through two screws. Maximum speed: 22 knots.

Armour: belt 6in, deck 2in. Complement: 700.

Armament: 4×7.5in; 6×6in; 2×12pdr, plus smaller weapons; 2×18in torpedo tubes.

Devonshire, Carnarvon, Antrim, Argyll, Hampshire, Roxburgh.

Argyll wrecked off east coast of Scotland, 1915.

Hampshire mined and sunk off Orkney, 1916, with Lord Kitchener aboard.

Duke of Edinburgh class

1906.

LOA: 505.5ft. Beam: 73ft. Displacement: 13,550 tons.

Triple-expansion steam engines delivering 23,500hp through two screws. Maximum speed: 23 knots.

Armour: belt 6in, deck 0.75–1.5in. Complement: 850.

Armament: 6×9.2in; 10×6in, plus smaller weapons; 3×18in torpedo tubes.

Duke of Edinburgh, Black Prince.

Black Prince sunk at Jutland, 1916.

Warrior class

1907. Effectively a modification of the above.

LOA: 505.5ft. Beam: 73ft. Displacement: 13,550 tons.

Triple-expansion steam engines delivering 23,500hp through two screws. Maximum speed: 23 knots.

Armour: belt 6in, deck 0.75–1.5in. Complement: 850.

Armament: 6×9.2in; 4×7.5in, plus smaller weapons; 3×18in torpedo tubes.

Warrior, Cochrane, Natal, Achilles.

Natal suffered an internal explosion at Cromarty, 1915.

Warrior sunk at Jutland, 1916.

Cochrane wrecked in the Mersey estuary, 1918.

Minotaur class

1908.

LOA: 519ft. Beam: 75ft. Displacement: 14,600–16,100 tons.

Triple-expansion steam engines delivering 27,000hp through two screws. Maximum speed: 23 knots.

Armour: belt 6in, deck 0.75–1.5in. Complement: 850.

Armament: 4×9.2in; 10×7.5in; 16×12pdr; 5×18in torpedo tubes.

Minotaur, Defence, Shannon.

Defence sunk at Jutland, 1916.

PROTECTED CRUISERS

Astrea class

1894–5. Originally eight ships, but converted to training or depot ships before the war.

LOA: 342ft. Beam: 49.5ft. Displacement: 4,360 tons.

Triple-expansion steam engines delivering 9,000hp through two screws. Maximum speed: 19.5 knots.

Armour: deck 2in. Complement: 326.

Armament: 2×6in; 8×4.7in, plus smaller weapons; 4×18in torpedo tubes.

Astrea, Charybdis, Fox.

Apollo class

1892–4. Originally twenty ships, but one wrecked and eight sold before the war.

LOA: 314ft. Beam: 42.6ft. Displacement: 3,600 tons.

Triple-expansion steam engines delivering 9,000hp through two screws. Maximum speed: 20 knots.

Armour: deck 2in. Complement: 273 (185 as minelayers).

Armament: 2×6in; 8×4.7in, plus smaller weapons; 4×18in torpedo tubes.

(6×6pdr guns and 150 mines for minelayers.)

Apollo*, Rainbow, Sirius, Iphigenia*, Thetis*, Brilliant, Sappho, Andromache*, Latona*, Naiad*, Intrepid.

* Converted as minelayers.

Brilliant, Sirius, Iphigenia, Intrepid, Thetis all sunk as blockships at Zeebrugge, 1918.

Crescent class

1893. Became depot ships, mainly for submarines, 1915–16.

LOA: 387ft. Beam: 60.6ft. Displacement: 7,700 tons.

Triple-expansion steam engines delivering 12,000hp through two screws. Maximum speed: 19.5 knots.

Armour: deck 2.5–5in. Complement: 550.

Armament: 1×9.2in; 12×6in, plus smaller weapons; 2×18in torpedo tubes.
Crescent, Royal Arthur.

Edgar class
1893–4. Generally similar to the above.
LOA: 387ft. Beam: 60.6ft. Displacement: 7,700 tons.
Triple-expansion steam engines delivering 12,000hp through two screws. Maximum speed: 19.5 knots.
Armour: deck 2.5–5in. Complement: 550.
Armament: 2×9.2in; 10×6in, plus smaller weapons; 2×18in torpedo tubes.
Edgar, Hawke, Endymion, Gibraltar, Grafton, Theseus.
Hawke torpedoed by U-9 in North Sea, 1914. Surviving ships retired November 1914 as mechanically and structurally unfit for service.

Eclipse class
1896–9. *Dido* and *Eclipse* became depot ships during the war years.
LOA: 370ft. Beam: 54ft. Displacement: 5,600 tons.
Triple-expansion steam engines delivering 9,600hp through two screws. Maximum speed: 19.5 knots.
Armour: deck 2.5–5in. Complement: 550.
Armament: 11×6in, 9×12pdr, plus smaller weapons; 3×18in torpedo tubes.
(5×6in, 6×4.7in, *Eclipse*)
Minerva, Talbot, Eclipse, Doris, Venus, Isis, Juno, Diana.

Pelorus class
1897–1900. Originally ten ships, but three sold before the war and one converted as submarine depot ship.
LOA: 314ft. Beam: 36.5ft. Displacement: 2,250 tons.
Triple-expansion steam engines delivering 7,000hp through two screws. Maximum speed: 20.5 knots.

Armour: deck 2in. Complement: 224.
Armament: 8×4in, plus smaller weapons; 2×14in torpedo tubes.
Pelorus, Pegasus, Proserpine, Pioneer, Psyche, Pyramus.
Pegasus sunk by light cruiser *Königsberg* at Zanzibar, 1914.

Vindictive
1899. Originally four-ship Arrogant class, but one lost and another two converted before the war. *Vindictive* herself sunk as blockship at Ostend, 1918, having earlier been heavily modified for the Zeebrugge raid.
LOA: 342ft. Beam: 57.5ft. Displacement: 5,750 tons.
Triple-expansion steam engines delivering 10,000hp through two screws. Maximum speed: 19 knots.
Armour: deck 3in. Complement: 480.
Armament: 10×6in, 9×12pdr, plus smaller weapons; 3×18in torpedo tubes.

Highflyer class
1900–1.
LOA: 370ft. Beam: 54ft. Displacement: 5,600 tons.
Triple-expansion steam engines delivering 10,000hp through two screws. Maximum speed: 20 knots.
Armour: deck 3in. Complement: 500.
Armament: 11×6in; 9×12pdr, plus smaller weapons; 2×18in torpedo tubes.
Highflyer, Hermes, Hyacinth.
Hermes converted to carry seaplanes, but reconverted before the war. Torpedoed by U-27 in the Straits of Dover, 1914.

Challenger class
1904–5.
LOA: 376ft. Beam: 56ft. Displacement: 5,915 tons.
Triple-expansion steam engines delivering 12,500hp through two screws. Maximum speed: 21 knots.

Officers aboard the elderly cruiser *Vindictive* before the successful raid on Zeebrugge. *(Private collection)*

Armour: deck 2–3in. Complement: 475.
Armament: 11×6in; 9×12pdr, plus smaller weapons; 2×18in torpedo tubes.
Challenger, Encounter.

Topaz or Gem class

1904–5.
LOA: 374ft. Beam: 40ft. Displacement: 3,000 tons.
Triple-expansion steam engines delivering 9,800hp through two screws. Maximum speed: 22 knots.
Armour: deck 2in. Complement: 296.
Armament: 12×4in, plus smaller weapons; 2×18in torpedo tubes.
Topaz, Amethyst, Diamond, Sapphire.

Diadem class

1898–1900. These were the only protected cruisers to have four funnels as opposed to two or three, and appearance resembled the Cressy-class armoured cruisers. During the war, most of them became training or accommodation ships, except for *Ariadne*, which became a minelayer.

LOA: 450ft. Beam: 69ft. Displacement: 11,000 tons.
Triple-expansion steam engines delivering 16,500hp through two screws. Maximum speed: 25 knots.
Armour: deck 4in. Complement: 700.
Armament: 16×6in; 14×12pdr, plus smaller weapons; 2×18in torpedo tubes.
Diadem, Niobe, Europa, Amphitrite, Argonaut, Ariadne.*
* Manned by Royal Canadian Navy.
Ariadne torpedoed off Beachy Head, 1917.

Sentinel class

1905.
First of a new class of cruiser designed to operate with destroyers in the escort role, mainly acting as a screen for major fleet units.
LOA: 360ft. Beam: 40ft. Displacement: 2,900 tons.
Triple-expansion steam engines delivering 17,500hp through two screws. Maximum speed: 25 knots.
Armour: deck 1.5in max. Complement: 296.

Armament: 9×4in; 1×3in AA; 2×14in torpedo tubes.
Sentinel, Skirmisher.

Forward class
1905. Almost identical to Sentinel class, but LOA 365ft, and 2in armour belt.
Forward, Foresight.

Pathfinder class
1905. Similar to Forward class, but LOA 70ft, and displacement 2,940 tons.

Adventure class
1905.
LOA: 374ft. Beam: 38ft. Displacement: 2,670 tons.
Triple-expansion steam engines delivering 16,000hp through two screws. Maximum speed: 25.5 knots.
Armour: deck 2in. Complement: 268.
Armament: 9×4in; 1×3in AA; 2×14in torpedo tubes.
Adventure, Attentive.

Boadicea class
1909–11.
LOA: 405.75ft. Beam: 41ft. Displacement: 3,400 tons.
Turbines delivering 18,000hp through two screws. Maximum speed: 26 knots.
Armour: none. Complement: 330.
Armament: 6–10×4in; 1×3in or 4in AA; 2×18in or 21in torpedo tubes.
Boadicea, Bellona, Blanche, Blonde.

Active class
1912–13.
As for Boadicea class, but 3,440 tons displacement, 10×4in guns and 2×21in torpedo tubes.
Active, Amphion, Fearless.
Amphion mined off Thames Estuary, 1914.

Bristol class
1910–11. The first of a number of 'Town' cruisers in five different classes, intended as useful dual-purpose ships capable of cruising or fleet duties. All had four funnels.

The light cruisers of the Forward class were designed to operate with the fleet and, despite appearances, at 2,900 tons standard displacement, *Forward*, shown here in the harbour at Mudros, was smaller than a modern destroyer. *(IWM SP 872)*

The first two classes, Bristol and Weymouth, retained ram bows, but the later classes had cut-away bows.

LOA: 453ft. Beam: 47ft. Displacement: 4,800 tons.

Turbines delivering 22,500hp through four (*Bristol*, two) screws. Maximum speed: 26 knots.

Armour: deck up to 2in. Complement: 500.

Armament: 2×6in; 10×4in; 1×3in AA; 2×18in torpedo tubes.

Liverpool, Newcastle, Bristol, Glasgow, Gloucester.

Weymouth class

1911–12.

LOA: 453ft. Beam: 48.5ft. Displacement: 5,250 tons.

Turbines delivering 23,500hp through four (*Yarmouth*, two) screws. Maximum speed: 26 knots.

Armour: deck up to 2in. Complement: 540.

Armament: 8×6in; 1×3in AA; 2×21in torpedo tubes.

Weymouth, Dartmouth, Falmouth, Yarmouth.

Falmouth torpedoed four times by *U-63* and *U-66* in North Sea, 1916.

Chatham class

1912.

LOA: 458ft. Beam: 48.75ft. Displacement: 5,400 tons.

Turbines delivering 25,000hp through four (*Southampton*, two) screws. Maximum speed: 26 knots.

Armour: deck up to 2in. Complement: 500.

Armament: 8×6in; 1×3in AA; 2×21in torpedo tubes.

Chatham, Dublin, Southampton; plus a further three ships, *Melbourne, Sydney* and *Brisbane*, built for Australia, 1913–15.

Birmingham class

1914.

LOA: 450ft. Beam: 50ft. Displacement: 5,440 tons.

Turbines delivering 25,000hp through four screws. Maximum speed: 26 knots.

Armour: belt 3in. Complement: 540.

Armament: 9×6in; 1×3in AA; 2×21in torpedo tubes.

Birmingham, Lowestoft, Nottingham.

Nottingham torpedoed by *U-52*, North Sea, 1916.

Birkenhead and Chester

1915–16. Both originally laid down for Greece, but taken over on the outbreak of war.

LOA: 446ft and 456.5ft respectively. Beam: 50ft. Displacement: 5,200 tons.

Turbines delivering 25,000hp and 31,000hp respectively through four screws. Maximum speed: 25 and 26.5 knots.

Armour: belt 3in. Complement: 550.

Armament: 10×5.5in; 1×3in AA; 2×21in torpedo tubes.

Chester famous for the heroism of Boy Cornwell VC at Jutland.

LIGHT CRUISERS

These were a compromise between scouting cruisers and the various Town classes, with a high speed to enable them to work with destroyers.

Arethusa class

1914–15.

LOA: 436ft. Beam: 39ft. Displacement: 3,512 tons.

Turbines delivering 40,000hp through four screws. Maximum speed: 30 knots.

Armour: belt 3in, deck 1in. Complement: 318.

Armament: 3×6in; 4×4in; 2×3in or 1×4in AA; 8×21in torpedo tubes.

Arethusa, Aurora, Galatea, Penelope, Undaunted, Inconstant, Phaeton, Royalist.

Arethusa mined in North Sea, 1916.

Caroline class

1914–15.

LOA: 446ft. Beam: 41.5ft. Displacement: 3,750 tons.

Turbines delivering 40,000hp through four screws. Maximum speed: 30 knots.

Armour: belt 3in, deck 1in. Complement: 325.

Armament: 4×6in; 1–2×3in or 4in AA; 4–8×21in torpedo tubes.

Caroline, Carysfort, Cleopatra, Comus, Conquest, Cordelia.

Cambrian class

1915–16. Similar to Caroline class but with two, instead of three, smokestacks. However, *Calliope* and *Champion* were the first British cruisers to have geared turbines, improving performance and reducing fuel consumption.

LOA: 446ft. Beam: 41.5ft. Displacement: 3,750 tons.

Turbines delivering 40,000hp through four screws. Maximum speed: 30 knots.

Armour: belt 3in (*Calliope* and *Champion* 4in), deck 1in. Complement: 325.

Armament: 4×6in; 1–2×3in or 4in AA; 4–8×21in torpedo tubes.

Cambrian, Calliope, Canterbury, Champion, Castor, Constance.

Centaur class

1916. As for *Calliope* and *Champion*, but with 5×6in and 2×3in AA guns, and 2×21in torpedoes.

Centaur, Concord.

Centaur mined in North Sea, 1917, but survived, despite having bow and stern blown off.

Caledon class

1917.

LOA: 450ft. Beam: 42ft. Displacement: 4,120 tons.

Turbines delivering 40,000hp through two screws. Maximum speed: 30 knots.

Armour: belt 3in, deck 1in. Complement: 344.

Armament: 5×6in; 2×3in; 8×21in torpedo tubes.

Caledon, Calypso, Caradoc, Cassandra.

Ships of this class were later converted to AA cruisers and served in the Second World War. *Cassandra* mined in Baltic, 1918.

Ceres class

1917–18. As Caledon class, but beam 43.5ft and displacement 4,190 tons.

Ceres, Cardiff, Curlew, Coventry, Curacoa. Ships of this class were later converted to AA cruisers and served in the Second World War.

Carlisle class

1918. As Ceres class, but LOA 451.5ft, displacement 4,290 tons.

Only *Carlisle* completed before Armistice, with four more ships completed after the war. Ships of this class were later converted to AA cruisers and served in the Second World War.

Danae class

1918.

LOA: 471ft. Beam: 46ft. Displacement: 4,650 tons.

Turbines delivering 40,000hp through two screws. Maximum speed: 29 knots.

Armour: belt 3in, deck 1in. Complement: 400.

Armament: 6×6in; 2×3in; 12×21in torpedo tubes.

Danae, Dauntless, Dragon.

Post-war Delhi class was similar, with five ships completed 1919–22.

DESTROYERS

The destroyer traces its origins to the torpedo-boat destroyer, created to combat the menace of the torpedo boat that so concerned the world's navies in the closing years of the nineteenth century. For a modern comparison, one has to consider the missile-carrying fast boats that worried the navies, especially those of the Western alliance, during the later years of the Cold War, as these were seen to give small navies considerable hitting power.

The destroyer started to grow in size during the early years of the twentieth century, to the extent that by the final quarter of the century, many were larger than the cruisers of the First World War. Of the first generation, the Admiralty took the bold step of ordering no less than forty-two from fourteen different yards, which were given considerable scope in their interpretation of the design and specification. By the time the First World War started, most of these ships had been sold or scrapped, although a significant number seem to have sunk as the result of collisions, no doubt due in part to the lack of radar. These early ships of the A, B, C and D classes were known as 'turtle-backs', because of their shape. Some of the ships had bow tubes as well as deck tubes for launching torpedoes. However, the bow tubes were a failure as the ships tended to overrun the torpedoes – a reflection of the comparatively high speed of these ships when first built, and the slow speed of the early torpedoes.

A class
1893–5. Forty-two ships built.
LOA: 180–206ft. Beam: 18.5–20.5ft.
Displacement: 220–300 tons.
Triple-expansion steam engines delivering 3,100–4,850hp through two screws.
Maximum speed: 27–8 knots.
Complement: 45–60.
Armament: 1×12pdr; 3–5×6pdr; 2×18in torpedo tubes.

Boxer, Conflict, Fervent, Handy, Lightning, Opossum, Porcupine, Ranger, Sunfish, Surly, Wizard, Zephyr.
Lightning mined in North Sea, 1915.

B class
1895–1901.
LOA: 210–18ft. Beam: 20–2ft. Displacement: 300–70 tons.
Triple-expansion steam engines delivering 5,800–6,700hp through two screws.
Maximum speed: 30 knots.
Complement: 50–60.
Armament: 1×12pdr; 5×6pdr; 2×18in torpedo tubes.
Quail, Earnest, Griffon, Locust, Thrasher, Virago, Panther, Seal, Wolf, Spiteful, Peterel, Kangaroo, Lively, Myrmidon, Orwell, Sprightly, Success, Syren.
Success sunk off Fife, 1914.
Myrmidon mined in the English Channel, 1917.

Albacore and *Bonetta*
1908. These differed from the B class, displacing 440 tons, using steam turbines and having three 12pdr guns; but maximum speed was just 27 knots.

Express and *Arab*
1896 and 1901. These differed by displacing 470 tons, developing up to 9,000hp and having a maximum speed of 32 knots.

C class
1896–1901. Similar to B class, but with three funnels, rather than four. Displacement rose to between 283 and 330 tons, except for *Albatross*, which was 360 tons and capable of 32 knots. A further three craft were lost before the war.
Avon, Bat, Brazen, Otter, Star, Crane, Whiting, Bittern, Cheerful, Fairy, Fawn, Flirt, Flying Fish, Gypsy, Leopard, Sylvia, Violet, Osprey, Albatross, Dove, Kestrel, Mermaid, Vulture, Greyhound,

Racehorse, Bullfinch, Electra, Falcon, Leven, Ostrich, Recruit, Roebuck, Thorn, Vigilant, Vixen.

Recruit torpedoed by *U-66* in Thames Estuary, 1915.

Flirt torpedoed in Straits of Dover, 1916.

Cheerful mined off Shetland, 1917.

Otter scrapped in Far East, 1917.

Bittern sunk in collision off Portland Bill, 1918.

Fairy rammed *UC-75* and sank, 1918.

Falcon sunk in collision in North Sea, 1918.

Velox

1902. *Velox*, 440 tons, was a larger variant of the above, turbine-driven with eight screws on four shafts, and quoted as disposing of 8,000hp and being capable of 27 knots. She was mined near the Nab lightship in 1915. A smaller and faster ship, *Viper*, was commissioned in 1899, but wrecked in 1901.

D class

1895–9. These were similar to the B class but with two funnels, and displacement varying between 275 and 285 tons; power varied between 5,500 and 5,800hp. Two ships, *Ariel*, wrecked in 1907, and *Foam*, sold in 1914, did not see war service.

Desperate, Angler, Fame, Mallard, Coquette, Cygnet, Cynthia, Stag.

Coquette was mined in the North Sea, 1916.

Taku

1898.

Captured from China in the Boxer Rising, 1900, and sold 1916.

LOA: 193.6ft. Beam: 20ft. Displacement: 305 tons.

Triple-expansion steam engines delivering 6,500hp through two screws. Maximum speed: 32 knots.

Complement: 62.

Armament: 6×3pdr; 3×18in torpedo tubes.

E or River class

1903–5 and 1909. *Garry** sunk in a collision, 1908; *Blackwater*** sunk in a collision 1909.

LOA: 220–5ft. Beam: 23–4ft. Displacement: 527–66 tons.

Triple-expansion steam engines delivering 7,000–7,500hp through two screws. Maximum speed: 25–6 knots.

Complement: 70.

Armament: 4×12pdr; 2×18in torpedo tubes.

*Arun**, Cherwell, Dee, Eden+, Erne, Foyle**, Itchen**, Kennet**, Waveney+, Ettrick, Exe, Teviot*, Usk*, Boyne+, Chelmer**, Jed**, Liffey**, Moy**, Derwent+, Doon+, Kale+, Rother, Ure, Ribble*, Swale, Wear, Gala*, Colne**, Ness**, Nith**, Ouse**, Stour**, Test**.*

* Four funnels in open pairs; others had four funnels in closed pairs.

** Two tall or medium funnels; *Stour* and *Test*, built as replacements for losses, had turbines.

+ Two short funnels; *Eden* had turbines.

Erne wrecked off Rattray Head, 1915.

Eden sunk in collision in the English Channel, 1916.

Derwent mined off Le Havre, 1917.

Foyle mined in the Straits of Dover, 1917.

Itchen torpedoed by U-boat in the North Sea, 1917.

Kale mined in the North Sea, 1918.

Arno

1915.

Being built at Genoa for Portugal but taken over. Sunk in 1918 in a collision in the Dardanelles. Similar to the above with two funnels, but with 3×18in torpedo tubes.

F or Tribal class

1907–9. These three-funnel destroyers marked a considerable increase in tonnage.

LOA: 250–79ft. Beam: 25–6ft. Displacement: 865–90 tons.

Turbines delivering 14,500hp through three

Having come into existence as torpedo-boat destroyers, small and with a fast turn of speed, the destroyer developed during the early years of the twentieth century and started to grow in size, notably with the F or Tribal class, of which HMS *Cossack* was one. *(IWM SP 2847)*

screws. Maximum speed: 33–6 knots.
Complement: 72.
Armament: 5×12pdr and 2×18in torpedo tubes*; otherwise 2×4in and 2×18in torpedo tubes.
Afridi*, Cossack*, Ghurka*, Mohawk*, Tartar*, Amazon, Saracen, Crusader, Maori, Nubian, Viking, Zulu, Zubian+.
Maori mined off Zeebrugge, 1915.
Nubian torpedoed off Folkestone, 1916.
Zulu mined off Dover, 1916.
Ghurka mined off Dungeness, 1917.
+ *Zubian* consisted of the undamaged remains of *Zulu* and *Nubian*, and on 4 February 1918 the 'new' ship sank *UC-50* off Essex.

Swift
1907. Flotilla leader, specially built, fastest ship in the fleet.

LOA: 353ft. Beam: 34.5ft. Displacement: 2,207 tons.
Turbines delivering 50,000-hp through four screws. Maximum speed: 40+ knots.
Complement: 138.
Armament: 4×4in, with the two forward guns replaced by a single 6in, 1916; 1×12pdr; 2×18in torpedo tubes.

G or Basilisk class
1909–10.
LOA: 266–75ft. Beam: 26.75–8ft. Displacement: 885–964 tons.
Turbines delivering 12,500hp through three screws. Maximum speed: 27–8 knots.
Complement: 96.
Armament: 1×4in; 3×12pdr; 2×18in torpedo tubes.
Beagle*, Bulldog*, Foxhound*, Harpy*, Grasshopper, Renard, Basilisk*, Grampus*,

Mosquito, Pincher, Racoon, Rattlesnake*, Savage, Scourge*, Scorpion, Wolverine.

All three funnels, but * with the third very small.

Wolverine sunk in collision off north-west Ireland, 1917.

Pincher wrecked off Scilly Isles, 1918.

Racoon wrecked off northern coast of Ireland, 1918.

H or Acorn class

1910–11. All with three funnels of differing height, but otherwise greater standardisation than in earlier classes..

LOA: 240ft. Beam: 25.5ft. Displacement: 780 tons.

Turbines delivering 13,500hp through three screws. Maximum speed: 30 knots.

Complement: 72.

Armament: 2×4in; 2×18in torpedo tubes.

Acorn, Alarm, Brisk, Cameleon, Comet, Goldfinch, Hope, Larne, Lyra, Martin, Nemesis, Nereide, Redpole, Rifleman, Ruby, Staunch, Fury, Minstrel, Nymphe, Sheldrake.

Martin and *Nemesis* transferred to Japan, 1917–19.

Goldfinch wrecked off Orkney, 1915.

Staunch torpedoed by U-boat off Palestine, 1917.

Comet torpedoed by U-boat in the Mediterranean, 1918.

I or Acheron class

1911. All two funnels.

LOA: 240ft. Beam: 25.75ft. Displacement: 780 tons.

Turbines delivering 13,500hp through three screws, or * 16,500hp through two screws. Maximum speed: 30 knots.

Complement: 72.

Armament: 2×4in; 2×12pdr; 2×21in torpedo tubes.

Acheron*, Archer*, Ariel*, Attack*, Badger*, Beaver*, Defender, Druid, Ferret, Forester, Goshawk, Hind, Hornet, Hydra, Jackal,
Lapwing, Lizard, Phoenix, Sandfly, Tigress.

Ariel completed as minelayer.

Attack mined off Alexandria, 1917.

Phoenix torpedoed by U-boat in the Adriatic, 1918.

Ariel mined in North Sea, 1918.

Modified Acheron class

1912.

As above, but LOA 255ft and displacement 790 tons, with 20,000hp and a maximum speed of 35 knots.

Firedrake, Lurcher, Oak.

A further six ships of 700 tons displacement were built for the Royal Australian Navy between 1910 and 1915.

NB: No J class.

K or Acasta class

1912–13.

LOA: 257–66ft. Beam: 26.5–8ft. Displacement: 935–1,000 tons.

Turbines delivering 22,500–5,000hp through three screws (* two screws).

Maximum speed: 30–2 knots.

Complement: 75–7.

Armament: 3×4in; 2×21in torpedo tubes.

Acasta, Achates, Christopher, Cockatrice, Shark, Sparrowhawk, Hardy*, Ambuscade, Contest, Lynx, Midge, Owl, Spitfire, Garland*, Paragon*, Porpoise*, Unity*, Victor*.

Lynx mined in Moray Firth, 1915.

Shark and *Sparrowhawk* sunk at Jutland, 1916.

Paragon torpedoed by destroyer in Straits of Dover, 1917.

Contest torpedoed by U-boat in the English Channel, 1917.

L class

1913–15.

LOA: 269ft. Beam: 27. 5ft. Displacement: 1,072 tons.

Turbines delivering 22,500–4,500hp

through two screws. Maximum speed: 31 knots.

Complement: 77.

Armament: 3×4in; 1×12pdr; 4×21in torpedo tubes.

Fortune (prototype, three funnels), *Ardent* (prototype, two funnels), *Lark, Laurel, Liberty, Linnet, Laertes*, Laforey*, Lawford*, Leonidas*, Llewellyn*, Louis*, Loyal*, Lucifer*, Lysander*, Landrail, Laverock, Lance*, Legion*, Lennox, Lookout*, Lydiard*, Lassoo*, Lochinvar*.*

* Three funnels. *Legion* completed as minelayer.

Louis wrecked in Suvla Bay during Gallipoli operation, 1915.

Lassoo mined in the North Sea, 1916.

Fortune and *Ardent* sunk at Jutland, 1916.

Laforey mined in the English Channel, 1917.

M class

1914–17. The most numerous single class of wartime destroyer, but with variations in size and number of funnels.

LOA: 271–6ft. Beam: 26.75ft. Displacement: 994–1,042 tons.

Turbines delivering 25,000hp through three screws. Maximum speed: 34 knots.

Complement: 80–98.

Armament: 3×4in; 1×12pdr; 4×21in torpedo tubes.

Mastiff (t), *Meteor* (t), *Manly* (y), *Minos* (y), *Miranda* (y), *Medea* (g), *Medusa* (g), *Melampus* (g), *Melpomene* (g), *Matchless* (a), *Milne* (a), *Morris* (a), *Murray* (a), *Maenad* (a), *Mameluke* (a), *Mandate* (a), *Manners* (a), *Marmion* (a), *Marne* (a), *Martial* (a), *Marvel* (a), *Michael* (a), *Millbrook* (a), *Mindful* (a), *Minion* (a), *Mischia* (a), *Mons* (a), *Moorsom* (a), *Myngs* (a), *Mystic* (a), *Nessus* (a), *Ossary* (a), *Moon* (y), *Morning Star* (y), *Mounsey* (y), *Musketeer* (y), *Mansfield* (h), *Mentor* (h), *Magic* (a), *Mary Rose* (a), *Medina* (a), *Medway* (a), *Menace* (a), *Moresby* (a), *Munster* (a), *Napier* (a), *Narborough* (a), *Narwhal* (a), *Negro* (a), *Nepean* (a), *Nereus* (a), *Nestor* (a), *Nicator* (a), *Nizam* (a), *Noble* (a), *Nomad* (a), *Nonpareil* (a), *Nonsuch* (a), *Norman* (a),

HMS *Onslaught* was one of the M class destroyers, the most numerous class in service during the war years, but with considerable variation in specification, including the number of funnels. *(IWM SP 1408)*

The destroyer *Obdurate* at sea. The two sets of torpedo tubes aft of the third funnel are noticeable and can be used to fire on either side. *(IWM SP 1354)*

Norseman (a), *Northesk* (a), *Obdurate* (a), *Obedient* (a), *Oberon* (a), *Observer* (a), *Octavia* (a), *Offa* (a), *Onslaught* (a), *Onslow* (a), *Opal* (a), *Ophelia* (a), *Opportune* (a), *Oracle* (a), *Orcadia* (a), *Orestes* (a), *Orford* (a), *Oriana* (a), *Oriole* (a), *Orpheus* (a), *Osiris* (a), *North Star* (a), *Nugent* (a), *Paladin* (a), *Parthian* (a), *Partridge* (a), *Pasley* (a), *Pelican* (a), *Pellew* (a), *Penn* (a), *Peregrine* (a), *Petard* (a), *Peyton* (a), *Pheasant* (a), *Phoebe* (a), *Pigeon* (a), *Plover* (a), *Plucky* (a), *Portia* (a), *Prince* (a), *Pylades* (a), *Nerissa* (y), *Relentless* (y), *Rival* (y), *Sabrina* (l), *Strongbow* (l), *Patrician* (t), *Patriot* (t), *Rapid* (t), *Ready* (t), *Surprise*(l), *Sybille* (l), *Truculent* (l), *Tyrant* (l), *Ulleswater* (l).

Meteor completed as minelayer.

(a) Admiralty M class, with three funnels.

(h) Hawthorn M class with four funnels, 27.5ft beam, 1,055 tons displacement, two screws, 27,000hp, 35 knots.

(y) Yarrow M class with two funnels, LOA 269.5–71.5ft, 880–900 tons, two screws, 23,000hp, 39 knots.

(l) Later Yarrow M class, 900–25 tons.

(t) Thornycroft M class with three funnels, 985–1,070 tons, two screws, 27,000hp, 37 knots.

(g) Admiralty M class originally intended for Greece and taken over in 1914.

Negro sunk in North Sea collision, 1916.

Nestor sunk at Jutland, 1916.

Medusa sunk in collision off Denmark, 1916.

Marmion sunk in North Sea collision, 1917.

Mary Rose sunk in action off Norway, 1917.

Partridge sunk in action off Norway, 1917.

Strongbow sunk in action off Norway, 1917.

Surprise mined in the North Sea, 1917.
Pheasant mined off Orkney, 1917.
Narborough wrecked off Scapa Flow, 1918.
Nessus sunk in North Sea collision, 1918.
North Star sunk in action off Zeebrugge, 1918.
Opal wrecked off Scapa Flow, 1918.
Ulleswater torpedoed by U-boat off Netherlands, 1918.

Botha class leaders

1914–15. Under construction as Chilean Almirante class and taken over by Royal Navy. Four funnels.
LOA: 331.3ft. Beam: 32.5ft. Displacement: 1,694–742 tons.
Turbines delivering 30,000hp through three screws. Maximum speed: 32 knots.
Complement: 205.
Armament: 4×4in; 2×12pdr; 4×21in torpedo tubes.
Botha, Broke, Faulknor, Tipperary.
Tipperary sunk at Jutland, 1916.

Talisman class

1916. Under construction for Turkey and taken over by Royal Navy. Three funnels.
LOA: 309ft. Beam: 28ft. Displacement: 1,098 tons.
Turbines delivering 25,000hp through three screws. Maximum speed: 32 knots.
Complement: 102.
Armament: 5×4in; 4×21in torpedo tubes.
Talisman, Termagant, Trident, Turbulent.
Turbulent sunk at Jutland, 1916.

Marksman class leaders

1915–16. Four funnels of differing size.
LOA: 325ft. Beam: 31.75ft. Displacement: 1,604–55 tons.
Turbines delivering 36,000hp through three screws. Maximum speed: 34 knots.
Complement: 116.
Armament: 4×4in; 1×3in AA; 2×2pdr; 4×21in torpedo tubes.
Marksman, Lightfoot, Nimrod, Gabriel*, Ithuriel, Kempenfelt, Abdiel+.
* Commissioned as minelayer.

The destroyer *Tyrant*, one of the M class destroyers built by a number of builders, in this case Yarrow. *(IWM SP 1237)*

+ Commissioned as minelayer, with armament of 3×4in and 72 mines.

Later Marksman class leaders

1916–17. Three funnels of differing size, otherwise similar to Marksman class, but with displacement of 1,670 tons.

Grenville, Hoste, Parker, Saumarez, Seymour, Anzac (Australia).

Hoste sunk in North Sea collision, 1916.

R class

1916–17. Similar to later M class, but smaller, with geared turbines and aft 4in gun mounted on bandstand.

LOA: 275ft. Beam: 26.75ft. Displacement: 1,036–96 tons.

Turbines delivering 27,000hp through two screws. Maximum speed: 36 knots.

Complement: 98.

Armament: 3×4in; 1×2pdr; 4×21in torpedo tubes.

Radstock, Raider, Restless, Rigorous, Rob Roy, Rocket, Romola, Rowena, Sable, Salmon, Sarpedon, Simoom (1), *Sorceress, Starfish, Rosalind* (t), *Recruit, Redgauntlet, Redoubt, Satyr, Sceptre, Setter, Sharpshooter, Skate, Skilful, Stork, Sturgeon, Sylph, Tancred, Tarpon*, Telemachus*, Tempest, Tenacious, Tetrarch, Thisbe, Thruster, Tormentor, Tornado, Torrent, Torrid, Radiant* (t), *Retriever* (t), *Taurus* (t), *Teazer* (t), *Tirade* (m), *Tower* (m), *Trenchant* (m), *Tristram* (m), *Ulster* (m), *Umpire* (m), *Undine* (m), *Urchin* (m), *Ursa* (m), *Ursula* (m).

* Commissioned as minelayer.

(t) Thornycroft R class with 29,000hp and up to 40 knots.

(m) Modified Admiralty R class with LOA 276ft and displacement 1,091 tons.

Recruit, Tornado, Torrent mined in North Sea, 1917.

Setter sunk in collision off Harwich, 1917.

Simoom sunk in action in North Sea, 1917.

S class

1918, with a further 31 ships completed in 1919, plus one each in 1922 and 1924. Two funnels.

LOA: 275–7ft. Beam: 26.6ft. Displacement: 1,075 tons.

Turbines delivering 27,000hp through two screws. Maximum speed: 36 knots.

Complement: 90.

Armament: 3×4in; 1×2pdr; 4×21in torpedo tubes, plus 2×14in, which later removed.

Sabre, Scimitar, Scotsman, Scout, Scythe, Seabear, Seafire, Searcher, Senator, Sepoy, Seraph, Shark, Sikh, Simoom (2), *Sirdar, Somme, Sparrowhawk, Spear, Splendid, Sportive, Swallow, Tactician, Tara, Tilbury, Tintagel, Tribune, Trinidad, Trojan, Speedy* (t), *Tobago* (t), *Torbay* (t), *Toreador* (t), *Tourmaline* (t), *Tomahawk* (y), *Torch* (y), *Tryphon* (y), *Tumult* (y).

(t) Thornycroft S class, 1,087 tons, 29,000hp, up to 38 knots.

(y) Yarrow S class, 930 tons, 23,000hp, up to 39 knots.

V and W classes

1917–18.

LOA: 312ft. Beam: 29.5ft. Displacement: 1,272–339 tons.

Turbines delivering 27,000hp through two screws. Maximum speed: 34 knots.

Complement: 110–20.

Armament: (V) 4×4in; 1×3in AA; 6×21in torpedo tubes.

(W) 3×4in; 1×3in AA; 6×21in torpedo tubes.

Valentine+, Valhalla+, Valkyrie+, Valorous+, Vampire+, Vanoc*, Vanquisher*, Vectis, Vega, Vehement, Vendetta, Venetia, Venturous*, Verdun, Verulam, Vimiera, Violent, Vivacious, Wakeful, Vancouver, Vanessa, Vanity, Velox, Versatile, Vesper, Vidette, Vittoria, Vivien, Vortigern, Voyager, Walker, Walpole, Walrus, Warwick, Watchman, Waterhen, Wessex, Westcott, Westminster, Whirlwind, Whitley, Winchelsea, Winchester, Windsor, Wolfhound, Wrestler,

Wryneck, Viceroy (t), *Viscount* (t), *Wolsey* (t), *Woolston* (t).

* Commissioned as minelayer.

+ Operated as destroyer leader.

(t) Thornycroft V and W types, with 37,000hp and up to 37 knots.

Vehement mined in North Sea, 1918.

Thornycroft leaders

1917, with a further ship built in 1919.

LOA: 329ft. Beam: 31.75ft. Displacement: 1,550–750 tons.

Turbines delivering 40,000hp through two screws. Maximum speed: 38 knots.

Complement: 181.

Armament: 5×4.7in; 1×3in AA; 2×2pdr; 6×21in torpedo tubes.

Shakespeare, Spencer.

Admiralty leaders

1918, with a further two ships commissioned in 1919, and one each in 1924 and 1925.

LOA: 332.5ft. Beam: 31.75ft. Displacement: 1,800–2,053 tons.

Turbines delivering 40,000hp through two screws. Maximum speed: 38 knots.

Complement: 181.

Armament: 5×4.7in; 1×3in AA; 2×2pdr; 6×21in torpedo tubes.

Bruce, Campbell, Douglas, Montrose, Scott, Stuart.

SEAPLANE CARRIERS

Ark Royal

1914.

LOA: 366ft. Beam: 50.75ft. Displacement: 7,020 tons.

Triple-expansion steam engines delivering 3,000hp through a single screw. Maximum speed: 10.6 knots.

Complement: 180.

Armament: 4×12pdr; 6×21in torpedo tubes.

Converted from collier.

The seaplane carrier *Ark Royal* was a long way from the three later aircraft carriers of the same name. *(FAAM)*

Converted packet ships

1914. A varied assortment of ships originally built between 1904 and 1911.

LOA: 311–75ft. Beam: 40–6ft. Displacement: 1,675–2,651 tons.

Turbines with three screws. Maximum speed: 21.5–4.5 knots.

Complement: 250.

Armament: 5×4.7in; 1×3in AA; 2×2pdr; 6×21in torpedo tubes.

Ben-my-Chree (x), *Empress* (s), *Engadine* (s), *Manxman* (m), *Riviera* (s), *Vindex* (x).

(m) ex-Midland Railway Irish Sea packet.

(s) ex-South East & Chatham Railway Channel packet.

(x) ex-Isle of Man Steam Packet Company.

Ben-my-Chree sunk by Turkish shore batteries, 1917.

Nairana

1917.

LOA: 352 ft. Beam: 45.5ft. Displacement: 3,042 tons.

Turbines delivering 6,700hp through two screws. Maximum speed: 20 knots.

Complement: 278.

Armament: 2×12pdr; 2×12pdr AA.

Seaplane carrier converted from passenger vessel.

Pegasus

1917.

LOA: 332ft. Beam: 43ft. Displacement: 2,070 tons.

Turbines delivering 9,500hp through two screws. Maximum speed: 21 knots.

Complement: 278.

Armament: 2×12pdr; 2×12pdr AA.

Seaplane carrier converted from passenger vessel.

Campania

1914.

LOA: 622ft. Beam: 65ft. Displacement: 18,000 tons.

Triple-expansion steam engines delivering 28,000hp through two screws. Maximum speed: 22 knots.

Complement: 600.

Armament: 6×4.7in, 1×3in AA.

Seaplane carrier converted from Cunard liner. In 1916, her fore-funnel was divided to allow a longer flying-off deck. In 1918, she was sunk in collision with the battlecruiser *Glorious* in the Firth of Forth.

Vindictive

Conversion incomplete at the Armistice and reconverted to a cruiser in 1925.

AIRCRAFT CARRIERS

(Sometimes referred to in the literature of the day as 'aerodrome ships')

Furious

1917.

LOA: 786.5ft. Beam: 88ft. Displacement: 22,000 tons.

Geared turbines delivering 94,000hp through four screws. Maximum speed: 32.5 knots.

Complement: 737.

Armament: 10×5.5in; 5×3in AA and smaller weapons. 20 aircraft.

Armour: belt 2–3in, deck 1–3in.

Originally laid down as a battlecruiser similar to *Glorious* and *Courageous*, but with 2×18in guns. Commissioned in 1917 with only the aft 18in gun, and a flying-off deck replacing the forward gun; but in 1918, an aft landing deck was added.

Argus

1918.

LOA: 565 ft. Beam: 68ft. Displacement: 15,775 tons.

Turbines delivering 22,000hp through four screws. Maximum speed: 20.5 knots.

Complement: 1495.

The first flush-deck carrier was HMS *Argus*, converted on the slipway from a liner. She entered service too late to see action in the First World War. *(FAAM CARS A/539)*

Armament: 6×4in AA and smaller weapons. 20 aircraft.

Laid down as a liner for Italy, she was completed as a carrier, and was the first to be built as a genuine 'flat top', with a through flight deck and no superstructure.

MONITORS

Humber, Mersey, Severn

1914. Originally intended for Brazil but taken over by the Admiralty.

LOA: 266.75ft. Beam: 49ft. Displacement: 1,260 tons.

Triple-expansion steam engines delivering 1,450hp through two screws. Maximum speed: 12 knots.

Armour: belt 2in. Complement: 100.

Armament: 3×6in; 2×4.7in howitzers, plus smaller weapons.

Mersey and *Severn* destroyed the German cruiser *Königsberg*, blockaded in the Rufiji estuary, in 1917, with the fall of shot guided by naval aircraft.

Glatton and Gorgon

1918. Originally intended for Norway.

LOA: 310ft. Beam: 73.6ft. Displacement: 5,700 tons.

Triple-expansion steam engines delivering 4,000hp through two screws. Maximum speed: 13 knots.

Armour: belt 2 in. Complement: 300.

Armament: 2×9.2in; 6×6in; 2×3in AA, plus smaller weapons.

Glatton caught fire and was scuttled in Dover Harbour, 1918.

Abercrombie class

1915.

LOA: 344.5ft. Beam: 90ft. Displacement: 6,150 tons.

The monitor *Lord Raglan* with the pre-dreadnought *Cornwallis* in the background. *(IWM SP 334)*

Triple-expansion steam engines delivering 2,000hp through two screws. Maximum speed: 8 knots.
Armour: deck 1.5in. Complement: 237.
Armament: 2×14in; 1-4×6in; up to 2×3in AA, plus smaller weapons.
Lord Abercrombie, Lord Havelock, Lord Raglan, Lord Roberts.

Lord Raglan sunk by *Goeben* off Imbros, 1918.

Lord Clive class

1915.
LOA: 335.5ft. Beam: 87.25ft. Displacement: 5,900 tons.
Triple-expansion steam engines delivering 2,300–500hp through two screws. Maximum speed: 8 knots.
Armour deck 1.5in. Complement: 237.
Armament: 2×12in (* 1×18in added, mid-1918); 1–4×6in; up to 2×3in AA, plus smaller weapons.
Earl of Peterborough, General Craufurd, general Wolfe*, Lord Clive*, Prince Eugene*, Prince Rupert, Sir John Moore, Sir Thomas Picton.

The Lord Clive class monitor *Earl of Peterborough* at anchor, with another monitor, *Lord Raglan*, in the background. *(IWM)*

Marshal class

1915.

LOA: 355.5ft Beam: 90.25ft. Displacement: 6,670 tons.

Diesel engines delivering 1,500hp through two screws. Maximum speed: 7 knots.

Armour: deck 1–3in. Complement: 228.

Armament: 2×15in; 8×4in; 2×3in AA; 2×12pdr.

Marshal Ney, Marshal Soult.

Marshal Ney had her 15in guns replaced by 6in guns in 1917 and became a guardship.

Erebus class

1916, plus a third ship cancelled in 1918.

LOA: 405ft. Beam: 88ft. Displacement: 8,000 tons.

Triple-expansion steam engines delivering 7,000hp through two screws. Maximum speed: 14 knots.

Armour: deck 1–4in. Complement: 223.

Armament: 2×15in; 8×4in; 2×3in AA; 2×12pdr.

Erebus, Terror.

M15 class

1915.

LOA: 177ft. Beam: 31ft. Displacement: 540 tons.

Initial ships had triple-expansion steam engines delivering 600–800hp through two screws. Maximum speed: 12 knots. Later ships included a number with diesel engines and some with four screws.

Complement: 67–82.

Original armament: 1×9.2in; 1×3in AA, but last five ships had a variety of main weapons.

M15, M16, M17, M18, M19, M20, M21, M22, M23, M24, M25, M26, M27, M28.

M21 mined off Ostend, 1918.

M28 sunk by *Goeben* off Imbros.

M29 class

1915.

Similar to M15 class, but 400hp, 10 knots, with 2×6in, 1×3in or 1×6pdr AA.

M29, M30, M31, M32, M33.

M30 sunk by Turkish shore batteries, 1915.

DEPOT SHIPS

Up to twelve elderly cruisers were converted as depot ships for destroyers and submarines, with one ship, *St George*, switched between these two roles. The destroyer depot ships were eventually replaced by five ex-merchant vessels from a number of lines, and commissioned into the Royal Navy as *Diligence, Greenwich, Hecla, Sandhurst* and *Tyne*. Displacement varied widely, from 3,380 tons up to 11,500 tons. All survived the war, and in one case, both wars, but most were disposed of between 1920 and 1926. Similarly, seven ships were taken up from trade as submarine depot ships, becoming *Ambrose, Lucia, Pandora, Titania, Adamant, Alecto* and *Maidstone; Lucia* being a former German ship. These varied even more widely between 935 tons and 6,480 tons, and while many were sold during the 1930s, a couple survived both wars.

In addition, five merchant ships were acquired as fleet repair ships over a number of years, some as early as 1900. These were *Aquarius, Assistance, Bacchus, Cyclops* and *Reliance*, varying between 2,800 tons and 9,600 tons.

Depot ships and repair ships were usually given some defensive armament, although 4in seems to have been the heaviest; others had much less, and a few had none at all.

MINELAYERS

As seen above, a number of destroyers were selected for minelaying duties, and later we will see that this also became a major duty for the more modern and larger submarines. Minelaying surface vessels needed to be fast, capable of making a sortie into enemy waters during the hours of darkness and getting clear again by daylight, yet they also had to have a good capacity. For this reason, two large, fast ships being built for the Pacific services of the Canadian Pacific Railway were obtained. These were augmented by a number of Channel packets and also a ship intended for inter-island services in New Zealand. In addition, during 1915, minelayers were ordered from the United States.

Princess Irene and Princess Margaret

1914 and 1915. Originally laid down for Canadian Pacific Railway.
LOA: 395.5ft. Beam: 54ft. Displacement: 5,070 tons.
Turbines delivering 15,000hp through two screws. Maximum speed: 23 knots.
Complement: 225.
Armament: 2×4in or 4.7in; 2×3in AA and smaller; 400 mines.
Princess Irene blew up at Sheerness, 1915.

ARMED MERCHANT CRUISERS

In both world wars, fast merchant ships were taken up from trade and converted into armed merchant cruisers. In the First World War, their main role was to patrol between Scotland and Iceland as the 10th Cruiser Squadron, helping to stop German surface raiders from breaking out into the wider Atlantic. Others searched for German surface raiders, usually also converted merchant ships, in the South Atlantic and Indian Ocean. Nevertheless, these ships proved themselves vulnerable to attack by U-boats, and the 10th Cruiser Squadron was paid off on 7 December 1917.

SLOOPS

The concerns over the danger posed by mines led to the creation of a new class of ship, the two-funnelled Flower class, known officially as fleet sweeping vessels (sloops),

The Flower class sloop HMS *Honeysuckle*. (IWM Q 43369)

but adaptable enough to be used on other duties. The design was such that yards with no previous experience of warship construction could be used and the ships themselves were simple enough to be built in six months.

Flower class

The class was divided into a number of batches, each named after the lead ship.

Acacia type, 1915.

LOA: 262.5ft. Beam: 33ft. Displacement: 1,200 tons.
Triple-expansion steam engines delivering 2,400hp through a single screw. Maximum speed: 17 knots.
Complement: 77–104.
Armament: 2×4in or 12pdr, plus smaller weapons.
Acacia, Anemone, Aster, Begonia*, Bluebell, Daffodil, Dahlia, Daphne, Foxglove, Hollyhock, Honeysuckle, Iris, Jonquil, Laburnum, Larkspur, Lavender, Lilac, Lily, Magnolia, Marigold, Mimosa, Primrose, Sunflower, Veronica.
* Converted to Q ship, 1916.
Aster mined in Mediterranean, 1917.
Begonia torpedoed in Atlantic, 1917.
Lavender torpedoed in Channel, 1917.

Azalea type, all 1915.

Similar to above but all with 2×4.7in guns and 79 men.
Azalea, Camellia, Carnation, Clematis, Heliotrope, Jessamine, Narcissus, Snowdrop, Zinnia.

Arabis type, 1915–16.

Similar to Azalea type, with LOA 267.75ft, beam 33.5ft, displacement 1,250 tons.
Alyssum, Amaryllis, Arabis, Asphodel, Berberis, Buttercup, Campanula, Celandine, Cornflower, Crocus, Cyclamen, Delphinium, Genista, Gentian, Geranium, Gladiolus, Godetia, Hydrangea, Lobelia, Lupin, Mallow, Marguerite, *Mignonette, Myosotis, Myrtle, Nasturtium, Nigella, Pansy, Pentstemon, Peony, Petunia, Poppy, Primula, Rosemary, Snapdragon, Valerian, Verbena, Wallflower, Wisteria.*
Arabis torpedoed in North Sea, 1916.
Genista torpedoed off Ireland, 1916.
Nasturtium mined in Mediterranean, 1916.
Primula torpedoed in Mediterranean, 1916.
Alyssum mined off Ireland, 1917.

MINESWEEPERS

Hunt class fleet minesweepers

1917.
LOA: 231ft. Beam: 28ft. Displacement: 750 tons.
Triple-expansion steam engines delivering 1,800hp through two screws. Maximum speed: 16 knots.
Complement: 71.
Armament: 1–2×12pdr, plus smaller weapons.
Belvoir, Bicester, Blackmorevale, Cattistock, Cotswold, Cottesmore, Croome, Dartmoor, Garth, Hambledon, Heythrop, Holderness, Meynell, Muskerry, Oakley, Pytchley, Quorn, Southdown, Tedworth, Zetland.
Blackmorevale mined off Scotland, 1918.

Later Hunt or Aberdare class

1918–19.
LOA: 231ft. Beam: 28.5ft. Displacement: 800–40 tons.
Triple-expansion steam engines delivering 2,200hp through two screws. Maximum speed: 17 knots.
Complement: 74.
Armament: 1×4in; 1×12pdr, plus smaller weapons.
Aberdare, Abingdon, Albury, Alresford, Appledore, Badminton, Bagshot, Banchory, Barnstaple, Battle, Blackburn, Bloxham, Bootle, Bradfield, Burslem, Bury, Caerleon, Camberley, Carstairs, Caterham, Cheam, Clonmel, Craigie, Cupar, Derby, Dorking, Dundalk, Dunoon,

Up close and dangerous. The minesweeper *Duchess of Rothesay* sits in the background while her crew tackle a German contact mine. *(IWM SP 280)*

Another minesweeper, HMS *Camberley*. *(IWM SP 2091)*

Elgin, Fairfield, Fareham, Faversham, Fermoy, Ford, Forfar, Forres, Gaddesden, Gainsborough, Goole, Gretna, Harrow, Havant, Huntley, Instow, Irvine, Kendal, Kinross, Leamington, Longford, Lydd, Mallaig, Malvern, Marazion, Marlow, Mistley, Monoghan, Munlochy, Nailsea, Newark, Northolt, Pangbourne, Penarth, Petersfield, Pontypool, Prestatyn, Repton, Ross, Rugby, Salford, Saltash, Saltburn, Selkirk, Sherborne, Shrewsbury, Sligo, Stafford, Stoke, Sutton, Swindon, Tiverton, Tonbridge, Tralee, Tring, Truro, Wem, Wexford, Weybourne, Widnes, Yeovil.

Three of these were mined in 1919, showing just how much the hazards of wartime survive into peacetime. Another thirty-four ships were cancelled and a further six completed as survey vessels.

Paddle Minesweepers, 1st Group
1916.
LOA: 245.75ft. Beam: 29ft, excluding paddleboxes. Displacement: 810 tons.
Inclined compound engines delivering 1,400hp. Maximum speed: 15 knots.
Complement: 52.
Armament: 2×12pdr, plus smaller weapons.
Ascot, Atherstone, Chelmsford, Chepstow, Croxton, Doncaster, Eglinton, Epsom, Eridge, Gatwick, Goodwood, Haldon, Hurst, Kempton, Lingfield, Ludlow, Melton, Newbury, Pontefract, Plumpton, Redcar, Sandown, Totnes.
Ludlow mined in North Sea, 1916.
Kempton and *Redcar* mined off Calais, 1917.
Ascot torpedoed off Farne Islands, 1918.
Plumpton mined off Ostend, 1918.

Paddle Minesweepers, 2nd Group
1918.
Similar to above, but LOA 249.75ft, displacement 820 tons, armament 1×12pdr; 1×3in AA.
Banbury, Harpenden, Hexham, Lanark, Lewes, Shincliffe, Shirley, Wetherby.

These minesweepers were augmented by a class of tunnel minesweepers. With their screws in tunnels and able to work in very shallow water, they drew just 3.5ft, and had a displacement of 290 tons. These were also known as the Dance class, with names such as *Hornpipe* and *Minuet*. In all, there were fourteen ships built in 1917 and 1918. Then there were the trawlers, some operated by the Admiralty, some hired in, with hundreds in service at any one time, suffering very heavy losses.

Q SHIPS

Q ships were decoy vessels designed to attract U-boats, which were expected not to waste a torpedo on a small merchant vessel, but instead surface and open fire using their deck gun or, possibly, send a boarding party with explosives to blow up the ship. Like the armed merchant cruisers, many of the Q ships were taken up from trade, but were smaller and slower ships. Unlike the AMCs, Q ships had their armament hidden behind dummy boats, deckhouses or cargo hatches. To make the Q ship more convincing, 'panic parties' would be seen running around the deck and launching lifeboats, while, of course, the rest of the crew would wait for the U-boat to stop within firing range.

The first success of this technique came in July 1915, when the converted coaster *Prince Charles* sank *U-36*.

A variation on this system was to pair an armed trawler with a submerged elderly B or C class submarine, connected with a towing wire and a telephone line, so that if a U-boat surfaced and threatened the trawler, the submarine would release the tow and torpedo the U-boat. The first success of this partnership was in June 1915 when the trawler *Taranaki* and *C24* sank *U-40* off Aberdeen.

Lt Gordon Campbell took most of his crew to his next ship, *Pargust*. Here, they are dressed in clandestine rig.

It is not possible to give an exhaustive list of ex-merchantman Q ships as there was no standard, with ships varying from cargo steamers of around 4,000 tons deadweight down to small sailing ships, which were still in service in many trades. It was vital that these remained looking like merchant ships. Twenty patrol boats were completed disguised as merchantmen to augment the Q ships, initially known as PQ boats and then PC boats. They were faster than the converted merchantmen and also had four torpedo tubes. There were also the Aubrietia type and Anchusa type Flower class sloops that were built as Q ships.

Aubrietia type
1916.
LOA: 267.5ft. Beam: 33.5ft. Displacement: 1,200 tons.
Triple-expansion steam engines delivering 2,500hp through a single screw, single funnel. Maximum speed: 17.5 knots.
Complement: 80.
Armament: 2×4in; 1×3pdr AA; depth-charge throwers.

Aubrietia, Heather, Salvia, Tamarisk, Tulip, Viola.
Salvia torpedoed off Ireland, 1917.
Tulip torpedoed in Atlantic, 1917.

Anchusa type
1917–18.
As above, but LOA 262.5ft, beam 35ft, displacement 1,290 tons and complement 93.
Anchusa, Arbutus, Auricula, Bergamot, Bryony, Candytuft, Ceanothus, Chrysanthemum, Convolvulus, Coreopsis, Cowslip, Dianthus, Eglantine, Gaillardia, Gardenia, Gilia, Harebell, Hibiscus, Ivy, Lychnis, Marjoram, Mistletoe, Montbretia, Pelargonium, Polyanthus, Rhododendron, Saxifrage, Silene, Sweetbriar, Syringa, Tuberose, Windflower.
Arbutus torpedoed off south-west Ireland, 1917.
Bergamot torpedoed in Atlantic, 1917.
Candytuft torpedoed in Mediterranean, 1917.
Anchusa torpedoed off north coast of Ireland, 1918.
Cowslip torpedoed off Morocco, 1918.

Gaillardia mined off Orkney, 1918.
Rhododendron torpedoed in North Sea, 1918.
Chrysanthemum and *Saxifrage* survive as RN drill ships on the River Thames, with the latter renamed *President II*.

24 class
1918–19.

Designed with straight stem and stern and a dummy bridge aft so that both ends of the ship appeared identical, and with dazzle painting, the effect was confusing. Many of these entered service after the war and so are outside the scope of this book, but were named after racehorses, as was a class of paddle minesweepers. There were twenty-two ships, with another two cancelled.
LOA: 276.5ft. Beam: 34.75ft. Displacement: 1,320 tons.
Triple-expansion steam engines delivering 2,500hp through a single screw. Maximum speed: 17 knots.
Complement: 82.
Armament: usually 2×4in, but some variation throughout the class.

TORPEDO BOATS, GUNBOATS AND PATROL BOATS

The fear of the torpedo almost amounted to a neurosis among the navies of the world. While the dreadnought battleships and battlecruisers were designed from the start as an all-big-gun category of vessel, it soon became apparent that smaller, quick-firing weapons capable of being depressed to catch fast-moving targets close to the ship were essential. Even better as a defensive measure was the creation of anti-torpedo-boat gun-boats, known initially as torpedo gunboats or 'catchers', and later as torpedo-boat destroyers, although the initial batch of such craft for the Royal Navy proved to be too slow to act as a credible defence. For offensive purposes, the Royal Navy also developed torpedo boats and even built a torpedo-boat mother ship, HMS *Vulcan*, to carry up to eight small craft close to their target. This was a theme that was to reappear during the Second World War, but it was one that did not justify itself. As the destroyer evolved, often carrying torpedoes itself, the dividing line between torpedo boat and destroyer became blurred, and even by the Second World War this blurring remained in the German Navy, which had large, ocean-going torpedo boats not much smaller than destroyers, as well as the famous E-boats.

By the outbreak of the First World War, the Royal Navy had around 130 small torpedo boats in service, some of them dating from as far back as 1885. They had pennant numbers prefixed with 'O' for the earlier boats, and unprefixed pennant numbers for later craft, which dated as recently as 1908 or 1909. These were all steam-powered, although one earlier boat had been used experimentally for an un-successful experiment with water-jet propulsion.

Gossamer class torpedo gunboat
1892–3.
LOA: 230ft. Beam: 27ft. Displacement: 735 tons.
Triple-expansion steam engines delivering 3,500hp through two screws. Maximum speed: 19 knots.
Complement: 90.
Armament: usually 2×4.7in, but some variation throughout the class; 5×14in torpedo tubes.
Gossamer, Seagull, Skipjack, Spanker, Speedwell.
Seagull lost in collision on Firth of Clyde, 1918.

Alarm class torpedo gunboat
1892–3. Three ships deleted before 1914.
Similar to Gossamer class, but 810 tons and 3×18in torpedo tubes.

The torpedo boat *Alarm* leaving harbour. *(IWM Q 20439)*

Circe, Hebe, Jason, Leda, Niger.
Niger torpedoed off Kent, 1914.
Jason mined off west coast of Scotland, 1917.

Dryad class torpedo gunboat
1893–4.
LOA: 250ft. Beam: 30.5ft. Displacement: 1,070 tons.
Triple-expansion steam engines delivering 3,500hp through two screws. Maximum speed: 18 knots. Complement: 120.
Armament: 2×4.7in and smaller; 5×18in torpedo tubes.
Hazard lost in collision off Portland, 1918, by which time she was a depot ship.

Kil class patrol gunboat
1917–18. Many converted for minesweeping.
LOA: 182ft. Beam: 30ft. Displacement: 890 tons.

Triple-expansion steam engines delivering 3,500hp through a single screw. Maximum speed: 13 knots.
Complement: 39.
Armament: 1×4in or 4.7in.
Kilberry, Kilbride, Kilburn, Kilcavan, Kilchattan, Kilchreest, Kilchrenan, Kilchvan, Kilclare, Kilcock, Kildalkey, Kildangan, Kildare, Kildary, Kildavin, Kildimo, Kildonan, Kildonough, Kildorry, Kildress, Kildwick, Kildysart, Kilfenora, Kilfinny, Kilfullert, Kilgarvan, Kilgobnet, Kilham, Kilkeel, Killena, Killerig, Killiney, Killour, Killowen, Killybegs, Killygordon, Kilmalcom.

Insect class large China gunboat
1915–16. Drew just 4ft.
LOA: 237.5ft. Beam: 36 ft. Displacement: 645 tons.
Triple-expansion steam engines delivering

2,000hp through two screws in tunnels. Maximum speed: 14 knots.
Complement: 57.
Armament: 2×6in; 2×12pdr; 2×3in AA.
Aphis, Bee, Cicala, Cockchafer, Cricket, Glowworm, Gnat, Ladybird, Mantis, Moth, Scarab.

These were augmented by the Fly class small China gunboat, also of 1915–1916, displacing just 98 tons, with a complement of 22. Sixteen were in service during the war years.

There were also a few survivors of the large fleet of gunboats that had operated throughout the Empire in the Victorian era.

Patrol boats were also introduced to hunt U-boats and were given hardened-steel rams in their bows. No less than eighteen shipyards were involved in their production.

During 1915 and 1916, and again in 1918, a series of motor launches was built, with engines and parts of the craft produced in the USA and Canada and shipped to the UK for final assembly. Altogether, 580 of these were produced, of which just thirty were built in 1918. These were given pennant numbers ML1–580. The initial fifty were 75ft in length, the remainder between 80 and 88ft. All had petrol engines.

A further step was the creation of coastal motor boats, or CMBs, built in three sizes, 40ft, 55ft and 70ft, and based originally on pre-war racing launches. The 40ft craft carried a single torpedo while the 55ft craft carried one or two 18in torpedoes. All were armed with Lewis guns. Once the depth charge was invented, some of the 55ft craft could carry up to four of these. The largest, 70ft craft were designed as minelayers, but did not enter service until 1919. They were soon withdrawn, as after the war there was no further use for them. The 40ft craft carried pennant numbers CMB1–61. The pennant numbers of the 55ft craft consisted of 'CMB' followed by a number, suffixed with A, B, BD, CE, CK, D or DE, depending on the type of machinery fitted.

SUBMARINES

The first British submarines were ordered in 1900, when a licence was obtained to use the patents held by the American A.P. Holland. Vickers at Barrow built the first five submarines, which were commissioned in 1902–3. The displacement of these boats on the surface was just 100 tons. Surface speed, propelled by the still-unreliable petrol engine, was just 8 knots, although submerged they could manage 5 knots for a short period. The Holland boats were substantially different from the submarine as it developed rapidly over the next few years, lacking a conning tower and having internal ballast tanks and a single bow torpedo tube. Nevertheless, they gave the fledgling submarine service much experience, allowing tactics and equipment, including the periscope, to be developed.

The A class that followed incorporated a conning tower and two bow torpedo tubes but, with the exception of the final boat, which had an experimental oil engine, all retained the use of petrol propulsion – unsatisfactory because of the danger of an explosion. It was not until the B class that a worthwhile amount of deck space became available. The C class offered little progress over the Bs, but the D class was the first to introduce diesel engines and external ballast tanks. Unusually, it had the bow torpedo tubes one above the other to give a smoother forward end, and there was for the first time a stern tube.

Before the war, pennant numbers were painted on the conning towers, while the serial numbers such as 'B5' were painted on the hull. Initially, the A class was excluded from this system and Roman numerals were used, but after 1910, all submarines used the same pennant number series and 10 was added to each to accommodate the surviving A class. By this time, the original Holland boats were being withdrawn.

A class

1903–5. Three of the four earlier boats were lost in accidents before the war.
LOA: 100ft (* 99ft). Beam: 11.5ft (* 12.75ft).
Displacement: 165 tons surface/180 tons submerged (* 180/207 tons).
Petrol engine delivering 450hp (* 550hp) through one screw. Maximum speed: 11.5 knots surface/7 knots submerged.
Complement: 11–14.
Armament: 2×18in torpedo tubes.
A2, A5*, A6*, A7*, A8*, A9*, A10*, A11*, A12*, A13*
A7 lost off Plymouth, 1914.

B class

1905–6. B2 lost before the war.
LOA: 135ft. Beam: 13.5ft. Displacement: 280 tons surface/313 tons submerged.
Petrol engine delivering 600hp through one screw. Maximum speed: 13 knots surface/9 knots submerged.
Complement: 16.
Armament: 2×18in torpedo tubes.
B1, B2, B3, B4, B5, B6, B7, B8, B9, B10, B11.
B10 bombed in dock at Venice, 1916.

C class

1906–10. C21 onwards had larger conning towers.
LOA: 143ft. Beam: 13.5ft. Displacement: 290 tons surface/320 tons submerged.
Petrol engine delivering 600hp through one screw. Maximum speed: 14 knots surface/10 knots submerged.
Complement: 16.
Armament: 2×18in torpedo tubes.
C1, C2, C3, C4, C5, C6, C7, C8, C9, C10, C11, C12, C13, C14, C15, C16, C17, C18, C19, *C20, C21, C22, C23, C24, C25, C26, C27, C28, C29, C30, C31, C32, C33, C34, C35, C36, C37, C38.*
C29 mined in North Sea, 1915.
C31 lost off Belgian coast, 1915.
C33 lost in North Sea, 1915.
C32 ran aground and blown up in Gulf of Riga, 1917.
C34 sunk by *U-52* off Shetland, 1917.
C26, C27, C35 scuttled off Helsingfors (Helsinki), 1918.

D class

1910–12.
LOA: 144.25ft. Beam: 15ft. Displacement: 313 tons surface/373 tons submerged.
Diesel engines delivering 1,200hp through two screws. Maximum speed: 16 knots surface/9 knots submerged.
Complement: 25.
Armament: 3×18in (two bow, one stern) torpedo tubes; one small gun.
D1, D2, D3, D4, D5, D6, D7, D8.
D2 lost in North Sea, 1914.
D5 mined off east coast, 1914.
D3 bombed by French airship, 1918.
D6 sunk by U-boat off north coast of Ireland, 1918.

E class

1913–16. E28 cancelled.
LOA: 181ft. Beam: 22.5ft. Displacement: 600 tons surface/800 tons submerged.
Diesel engines delivering 1,600hp through two screws. Maximum speed: 16 knots surface/10 knots submerged.
Complement: 30.
Armament: 5×18in (two bow, two beam, one stern) torpedo tubes; 1×12pdr gun.
E1 type: *E1, E2, E3, E4, E5, E6,* plus two boats for the Royal Australian Navy.
E7 type: *E7, E8, E9, E10, E11, E12, E13, E14, E15, E16, E17, E18, E19, E20.*
E21 type: *E21, E22, E23, E24*, E25, E26, E27, E29, E30, E31, E32, E33, E34*, E35, E36,*

Predecessor of the famous E class submarines were the D class. *D3* is seen here leaving port.
(IWM Q 22044)

E37, E38, E39, E40, E41*, E42, E43, E44, E45*, E46*, E47, E48, E49, E50, E51*, E52, E53, E54, E55, E56.

* Minelayers without beam torpedo tubes and instead fitted with tubes for 20 mines.

E3 torpedoed by *U-27* off Borkum.

E7 sunk at Dardanelles, 1915.

E10, E26 lost in North Sea, 1915.

E6 mined in North Sea, 1915.

E13 ran aground on Danish coast, 1915, interned and later scrapped.

E15 stranded at Dardanelles, 1915.

E20 torpedoed by *UB-14* in Sea of Marmara, 1915.

E5 sunk by cruiser *Strassburg* in North Sea, 1916.

E16 and *E24* mined in Heligoland Bight, 1916, *E24* on minelaying mission.

E17 wrecked off Texel, 1916.

E18 mined in Baltic, 1916.

E22 torpedoed by *UB-18* in North Sea, 1916.

E30, E37 lost in North Sea, 1916.

E36 lost in North Sea collision, 1917.

E47 lost in North Sea, 1917.

E49 mined off Shetland, 1917.

E8, *E9*, *E19* scuttled off Helsingfors (Helsinki), 1918.

E14 sunk at Dardanelles, 1918.

E34 mined in Heligoland Bight, 1918.

E50 lost in North Sea, 1918.

F class

1915–17, but none seem to have entered service and later boats were cancelled.

LOA: 151.5ft. Beam: 16ft. Displacement: 353 tons surface/525 tons submerged.

Diesel engines delivering 900hp through two screws. Maximum speed: 14.5 knots surface/9 knots submerged.

Complement: 20.

Armament: 3×18in (two bow, one stern) torpedo tubes; 1 small gun.

G class

1915–17. G15 cancelled.

LOA: 187ft. Beam: 22.6ft. Displacement: 700 tons surface/975 tons submerged.

Diesel engines delivering 1,600hp through two screws. Maximum speed: 14.5 knots surface/10 knots submerged.

This is another famous submarine, *E7*, although her number is obscured by the bow wave. *(IWM Q 22911)*

Complement: 30.

Armament: 1×21in (stern), 4×18in (two bow, two beam) torpedo tubes; 1×3in AA gun.

G1, G2, G3, G4, G5, G6, G7, G8, G9, G10, G11, G12, G13, G14.

G7 and *G8* lost in North Sea, 1918.

G8 wrecked 1918.

H class

H1 type: 1915. Built in Canada and the United States*, with the latter not released until 1917, when, apart from *H11* and *H12*, they were sent to Chile in payment for Chilean ships taken over in British yards.

LOA: 150.25ft. Beam: 15.75ft. Displacement: 364 tons surface/434 tons submerged.

Diesel engines delivering 480hp through two screws. Max. speed 13 knots surface/10 knots submerged.

Complement: 22.

Armament: 4×18in (bow) torpedo tubes; 1 small gun.

H1, H2, H3, H4, H5, H6, H7, H8, H9, H10, H11, H12*, H13*, H14*, H15*, H16*, H17*, H18*, H19*, H20*.*

H3 sunk in Adriatic, 1916.

H6 stranded on Dutch coast and taken over by Netherlands.

H5 sunk in Irish Sea collision, 1918.

H10 lost in North Sea, 1918.

H21 type: 1918, with a further fourteen built 1919–20.

As H1 but LOA 171ft, displacement 440 tons surface/550 tons submerged.

H21, H22, H23, H24, H25, H26, H28, H29, H30, H31.

J class

1916–17.

LOA: 275.5ft. Beam: 23ft. Displacement: 1,210 tons surface/1,820 tons submerged.

Diesel engines delivering 3,600hp through three screws. Maximum speed: 19.5 knots surface/9.5 knots submerged.

Complement: 44.

Armament: 6×18in (four bow, two beam) torpedo tubes; 1–2×3–4in guns mounted on superstructure.

J1, J2, J3, J4, J5, J6, J7.*

* Modified with displacement of 1,760 tons submerged.

J6 sunk in North Sea, 1918.

K class

1916–18. Steam-powered submarines distinguished by three collapsible smokestacks. An improved K class was ordered, but only one boat was completed and the remaining five were cancelled, all after the war.

LOA: 338ft. Beam: 26.6ft. Displacement: 1,883 tons surface/2,565 tons submerged.

Geared steam turbines delivering 10,500hp through two screws. Maximum speed: 25 knots surface/9 knots submerged.

Complement: 60.

Armament: 8×18in (four bow, four beam) torpedo tubes; 1–2×4in, 1×3in AA guns.

K1, K2, K3, K4, K5, K6, K7, K8, K9, K10, K11, K12, K13, K14, K15, K16, K17, K22.*

* Originally *K13*, salvaged and restored.

K1 sunk in North Sea collision, 1917.

K13 foundered in the Gare Loch, but raised and became *K22*.

K4, K17 sunk in Firth of Forth collision, 1918.

M class corsair or monitor submarines

1918. A third boat was commissioned in 1920, and a fourth was not completed.

LOA: 296–305ft. Beam: 24.5ft. Displacement: 1,600 tons surface/1,950 tons submerged.

Diesel engines delivering 2,400hp through two screws. Maximum speed: 15.5 knots surface/9.5 knots submerged.

Complement: 70.

Armament: 4×18in (bow) torpedo tubes; 1×12in and 1×3in AA guns.

M1, M2.

M2 modified after the war to become an aircraft-carrying submarine with a hangar in place of her 12in gun.

L class
1917–18 (L1), 1918–27 (L9), 1918–24 (L50). L1 type: LOA: 231ft. Beam: 23.5ft. Displacement: 890 tons surface/1,070 tons submerged.
Diesel engines delivering 2,400hp through two screws. Maximum speed: 17.5 knots surface/10.5 knots submerged.
Complement: 36.
Armament: 6×18in (four bow, two beam) torpedo tubes; 1×4in or 1×3in AA.
L1, L2, L7, L3, L4, L5, L6, L8.
L9 type: LOA: 238.5ft. Beam: 23.5ft. Displacement: 900 tons surface/1,080 tons submerged.
Diesel engines delivering 2,400hp through two screws. Maximum speed: 17.5 knots surface/10.5 knots submerged.
Complement: 36.
Armament: 4×21in (bow) and 2×18in (beam) torpedo tubes or minelaying chutes for 16 mines; 1×4in or 1×3in AA.
L9, L10, L11, L12*, L14*, L15, L16, L17*,* plus a further eleven delivered after the war and one uncompleted, as well as the L50 type, of which eight were delivered after the war and the remainder cancelled.
* Minelayer.
L10 sunk by German destroyer off the Texel.

R class submarine hunters
1918–19.
LOA: 163ft. Beam: 15.75ft. Displacement: 420 tons surface/500 tons submerged.
Diesel engines delivering 1,200hp through one screw. Maximum speed: 15 knots surface/9.5 knots submerged.
Complement: 22.
Armament: 6×18in (bow) torpedo tubes; 1×4in.

R1, R2, R7, R8, R9, R11, R12, plus three completed in 1919. *R5* and *R6* were cancelled.

The following were experimental classes to attract new builders.

S class
1914–15.
LOA: 148ft. Beam: 14ft. Displacement: 265 tons surface/386 tons submerged.
Diesel engines delivering 650hp through two screws. Maximum speed: 13.25 knots surface/8.5 knots submerged.
Complement: 21.
Armament: 2×18in (bow) torpedo tubes.
S1, S2, S3.
Sold to Italy, 1916.

W class
1915–16.
LOA: 171.5ft. Beam: 15.5ft. Displacement: 340 tons surface/508 tons submerged.
Diesel engines delivering 710hp through two screws. Maximum speed 13 knots surface/8.5 knots submerged.
Complement: 19.
Armament: 2×18in (bow) torpedo tubes; 1 small gun.
W1, W2, W3*, W4*.*
* Similar to above, but LOA 149.75ft, beam 17ft and 760hp.
All sold to Italy, 1916.

V class
1915–16.
LOA: 147.5ft. Beam: 16.25ft. Displacement: 364 tons surface/486 tons submerged.
Diesel engines delivering 900hp through two screws. Maximum speed: 14 knots surface/9 knots submerged.
Complement: 18.
Armament: 2×18in (bow) torpedo tubes; 1 small gun.
V1, V2, V3, V4.

Nautilus

1917.

LOA: 242.5ft. Beam: 26ft. Displacement: 1,270 tons surface/1,694 tons submerged.

Diesel engines delivering 3,700hp through two screws. Maximum speed: 17 knots surface/10 knots submerged.

Complement: 42.

Armament: 2×21in (one bow, one stern), 4×18in (beam) torpedo tubes; 1×12pdr gun.

Later designated N1. Became battery-charging vessels 1918.

Swordfish

1916.

LOA: 231.25ft. Beam: 23ft. Displacement: 932 tons surface/1,475 tons submerged.

Diesel engines delivering 3,750hp through two screws. Maximum speed: 18 knots surface/10 knots submerged.

Complement: 42.

Armament: 2×21in (one bow, one stern), 4×18in (beam), torpedo tubes; 2×12pdr guns.

Later designated *S1*, relegated to surface patrols, 1918.

Chapter Fifteen

Naval Bases

When thou givest to thy servants
to endeavour any great matter
Grant us also to know that it is not the beginning
but the continuing of the same unto the end
until it be thoroughly finished.
Sir Francis Drake

The Royal Navy's main bases in 1914 reflected the long tradition of wars with France and, to a lesser extent, Spain and the Netherlands. The main bases were in the south, at Devonport, really part of Plymouth, Portsmouth and the Nore, close to Chatham. Each of these was more than simply a port and a dockyard, but also included a number of shore stations for training and specialised aspects of the work of the fleet. Augmenting these bases were those at Rosyth, Scapa Flow, Harwich, Dover, the Cromarty Firth and Gibraltar and Malta.

Chatham

Chatham was the last of the three great naval ports and dockyards to be built, dating from 1613. Often associated with Sheerness, Chatham was the main base, with Sheerness providing support facilities. The rationale for building a naval base at Chatham was the need to defend London, and other dockyards built in the early days with the same objective included Harwich, Woolwich

and Deptford. Nevertheless, as wars with the Dutch passed and France became the main enemy, the importance of these ports declined, and only Chatham survived.

While Portsmouth built the first modern battleship, Chatham found itself at the same time engaged on the construction of the naval vessel of the future, the submarine, launching its first 'boat' in 1908. The proximity of Eastchurch on the Isle of Sheppey to Chatham was no doubt a major factor in this becoming as near a birthplace for British naval aviation as could be found. The Medway also offered a sheltered stretch of water from which the frail early aircraft could be operated.

Cromarty

Essentially, Cromarty meant the Cromarty Firth, and the part of the firth used by the Royal Navy was Invergordon, the small town of Cromarty itself having just a very small harbour and in any case being fairly difficult to reach by road or rail. The narrow entrance to the firth, with cliffs on either

Scapa Flow was the naval anchorage that enabled the Royal Navy to maintain a blockade of Germany, but it was situated far from dock facilities. Before the war, while at the Admiralty, Jellicoe had a floating dock taken to Invergordon on the Cromarty Firth, part-way between Scapa Flow and Rosyth, which was still to be completed. *(IWM Q 20263)*

side, meant that the anchorage was easy to defend, but also easy to block.

One of Jellicoe's achievements while at the Admiralty was to locate a large floating dock near Invergordon, reducing the need for major units of the fleet to make the long voyage to Portsmouth or Plymouth for repairs, and this was used extensively by cruisers, especially during the war years.

DEVONPORT

Although Plymouth was a naval base from the time of Edward I and used in wars with the French, it is perhaps best known for its connection with Sir Francis Drake and the defeat of the Spanish Armada in 1588, although Drake's early naval reputation was gained as a privateer. In 1824, the dockyard area became independent of Plymouth itself and known as Devonport. During the eighteenth and nineteenth centuries, Plymouth, or Devonport, became the second-largest base for the Royal Navy. It was conveniently placed close to the Royal Navy's training school for officers at Dartmouth.

DOVER

Dover was the main continental packet port by the turn of the century. It was closed to civilian traffic on the outbreak of war so that the British Expeditionary Force could be moved to France and Belgium and then kept reinforced and resupplied throughout the war. The need to protect the movements of the BEF and to guard the Straits of Dover gave rise to the Dover Patrol, a counter to German attempts to attack shipping in the Channel and to German mine-laying, while also helping to prevent the German navy sending its ships out to the oceans by what would have been the most direct route.

HARWICH

By the time war broke out, the port of Harwich had become the main packet port for steamers to and from the Netherlands, with some services operating further north to Germany and Denmark. It was the natural choice for a secure port, with good railway connections to London, for naval vessels guarding the northern approach to the Thames and the English Channel, and for offensive operations against German North Sea ports and in the Heligoland Bight. Harwich had two flotillas: one for submarines commanded by Cdre, later Rear Adm, Roger Keyes, and the other for destroyers, commanded by Cdre, also later Rear Adm, Reginald Tyrwhitt. In fact, the Harwich flotillas were often more than a

single flotilla apiece, Tyrwhitt, for example, having two flotillas and more than twenty destroyers, and using light cruisers as destroyer leaders.

PORTSMOUTH

Portsmouth, on Portsea Island, was strategically well placed to become the Royal Navy's main port and dockyard, and as early as 1194, King Richard I had ordered the construction of a dockyard. Henry VII had the world's first dry dock completed there in 1496. The large size of Portsmouth harbour meant that there was considerable space for mooring the reserve fleet during times of peace. The Solent and Spithead provided a sheltered anchorage, and during the eighteenth and nineteenth centuries it also provided a well protected assembly point for convoys.

Over the years, almost 300 warships were built at Portsmouth, perhaps the most notable being the first battleship of the modern era, *Dreadnought*. Lack of space meant that when the submarine arrived, it was based across the harbour at HMS *Dolphin*, Gosport. Gosport also provided one of the Royal Naval Air Service's early aerodromes.

ROSYTH

While for most of British history the threat had come from the south, with France, Spain, the Netherlands and then France again being seen as the most likely enemy, by the early twentieth century it was clear that a newly united and ambitious Germany posed the biggest threat. This led to the search for a convenient dockyard on the east coast of Scotland, an area notably lacking in sheltered anchorages. The choice fell on Rosyth on the north bank of the Firth of Forth and not too far from

Edinburgh. Construction work began in 1909, although by the time it was completed, in 1916, the nation was already at war with Germany. The dockyard had been opened the previous year, on 8 June 1915, by King George V. Unlike Chatham, Devonport and Portsmouth, Rosyth was not a manning port, and did not undertake construction of warships but concentrated instead on refitting and repair work. In fact, after the First World War, Rosyth was closed until war broke out in 1939.

Rosyth was unpopular with many senior officers, including Fisher, First Sea Lord from 1904 to 1910, and then again in 1914 to 1915, because it was too far upstream in the Firth of Forth, and so was distant from the open sea, and because the famous railway bridge, if damaged, could close the port. Nevertheless, in the desperate search for a base further south than Scapa Flow, Rosyth was used by the battlecruiser squadrons.

SCAPA FLOW

Scapa Flow is a massive anchorage in Orkney, on the south side of the mainland of Orkney. Its main advantages were its proximity to German waters, making it ideally suited for the blockade, and the sheer size of the anchorage, so that much training could be handled within its waters and almost any size of fleet could be accommodated. Its weaknesses were the difficulties in keeping the many entrances to the anchorage secure, its remoteness, the absence of any railway connection, so that supplies and men had to come by sea, and the absence of any repair facilities. The very size of the anchorage was also a weakness, since the huge waves that could sweep across it could easily wash men overboard, and often did so.

The problems with security were at first such that Jellicoe at one stage took the Grand Fleet away to bases on the west of Scotland and to Lough Swilly in Co. Donegal, on the north coast of Ireland. On one occasion, he remarked to a visiting admiral, 'I wonder if we will still be here in the morning.' He referred to the danger of submarine attack.

Shortly before the outbreak of war, there was an urgent programme of preparing 'Scapa' for the fleet. A small headquarters was established ashore, and the seagoing repair ships *Cyclops* and *Assistance* were moored off the pier, with a telegraph cable running from *Cyclops* to Kirkwall and then on to the mainland of Scotland, down to the Admiralty in London. Defensive measures included placing two elderly battleships, *Hannibal* and *Magnificent*, with their four 12in guns, at the two main entrances to Scapa Flow, while shore batteries of 4in and 6in guns were also provided. Elementary anti-submarine defences were installed, initially consisting of buoys across the channels with nets strung between them, but the nets soon proved too weak to withstand the winter weather and stronger nets, after which herring drifters with nets between them, were installed. Fifty trawlers armed with guns and towing explosive sweeps began to patrol the entrances, while contact mines were laid in defensive minefields. Yet, it was not until May 1915, that Scapa Flow could be said to be secure.

Much was eventually done to strengthen the defences, with booms and nets, and mines that could be detonated remotely once a visiting U-boat triggered off the acoustic and electro-magnetic sensors. Nevertheless, for the first autumn and winter of war the lack of any German intrusion was simply down to the fact that no one in Germany believed that the main forward anchorage for the Grand Fleet could be so badly defended.

OVERSEAS BASES

GIBRALTAR

Gibraltar provided refit and repair facilities and easy access to both the Mediterranean and the Atlantic. Before the war, it had been the main base for the Atlantic Fleet.

MALTA

Malta's connection with the British came in 1799 when a delegation reached one of Nelson's ships to seek help in evicting the French, who had occupied the island. Despite its excellent Grand Harbour, Malta remained something of a backwater until the opening of the Suez Canal in 1869 put it on the main shipping routes to India and Australia. It was the main base for the Mediterranean Fleet, but it had a relatively quiet war because the Royal Navy and Italian Navy were by and large very successful in keeping the Austro-Hungarian navy bottled up in the Adriatic (but see Appendix III on VCs).

CHAPTER SIXTEEN

NAVAL AIR UNITS

An aviator bold am I –
Yo ho, my lads, yo ho!
With joy I cleave the Eastern sky –
Yo ho, my lads, yo ho!
I love the roaring of the gale and hate the gentle breeze,
I hate a calm and placid day, but welcome storm-tossed seas.
The Fleet Air Arm Songbook (RNAS song originating with east coast air stations)

The concept of the flight, squadron, wing and group was already understood by the outbreak of the First World War, as indicated by the ranks of the Royal Naval Air Service. Nevertheless, when it came to allocating designations to these units, there was still some uncertainty. Should they be referred to by their base or the part of the fleet to which they belonged? Should there be numbers or letters? How many aircraft should a squadron have? Initially, the RNAS squadrons were far larger than would have been the case in later years, with as many as sixty-six aircraft in No. 1 squadron at one time. Flights were provided for many of the Royal Navy's main bases, including air defence flights at Dover, seen as vulnerable because of its proximity to France. There were difficulties at first in identifying squadrons, since the temptation was to describe them as being part of a particular naval unit, including their home base. It was not until 1916 that a logical and consistent system was introduced, and even then there were many exceptions. The eventual

formation of the Royal Air Force in 1918 meant that the new service found itself with many squadron numbers duplicated in the RNAS and RFC, and resolved this problem by simply adding 200 to all of the naval air squadron designations.

It is worth looking at the order of battle for the RNAS on 31 March 1918, on the eve of the merging of the service with the Royal Flying Corps into the new Royal Air Force:

1 Wing (Dunkirk): Squadrons 2, 13, 17
2 Wing (Mudros): Squadrons: A, B, C, D, E, F, G, Z (Greek)
3 Wing disbanded 1917
4 Wing (La Panne): Squadrons 4, 8
5 Wing (Malo-les-Bains): Squadrons 7, 11, 12, 14, 15
6 Wing (Otranto): Squadrons 1, 2
10, 11, 13, 22, 41 Wings under RFC control

THE SQUADRONS

Eastchurch Mobile Squadron: Formed 8 August 1914, became No. 3 Squadron

1 September. Aircraft included Short S.38, Royal Aircraft Factory BE2a, Sopwith Tractor, DFW.

No. 1: Formed at Antwerp, 1 September 1914, various bases in Belgium and northern France before disbanding in retreat, 14 October. Reformed Gosport (Grange Field), 15 October 1914. Flights deployed Dover, Westgate, St Pol, Farnborough, Gosforth, Whitley Bay, then became No. 1 Wing, 21 June 1915. Reformed as A Squadron within No. 1 Wing, July 1916, before becoming No. 1 Squadron December 1916, then No. 1 (Naval) Squadron February 1917. Operated from many bases in France, being at La Targette at the Armistice. More than twenty different aircraft types operated, including Royal Aircraft Factory BE2a and BE8, Sopwith Tabloid, Morane Parasol, Vickers FB5, Nieuport 10 and 11, Curtiss N. Became No. 201 Squadron, RAF, 1 April 1918.

No. 2: Formed at Eastchurch, 10 September 1914, before moving to Dunkirk and then Belgium, disbanding back in UK, 10 October. Reformed at Eastchurch 17 October 1914 for training duties, then became No. 2 Wing, June 1915. Detachments sent to Dover, Westgate and Eastchurch. Reformed out of B Squadron No. 1 Wing at St Pol, November 1916, and remained in France. Around twenty aircraft types operated at various times, including Blériot XI, Curtiss N, Avro 504B, Bristol Scout and Henri Farman F40. Became No. 202 Squadron, RAF, 1 April 1918.

No. 3: Formed from Eastchurch Mobile Squadron at St Pol, 1 September 1914. Served in France and Belgium and may have absorbed elements of No. 1 and No. 2 squadrons in October. Moved to Dover, February 1915, and sailed for Dardanelles,

being based at Tenedos. Became 3 Wing, June 1915. Reformed out of C Squadron, 1 Wing, St Pol, November 1916. Served at various bases in France before returning to the UK, with a rest period at Walmer in late 1917. Returned to France, February 1918, initially with training on RFC aerial gunnery range at Berck-sur-Mer, then operated from a number of bases in France, including Bruille at the Armistice. Some twenty-five aircraft types operated, including Sopwith 1½-Strutter and Camel, landplanes and seaplanes. Became No. 203 Squadron, RAF, 1 April 1918.

No. 4: Believed formed 25 March 1915, from the Air Defence Flight, Dover, although some sources suggest formed from No. 4 Wing. Operated from Dover and Eastchurch before becoming 4 Wing, October. Reformed at Coudekerque, December 1916 from A Squadron, 4 Wing. Based mainly in UK until going to France, spring 1918. Only about ten different aircraft types operated, including Avro 504B, BE2c, Nieuport 10. Became No. 204 Squadron, RAF, 1 April 1918.

No. 5: Formed Dover 2 August 1915 from part of No. 4 Squadron, then disbanded into RNAS Dover, although it is possible that it may have become 5 Wing. Reformed from B Squadron, 5 Wing, at Coudekerque, December 1916. Served at various bases in France, many of which unrecorded. Aircraft included Sopwith Spinning Jenny and 1½-Strutter, DH4 and DH9A, and Avro 504B. Became No. 205 Squadron, RAF, 1 April 1918.

No. 6: Although elements were assembled at Dover, the squadron formed at Petite Synthe, December 1916, from A Squadron, 4 Wing. Served at various bases in France with a spell in the UK, disbanded into 9 and

The view forward from the bridge of the *Ark Royal* in 1915, with Short seaplanes being handled.
(FAAM CARS A265)

10 squadrons, Dunkirk, August 1917. Reformed Dover, January 1918, from Defence Flight Walmer and No. 11 Squadron. Returned to France later that month, operating from a number of different bases. Aircraft included Nieuport 10, 11, 12, 17bis and Sopwith Camel. Became No. 206 Squadron, RAF, 1 April 1918.

No. 7: Formed in UK and almost immediately deployed to German East Africa, April 1916, operating from a number of locations, including Dar-es-Salaam, before disbanding January 1917, and

personnel returning to UK. Meanwhile, another 7 Squadron was formed from B Squadron, 4 Wing, at Petite Synthe, end of December 1916. Served in France and at Redcar and Manston in UK. Aircraft included Voisins, BE2cs, Caudron GIV, Sopwith 1½-Strutter, Short Bomber and Handley Page 0/100, 0/400. Became No. 207 Squadron, RAF, 1 April 1918.

No. 8: Formed in UK and also almost immediately deployed to German East Africa, January 1916, reaching Zanzibar. Later referred to as 'Cape Squadron' and 'East Africa Force', before disbanding

December 1917. Meanwhile, another 8 Squadron was formed at St Pol, October 1916, with aircraft and personnel from a number of flights in 1, 4 and 5 Wings. Served in France, and at Walmer and Dover. Aircraft included Nieuport 11, 17bis, 21 and Sopwith Camel, Pup, Snipe and 1½-Strutter. Became No. 208 Squadron, RAF, 1 April 1918.

No. 9: Formed from part of No. 8 squadron at St Pol, 1 February 1917. Served in France and Belgium, with a break at Dover, February 1918. Aircraft included Nieuport 10, 11, 12, 17bis, 21 and Sopwith Camel, Pup, Snipe and 1½-Strutter. Became No. 209 Squadron, RAF, 1 April 1918.

No. 10: Formed in 4 Wing at St Pol, 12 February 1917. Operated mainly in Belgium. Aircraft included Nieuport 12, Sopwith Triplane and Camel. Became No. 210 Squadron, RAF, 1 April 1918.

No. 11: Believed to have been a No. 11 in East Africa during 1915/16, possibly derived from No. 7 Squadron, then reformed at Petite Synthe, March 1917, within 4 Wing. Operated in Belgium before disbanding due to shortage of pilots, August 1917. Reformed at Petite Synthe, March 1918, within 5 Wing, and remained in France. Aircraft included Nieuport 10, 11, 17bis, and Sopwith Camel, Pup and Triplane. Became No. 209 Squadron, RAF, 1 April 1918.

No. 12: Formed Hondschoote, 8 June 1917, within 5 Wing. Disbanded 1 April 1918. Reformed at Great Yarmouth as 212 Squadron, RAF, 20 August, 1918. Aircraft included Sopwith Pup, Triplane and Camel, DH4 and DH9A.

A look down into the hangar deck, or hold, of the *Ark Royal* with aircraft under repair or being assembled. *(FAAM CARS A273)*

No. 13: Formed from Seaplane Defence Squadron at St Pol, 15 January 1918, remaining in France. Operated Sopwith Camels. Became No. 213 Squadron, RAF, 1 April 1918.

No. 14: Formed from 7A at Coudekerque, 9 December 1917, within 5 Wing. Remained in Belgium. Operated Handley Page 0/100, 0/400. Became No. 214 Squadron, RAF, 1 April 1918.

No. 15: Formed from personnel of Nos 7 and 14 squadrons at Coudekerque, 10 March 1918, within 5 Wing. Operated from Netheravon and Andover, before returning to continent. Operated Handley Page 0/100, 0/400. Became No. 215 Squadron, RAF, 1 April 1918.

No. 16: Formed from A Squadron, 8 January 1918, at Ochey, and remained in Europe. Operated FE2b, Handley Page 0/100, 0/400. Became No. 216 Squadron, RAF, 1 April 1918.

No. 17: Formed to replace RNAS Seaplane Base Dunkirk, 14 January 1918, within No. 1 Wing. Operated DH4 and DH9 bombers. Became No. 217 Squadron, RAF, 1 April 1918.

Sopwith Camel taking off from the battlecruiser *Renown*, using a platform built over B turret, which seems to have been rotated into the wind. *(FAAM CAM 2)*

No. 218: Formed within RAF at Dover, 24 April 1918. Moved to France. Operated DH4 and DH9 bombers.

No. 219: Formed within RAF at Westgate, 22 July 1918, from aircraft belonging to five flights. Aircraft included Sopwith Baby and Camel.

No. 220: Formed within RAF at Imbros, 1 April 1918, having been Reconnaissance Squadron Aegean. Aircraft included DH4 and DH9 bombers and Sopwith F1 Camel fighters.

No. 221: Formed within RAF at Stavros, 1 April 1918, having been Anti-Submarine Squadron, Aegean. Disbanded into 222 Squadron at Mudros, October 1918. Aircraft included DH4 and DH9 bombers and Sopwith F1 Camel fighters.

No. 222: Formed within RAF at Thasos, 1 April 1918, having been A and Z squadrons, 2 Wing. Remained in eastern Mediterranean until after the Armistice and disbanded early 1919. Aircraft included DH4, DH6 and DH9 bombers and Sopwith F1 Camel and 1½-Strutter fighters.

No. 223: Formed within RAF at Mitylene, 1 April 1918, having been B squadron, 2 Wing. Disbanded July. Reformed at Otranto from Seaplane Unit Otranto, July 1918, then redesignated as 263 Squadron in September. Reformed as mobile bomber squadron, September 1918, and disbanded the following May. Aircraft included DH4, DH6 and DH9 bombers, Sopwith F1 Camel fighters and Short 184 seaplanes.

No. 224: Formed within RAF at Otranto, 1 April 1918, from Anti-Submarine Squadron Otranto. Disbanded April 1919. Aircraft included DH4 and DH9 bombers and Sopwith F1 Camel and 1½-Strutter fighters.

No. 225: Formed within RAF at Otranto, 1 April 1918, from Fighter Squadron Otranto. Disbanded in December. Aircraft included Sopwith F1 Camel and 1½-Strutter fighters.

No. 226: Formed within RAF at Pizzone, 1 April 1918, from DH4 Bombing Squadron Pizzone. Disbanded in December. Aircraft operated included DH9 and DH9A as well as DH4, and also Sopwith 1½-Strutter fighters.

No. 227: Formed within RAF at Pizzone, 1 April 1918, and formerly Caproni Squadron, Taranto. Believed to not have been fully established. Disbanded December 1918. Aircraft operated included DH4 and DH9 as well as Caproni Ca4, and also Sopwith 1½-Strutter fighters.

No. 228: Formed within RAF at Great Yarmouth, 20 August 1918, from Boat Flight, Yarmouth. Disbanded in June 1919. Aircraft operated included H16 and Felixstowe F2A.

No. 229: Formed within RAF at Great Yarmouth, 20 August 1918, and formerly Short and Schneider Flights, Yarmouth. Aircraft operated included Short 184, Sopwith Baby, Schneider and Fairey IIIC.

No. 230: Formed within RAF at Felixstowe, 20 August 1918, from Anti-Submarine Patrol Unit, Felixstowe. Aircraft operated included H12, H16, Felixstowe F2A, Short 184 and Sopwith F1 Camel.

No. 231: Formed within RAF at Felixstowe, 20 August 1918, from Anti-Submarine Patrol Unit, Felixstowe. Disbanded July 1919. Operated Felixstowe F2A flying boats.

No. 232: Formed within RAF at Felixstowe, 20 August 1918, from a number of flights. Disbanded January 1919. Operated Felixstowe F2A flying boats.

No. 233: Formed within RAF at Dover, 31 August 1918, from a number of flights. Disbanded May 1919. Aircraft operated included Short 184, Felixstowe F2A, Sopwith F1 Camel, Wright SP, and DH4 and DH9.

No. 234: Formed within RAF at Tresco, Isles of Scilly, 20 August 1918, from a number of flights. Disbanded May 1919. Aircraft operated included Short 184, Felixstowe F3, Lockheed H12B.

No. 235: Formed within RAF at Newlyn, 20 August 1918, from 424 and 425 flights. Disbanded February 1919. Operated Short 184 seaplanes.

No. 236: Formed within RAF at Mullion, 20 August 1918, from a number of flights. Disbanded May 1919. Aircraft operated included DH6 and DH9, and Sopwith 1½-Strutter.

No. 237: Formed within RAF at Cattewater, 20 August 1918, from several flights. Disbanded May 1919. Operated Short 184 seaplanes.

No. 238: Formed within RAF at Cattewater, 20 August 1918, from several flights. Disbanded May 1919. Aircraft operated included Felixstowe F3, F5 and Lockheed H16.

No. 239: Formed within RAF at Torquay, 20 August 1918, from several flights. Disbanded May 1919. Operated Short 184 seaplanes.

No. 240: Formed within RAF at Calshot, 20 August 1918, from several flights.

Disbanded May 1919. Aircraft operated included Short 184 and 320, Fairey Campania, Felixstowe F2A and Lockheed H12.

No. 241: Formed within RAF at Portland, 20 August 1918, from several flights. Disbanded June 1919. Aircraft operated included Short 184, Fairey Campania, Felixstowe F2A, DH6 and Wright SP.

No. 242: Formed within RAF at Newhaven, 15 August 1918, from several flights. Disbanded May 1919. Aircraft operated included Short 184, Fairey Campania, DH6.

No. 243: Formed within RAF at Cherbourg, 20 August 1918, from several flights. Disbanded March 1919. Aircraft operated included Short 184 and Wright SP.

No. 244: Formed within RAF at Bangor, north Wales, 15 August 1918, from several flights. Disbanded January 1919. Operated DH6.

No. 245: Formed within RAF at Fishguard, 20 August 1918, from 426 and 427 flights. Disbanded May 1919. Aircraft operated included Short 184 and Hamble Baby flying boat.

No. 246: Formed within RAF at Seaton Carew, Co. Durham, 15 August 1918, from several flights. Disbanded May 1919. Aircraft operated included DH6, Short 184.

No. 247: Formed within RAF at Felixstowe, 20 August 1918, from a number of flights. Disbanded January 1919. Operated Felixstowe F2A flying boats.

No. 248: Formed within RAF at Hornsea, 20 August 1918, from a number of flights.

Disbanded March 1919. Aircraft operated included Short 184, Sopwith Baby and Schneider.

No. 249: Formed within RAF at Dundee, 18 August 1918, from a number of flights. Disbanded October 1919. Aircraft operated included Short 184 and Sopwith Baby.

No. 250: Formed within RAF at Padstow, 1 May 1918, from a number of flights. Disbanded May 1919. Aircraft operated included DH6 and DH9.

No. 251: Formed within RAF at Hornsea, 1 May 1918, from a number of flights. Disbanded June 1919. Operated DH6.

No. 252: Formed within RAF at Tynemouth, 1 May 1918, from a number of flights. Disbanded June 1919. Aircraft operated included DH6, Sopwith Baby and Kangaroo.

No. 253: Formed within RAF at Bembridge, 7 June 1918, from a number of flights. Disbanded May 1919. Operated DH6 and Short 184.

No. 254: Formed within RAF at Prawle Point, Devon, 31 May 1918, from a number of flights. Disbanded February 1919. Aircraft operated included DH6 and DH9.

No. 255: Formed within RAF at Pembroke during May 1918, from a number of flights. Disbanded May 1919. Operated DH6.

No. 256: Formed within RAF at Seahouses, Northumberland, during June 1918, from a number of flights. Disbanded June 1919. Aircraft operated included DH6 and Kangaroo.

No. 257: Formed within RAF at Dundee during July 1918, from 318 and 319 flights. Disbanded June 1919. Aircraft operated included Lockheed H16 and Felixstowe F2A flying boats.

No. 258: Formed within RAF at Luce Bay, Wigtownshire, 15 August 1918, from a number of flights. Disbanded March 1919. Operated DH6.

No. 259: Formed within RAF at Seahouses, Northumberland, during July 1918, from a number of flights. Disbanded August 1919. Operated Felixstowe F2A.

No. 260: Formed within RAF at Westward Ho! 15 August 1918, from 502 and 503 flights. Disbanded February 1919. Operated DH6.

No. 261: Formed within RAF at Felixstowe, 20 August 1918, from a number of flights. Disbanded September 1919. Operated Felixstowe F2A.

No. 262: No record of this squadron.

No. 263: Formed within RAF at Otranto, 27 September 1918, from a number of flights. Disbanded May 1919. Aircraft operated included Short 184 and 320, Sopwith Baby and Felixstowe F3.

No. 264: Formed within RAF at Suda Bay, 27 September 1918, from 439 and 440 flights. Disbanded March 1919. Operated Short 184.

No. 265: Originally intended to form at Gibraltar as an F3 squadron, but did not come into existence.

No. 266: Formed within RAF at Mudros, 27 September 1918, from 437 and 438 flights.

Disbanded September 1919. Operated Short 184 and 320.

No. 267: Formed within RAF at Kalafrana, 27 September 1918, from several flights. Operated Short 184, Felixstowe F2a, F3 and Fairey IIID.

No. 268: Formed within RAF at Kalafrana, 27 September 1918, from 433 and 434 flights. Disbanded September 1919. Operated Short 184 and 320.

No. 269: Formed within RAF at Port Said, 6 October 1918, from 431 and 432 flights. Redesignated 481 Flight, November 1919. Operated Short 184, BE2e, DH9.

No. 270: Formed within RAF at Alexandria, 6 October 1918, from several flights. Disbanded September 1919. Operated Short 184, Felixstowe F3, and DH9.

No. 271: Formed within RAF at Taranto, 27 September 1918, from several flights. Disbanded December 1918. Operated Short 184 and Felixstowe F3.

No. 272: Formed within RAF at Machrihanish, near Campbeltown, 15 August 1918, from several flights. Disbanded March 1919. Operated DH6.

No. 273: Formed within RAF at Great Yarmouth, 20 August 1918, from several

The Fairey Campania was supposed to mark a big step forward in naval air power, being able to take off from the ship of the same name on a trolley. However, it was still penalised by the drag of the floats. *(IWM Q 69382)*

flights. Disbanded July 1919. Aircraft operated included DH4, DH9, DH9A, Sopwith F1 Camel, BE2c.

No. 274: Originally intended to be an anti-submarine squadron and would have formed just before the Armistice, but instead formed as a bomber squadron in 1919.

A Squadron: Formed at Manston, 5 October 1917, and moved to France. Redesignated No. 16 Squadron, January 1918. Operated FE2b, Handley Page 0/100 and 0/400 bombers.

Handley Page Squadron: Formed at Manston, 1 July 1916, moved to Europe and may have disbanded only to reform in late 1917. Disbanded again April 1918. Operated Handley Page 0/100 and 0/400 bombers.

Seaplane Defence Flight/Squadron: Formed as a flight at St Pol, 30 June 1917, and became a squadron on 23 September 1917, before being redesignated as No. 13 Squadron, January 1918. Aircraft operated included Sopwith Bay, Triplane, Pup, F1 Camel.

NAVAL WINGS

The rapid expansion of the RNAS was accommodated to a great extent by taking the early squadrons and redesignating these as naval wings, with No. 1 Squadron becoming 1 Wing, for example. The RFC's own Naval Wing had itself been renamed the Royal Naval Air Service on 1 July 1914, although it was another year before the RNAS truly became independent of the RFC. Initially, the wings maintained their operational units as flights, but these became squadrons again, being designated A, B or C squadrons rather than having numbers; there would also be a head-

quarters squadron. Confusingly, given the structure of the RAF, and the RNAS's own rank structure, within the wings there would also be groups, such as A Group, or the Eastchurch Group within 1 Wing.

The decision to create squadrons in a consecutive numbering system as shown above was to simplify matters considerably, as it was no longer possible to mistake A or B squadron for 1, 2 or 3 wing. The squadrons had to be known as naval squadrons to avoid confusion with the RFC. Despite the eventual allocation of numbers in the 700 and 800 range to naval air squadrons, this remains the case today.

FLIGHTS

In addition to the squadrons, a large number of flights were formed within the newly created Royal Air Force, largely as a temporary tidying-up measure, taking in the locally titled units scattered around the coast and overseas. Most of these were absorbed into squadrons or, often, a new squadron was formed from between two and six flights, so that the period during which the flights were extant ranged from late May 1918 to late 1919. The system was revived when the Fleet Air Arm was recreated within RAF Coastal Area in 1923, and then again these disappeared later when the RAF allocated squadron numbers in the 700 and 800 series to Fleet Air Arm units.

The flights were allocated in blocks, depending on the type of operations envisaged, as follows:

300–32: Large flying boats.
333–44: Special service units, usually with large flying boats.
345–58: Float seaplanes.
450–5: Sopwith Baby seaplanes.
470–87: Land fighters for defence against torpedo-carrying seaplanes.

490–9, **534**, **550–61**: Anti-submarine light bombers.

500–33: Special service, anti-submarine patrols, initially using DH6 bombers, although there were plans, later abandoned, to replace these with DH9s.

562: Malta anti-submarine flight.

NAVAL AIR STATIONS IN THE UNITED KINGDOM 1914–1918

The rapid growth of the RNAS and its commitment to providing air defence for the United Kingdom, as well as its anti-submarine commitments, meant that a substantial network of naval air stations was quickly established. Some were RFC stations, where the RNAS had what would later be described as 'lodging facilities'. Abroad, the seaplanes and flying boats managed to settle down reasonably quickly alongside the naval bases, but ashore in France and Belgium, in particular, a large number of air stations were used, with units often moving at extremely short notice as the frontline varied according to the ebb and flow of the conflict. Many air stations were used, some for very short periods, as in the retreat of late 1914. Many were used either by the RFC or the RNAS, or, of course, by the French and Belgians, as seemed expedient at the time.

While the bases were known as Royal Naval air stations, none seemed to have attracted ships' names at the time, possibly because a high degree of impermanence existed, or perhaps because the RNAS was still officially part of the army-dominated RFC until 1915.

The main bases in the UK for aeroplanes were:

Aldeburgh, Suffolk – a substation or satellite for Great Yarmouth.

Anglesey – doubled up as an airship station.

Ashington, Northumberland – basically an RFC station.

Atwick/Hornsea, Yorkshire – basically an RFC station.

Bacton, Norfolk – a substation for Great Yarmouth.

Bangor, north Wales.

Barrow in Furness, Lancashire – doubled up as an airship station.

Bembridge Harbour, Isle of Wight – a substation for Calshot.

Bembridge or New Bembridge, Isle of Wight – airfield.

Bowness on Windermere, Westmorland – a private seaplane station used temporarily for training.

Brading, Isle of Wight – basically an RFC station.

Burgh Castle, Suffolk – a substation for Great Yarmouth.

Butley, Suffolk – existed as an experimental station 1918/19.

Cairncross, Berwickshire – basically an RFC station.

Calshot, Hampshire – seaplane station at the mouth of Southampton Water.

Carnoustie, Forfarshire – provided temporary lodging facilities until RNAS Dundee was ready.

Catfirth, Shetland – flying boat base.

Cattewater, Devon – seaplane and flying boat base close to Devonport.

Chickerell, Dorset – special duties station.

Chingford, Essex – training station.

Clacton, Essex – seaplane station.

Covehithe, Suffolk – night substation for Great Yarmouth.

Cramlington East, Northumberland – special duties station.

Cranwell North (HMS *Daedalus*), Lincolnshire – training station.

Cranwell South (HMS *Daedalus*), Lincolnshire – training station.

Cromarty, Ross and Cromarty – seaplane station convenient for Invergordon base.

Detling, Kent – night landing alternative for Eastchurch.

Donibristle, Fife – shore station for shipboard seaplanes when ships visiting Rosyth.

Dover Harbour – seaplane and flying boat station.

Dover Guston Road – landplane base mainly for fighters.

Dundee Stannergate, Forfar – seaplane and flying boat base.

Eastbourne, Sussex – training school originally in private hands.

Eastchurch, Isle of Sheppey, Kent – first RN air station and flying school.

East Fortune, East Lothian – originally an airship station but then became a fighter station and also used for carrier aircraft in 1918.

Fairlop, Essex – a substation for Chingford.

Felixstowe, Suffolk – seaplane and flying boat station.

Fishguard, Pembrokeshire – seaplane station.

Freiston – a substation for Cranwell, for bomb-aiming and aerial gunnery training.

A Curtiss Large America flying boat on the slipway, most probably at Felixstowe. *(IWM Q 67581)*

Gosforth, Northumberland – manufacturer's aerodrome with lodging facilities for RNAS units.

Gosport, Hampshire – used early in war.

Grain, Kent – initially a substation for Eastchurch, but also used for air defence of fleet at the Nore and then marine aircraft experimental station.

Great Yarmouth, Norfolk – major seaplane and flying boat base.

Greenland Top, Lincolnshire – basically an RFC station.

Hawkcraig Point, Fife – experimental station in 1917/18.

Hendon, Middlesex – civil aerodrome taken over as flying school and aircraft park.

Holt – a substation for Great Yarmouth for night landings.

Hornsea Mere, Yorks – seaplane substation for Killingholme.

Houton Bay, Orkney – seaplane and flying boat station close to Scapa Flow.

Immingham, Lincolnshire – used by Eastchurch Mobile Squadron, then became kite balloon base.

Killingholme, Lincolnshire – mainly seaplane and flying boat base, but some landplane facilities.

Lee-on-the-Solent, Hampshire – seaplane training station originally intended as substation for Calshot, but also became landplane base in due course.

Leuchars, Fife – a training station, later became Grand Fleet School of Aerial Gunnery and Fighting on 10 November 1918.

Leysdown, Isle of Sheppey – substation for Eastchurch.

Luce Bay, Wigtownshire – airship station later used by aircraft.

Machrihanish, Argyll – originally airship station but later used by landplanes.

Manston, Kent – essentially a substation for Westgate.

Martlesham Heath, Suffolk – basically an RFC station but also used as a substation for Felixstowe.

Mullion, Cornwall – originally an airship station, but later used by landplanes.

New Haggerston, Northumberland – basically an RFC station.

Newhaven, Sussex – a seaplane substation for Calshot, despite being some distance away.

Newlyn, Cornwall – seaplane station.

North Coates Fittes, Lincolnshire – basically an RFC station.

Owthorne, Yorkshire – basically an RFC station.

Padstow, Cornwall – originally for seaplanes and flying boats, but also used by DH9 units.

Pembroke, Pembrokeshire – airship station soon joined by aircraft.

Peterhead, Aberdeenshire – seaplane station.

Portholme Meadow, Huntingdonshire – private airfield used as a testing station.

Portland Harbour, Dorset – seaplane substation to Calshot, despite distance.

Prawle Point, Devon – seaplane and flying boat station.

Redcar, Yorkshire – fighter and training station.

Rennington, Northumberland – basically an RFC station.

Ringmer, Sussex – night landing station for Eastbourne.

Rochford, Essex – fighter station.

Rosyth, Fife – kite balloon station, also used for ships' aircraft.

Scapa, Orkney – seaplane station but also became aircraft base and repair depot for aircraft from Grand Fleet.

Scarborough, Yorkshire – fighter station.

Seahouses, Northumberland – basically an RFC station.

Seaton Carew/West Hartlepool, Durham – basically an RFC fighter station.

Seaton Carew/Tees, Durham – seaplane station.

Skegness, Lincolnshire – used by Eastchurch Mobile Squadron, briefly.

Smoogroo, Orkney – practice and training station for Grand Fleet.

South Shields, Durham – seaplane station and depot.

Stenness Loch, Orkney – flying boat station.

Stonehenge, Wiltshire – an RFC station.

Strathbeg Loch, Aberdeenshire – seaplane substation for Peterhead.

Tallaght, Co. Dublin – opened August 1918 by RAF.

Telscombe Cliffs, Sussex – basically an RFC station.

Torquay Harbour – seaplane and kite balloon station.

Tregantle, Cornwall – storage depot for naval aircraft.

Tresco, Isles of Scilly – seaplane and flying boat station.

Trimley, Suffolk – substation for Felixstowe.

Turnhouse, West Lothian – basically an RFC

RNAS personnel at Imbros, many of them dressed in khaki. *(FAAM PERS 2937)*

RNAS wireless telegraph staff at Imbros. Note the mixture of uniforms, and that ratings wore peaked caps with white vests, khaki trousers, and puttees. *(FAAM PERS 2936)*

station but later used for a fleet aeroplane depot.

Tynemouth, Northumberland – basically an RFC station.

Walmer, Kent – rest station for RNAS units from the Western Front.

Westgate/Mutrix Farm, Kent – landplane base until replaced by Manston.

Westgate/St Mildred's Bay, Kent – seaplane station.

Westray, Orkney – flying boat station used as substation for Houton Bay.

Westward Ho! Devon – air station briefly in summer, 1918.

Whitley Bay, Northumberland – fighter station.

Withnoe, Cornwall – storage depot for aircraft.

NAVAL AIR STATIONS ABROAD

France: Bray Dunes, Petite Synthe, Couderkerque.

Belgium: La Panne, Furnes.

Italy: Otranto (with a substation at Santa Maria di Lucia), Taranto (all seaplane stations).

Other seaplane stations at Alexandria, Cherbourg, Gibraltar, Kalafrana (Malta), Mudros, Port Said, Suda Bay, Syra Island.

There were also stations, substations or sheds for airships, which included:

Anglesey, Isle of Anglesey.
Auldbar*, Angus.
Ballyliffan*, Donegal.
Bridport*, Dorset.
Bude*, Cornwall.
Capel, Kent.
Chathill*, Northumberland.
Cranwell, Lincolnshire, with training facilities.
East Fortune, East Lothian.
Godmersham Park*, Kent.
Howden, Yorkshire.
Killeagh*, Co. Cork.
Kingsnorth, Kent.
Kirkleatham*, Yorkshire.
Laira*, Devon.
Larne*, Antrim.
Longside, Angus.
Lowthorpe*, Yorkshire.
Luce Bay, Wigtownshire.
Malahide*, Co. Dublin,
Mullion, Cornwall.
Pembroke, Pembrokeshire.
Polegate, Sussex.
Pulham, Norfolk.
Ramsay*, Isle of Man.
Slindon*, Sussex.
Upton*, Dorset.
West Mersham*, Kent.

* Substation or mooring-out site.

The only overseas airship station was at Mudros.

In addition there were overseas kite balloon stations at Alexandria, Bizerte, Brindisi, Corfu, Gibraltar, Malta.

Airships had a number of advantages compared to the early aeroplane, including a better rate of climb, as ballast – often water – was discharged, a far better range and superior load-carrying ability. They also did not need a runway. Nevertheless, there were many drawbacks. Handling on the ground was one of these, especially in strong winds. Small, non-rigid airships could require as many as 100 men to handle them on the ground, more if there was a high wind. It became necessary to ensure that airships were stored in their own sheds, protected from the elements, rather than left in the open, battling against their mooring masts. Initially, the pioneers used the same shed in which the airship had been built as its base, but as airship production grew and the craft were sold to other users, it became necessary to produce a standard shed. Even by the time the RNAS took over airships from the RFC, not only had much experience been gained in finding suitably sheltered spots in woods or quarries, but a portable shed had been developed with mobile warfare in mind. A simple shed was produced for the early SS-class airships and this was followed by the 'coastal' shed, 320ft long, 120ft wide and 80ft high, which could accommodate two coastal airships side-by-side, and two SS airships as well. The large, rigid airships required something more, and the Admiralty decreed that these would also be housed side-by-side, with the result that the No. 1 shed at Howden was 703ft long, 150ft wide and 100ft high. However, the advent of the R33 class meant that the No. 2 shed was 750ft long, 300ft wide and 130ft high. In many stations, a second shed had to be added because the size of the class-33 airships.

The task of building these sheds came under a special unit, the Air Construction Corps, formed to build air stations. Most of the airship stations were built down the east coast, simply because this was a convenient point both for air raids against German-occupied territory and for convoy protection. The latter was catered for by sheds at Longside, East Fortune, Howden, Pulham and Kingsnorth, and would have been augmented by a shed at Lough Neagh in the north of Ireland for Atlantic patrols by the class-33 airships, had not the Armistice intervened before it could be completed. A further shed was built at Cranwell to train airship crews.

The airships were heavily dependent on hydrogen gas for their lift, and this was produced in Silicol plants in special gas houses close to the sheds. Given the highly flammable nature of hydrogen, this was a dangerous business, but there was just one serious accident when, on 14 April 1917, the Silicol plant at Pulham exploded, killing an officer and a rating. Caustic soda badly burned another officer and a civilian workman, while a number of others were less seriously injured.

APPENDIX I

BOARD OF ADMIRALTY

The proper title of the Board of Admiralty was the Commissioners for Executing the Office of Lord High Admiral of the United Kingdom of Great Britain and Ireland, and remains much the same today except, of course, that 'Northern Ireland' replaced 'Ireland' in 1922.

The Admiralty differed completely from the War Office and the Air Ministry in that it was not only the department of state for naval matters but also an operational head-quarters. While the Royal Navy operated its ships in fleets and squadrons, with the former usually headed by a commander-in-chief and the latter by a flag officer, the Admiralty could, and often did, by-pass the local chain of command and would communicate directly with the commanding officer of a warship. This ability was used much more often as wirelesss telegraphy eased communications, and indeed the Admiralty has been criticised for not using the intelligence resources available to it at Jutland and communicating more efficiently and effectively with the commanders at sea. On the other hand, communication can be overdone, and the still-new technology was a godsend to an overactive First Sea Lord such as Churchill, and a curse to everyone else.

The nature of the Admiralty's dual function has been one that developed over the centuries and reflected the complete-ness of a warship as a fighting unit, with a mix of skills and specialisations aboard, unlike an army unit that would be infantry, artillery or cavalry, later tanks, and which would need to cast around for its supporting arms.

In 1914, the Board of Admiralty consisted of:

First Lord – The Right Honourable Winston Churchill MP

First Sea Lord – Admiral His Serene Highness Prince Louis of Battenberg

Second Sea Lord – Vice Adm Sir John Jellicoe

Third Sea Lord – Rear Adm Archibald Wilson Moore

Fourth Sea Lord – Capt, later Rear Adm, Cecil Foley Lambert

Civil Lord – The Right Honourable George Lambert MP

Additional Civil Lord – The Right Honourable Sir Francis Hopwood MP

Parliamentary and Financial Secretary – The Right Honourable Thomas Macnamara MP

Permanent Secretary – Sir William Graham Greene

Naval Secretary to the First Sea Lord – Rear Adm The Honourable Henry Jackson

There was also an Admiralty War Staff of still recent vintage, headed by Adm Sir

Henry Jackson, and a Director of the Intelligence Division, headed by Rear Adm Arthur Leveson.

The First Sea Lord apart, the officers on the Admiralty Board were not always the most senior at the time, with many officers outranking them heading the fleets and, in some cases, even the squadrons. This was to change in later years, but commanders-in-chief had substantial powers dating from the time when it could take a year or more to get a message to a distant fleet.

On 23 October 1917, an Order in Council revised the membership of the Board as follows:

The First Lord of the Admiralty
The First Sea Lord and Chief of Naval Staff
The Deputy First Sea Lord
The Second Sea Lord and Chief of Naval Personnel
The Third Sea Lord and Chief of Naval Materiel
The Fourth Sea Lord and Chief of Supplies and Transport
The Fifth Sea Lord and Chief of Naval Air Service
The Deputy Chief of Naval Staff
The Assistant Chief of Naval Staff
The Civil Lord
The Controller
The Parliamentary and Financial Secretary
The Permanent Secretary

The Fifth Sea Lord position was dropped with the formation of the Royal Air Force, but reinstituted when the Fleet Air Arm passed back into naval control.

APPENDIX II

BATTLE AND CAMPAIGN HONOURS

Belgian Coast 1914–1918

The British army on the Western Front had its left flank extended into Belgium, with the right flank and the rear of the German army in France and Belgium similarly exposed. Attempts to defend the port of Antwerp failed despite the deployment of substantial forces at the insistence of the First Lord of the Admiralty, Winston Churchill. It fell to the Royal Navy to evacuate these forces back to England and safety. The need to keep the most modern and powerful ships in safer northern waters where they might have a chance of engaging the German High Seas Fleet meant that the work of coastal bombardment to help the army fell upon elderly ships. There were also minelaying and anti-submarine operations. More than 150 ships were involved, ranging from coastal motor boats, CMBs, through monitors to obsolete pre-dreadnought battleships.

Cameroons 1914

A German colony on the west coast of Africa, the main value of Cameroon was that it was home to a major wireless station enabling Germany to keep in touch with warships operating in the mid-Atlantic. Around 4,500 British, Belgian and French troops landed to attack the capital, Douala, while the Germans sank eleven ships in the river in an unsuccessful attempt to form a

barrier. The town was soon taken, along with 1,200 prisoners, after which it was decided to seize the entire territory, which took until February 1915. Fourteen naval vessels, many of them river gunboats from the Niger Flotilla, were involved, although just four ships were awarded the battle honour.

Dardanelles
19 February 1915–8 January 1916

The landings at Gallipoli are covered in Chapter 4, as are the successful operations by British submarines in the Sea of Marmara in Chapter 10. The Royal Navy's first venture was to bombard the forts alongside the coastline of Gallipoli, although this basically alerted the Turks to the looming British threat and, with German help, strong defensive measures were put in place. Incredibly, major surface units attempted to force their way through to the Sea of Marmara and to Constantinople, only to find extensive Turkish fortifications guarding the Dardanelles, which also had minefields laid across them. The casualties included the battlecruiser *Inflexible*, which struck a mine but managed to retire to Malta for repairs, while two pre-dreadnought battleships, *Irresistible* and *Ocean*, were unluckier still and sank. Later, another pre-dreadnought, *Goliath*, was sunk by a Turkish torpedo boat, while two more

pre-dreadnoughts, *Triumph* and *Majestic*, were both torpedoed and sunk by *U-21*, just two days apart. In January 1916, the pre-dreadnought *Russell* struck a mine and sank off Malta.

Strangely, despite the heroic efforts by the Royal Navy to put the Gallipoli invasion force ashore, and the great skill with which the evacuation was carried out, Gallipoli itself is not a campaign honour.

More than a hundred warships, including monitors and a torpedo boat, share this honour along with ten submarines.

Dogger Bank
24 January 1915

During the First World War, both sides were on the lookout for a fleet action, with the one proviso that neither side dared risk losing its major fleet units. Rear Adm Franz von Hipper in the battlecruiser *Seydlitz* took his First Scouting Group, consisting of two other battlecruisers and an armoured

cruiser, with four light cruisers and two destroyer flotillas, to strike at British patrols around the Dogger Bank. The Admiralty, on learning of German intentions through a signals intercept, sent Vice Adm Sir David Beatty's five battlecruisers, escorted by light cruisers and torpedo boats, from Rosyth, while Cdre Tyrwhitt's Harwich destroyer flotilla was also ordered to sea. Beatty aimed to block the route between the German ships and their home base of Wilhelmshaven.

The two forces clashed early on 24 January 1915, and at first the battle went Beatty's way, with *Seydlitz* losing her two aft turrets to a direct hit from Beatty's flagship, *Lion*, while the armoured cruiser *Blücher* was crippled. *Lion* was then hit by three shells and began to fall astern, with Rear Adm Arthur Moore taking command, but instead of chasing after the rest of the German force, he had the British ships concentrate their fire on the *Blücher*.

This battle was credited with teaching the Germans the dangers of flash from bursting shells reaching down into the magazines, and so their ships did not confront this danger at Jutland, unlike those of the British. Nevertheless, it was also a lost opportunity because of British bungling.

Some forty-six ships share this honour.

Dover
20/1 April 1917

The ships of the Dover Patrol were at sea on their normal defensive dispositions and not aware of an impending German attack. Twelve German destroyers attacked the six British ships, which included the two destroyer leaders *Broke*, captained by Cdr Evans, and *Swift*, under Cdr Peck. In the high-speed action that ensued, two German destroyers were sunk, despite serious damage and heavy casualties aboard *Broke*. The Germans were driven off. This honour belongs to just the two ships named.

Falklands
8 December 1914

The Falklands marked a serious failure of intelligence and communication on the part of the Germans, and a prompt response to a perceived threat by the Admiralty. The bad news from Coronel took some time to reach the Admiralty, but the immediate reaction of Churchill, the First Lord, and Fisher, the First Sea Lord, was to send two modern dreadnought battlecruisers, *Invincible* and *Inflexible*, under the command of Vice Adm Sir Doveton Sturdee, to the South Atlantic, where Rear Adm Stoddart, whose squadron was patrolling the east coast of South America, was already assembling all available warships. The combined force reached Port Stanley in the Falkland Islands on 7 December 1914. This was the first time in the war that modern, powerful British warships had been deployed away from home waters.

Adm Graf von Spee's plan was to attack the Falklands and destroy the base, possibly being able to seize coal and provisions for his ships, and then head north, break through the British blockade and finally reach Germany. Crucial to his plans was the assumption that the Falklands would be undefended. Lacking aerial reconnaissance or submarines that might have remained undetected, he dispatched the armoured cruiser *Gneisenau* and the light cruiser *Nürnberg* on reconnaissance, but as they neared Port Stanley during the morning of 8 December, those aboard saw the distinctive tripod masts of British battlecruisers in the outer anchorage, while at the same time they were spotted by the British. Had they pressed ahead, they would have caught the British at a disadvantage, as the two ships were coaling, but within two hours, the British ships were at sea, chasing after von Spee, who was heading south-east.

While the German squadron hoped that nightfall would enable it to escape, by 1300 the flagship, the light cruiser *Leipzig*, was taking British fire. Von Spee dispersed his light cruisers while the two armoured cruisers *Scharnhorst* and *Gneisenau* faced the advancing British ships. The Germans were heavily outgunned, facing the 12in guns of the Royal Navy with 8in guns, and at 1615 *Scharnhorst* went down with all hands aboard, followed by *Gneisenau* at 1800.

Von Spee's gallant defence did little for the light cruisers. *Leipzig* was eventually sunk by the British cruisers *Cornwall* and *Glasgow*, while *Kent* chased after *Nürnberg* and sank her. For the time being, *Dresden* managed to evade the pursuers, but she was found three months later to the west of Chile and, when *Kent* and *Glasgow* approached, her commanding officer ordered her to be scuttled.

Eight warships shared this honour.

Cdr Loftus Jones commanded the 4th Destroyer Flotilla at the Battle of Jutland and won the Victoria Cross defending British battlecruisers from a German destroyer attack. *(RNM)*

Heligoland
28 August 1914

The first clash between British and German naval forces of the war in the Heligoland Bight. The idea was to try to bring the Germans to battle, the Admiralty hoping that they would allow themselves to be drawn within range of Vice Adm Beatty's battlecruisers. Cdre Tyrwhitt commanded his Harwich force of two flotillas with a total of twenty-one destroyers, led by the light cruisers *Arethusa* and *Fearless*, with cover by the 1st Battle Cruiser Squadron supported by the 1st Light Cruiser Squadron.

The Harwich force entered the Bight shortly after dawn on a sweep looking for German warships, and found two destroyers on patrol, sinking one of them. Six German light cruisers then appeared, led by Rear Adm Maas in *Köln*, and a number of high-speed actions followed. Beatty responded quickly to Tyrwhitt's call for assistance, arriving in *Lion* with another four battle-cruisers and an escort of eight light cruisers and a number of destroyers. Three German cruisers, *Köln*, *Ariadne* and *Mainz*, were soon sunk, while the other three disappeared into the morning mist. The Germans lost 1,200 men killed or taken prisoner.

This honour is shared by sixty-six ships and eight submarines.

Jutland
31 May 1916

This confrontation between the heavy battle fleets of Britain and Germany had been long sought after by the Royal Navy as a means of bringing to bear its naval superiority over its enemy. The Germans, for their part, were keen to reduce the numerical superiority over their own forces of the Royal Navy's Grand Fleet, and for this reason the plan was that the British ships would first have to cross a line of U-boats which would inflict heavy losses on the Grand Fleet's dreadnoughts. For a detailed account of this controversial engagement, see Chapter 7.

When the guns fell silent, the Royal Navy had lost three battlecruisers, three armoured cruisers and eight destroyers, with the lives of 6,090 men. The cost to the Germans had been one battlecruiser and an obsolete pre-dreadnought battleship, four light cruisers and five destroyers, taking with them 2,550 men. Jellicoe and Scheer were both criticised for their conduct, and in fact only Hipper came out of the engagement with his reputation undiminished. The Admiralty failed to give Jellicoe the information that they held, and Beatty was also guilty of neglecting the needs of his superior. On paper, it was a German victory, but Jellicoe's caution had stopped it becoming a complete disaster for the Royal Navy. In practice, because the High Seas Fleet only ever ventured out again to surrender, Jellicoe had retained British control of the seas.

This honour is shared by no fewer than 150 ships.

Mesopotamia
1914–1918

Mesopotamia was important as the source of much of Britain's oil during the war, but it was part of the vast Ottoman Empire. Indian troops were landed on 23 October 1914 and within a month had captured the key objective of Basra, then, as now, the main outlet for the area. Reinforcements early the following year encouraged the British to march on Baghdad. Supported by river gunboats and gun crews forming naval brigades, the British force won a number of victories but, after taking Kut-el-Amara and advancing on Baghdad, was forced back and surrounded. Despite valiant attempts to run supplies through on the river, eventually 8,000 British and Indian troops were forced to surrender. A fresh expeditionary force retook Kut in February 1917 and, with the continued support of river gunboats, eventually took Baghdad and, finally, the Mosul oilfields.

This honour is shared by thirty-five ships, many of them river gunboats.

Ostend
10 May 1918

The operation was the second attempt to block the port of Ostend after the earlier attempt in April, which was timed to coincide with a similar assault on Zeebrugge, had failed. The cruiser *Vindictive*, which had been heavily modified for the Zeebrugge raid and badly damaged during the operation, was patched up and sent off again, this time to act as a blockship with another ship, the *Sappho*. In the event, *Sappho* had to return with engine trouble, leaving it to *Vindictive* to block the port. The operation encountered further problems when Cdr Godsal encountered thick fog.

The damaged mole at Zeebrugge after the raid in 1918. *(FAAM)*

However, he managed to place his ship right in the harbour mouth before he was killed by a direct hit as he was attempting to turn *Vindictive* across the channel. The first lieutenant took control but the ship had run aground and could not be moved. He blew *Vindictive*'s scuttling charges and she settled, partially blocking the entrance. There is more on this operation in Appendix III, on Victoria Cross awards.

Seven ships share this award with six coastal motor boats and two minelayers.

Scandinavian Convoys
17 October and 12 December 1917

It was not until late 1917 that British convoys to the neutral Scandinavian countries came under attack. On 17 October, off the Norwegian coast, the two British gunboats *Mary Rose* and *Strongbow* were attacked by two German gunboats fitted with a single 8.2in gun each, against their three 4in guns. Outgunned, both British ships were sunk.

Again, on 12 December, four German destroyers attacked *Partridge* and *Pellew*, sinking both.

All four ships qualified for this honour.

Suez Canal
2–4 February 1915

Turkish forces attacked the Suez Canal in February 1915, but were repulsed by British forces guarding the canal zone, aided by an assortment of British and some French warships and armed tugs in the area.

Nine British warships and six armed tugs share this battle honour.

Zeebrugge
23 April 1918

The Belgian ports of Zeebrugge and Ostend were not only vital to the German armies ashore but also provided excellent bases for German torpedo boats, minelayers and submarines within easy reach of the Thames Estuary, the Nore and the English Channel. It was decided to put both ports out of use by sinking blockships at the entrances, while also mounting an amphibious assault on the mole, and the viaduct connecting this to the mainland at Zeebrugge. So important were these two operations that more than 160 British warships were involved, including the Harwich Force.

The Ostend operation ran into difficulties once the wind swept away the smokescreen; moreover, a vital navigation aid had been moved, causing two of the ships to run aground offshore.

The Zeebrugge operation is described more fully in Appendix III on the Victoria Cross awards (see Bamford, Carpenter, etc). It involved placing the elderly cruiser *Vindictive* alongside, so that marines could seize the mole and attack its gun emplacements. Two out of the three British minelayers used as blockships were sunk, blocking the entrance canal, while two submarines, *C1* and *C3*, were used to bring down the viaduct.

In addition to the two submarines, this honour was shared by another twenty-eight warships, plus eighteen coastal motor boats and thirty-three minelayers.

Despite the failure at Ostend, sufficient heroism was shown in adverse circumstances for sixteen warships and three monitors, plus six coastal motor boats and twelve minelayers, to receive an award.

APPENDIX III

VICTORIA CROSS AWARDS

The Victoria Cross was well established as the top decoration for valour by the outbreak of the First World War, while for other acts of gallantry there existed the Albert Medal, later to be retitled the George Cross. The war saw the first award of the Victoria Cross to a member of the Royal Naval Volunteer Reserve, but was perhaps most famous for the award to fatally wounded young Jack Cornwell, just 16 years old and the youngest ever to be awarded the VC, at the Battle of Jutland. War service also saw the Albert Medal awarded to PO Michael Keogh of HMS *Ark Royal* for rescuing a fatally injured pilot from a burning aircraft, while later Lt D.P.T. Stembridge also received the medal for a similar deed. On 6 March 1918, it was awarded to Flt Lt V.A. Watson for saving the life of a crewman in a blazing naval airship, while on 12 April 1918, Lt A.G. Bagot RNVR of *ML356* received the award for saving life following a fire at sea. On one occasion three men received the award when they rescued a pilot whose seaplane crashed into a mast 360ft off the ground on Hornsea Island; these brave men were OS G.E.P. Abbott, OS R.J. Knowlton and OS Gold. Not all of the awards were connected with aircraft or airships; a good example was the award to A.W. Newman, a mate, for disposing of burning ammunition on 10 October 1917. A similar example of bravery on 6 December 1917 saw the award given to LS T.N. Davis. Deckhand J.G. Stanners also won the award for fighting a fire in a magazine on 29 December 1917.

The Victoria Cross (VC) had a blue ribbon, while the current dark-red ribbon was reserved for army use only.

Cdr Henry Peel Ritchie, Dar-es-Salaam, 28 November 1914, aboard HMS *Goliath*.

Ironically, the name Dar-es-Salaam means 'Abode of Peace'. In 1914, it was the capital of German East Africa, and it was also harbouring the fugitive German commerce raider, the cruiser *Königsberg*, which had been trapped in the River Rufiji. One of the warships responsible for the plight of the *Königsberg* was the pre-dreadnought battle-ship HMS *Goliath*. Ritchie was second in command of *Goliath*, but he was given the independent command of a captured German cable vessel that had been turned into an armed auxiliary vessel, *Duplex*, so that he could enter the harbour at Dar-es-Salaam and sink the supply vessels that were supporting the *Königsberg*. Unfortunately, *Duplex* had unreliable machinery, so a Maxim machine gun and extra protection, including two steel lighters lashed to either side, were fitted to *Goliath*'s steam pinnace, which Ritchie himself drove into the harbour. He was accompanied by another of the battleship's officers, Lt Paterson, in a captured German tug, *Helmuth*, and an officer from the elderly protected cruiser *Fox* in that ship's steam cutter.

This improved force entered the harbour, where white flags of truce were flying, and the local governor had agreed that any German ships would be British prizes of war or could be destroyed. Paterson put the *Helmuth* alongside the German *Feldmarschall* to board her and lay demolition charges, while Surgeon Lt Holtom, also from *Goliath*, checked a hospital ship, *Tabora*. Meanwhile, Ritchie boarded the *Königsberg*, finding her almost deserted, and after those aboard were ordered into her boats, demolition charges were placed under her engines. He then went aboard the *Kaiser Wilhelm II*, but his suspicions were aroused when he saw a discarded ammunition clip from a Mauser, with the ends of the bullets sawn off.

Almost immediately, despite the flags of truce, small arms fire opened up, initially aimed at the cutter from *Fox*, and Ritchie returned to his pinnace, ready to pull out of the harbour. As they started to move, artillery fire was added to that of the small arms. PO Clark, the coxswain, was hit, leaving Ritchie to take over. Ritchie, in turn, was hit eight times in twenty minutes, including wounds to his head, both arms and then two in his right leg, which caused him to fall, although he was already faint from loss of blood. First, AB Upton took over, and then Clark, by this time roughly bandaged, resumed control, taking the pinnace alongside the battleship, which then opened fire with her 12in main armament and flattened the governor's house.

The cutter from *Fox* had also run into trouble; her stoker was fatally wounded, so that Lt Corson, in command, had to take over and stoke the fire.

Corson received the DSC, Clark the CGM and Upton the DSM. Holtom had been left aboard the *Tabora* and became a prisoner of war, but when later released he confirmed that she had been a fake. Ritchie's VC was gazetted on 10 April 1915. Meanwhile, he had spent six weeks in hospital at Zanzibar. Ritchie survived the war, retiring in 1917, but remained on the retired list and was promoted captain in 1924.

Lt Cdr Norman Douglas Holbrook, the Dardanelles, 13 December 1914, aboard HM Submarine *B11*.

B11 was an obsolete submarine and one of three of her class based with three French submarines at Tenedos, to keep a watch on the Dardanelles and ensure that Turkish warships did not attempt to break out. It was decided to attempt a submerged pene-tration of the Dardanelles, a narrow channel, in places just two miles wide and with strong currents, sandbanks and shallows. The channel was heavily patrolled by the Turks, who had forts with guns lining the shore and had also sown minefields. The maximum submerged speed of *B11* was just 1 knot faster than the maximum 5kt current that could be expected, and she could only make that for two hours before her battery needed to be recharged.

Before dawn on Friday 13 December 1914, *B11* left Tenedos, diving off Cape Helles to enter the Dardanelles, only to resurface shortly afterwards as severe vibration was felt on the hull. The culprit was a metal guard fitted to ward off mine cables that had twisted itself into a hook and was more likely to pull a mine cable on to the submarine than ward it off. The crew worked waist-deep in water to jettison the hook as the vessel remained partially submerged to avoid being seen. The submarine then went down to 80ft to move slowly for four hours, eventually rising to periscope depth just 10 miles into the Dardanelles, and 2 miles from the Narrows. Holbrook could see the 10,000-ton battleship *Messudieh* at anchor in Sari Sighlar Bay on the Asiatic side of the Dardanelles. *B11*'s starboard torpedo was fired, hitting the battleship which began to sink stern-first, before capsizing, all in just ten minutes.

As *B11* turned to head back down the straits, her torpedo was noticed and the Turks opened fire. The submarine then grounded on a sandbank, which forced her conning tower out of the water. Given this target, the Turkish fire intensified, but fortunately the submarine slid off the sandbank and into deeper water, eventually reaching the Mediterranean after being submerged for nine hours. One indication of the conditions aboard was that when she returned to the surface, it was some time before her engine could be started, because of the lack of oxygen in the air.

Holbrook and his crew were cheered back into port and the crews of the other submarines presented him with a large, cardboard Iron Cross. The more substantial Victoria Cross was gazetted on 22 December, while his first lieutenant received a DSO and the rest of the crew, all ratings, received DSMs. The entire crew shared a prize bounty of £3,500.

Holbrook survived the war and retired in 1920, being promoted to commander on the retired list in 1928. He was recalled to service at the Admiralty for the Second World War.

Lt Cdr Eric Gascoigne Robinson, the Dardanelles, 26 February 1915.

As the Gallipoli campaign ground to a halt, in February 1915, the Mediterranean Fleet began to see if it could break the deadlock by forcing the Dardanelles. This involved heavy bombardments, starting on 19 February, while on 26 February a force of fifty Royal Marines from the pre-dreadnought battleship HMS *Vengeance*, with a demolition party led by her torpedo officer, Lt Cdr E.G. Robinson, was landed at 1430 near Kum Kale. Here, they were to deal with the guns and also destroy a battery inland at Orkanie, as well as destroying two AA guns and a bridge across the Mendere river.

The party was soon held up by heavy fire, which killed a sergeant and two marines. Robinson's team could not get to the battery at Orkanie; he thought that he could reach the two AA guns at Achilles' Tomb, but realised that the white tropical uniforms of his men would make them easy targets. He left his men behind and went on ahead with a charge of gun-cotton. Finding the AA battery deserted, Robinson blew up one gun, before returning to his men, picking up a second charge and going back to blow up the second. Meanwhile, the guns of the cruiser *Dublin* had successfully subdued the fire that had held up the marines, and Robinson was able to destroy the battery at Orkanie. He did not have sufficient time to destroy the bridge, but nevertheless, his entire party was able to return to the landing site at Kum Kale.

Later, on the night of 26/7 April 1915, while reconnoitring a new minefield, the submarine *E15* was forced off course by the strong current in the Dardanelles and ran aground with her conning tower clear of the water. When the Turks opened fire, her commanding officer and several members of the crew were killed, and the rest had no choice but to surrender. To stop the boat falling intact into enemy hands, several attempts were made to destroy her, using bombs from aircraft, shells from battleships and torpedoes from submarines, all of which failed. Two steam picket boats from the battleships *Triumph* and *Majestic*, with *Triumph*'s boat commanded by Robinson, were sent with torpedoes mounted on outriggers to destroy *E15*. Lieutenant Godwin, in command of the boat from *Majestic*, managed to destroy the submarine with his second torpedo, but his boat was damaged and he was wounded. Robinson's crew rescued the men from Godwin's boat and took them back to safety with the loss of just one man.

Godwin received the DSO, two other officers the DSC, and all of the men in the two boats received the DSM. For these two actions and other sorties into the minefields, Robinson received the Victoria Cross, with the award gazetted on 16 August 1915. Robinson was also promoted to commander. He was promoted to captain in 1920, becoming Captain (D), commanding destroyers on the China Station aboard the cruiser *Berwick*. He retired and was promoted to rear admiral on the retired list in 1933. Recalled in 1939, he served for two years as a convoy commodore, before ill health forced him to retire again in 1941.

Cdr Edward Unwin RN; Mid George Leslie Drewry RNR; Mid Wilfred St Aubyn Malleson RNR; AB William Charles Williams RN; AB George McKenzie

Cdr Unwin and AB Williams both won the VC, for their prompt action in saving from breaking away the pontoon over which troops were running ashore at the Dardanelles. *(IWM)*

Samson, RNR; V Beach, Gallipoli, April 1915.

The problems inherent in the Dardanelles operation were consistently underestimated by the Admiralty and the War Office, as indeed were the fighting qualities of the Turks and their German mentors.

On the southern end of Cape Helles, V Beach was to be taken after a bombardment of the village and fort of Seddul Bahir by the pre-dreadnought battleship *Albion*, which would also blow holes in the barbed wire on the beach. While this was going on, the converted collier *River Clyde* would approach the beach bringing three lighters carrying troops and a converted hopper barge. The hopper would be sent to ground on the beach, while the lighters were used to create a pontoon, so that 2,000 troops from three regiments could rush out from the lighters and from specially cut ports in the collier's sides, to cross the pontoon bridge and storm the beach. Following this, they would advance inland and meet up with troops from W, X and Y beaches, who would have made successful landings elsewhere. The force would regroup, take the town of Krithia and scale the heights of Achi Baba.

Beginning at 0600 on Sunday 25 April 1915, *Albion* bombarded her targets for an hour. Meanwhile the *River Clyde* made her run to the shore and the lighters and hopper were duly positioned, with no more than a few hitches and premature groundings. The bombardment ceasing, the landing force raced towards the shore, while Turkish troops crept back to their machine guns and opened fire. The British troops became trapped on the beach by barbed wire that had been hardly touched by the bombardment. The pontoon was smothered by the dead and the wounded, while more troops struggled out of the collier. This went

on for three hours, with just 200 troops actually getting ashore and then being forced by the heavy fire to remain trapped in the shelter of a bank. Covering fire from guns aboard the *River Clyde* was no match for the Turkish artillery.

There were other problems. Before the landings started, the current started to pull the lighters away, whereupon the *River Clyde*'s commanding officer, Cdr Edward Unwin, whose idea it was, swam ashore with a line and secured the first lighter and then towed it ashore. Finding nothing to which he could secure the lighter, he remained in the water with the line wrapped around his waist while the first troops rushed past him. He stayed at his post, although more than 50 years old, until he was numb and had to be rescued and taken to his ship, where the surgeon wrapped him in blankets. However, as soon as his circulation returned, he went back into the water, where he was wounded three times. He then found a launch, secured her stern to his ship, and pushed the launch ashore to rescue the wounded lying in the shallow water, succeeding in rescuing at least seven men before he was forced to stop by sheer exhaustion. Other members of the collier's crew also had to get into the water to manhandle the lighters into position under heavy fire. Mid Drewry was wounded in the head but continued passing lines between the lighters until he collapsed from exhaustion. AB Williams remained up to his neck in water for an hour, but held on to his lines until he was killed, dying in the arms of Unwin. Another AB, George Samson, worked in the lighters and remained there all day under heavy fire, until he was so badly wounded that he had to be relieved; he carried thirteen pieces of shrapnel in his body for the rest of his life. Drewry was relieved by Mid Malleson, and when the line broke twice, had to retrieve it.

All five awards were gazetted on 16 August 1915, the ratings being the first from the lower deck to receive the VC for more than fifty years.

Unwin was sent to Haslar for an operation, but was soon back at Mudros in command of the light cruiser *Endymion*, and was beachmaster for the landings at Suvla Bay on 7 August 1915. The following March, during the withdrawal, he was last to leave the beaches. As the boat pulled away from the shore, a man fell overboard, and Unwin dived in to rescue him. He was promoted acting commodore in 1919, while his substantive rank of captain was backdated to 11 November 1918 in recognition of his outstanding war service.

Drewry was promoted to acting lieutenant in 1916 and posted to the battleship *Conqueror*, later taking command of HMT *William Jackson* at Scapa Flow. He died shortly after receiving serious head and other injuries in an accident.

Malleson was promoted to acting sub-lieutenant in 1916 and joined the battleship *Lord Nelson*, later moving to *Dolphin* for submarine training. In March 1918, he was promoted to lieutenant and joined the depot ship *Lucia*. After the war, he commanded submarines. He retired with the rank of commander during the late 1930s, after some years in back-office roles, before returning to the service for the Second World War, eventually reaching the rank of captain. Retiring again, at his own wish he faded into obscurity and spent the rest of his life in Cornwall until his death in 1975, refusing to join the VC and GC Association or to attend any functions.

Samson, the first RNR rating to win a VC, went to hospital in Port Said and then to Haslar. He arrived home at Carnoustie in Scotland in civilian clothes, his uniform not having been replaced, to find that he was taken for a shirker by the assembled local

dignitaries and pipe band. A couple of months later, when he arrived after receiving his VC, clearly still not in uniform, he was presented with a white feather. He was promoted petty officer before he returned to sea, and after the war, he returned to the Merchant Navy. He died of pneumonia in 1923 in Bermuda.

Sub Lt Arthur Walderne St Clair Tisdall RNVR, V Beach, Gallipoli, April 1915.

Sub Lt St Clair Tisdall was commanding 1 Platoon, Anson Company, Royal Naval Division, taking passage aboard the *River Clyde* in order to serve ashore with the army. He was still aboard the ship waiting to go ashore with his men as the first troops ashore were being mown down by Turkish machine-gun fire. He jumped over the side of the ship and into the water, wading ashore and, with the help of a leading seaman, joined Unwin in rescuing the wounded from the shallows. Between them, Tisdall and LS Malia took two boatloads of wounded back to the *River Clyde* and, after being joined by a chief petty officer and two more leading seamen, made at least another four trips.

On 6 May, Tisdall was leading his men during the first battle of Achi Baba, during which they occupied an enemy trench. He stood up on the parapet of the trench to look for the enemy when he was shot in the chest and died immediately. His award was gazetted on 31 March 1916, after some delay in establishing the facts. His comrades in the rescue mission received the CGM, with the exception of LS Curtiss, who was posted missing in action in June 1915.

L/Cpl Walter Richard Parker RMLI, Gaba Tepe, Gallipoli, April/May 1915.

L/Cpl Parker was a member of the Royal Marine Light Infantry serving with the Portsmouth Battalion of the Royal Naval

Division. His unit was landed at Anzac Cove on 28 April 1915, to relieve Australian troops at Gaba Tepe, and he soon showed commendable courage in leading stretcher parties, being relegated to this duty because of his poor eyesight. On the night of 30 April/1 May, volunteers were sought to take food, water, ammunition and medical supplies to an isolated position at MacLaurin's Hill. Many men had already been killed or wounded while attempting this mission. The position seemed so hopeless that an Australian officer threatened to shoot Parker if he went on his mission – Parker ignored him. It was daylight by the time Parker and his comrades set out, and one man was soon wounded. Parker organised a stretcher party for him and then continued, eventually reaching the isolated position alone, but already wounded. He immediately started to give first aid to the many wounded at MacLaurin's Hill, and later helped in the evacuation, despite having received further wounds while in the trench.

It took some time before Parker's valour could be validated, and so his award was not gazetted until 22 June 1917. By this time, following treatment at the Military Hospital at Netley, near Southampton, he had already been discharged from the service in June 1916 as being unfit for further service. He died in 1936.

Lt Cdr Edward Courtney Boyle RN, Sea of Marmara, April/May 1915, aboard HM Submarine E14.

The E class submarines were among the most up-to-date in service with the Royal Navy in 1915. As the difficult terrain meant that Gallipoli was seven days by land from Constantinople, but only a day by sea, coastal shipping was important to the Turks, while the Dardanelles offered a short cut for an offensive fleet into the heart of Turkey.

Following the success of *B11*, it seemed that submarine warfare was the only way forward, as repeated attempts by surface units had been repulsed by the Turks.

One of the Royal Navy's most experienced submariners, Lt Cdr Boyle was in command of *E14* when she was detached from the fleet on 27 April 1915 to make her foray into the Sea of Marmara. The passage of the Dardanelles took seventeen hours, sixteen of them submerged. During the passage, Boyle found the torpedo gunboat *Paykisevki*, a 700-ton ex-German vessel, and his second torpedo sank her. This, of course, alerted the Turks to his presence, and the intensity of the anti-submarine patrols was such that he had difficulty finding opportunities to surface and recharge his batteries.

Despite the anti-submarine patrols, Boyle had, on 1 May, already forced the Turks to reroute their troop movements over land. That same day, *E14* sank the gunboat *Nour el Bahr*. A week later, he went into the harbour at Rodosto looking for targets, surfaced and exchanged rifle fire with troops, as the E class submarines had not been fitted with 6pdr guns at this stage. On 10 May, he sank the ex-White Star liner *Guj Djemal*, 5,000 tons, carrying no less than 6,000 troops and an artillery battery to Gallipoli. The lack of a gun was felt most strongly on 13 May, when, with only one torpedo left, and that defective, he encountered a small steamer, and had to force her to run aground, using only rifle fire. He remained on station despite lacking offensive armament, until 18 May, because the presence of the submarine effectively stopped all shipping movements in the Sea of Marmara.

Running through the Dardanelles on 18 May to rejoin the fleet, *E14* made two more offensive patrols, spending some seventy days in the Sea of Marmara between June and August.

Boyle was gazetted on 21 May 1915, by which time he had already been promoted to commander in recognition of his courage and initiative. Both his officers were awarded the DSC and all of the ratings received the DSM. While prize money was paid for the two naval vessels and steamer, totalling £375, the claim of £31,000 for the troopship was disallowed because she was not an armed ship. After promotion to captain and a period as King's Harbourmaster at Devonport from 1926 to 1928, Boyle took command of *Iron Duke* from 1929 to 1931. He retired

the day after being promoted to rear admiral in 1932, and returned to the RN in 1939, serving as Flag Officer in Charge, London, until 1942. He died on 16 December 1967 as a result of injuries suffered when he was knocked down by a lorry near his home in Sunningdale the previous day.

Lt Cdr Martin Eric Nasmith, Sea of Marmara, May/June 1915, aboard HM Submarine *E11*.
One of the first things that Boyle had to do when he returned from his first trip into the

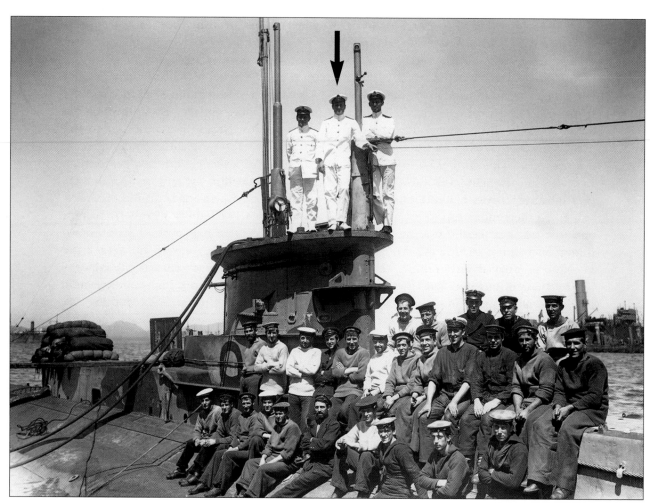

Lt Cdr Martin Nasmith (arrowed), who won the VC for his exploits in the Sea of Marmara, with the crew of *E11*. (IWM Q 13260)

Sea of Marmara was to brief Lt Cdr Martin Nasmith, already one of the most successful submarine commanders. Nasmith had been ordered by Commodore (S), Roger Keyes, to 'Go and run amuck in the Marmara.'

Nasmith left on 19 May, commanding another E class boat, *E11*. Nothing if not diligent, Nasmith had taken the unusual step of flying over the Dardanelles and the Marmara in a Farman biplane on a personal aerial reconnaissance. When *E11* entered the Sea of Marmara, the havoc he created was even worse than that of *E14*, persuading many Turks that a large Allied submarine force had penetrated the Dardanelles and was approaching the Bosporus. None of this was surprising, as Nasmith showed that he was also a master of propaganda.

Nasmith's patrol saw *E11* sink a large gunboat, an ammunition ship, three store ships and two transports, as well as four minor vessels, including a large troop-carrying barge which he encountered on one of two trips into the harbour at Constantinople. He also took the first photographs through a submarine periscope. His most unusual exploit occurred as he was chasing a paddle steamer aground. Being too close to the shore, he was engaged by Turkish cavalry, and returned their rifle fire, but decided to leave once holes started to appear in his conning tower. The dying act of the gunboat he torpedoed was to shoot a hole in his periscope: After making emergency repairs, he signalled for a replacement to be flown out. At one stage, he hid his submarine by lashing it alongside a sailing ship. He also gave an interview to an American journalist, before sending his first lieutenant across to place charges and blow the ship up; but before he did so he informed her master that there were eleven British submarines in the Sea of Marmara.

One reason for the high rate of success enjoyed by Nasmith was that he never wasted a torpedo. When torpedoes missed, they normally ran on until they sank to the bottom, but Nasmith modified his so that they surfaced. The surfaced torpedoes had their firing pistols disabled, before being manhandled back into a flooded torpedo tube and into *E11*.

Of the two transports sunk, one was a substitute for a battleship that Nasmith had expected to find in the Dardanelles on his homeward passage. Rather than return to base with two unspent torpedoes, when he discovered that the battleship was not there he managed to turn round, despite the strong current, and return up the Dardanelles, until he found the transport and sank her with the two torpedoes. All of this success may have seemed to be tempting fate, and *E11* nearly met her end when she became entangled in the mooring cable of a mine on her way out through the Dardanelles. Nasmith was alerted to the problem by a grating sound and, checking through his periscope, he could see a mine cable entangled in his port hydroplane. He could not surface because of the proximity of Turkish shore batteries in the narrowest part of the strait, and could not slow down lest the mine swung round and struck the submarine. Without mentioning the danger to any of his men, Nasmith towed the mine for eleven miles, before finally putting *E11* full astern and surfacing, on which the mine floated free.

Nasmith's VC was gazetted on 25 June 1915, with promotion to commander five days later, and once again his officers both received DSCs, while the rest of the crew received DSMs. Like Boyle, Nasmith went back into the Sea of Marmara twice. On the first of these patrols, in July and August, he finally achieved his ambition of sinking a battleship, the *Heireddin Barbarossa*, a gunboat, six transports, one steamship and twenty-three sailing vessels. In a further patrol lasting forty-seven days in November and December, he sank a destroyer, the *Yar Hissar*, as well as eight sailing vessels, five of them large.

After his third venture into the Sea of Marmara, Nasmith returned to the UK, and became a captain exactly a year to the day after becoming commander. In January 1928, he was promoted to rear admiral, naturally enough becoming Admiral (S). After a spell as a vice-admiral, he became a full admiral in 1936 and, after being C-in-C Plymouth and Western Approaches from 1938 until 1941, he took over from his friend Boyle as Flag Officer in Charge, London, until 1946. After the war, Nasmith was Vice-Chairman of the Imperial War Graves Commission, and retired to Morayshire, where he died in hospital in Elgin in June 1965.

Flg Sub Lt Reginald Alexander John Warneford, Belgium, June 1915, with No. 1 Squadron, RNAS.

A member of the Royal Naval Air Service, like most of his peers Warneford had been trained at Eastchurch on the Isle of Sheppey. He soon achieved a reputation as a daring pilot. Early on 17 May 1915, he was flying on patrol with his commanding officer, Sqn Cdr Spenser Gray, when they sighted the Zeppelins *LZ-37*, *LZ-38* and *LZ-39* off Dunkirk, heading east, at around 0330. Both aircraft attacked *LZ-39* with machine-gun fire, coming in from below, as it would have taken too long to climb above the airship. The Zeppelin immediately jettisoned its water ballast, which allowed it to soar at 1,000ft a minute out of range. All three Zeppelins returned safely to the shed.

The same three Zeppelins bombed Calais on the night of 6/7 June. Wg Cdr Arthur Longmore sent Warneford with another pilot to intercept, but the other pilot's aircraft suffered engine trouble and had to return. Warneford, flying a Morane-Saulnier Type L parasol monoplane, armed with a Vickers machine gun firing forwards through the propeller and six 10lb bombs that could be released using an improvised toggle and release wire, continued towards the Zeppelins. At around 0105, he saw *LZ-37* north of Ostend at about his altitude. His problem became one of how to approach without the Zeppelin jettisoning her ballast and ascending out of reach. The situation was made more difficult by the fact that hunter and hunted were moving at roughly the same speed. At 0150, near Bruges, the Zeppelin opened fire with her Maxim machine guns; Warneford turned away, on which the airship gave chase. This continued until 0215, by which time Warneford had climbed to a high altitude. Once the firing stopped, he turned, finding himself behind the Zeppelin and well above it. He switched off his engine and dived towards the airship from 11,000ft. At 7,000ft and just above the Zeppelin, he released his bombs, and as the last one went, the first exploded and rolled his aircraft over. He struggled to regain control, but once he had done so and had time to look around, he found that the Zeppelin was on the ground in flames.

LZ-37 had crashed on top of a convent just outside Ghent, killing two nuns and two orphans, while many more were injured. Only the coxswain of the airship survived.

Meanwhile, unable to restart his engine, Warneford landed to make repairs, finding that a joint on a petrol pipe had fractured. Having fixed the pipe, he managed to restart the engine and took off again at 0315. He lost his way and had to land for fuel, but eventually rejoined his unit at 1030.

This was the first success against the dreaded Zeppelin scourge that had already attacked east coast towns and, a week

An early VC for naval aviation was that awarded to Flying Sub Lt Reginald Warneford, who shot down a Zeppelin over Belgium. Here he is on the right with fellow officers. Note the eagle badge on his sleeve above the curl, rather than the wings of later years. *(IWM Q 69479)*

earlier, had made the first attack on London. Warneford heard of his Victoria Cross from King George V himself by telegram on 8 June, with the official citation on 11 June – the shortest interval between deed and award in the entire history of the VC.

Warneford had become a hero figure overnight. The American journalist Henry Needham visited him for an interview and, on 17 June, Warneford took Needham for a flight in a Farman biplane. Both men were thrown out when the aircraft turned over, and killed.

Lt Frederick Daniel Parslow RNR, in the Atlantic, July 1915, aboard HM Horse Transport *Anglo Californian.*

One of the oldest VC winners, Lt Parslow was 59 years of age and in command of HM Horse Transport *Anglo Californian*, an unarmed converted nitrate carrier, bringing 927 horses from Montreal to Avonmouth. At 0800 on 4 July 1915, when the transport was 90 miles south-west of Queenstown, in the south of Ireland, a large U-boat surfaced about a mile from the ship. The only means of defence was the *Anglo Californian*'s speed, and Parslow immediately turned away from the U-boat and called for full speed, eventually reaching 14kts. He also ordered that signals should be transmitted warning that his ship was under attack. At 0900, the U-boat commander realised that the ship could not be boarded and opened fire with his deck gun, and, maintaining a steady rate of fire, scored a small number of hits on the superstructure and hull.

This hot pursuit continued until 1030, when the U-boat commander hoisted the signal to abandon ship. Realising that he could not shake off his pursuer and that, if the transport were torpedoed, many of the 150 members of the ship's company, which included vets and grooms, would be killed, Parslow ordered the engines to stop and the lifeboats to be launched. Before this could happen, two destroyers, *Mentor* and *Miranda*, signalled that they were coming to his aid and urged him to delay abandoning ship. Parslow got the ship under way again, all the while continuing to transmit signals to provide a homing beacon for the warships. This provoked a fresh volley of fire from the U-boat, concentrating as far as possible on the bridge, but also wrecking the lifeboats on the port side; the occupants of one which had been filling up as the order to abandon ship was giving, were thrown into the sea. The ship's wheel was blown away, so that Parslow's son, who was steering, had to lie on the bridge deck and steer using the spokes. Parslow himself was also on the deck, but had to raise himself from time to time to see where the ship was headed. On one of these occasions, a shell burst nearby, blowing off his head and an arm. Closing to around 50yd, the U-boat crew then appeared on deck and aimed rifle fire at those on the bridge.

Shortly afterwards, the two destroyers arrived, forcing the U-boat to dive at around 1100.

Parslow's determined struggle neverthe-less saved the ship and her cargo. Despite

this, there was a long interval before the VC was gazetted, on 24 May 1919, because the conditions governing the award of the VC had to be widened to allow it to be granted to members of the Merchant Navy, despite Parslow's holding RNR rank at the time. His son was awarded the DSC and promoted to sub-lieutenant.

Lt Cdr Edgar Christopher Cookson, Kut-el-Amara, September 1915, aboard HMS *Comet*.
Lt Cdr Edgar Cookson was in command of the armed paddle-steamer *Comet*, one of an improved flotilla of assorted craft intended to control the Tigris and Euphrates after the British army had secured the province of Basra in Mesopotamia, now Iraq, to safeguard the oilfields in the Middle East and ensure Arab neutrality. The British next felt that they could march on Baghdad, displacing the Turks who occupied the region.

The Turkish defences included a barrier across the Tigris at Es Sinn. The barrier consisted of two iron barges run aground on either bank, connected to a dhow sunk in midstream. The barrier itself was under the control of shore-based artillery, in addition to large numbers of Turkish troops in trenches with machine guns.

On 28 September 1915, just before dark, Cookson took *Comet*, with two armed launches, to destroy the dhow by gunfire. This seemed to have little effect, while Turkish fire had badly damaged *Comet*, wounding many of her crew and putting her guns out of action. In response, *Comet* worked up to full speed and charged the barrier, but the chains held. Cookson then placed his ship alongside the barrier, jumped on to the dhow and began to chop at the cables with an axe. He was hit several times, and was dragged back on board his ship, badly wounded. He ordered his men to return downstream at full speed, telling

Artist's impression of Lt Cdr Edgar Cookson, in command of the armed paddle-steamer *Comet*, attempting to cut through Turkish obstructions in a desperate bid to relieve the garrison at Kut-el-Amara. *(IWM)*

them that the operation was a failure and that he was done for.

Cookson died shortly afterwards. His VC was gazetted on 21 January 1916.

British forces advanced the next day, and after the Turks withdrew, the barrier was dismantled.

Sqn Cdr Richard Frederick Bell Davies, Ferrijik Junction, Thrace, November 1915, with No. 3 Squadron, RNAS.

On 19 November 1915, Sqn Cdr Bell Davies, flying a Nieuport, and Flt Sub Lt Gilbert Smylie, flying an Henri Farman, of No. 3 Squadron, RNAS, were sent to bomb Ferrijik Junction on the mainland of Thrace, north-west of Gallipoli. Both aircraft carried six 20lb bombs. On their way to the target, Smylie's aircraft was hit and the engine failed. Nevertheless, he managed to glide over the target and release five of his bombs before gliding on and force-landing safely on a mudbank beside the Maritsa river. The mudbank had been baked hard by the summer heat and, to keep his aircraft from falling into enemy hands, Smylie set fire to it. As he walked back towards the railway station, Smylie saw Bell Davies circling above him and realised that he was about to land, being unaware of the danger from the unexploded bomb aboard the burning aircraft. Smylie immediately returned to his aircraft and fired his service revolver at the bomb, which exploded, much to the surprise of Bell Davies, who then landed and took Smylie aboard. The passenger seat had been removed from the aircraft to save weight, so Smylie had to crouch under the engine cowling. With the extra weight aboard, Bell Davies needed 150yd to get his aircraft into the air, but both men returned safely to their unit.

Bell Davies's VC was gazetted on 1 January 1916, and at the same time Smylie was gazetted for a DSC.

During his period in the eastern Mediterranean, Bell Davies had been one of the naval airmen taking Nasmith on his reconnaissance flights over the Dardanelles. Later, he commanded the naval air station at Killingholme and then became Senior Flying Officer, Grand Fleet, aboard the seaplane carrier *Campania*. When the RAF was formed, RFC ranks were initially used and he became a lieutenant-colonel, so it is fair to assume that he would have become a wing commander later; but he chose to return to the Royal Navy in the rank of commander. He was promoted to captain in 1926 and spent two years in the Naval Air Section at the Admiralty. He continued to advance in his career and, in 1937 on the return of the Fleet Air Arm to the Royal Navy, he became the first Rear Admiral Naval Air Stations, at a time when all the RN had were those at Lee-on-Solent, Ford, Worthy Down, Donibristle and Bermuda. He retired in 1941, but returned in 1944 in command of the escort carrier *Pretoria Castle*. He died in Haslar Royal Naval Hospital in 1966.

Lt Humphrey Osbaldeson Brooke Firman RN; Lt Cdr Charles Henry Cowley RNVR; River Tigris, 24/5 April 1916, aboard SS *Julnar*.

After the capture of Kut, British forces advanced within 20 miles of Baghdad, before being force back on Kut by the Turks, who then besieged the British garrison. A number of attempts were made to relieve the garrison, the last of which involved the river steamer SS *Julnar*. Volunteers were sought for this hazardous mission, and eventually Lt Humphrey Firman was placed in command with, unusually, a lieutenant-commander as his second in command – Henry Cowley from the Lynch Brothers steamer *Mejidieh*, which also provided the *Julnar*'s engineering officer. The crew was completed by twelve ratings from the river gunboat flotilla.

At around 2000 on 24 April 1916, the *Julnar* left Fallahiya with 270 tons of supplies, but despite a heavy artillery barrage, designed to keep the Turks preoccupied, and a heavy overcast sky, within ninety minutes her presence was known to the Turks, who sent up star shells. The river was in full flood, and against the strong current the *Julnar* could only make 6kts. She had to cover some 25 miles, but, before the first 5 miles were covered, she was already riddled by machine-gun fire, and at Es Sinn, heavy artillery opened up on her. On reaching Magasis, the site of a fort and a sharp right hand bend in the river, they found a barrier made of steel hawsers, with strong Turkish forces on both banks. They attempted to force the barrier, but heavy fire destroyed *Julnar*'s bridge, killing Firman, while the ship's rudder became entangled in the steel hawsers and she ran aground. Turkish troops then stormed aboard, capturing the survivors and taking the supplies intended for Kut.

Cowley had minor wounds when captured, but he was separated from the other survivors and, although the Turks maintained that he died in an escape attempt, there seems to be little doubt that he was executed. He had spent most of his life in Mesopotamia and the Turks regarded him as an Ottoman subject, and therefore a traitor.

Both men were gazetted for posthumous VCs on 2 February 1917.

Cdr The Hon. Edward Barry Stewart Bingham RN; Boy First Class John Travers Cornwell RN; Cdr Loftus William Jones RN; Francis John William Harvey RMLI; at the Battle of Jutland, 31 May 1916.

As mentioned earlier in Chapter 7, Jutland, on 31 May 1916, was the major sea battle that both the Grand Fleet and the High Seas Fleet had been planning for since the outbreak of war, if not earlier.

Boy First Class Jack Cornwell, who remains the youngest-ever naval recipient of the Victoria Cross, killed in the Battle of Jutland at the age of just 16 years. *(IWM)*

Cdr The Hon. Edward Bingham was in command of the 13th Destroyer Flotilla aboard *Nestor*, which, accompanied by her sister ships *Nomad* and *Nicator*, was sent on ahead to torpedo the German battlecruiser fleet. Shortly after 1615, as they were within 3,000yd of the battlecruisers, the destroyers came under heavy fire from the secondary armament of the German ships. First, *Nomad* was hit and had to stop, and then *Nestor* was also badly damaged by shellfire and swerved, narrowly missing *Nicator*, which escaped with minimal damage.

The two crippled destroyers were left behind by the battlecruisers, but they soon saw the main force of the battle fleet steaming directly towards them. *Nomad* was soon taking heavy gunfire, while those aboard *Nestor* were busy destroying confidential papers, including the code books and charts, as they awaited their fate. Their last torpedo was fired at the Germans, and then it was their turn to take the German fire. As the shells exploded, the ship began to settle by the stern, and Bingham gave the order to abandon ship. Bingham was among those picked up by German ships and became a prisoner of war.

Shortly afterwards, the 3rd Battle Cruiser Squadron sent the light cruiser *Chester* to investigate gun flashes to the south-west. At 1740, *Chester* was in action against four German light cruisers, outgunned with her six 5.5in guns facing thirty 5.9in guns. Within a few minutes, *Chester* had been hit seventeen times, losing her fire control and the crews of half her guns, with thirty men dead and another forty-six wounded. The casualties included the crew of the forward 5.5in turret, but after the battle, just one member of the gun crew remained, Boy First Class Jack Cornwell, the sight-setter, not yet 16 years old. Mortally wounded, he had remained at his post awaiting orders. He died from his wounds in hospital at Grimsby on 2 June.

Chester fell back on the 3rd Battle Cruiser Squadron, which managed to surprise the German light cruisers and damage three of them. The Germans then sent destroyers to engage the British battlecruisers, and these ran into a counter-attack by the British 4th Destroyer Flotilla led by Cdr Loftus Jones aboard *Shark*. An early victim was the German destroyer *B-98*, but then *Shark* was badly damaged, with her fo'c'sle wrecked and the forward 4in gun lost. Jones refused help from another ship for fear that she would be lost if she stopped. Three German cruisers now concentrated their fire on *Shark* as she drifted helplessly, wrecking her after gun. When the boats were turned out so that they could abandon ship, they, too, were blown away. Once again aboard a destroyer, confidential papers were destroyed and rafts readied. Jones himself had been badly wounded in the leg, but he went to the midships gun and, with three ABs, started to fire at a German destroyer, *V-48*, damaging her. The German destroyers then came close and poured their concentrated fire into *Shark*, blowing Jones's leg away above the knee. As his wound was being attended to, he realised that the ensign had been destroyed in the blast and ordered another one to be raised. As the ship settled in the water, a German destroyer fired a torpedo and the destroyer then sank quickly. Jones was seen later on a liferaft wearing a lifejacket, encouraging other survivors to sing, before the loss of blood and exhaustion took their toll, and he was not among those picked up.

Because of delays in getting the full story of his courage, his VC was not gazetted until 6 March 1917. The ratings who had stood by him on the midships gun all received the DSM.

Maj Francis Harvey of the Royal Marine Light Infantry was in command of the Royal Marine detachment aboard the battlecruiser *Lion*. When the ship was hit amidships on Q turret, the shell penetrated the turret and exploded, blowing the roof out and killing the gun's crew, as well as starting a fire. This was a moment of extreme danger as, to expedite the rate of fire, magazine doors were left open and cordite charges were left in their cages or on the deck of the turret. The danger was that a flash from a hit on the turret could travel down into the magazine and cause a tremendous explosion that could tear the ship apart. Already, two battlecruisers, *Indefatigable* and *Queen Mary*, had blown up, the first with just two survivors from her 1,017 crew, and the second with twenty from a ship's company of 1,266.

Mortally wounded, with severe burns and suffering from shock, Harvey managed to give the order to close the magazine doors and flood the magazine, and so, although the fire ignited the cordite in the turret and the resultant flash went through to the magazine handling room, killing every man there, the magazine itself was saved, and so, too, was the ship.

Cornwell, Harvey and Bingham were gazetted on 15 September 1916.

Lt Gordon Campbell RN; Lt Ronald Niel Stuart RNR; Seaman William Williams RNR; Lt Charles George Bonner RCNR; AB Ernest Herbert Pitcher RNR; Atlantic and Bay of Biscay, 1917, serving in Q ships.

The Q ship HMS *Farnborough* beached after her engagement with *U-83*, for which her commanding officer, Lt Gordon Campbell, won the VC.

Seaman William Williams RNR was the other recipient in the crew ballot for the two VCs awarded to the ship's company of *Pargust*. (*Private Collection*)

The Admiralty's reluctance to instigate a convoy system during the First World War meant that a number of other expedients had to be tried, including the Q ships. As mentioned in Chapter 8, these consisted mainly of a variety of merchantmen intended to attract a U-boat, and then, once the submarine was within range, uncover a variety of weapons, including guns and torpedoes and, later, depth charges. The crew of the Q ship had to lie motionless out of sight until it was time to attack the U-boat, although a variation on this was to have a number of members of the crew as a 'panic party', who could be seen by the U-boat crew to be getting ready to abandon ship.

Lt Gordon Campbell's Q ship was the *Loderer*, an ex-collier with a 12pdr hidden in a steering house aft, another two behind hinged flaps on the main deck, and two more in cabins on the upper deck. For good measure, there was also a 6pdr on each end of the bridge and a Maxim machine gun in a hen-coop amidships. Campbell was the sole regular among the ship's company of sixty-seven men. The ship was renamed *Farnborough* during a passage from Devonport to Queenstown in the south of Ireland early in 1916, and later again renamed *Q5*.

At 0640 on 22 March 1916, *Farnborough* sighted a submarine, partially submerged, which fired a torpedo that missed. When the submarine surfaced, the 'panic party' started their routine, taking to the boats while one of them carried a stuffed parrot in a cage. *U-68* then moved closer to the ship, ready to sink her, but at 800yd, *Farnborough*'s guns opened fire, hitting the submarine several

times before using depth charges to deliver the *coup de grâce*. There were no survivors. For this, Campbell was promoted to commander and received the first of three DSOs.

There was a further incident, in which a U-boat just managed to get away. Then, at 0945 on 17 February 1917, west of Ireland, *Q5* was hit by a torpedo by the engine room bulkhead and started to settle by the stern. This would have been sufficient for the whole ship's company to abandon ship, but only the 'panic party' did so. The submarine then approached so close – to within 20yd of the ship – that those left aboard could see her shape beneath the surface of the water, while to keep concealed in the flooded machinery spaces, the engineers and stokers had to lie flat on gratings. The U-boat did not surface until 1005, at 300yd, but in a position where none of *Q5*'s guns could be brought to bear on her. It was not until she passed down the ship's port side towards the panic party boats that an opportunity to open fire occurred, and at 1010 *Q5* opened fire at just 100yd. Most of the forty-five shells fired found their target, sinking *U-83* and leaving just two survivors.

It looked as if *Q5* herself was finished, but a destroyer and sloop appeared to take her in tow and she was safely beached. Campbell received the VC, and the ship's first lieutenant the DSO.

Campbell's crew followed him to his next ship, yet another converted collier, originally named *Vittoria*, but for Q ship purposes renamed *Pargust*. This ship had a heavier armament, with a 4in gun, four 12pdrs, two 14in torpedo tubes and depth charges. Improvements had also been made to the concealment and to the accommodation, and there was a more up-to-date wireless.

At 0800 on 7 June 1917, in mid-Atlantic, a torpedo hit the ship from close range. Once again, the panic party abandoned ship, still with the stuffed parrot. The U-boat's periscope was first spotted at around 0815, but it did not surface until around 0835. The guns opened fire at about 50yd range, firing thirty-eight rounds, and before she could get away, *UC-29*, a minelaying submarine, blew up and sank, again leaving just two survivors. *Pargust*, too, was saved, being towed back to Queenstown. The King awarded the VC to the entire ship, but under the rules the crew had to ballot for one officer and one seaman to receive the award. They chose Lt Ronald Niel Stuart RCNR and Seaman William Williams RNR. Several other members of the crew also received medals, while Campbell got a bar to his DSO and was promoted to captain.

Once again, Campbell was given another ship, losing his first lieutenant to go off to his first command, but otherwise retaining almost all of his crew. The next ship was yet another collier, *Dunraven*.

On 8 August 1917, at 1058, a U-boat was sighted ahead on the horizon while *Dunraven* was some 130 miles south-west of Ushant, off Brittany. The Q ship continued as if she had not seen the submarine, which dived and then surfaced astern of her, opening fire at a range of 3 miles. By this time, many merchantmen had defensive measures in place, and so Campbell was able to make smoke, while his men were able to man a 2.5pdr and let off a number of inaccurate and panicky shots. *UC-71* shelled the Q ship for half an hour without hitting, and so closed to 1,000yd, at which point Campbell stopped his vessel, let off steam amidships as if there had been a hit, and sent away his panic party. Unfortunately, as he turned to prepare to fire, the submarine finally scored three hits on the poop deck, detonating a depth charge, blowing Lt Bonner out of his hiding place and starting a fire on the deck, leaving several men still in hiding near the ammunition lockers while a fire raged around them. By this time, the U-boat was hidden by the smoke, but at 1258, she emerged again and Campbell prepared to open fire. There was then a tremendous explosion aft, blowing the 4in gun and its crew into the air, one man landing in the sea and others falling on to the 'deck cargo' of mock railway wagons, whose canvas broke their fall.

Realising that *Dunraven* was a decoy, the U-boat dived, even though one of two shots that were fired might have hit her. Campbell sent away a second panic party, but at 1320 *Dunraven* was torpedoed. A third panic party was sent away, leaving just two guns manned. As the fire aft raged and ammunition continued to explode, the submarine surfaced and again started firing shells at the Q ship, before submerging again at 1450. Campbell fired two torpedoes at the periscope, but missed. By this time *UC-71* was also out of torpedoes and, in any case, would not surface, as help for *Dunraven* was on its way. Nevertheless, the submarine was never seen again.

Once again the ship was awarded the VC, and on this occasion the ballot choose Lt Charles Bonner, RNR and the 4in gunlayer AB Ernest Herbert Pitcher, RNR.

Campbell then went ashore to become flag captain to Adm Bayly, who was in command of the Q ships. After the war, Campbell's commands included the battlecruiser *Tiger* and the Simonstown naval base in South Africa. Later, he became naval ADC to the King and was then promoted to rear admiral, before retiring in 1928. He subsequently became an MP, but retired after a severe illness, although by this time he was a vice-admiral on the retired list. He died in 1953.

Capt Archibald Bisset Smith, Atlantic, 10 March 1917, aboard SS *Otaki*.

The threat posed by German commerce raiders had eased considerably by 1917, but on 10 March, the New Zealand Shipping Company steamer *Otaki* was 350 miles east of the Azores, on a voyage from London to New York, when she encountered the *Mowe*, a converted fruit carrier. *Otaki*'s master, Capt Archibald Bisset Smith, first saw the German ship at around 1430, at about 3 miles on his port quarter, in poor visibility due to heavy rain squalls. Suspecting an enemy ship, he did not stop, but increased his speed to Otaki's maximum 15kts.

Mowe was smaller than *Otaki*, but faster, and in addition to some armour plating, her conversion had included fitting four 5.9in, one 4.1in and two 22pdr guns, a formidable armament that had seen her sink or seize twenty-one ships on her second raiding mission. She had been at sea since the previous November. By comparison, *Otaki* simply mounted a single 4.7in gun on her stern.

Mowe gave chase, needing to get closer to *Otaki* in the poor visibility and heavy swell to ensure accuracy once firing started. When the range had closed to about a mile, a warning shot was fired, but *Otaki* continued on her way and those aboard the German ship could see the stern gun being uncovered and manned. The gunners aboard *Mowe* opened fire without further warning, and both ships exchanged fire for around twenty minutes. Several shots from *Mowe* landed on *Otaki*, killing some members of her crew and starting fires. Nevertheless, the battle was far from one-sided, and *Otaki* landed seven shells on her pursuer, hitting the signal bridge and a coal bunker, starting a fire that lasted for three days, and also putting one shell alongside the funnel as well as others on the superstructure. It was, in fact, excellent gunnery that not only surprised the Germans, but also caused considerable damage and killed or wounded fifteen men. Yet *Otaki* was heavily outgunned; no less than thirty shells hit her and, as evening approached, she was on fire. Despite the heavy seas, Bisset Smith decided to abandon ship to save as many lives as possible, since six men had been killed and another nine wounded out of her ship's company of seventy-one. The boats were lowered, leaving just Bisset Smith, his chief officer and the ship's carpenter on board. Expecting the master to follow them, the two men jumped into the sea, but Bisset Smith remained aboard to go down with his ship, which sank with her red ensign still flying. *Mowe* picked up the survivors, who became prisoners of war.

Bisset Smith's VC was gazetted on 24 May 1919, after the award had been extended to Merchant Navy personnel. His chief officer was awarded the DSO, and the gun crew received the DSM.

Maj Frederick William Lumsden RMA, Francilly, France, 3/4 April 1917.

One of the most decorated members of the Royal Marine Artillery – he won the DSO with three bars, a CB and a Croix de Guerre – Maj Frederick Lumsden was with his unit when it took part in the capture of the village of Francilly in the run up to the major battle at Arras, which opened on 9 April. The advancing troops discovered that the Germans had left behind, in no man's land, a battery of six field guns, which Lumsden was determined to take, even though their position was under heavy fire, as the Germans in turn were determined that the guns should be destroyed rather than captured.

After dark, Lumsden led four teams of horses covered by a force of infantry into no man's land, but lost one team, which had to withdraw because it had taken such heavy casualties. Lumsden went on with the infantry to secure the guns under heavy fire, then called the three remaining teams forward, sending two of them back with guns before taking the third team and its gun to his own lines. Lumsden then went back with his team and took two more guns. The Germans then counter-attacked and disabled the one remaining gun, but Lumsden was soon back to drive them off and seize the sixth gun.

For his courage and daring, Lumsden was given temporary promotion to brigadier-general and command of 14th Brigade. He was gazetted for the VC on 8 June 1917.

On 1 June 1918, Lumsden was awarded the CB, but may not have known of this before he was killed by a sniper's bullet on 3 June at Blairville, near Arras.

A/Lt William Edward Sanders RNR, Atlantic, 30 April 1917, aboard the Q ship *Prize*.

A/Lt William Sanders was in command of the Q ship *Prize*. The ship was aptly named,

as she had been the first prize captured from the Germans at the start of the war, having originally been the *Else*, and her new name on being taken by the British at first had been *First Prize*. She was a 200-ton schooner and was chosen for Q ship duties because, although the U-boat commanders had become suspicious of steamers, they still seemed willing to attack sailing ships. When she was converted into a Q ship in 1917, she was given two 12pdrs and two Lewis guns.

On 30 April 1917 soon after 2000, a submarine surfaced off *Prize*'s port quarter. This was *U-93*, on her first patrol, although her commander had considerable experience and had already accounted for eleven British ships. *U-93* opened fire at 2040 at a range of 3,000yd, holing *Prize* in three places along the waterline, setting her engine room on fire. Two shells also hit her main mast. This justified the panic party taking to the boats. At 2105, *U-93* approached the crippled ship, coming within 80yd, at which point Sanders ran up the white ensign and the gun ports fell open. The first shell from the forward 12pdr hit the U-boat's forward 4.1in gun, knocking the gun and its crew into the sea. The Lewis guns sprayed the deck of the U-boat while the 12-pdrs continued to punish her, wrecking her conning tower and starting fires within the submarine. *U-93* attempted to ram *Prize*, but sheered off under the heavy fire, and shortly afterwards seemed to sink.

The panic party in their boats picked up the submarine's commanding officer, one of his officers and a petty officer, who helped *Prize*'s crew plug the holes along the waterline and pump out, so that she eventually reached Kinsale safely.

Sanders was promoted to lieutenant-commander, and his fellow officers at the Milford Haven naval base presented him with a sword of honour.

Meanwhile, *U-93* had not been sunk, and her first lieutenant managed to take her back to Germany despite the fact that she could not dive because of the damage to her conning tower. This also meant that *Prize*'s cover was blown, and when she was discovered by *U-48* in the Atlantic on 14 August 1917, she was immediately torpedoed and went down with all hands.

Skipper Joseph Watt RNR, Straits of Otranto, 14/15 May 1917, aboard drifter *Gowan Lea.*

The Straits of Otranto were the way for the Austro-Hungarian navy to leave the Adriatic and enter the Mediterranean, and because of this, a substantial barrage was placed across it, strung between no less than 120 net drifters and thirty motor launches, all carrying depth charges to drop on submarines, as well as a small gun. The Italian navy provided destroyers and sloops, with limited aerial observation from kite balloons. This massive construction only succeeded in stopping two submarines, but it had a massive irritant effect on the Austrians, who attacked the barrage on four occasions during March and April 1917.

On the night of 14/15 May, three light cruisers, *Novara*, *Saida* and *Helgoland*, were sent down the Adriatic to attack the barrage, each being assigned to one-third of its length. Before attacking the drifters, clearly massively outgunned by the light cruisers, the Austrians offered their crews the opportunity to surrender and take to their boats, and some did accept this offer. Most of the drifter crews did not leave their ships until they were crippled by gunfire, and even then some crewmen continued to fire their small guns until they were killed at their posts. The Austrians later described the fighting of the drifters as a 'mad resistance'.

When *Novara* came within 100yd of the drifter *Gowan Lea*, her skipper, Joseph Watt, ignored the call to surrender and ordered full speed ahead, while his crew were called to give three cheers and fight to the finish. They got off just one shot from their 57mm gun before it was knocked out by a 4.1in shell from the cruiser. The drifter's crew struggled to get their gun working again, although their efforts were hampered when a shell exploded a box of ammunition on deck, wounding one man seriously. *Novara*

Skipper J. Watt and the crew of the drifter *Gowan Lea*. *(Private Collection)*

had by this time moved on, convinced that the drifter must be sinking having taken such punishment, but the crew of *Gowan Lea* then went alongside another drifter, whose crew were all dead or wounded, to render assistance, before proceeding to Otranto themselves.

Out of forty-seven drifters on duty that night, fourteen were sunk and another three badly damaged, while seventy-two men were taken prisoner.

Skipper Watt's VC was gazetted on 29 August 1917, while he also received French, Serbian and Italian awards. Altogether, the men aboard the drifters won five DSCs and a bar to a DSC, five CGMs, eighteen DSMs and a bar to a DSM.

After the war, Watt returned to his peacetime trade as a fisherman, with his own herring drifter, working from Fraserburgh and later from Lowestoft, being known to his friends as 'VC Joe'. In the Second World War, he was regarded as being too old for active service, but his drifter was one of many supporting the ships of the Home Fleet. He died back in Fraserburgh in 1955.

Skipper Thomas Crisp RNR, North Sea, 14 August 1917, aboard HM Special Services Smack *Nelson.*

Skipper Thomas Crisp was fishing aboard his smack in company with another smack, *Ethel and Millie*, in the North Sea on 14 August 1917 when at 1445, he saw a submarine more than 3 miles away in a light mist. As he ordered the crew to clear the decks for action, a shell from the U-boat exploded 100yd off his port bow. While *Nelson*'s gun was manned, the range was too great, and Crisp ordered that fire was to be held until the U-boat came closer. A fourth shell from the U-boat holed the smack beneath the water line; the seventh shattered Crisp's legs at the hip and

partially disembowelled him. Despite his terrible wounds, Crisp remained at his post and ordered his gunners to fire, while his boat's carrier pigeon was readied to fly, carrying the message that they were under attack and giving their position. The U-boat then turned its attention to the *Ethel and Millie.*

As the smack settled in the water, Crisp gave the order to abandon ship, refusing his son's request that he join the rest of the crew in the boat, and remained aboard as *Nelson* sank a quarter of an hour later, her white ensign still flying. The other smack's crew were taken prisoner by the Germans, but the *Nelson*'s men rowed away and escaped, thanks to the mist that was by this time falling. They were not picked up until the following day by a destroyer.

Crisp's VC was gazetted on 2 November 1917. His son was awarded a DSM and LS Ross, the gunner, a bar to his DSM, which he had won in an earlier action.

By the time of this, her last action, the *Nelson* was no stranger to Royal Navy service. F.W. Moxey of Lowestoft offered his smack *G & E* (named after his children, Gladys and Edward) to the Admiralty as early as 1915, when U-boats first started attacking the fishing fleets, with the suggestion that she be armed with a gun. The initial reaction of the Admiralty was to refuse this offer, but before long there was a change of mind and many trawlers and drifters were taken up and guns fitted, their crews enlisted into the RNR. Names were changed as well, and *G & E* soon became *I'll Try*, and then later *Nelson*. On 11 August 1915, under the command of Lt Cdr Hammond, she sank *UB-4*, from which Hammond succeeded in bringing the German ensign and flagstaff back to Lowestoft. Under Crisp's command, as *I'll Try*, she scored hits on a U-boat in a game of cat and mouse over several hours, for which Crisp received the DSC.

OS John Henry Carless RNR, Heligoland Bight, 17 November 1917, aboard HMS *Caledon*.

OS John Carless was a rammer manning one of the guns aboard the light cruiser *Caledon* during the Battle of the Heligoland Bight on 17 November 1917. The battle occurred when German minesweepers were operating more than a hundred miles from the main submarine bases, anxious to keep the approaches clear of mines. On becoming aware of this, Beatty, by this time in command of the Grand Fleet, ordered a force of light cruisers into the Bight, with battleship cover in case the two German battleships covering the minesweepers intervened. An action duly erupted, during which the German battleships *Kaiser* and *Kaiserin* fired salvoes that straddled the light cruiser *Caledon* and her sister ship *Calypso*. One of the guns aboard *Caledon* was hit and the entire gun crew was killed or wounded. Although Carless was fatally wounded in the stomach, he continued to serve his gun and helped to remove the other wounded. When he collapsed, he recovered and got to his feet, and cheered in the replacement gun crew, before he collapsed for a second time and died.

His VC was gazetted on 17 May 1918.

Lt Cdr Geoffrey Saxton White RN, Dardanelles, 28 January 1918, aboard HM Submarine *E14*.

E14 was, of course, the submarine in which Lt Cdr Boyle had penetrated the Dardanelles earlier in the war, but by January 1918, she was under the command of Lt Cdr Geoffrey White. White had undertaken aerial reconnaissance over the Dardanelles, where the German battlecruiser *Goeben* had run aground off Nagara Point after being damaged by mines during a sortie with the light cruiser *Breslau*. The *Breslau* had been sunk by mines after she and *Goeben* had sunk the British monitors *M28* and *Lord Raglan*. White and *E14* were on patrol near the Straits of Otranto and were ordered to Mudros to prepare for an attack on the *Goeben*.

E14 left Mudros on 27 January, and made her way through the series of obstacles, natural and man-made, that were a feature of all such operations in the Dardanelles, only to find that *Goeben* had been refloated and had left. Turning round, White took *E14* down the Dardanelles and, at 0845 on 28 January, he attacked a Turkish ship, firing a torpedo. Eleven seconds after the torpedo had been fired, there was an explosion ahead of the submarine, either from the torpedo exploding prematurely or from a depth charge attack. The explosion sprang open the forward torpedo hatch and water flooded into the submarine. The lights failed and, losing her trim, *E14* started to float towards the surface. As she surfaced, the shore batteries opened fire, but she dived again before they could find their range. Nevertheless, the air inside the submarine, having been submerged for so long, was by this time so bad that White decided to make a dash for it on the surface. The artillery fire resumed as the submarine raced down the Dardanelles and, as several shells hit *E14*, she was soon badly damaged. White decided to run the submarine aground to give his crew a better chance of survival as she was so badly damaged that diving again was no longer an option but, before he could do so, a shell blew him out of the conning tower. Just seven members of his crew survived to become prisoners of war.

White's posthumous VC was gazetted on 24 May 1919.

Cdr Arthur Francis Blakeney Carpenter RN; Sgt Norman Augustus Finch RMLI; Lt Cdr Arthur Leyland Harrison RN; Capt Edward Bamford RMLI; AB Albert Edward McKenzie RNR; Zeebrugge, 22/3 April 1918.

Throughout the First World War, the Royal Navy had planned to seal off the Belgian ports of Zeebrugge and Ostend once they fell into German hands. At Zeebrugge, more than thirty destroyers and torpedo boats were based, and about the same number of U-boats. Attempts by the British army to reach the ports had failed in 1917, and so the task was given to the Dover Patrol, by this time under the command of the gung-ho Vice Adm Roger Keyes. The plan was to sink blockships in the entrance to the canal at Zeebrugge using a smoke-screen as cover, while infantry attacked the mole batteries. A section of the mole would also be blown up to prevent the Germans sending reinforcements. The assault would be conducted by the 4th Battalion, Royal Marine Light Infantry, augmented by a force of 200 naval personnel who had been given training in fighting with rifle and bayonet and hand grenades. Another fifty naval volunteers formed the demolition party.

The assault force would be landed in the elderly cruiser *Vindictive*, modified with special ramps cut into her side so that large numbers of men could storm ashore, and special fenders and derricks to enable her to stay alongside. Her upperworks were given additional protection, and Lewis guns were mounted above the bridge position. An 11in howitzer was placed on the quarterdeck, along with two extra 7.5in guns and flame-throwers for use against German troops. Two former Mersey ferries, *Iris II* and *Daffodil*, were also to carry troops.

The assault would have to cover some 70 miles, with the final stages including German minefields, narrow channels and sandbanks. The date chosen was the night of 22/3 April, when moonless conditions

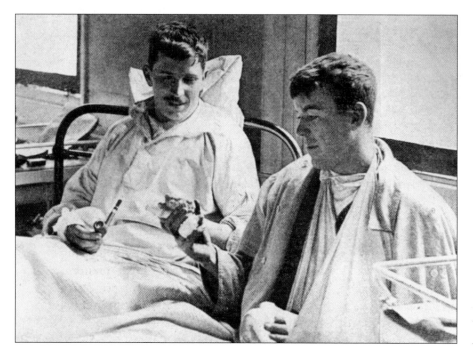

Sergeant Norman Finch RMLI (left) was one of several VCs in the raid on Zeebrugge. He is seen here in bed in hospital, recovering from his wounds. (*via Steve Snelling*)

coincided with a high tide at Zeebrugge just before midnight.

Commanded by Cdr Alfred Carpenter, *Vindictive* was spotted while she was some 300yd off the mole, and immediately heavy German fire was brought down upon her. Her superstructure, including the wheelhouse and bridge, funnels and ventilators, were soon badly damaged. The commander of the naval assault force, Capt Halahan, and of the Marines, Col Elliot, were both killed, as were many of their officers, and others were wounded. Despite this hail of fire, Carpenter brought the old cruiser alongside the mole just a minute late, although some 300yd further from the batteries than planned, and then went down to the upper deck to supervise the landings, made more difficult as the tide had started to turn. Damage to the ship and the swell made it difficult to get her tight alongside until the ferry *Daffodil* managed to push her in, even though her own captain had been half-blinded by a shell exploding.

Meanwhile, Lt Rigby had directed the Marines in the improvised fighting top above the bridge to bring down fire on the enemy guns (although locating them in the dark was difficult), spraying the mole with bullets. Just as *Vindictive* drew alongside, the fighting top was hit by two shells, killing Rigby and wounding or killing everyone else. However, the second in command, Sgt Finch, who remounted a Lewis gun, got it back into action and, despite being seriously wounded, kept up a heavy fire that was credited with saving many lives among the troops storming the mole. He only abandoned his position when a further shell wrecked the fighting top completely.

With Halahan dead, Lt Cdr Harrison took command of the naval party, even though his jaw had been broken by a shell splinter as the cruiser had approached the mole. In great pain, he led his men towards the seaward batteries on the mole, but he was killed and all of his men either killed or wounded. At his side was AB Albert McKenzie, in charge of a Lewis gun, who advanced down the mole firing his gun with devastating effect.

Capt Edward Bamford landed on the mole with No. 5 Platoon and immediately led his men on to the upper promenade of the mole, where they attacked snipers who had been firing at men on the deck of *Vindictive*. They hailed *Iris II*, but found that she could not get alongside to land her troops. Bamford then gathered the survivors of his platoon and collected men from two other platoons before leading an attack on the batteries at the end of the mole. When they heard the recall signals from the ferries at 1250, they returned in small groups so as not to clog the scaling ladders.

Vindictive needed the help of *Daffodil* to pull away from the mole, but not before two of the three blockships had slipped past and been scuttled in the canal entrance. For their part in the operation, both ships had the prefix 'Royal' added to their names at the behest of King George V.

Carpenter's VC was as a result of a ballot by the ships' companies of the three assault ships, as was that of McKenzie. Capt Bamford and Finch were elected similarly by the officers and men of the RMA and RMLI. All four were gazetted on 23 July 1918. Harrison's VC was gazetted on 17 March 1919.

Carpenter was promoted to captain and, after the war, remained in the service with a number of commands. He was promoted to rear admiral in 1929 and retired, although he was appointed vice-admiral on the retired list in 1934. He did not return to sea during the Second World War, but commanded his local Home Guard battalion. In 1945, he returned to the Admiralty as Director of Shipping. He died at Lydney, Gloucestershire, in 1955.

Bamford was promoted to brevet major. He was the only one of the VCs at Zeebrugge not to be wounded. He became a full major in 1928 while serving in Hong Kong. He died from a mysterious illness in September of that year.

Finch remained in the Royal Marines after the war, until his retirement in 1929, but rejoined in 1939 and was soon promoted to quartermaster sergeant and later to temporary lieutenant (QM). He died in Portsmouth in 1966.

McKenzie seemed to be recovering from the wounds he received during his charge along the mole, but died from influenza during the epidemic of 1918.

Lt Cdr George Nicholson Bradford RN, Zeebrugge, 22/3 April 1918.

Lt Cdr George Bradford was in command of the naval storming party aboard the ex-Mersey ferry *Iris II* at Zeebrugge. The ferries were used because they drew just 11ft, and it was recognised that the great draught of *Vindictive* would make it difficult for her to draw alongside the mole, and could even result in her grounding or being mined during the approach. Both ships received extensive armour protection for the upper deck and special anchors were fitted to catch the mole parapet.

Iris II came alongside the mole at 1215, some way ahead of where *Vindictive* was attempting to draw alongside. In the swell, it was going to be difficult to use the parapet anchors, and when Lt Claude Hawkins did manage to get to the top of the mole using a scaling ladder, he was attacked and killed. Bradford then climbed a derrick that was protruding from the ship over the mole, and despite the fact that it was crashing into the mole as the ship tossed and rolled in the swell, managed to jump with the anchor on to the mole amid heavy fire. He had only just placed the anchor in position when he

was killed, his body, riddled with machine-gun bullets, falling into the water between the ferry and the mole.

Seeing the difficulties facing *Iris II*, Carpenter aboard *Vindictive* signalled her to leave, but at that moment the anchor cable either parted or was shot away, so that Bradford's sacrifice had been in vain. *Iris II* went alongside *Vindictive* so that her storming party could reach the mole through the cruiser, but only a few men had gone across when the recall signal was given. In her withdrawal, the ferry was hit twice by heavy artillery fire, with heavy loss of life among the sailors left down below.

Bradford's VC was gazetted on 17 March 1919. His body was recovered by the Germans some miles down the coast at Blankenberge.

Lt Richard Douglas Sandford RN, Zeebrugge, 22/3 April 1918.

Lt Richard Sandford was in charge of one of the submarines used by the naval demolition party, intending to blow up the 300yd-long viaduct that would be used by the Germans to reinforce the mole. The original idea had been to use rafts loaded with demolition charges, but in the end Keyes decided to use two obsolete submarines, *C1* and *C3*. Both submarines were loaded with demolition charges, about 5 tons of Amatol explosive in each, and each was manned by crews of two officers and four men. Special gyroscopic steering gear was fitted so that the crews could set the course and then take to the motor skiffs provided, before the submarine hit the viaduct and exploded. The submarines were towed to the area, but *C1* broke her tow and was unable to go any further.

C3 got to within reach of Zeebrugge and slipped her tow under cover of a smokescreen. At around midnight, she emerged from the smokescreen and was immediately

HMS *Thetis*, sunk as a blockship at Zeebrugge, 1918. *(IWM Q 745)*

picked up by the Germans, although they did not open fire, possibly believing that she was one of their own craft returning. Sandford decided not to risk using the gyroscopic steering and conned the submarine towards the target. He called the crew upon deck before making his last course correction and at 0015 he ran *C3* straight into the viaduct support at more than 9kts, buckling the steel girders, so that her bows stuck out from the other side and her conning tower was wedged among the girders. He set the fuses, which had a twelve-minute delay, and ordered the crew into the motor skiff. The collision had dispelled any notion in the minds of the Germans that this was one of their own; they opened fire, hitting Sandford, his coxswain and the stoker. The crew got into the skiff, but the motor would not start and they had to resort to oars and row. Sandford and the two oarsmen were hit again, but two others took their place. They were just 300yd away when *C3* blew up, destroying around 100ft of the viaduct and preventing reinforcements from using it. Sandford and his companions were then picked up by a picket boat from a destroyer.

Sandford's VC was gazetted on 23 July 1918. He spent three months in hospital recovering from wounds in his hand and thigh. His second in command received the DSO, and the four ratings all received the CGM. Sandford died from typhoid fever in Grangetown, Yorkshire, in November 1918.

Lt Percy Thompson Dean RNVR Zeebrugge, 22/3 April 1918.

Lt Percy Dean was the first RNVR officer to win a VC. The main aim of the Zeebrugge raid was to scuttle three blockships, the elderly light cruisers *Thetis*, *Intrepid* and *Iphigenia*, in the canal entrance. The three ships rounded the mole at 1220, whereupon the guns on the mole opened fire immediately. *Thetis*, in the lead, took most of the fire, but shielded her two companions. She missed the gap in the net defences, doubtless because of the heavy fire, and the nets wound around her screws, so that she ran aground short of the entrance. *Intrepid* nevertheless arrived at the canal mouth unharmed and was placed across the channel when *Iphigenia* collided with her. Lt Bonham-Carter, *Intrepid*'s commanding officer, immediately blew the charges and his ship settled, almost blocking the canal. *Iphigenia* was placed alongside her, effectively blocking the canal entrance.

The blockships had been followed by ML *282*, commanded by Lt Percy Dean, who had endured the heavy fire that had been aimed at the three cruisers. Despite this, he was described as handling his motor launch as 'calmly as if engaged in a practice manoeuvre' and took off more than 100 officers and men from the three ships. Three men were shot down beside him, and

at one moment he found German troops looking down on him; he emptied six revolvers at them. He kept close to the side of the channel so that the Germans could not depress their guns at him, and when the steering gear broke down as he was about to clear the canal, he manoeuvred on engines. The motor launch had reached open water when Dean was told that an officer had fallen overboard, and so he turned back, putting one engine ahead and the other astern, to pick the man up. Although the small No. 282 was hit several times, she was not sunk and was able to transfer her passengers to a destroyer.

Dean's VC was gazetted on 23 July 1918.

After the war, Dean entered the Commons as one of the members for Blackburn, and remained in Parliament until 1922. He died in March 1939, in London.

Lt Victor Alexander Charles Crutchley RN; Lt Geoffrey Henage Drummond RNVR; Lt Roland Richard Louis Bourke RNVR; Ostend, 9/10 May 1918.

The Ostend raid was intended to take place on the same night as the Zeebrugge raid, but the Germans seemed to have been expecting the attack and changed the navigation marks. This, with a change in the wind that blew the smokescreen away, saw the raid aborted when one of the blockships ran aground and the other collided with it. The ships' scuttling charges were exploded so that they would not fall into enemy hands, and the crews were taken off.

Vice Adm Keyes was pressed to allow a second attempt. Possibly believing that she was a lucky ship, or because the modifications for the Zeebrugge raid meant that she was no longer suitable as a cruiser, *Vindictive* was chosen as one of the blockships, with another old cruiser, *Sappho*, as the other. *Sappho* had to return with engine trouble, and so it was left to *Vindictive* on her own to block the port.

Aboard *Vindictive*, Cdr Godsal encountered thick fog but he managed to place his ship right in the harbour mouth and was attempting to turn her across the channel when a shell hit the bridge and killed him, also badly wounding his navigator. Lt Victor Crutchley, the first lieutenant, took control and continued the attempt to swing the ship around, but she had run aground and could not be moved. He ordered the crew to abandon ship and toured the ship to make sure that no one was left aboard, before setting the charges and following them into *ML254*. *Vindictive* blew up as *ML254* pulled away, and she settled, partially blocking the entrance.

Lt Drummond, in command of *ML254*, had been wounded as he followed the cruiser into the port, and his second in command had been killed. Despite this, he had taken off forty men, although some were killed and others wounded while aboard his craft. He remained conscious until they were heading back to Dover, when he collapsed and Crutchley took over from him. *ML254* was badly holed in the bows, and Crutchley had to organise a bucket party, while the rest of those aboard were told to stand in the stern to help raise the bows. Nevertheless, the frail craft survived to take her passengers to Keyes's flagship, the destroyer *Warwick*.

Lt Roland Bourke was in command of the other motor launch, *ML276*, intended to pick up survivors. The two launches actually collided as *ML254* was leaving the harbour and *ML276* was on her way in, but neither suffered serious damage. Bourke took his launch close to *Vindictive* to ensure that no one was left aboard, remaining for ten minutes under heavy fire. He was about to leave when he found three men in the water, including the cruiser's navigator, all badly

wounded, clinging to an upturned boat. He picked all three up and turned for the open sea, but *ML276* was then hit by a 6in shell, which caused severe damage and killed two of her ratings. All in all, she was hit fifty-five times. Bourke took her to a monitor, which took the launch in tow.

All three officers were gazetted on 28 August 1918.

Crutchley remained in the navy after the war, being promoted to lieutenant-commander in 1923, commander in 1928, and then captain in 1932. He also spent time on secondment in New Zealand and, later, Australia. He was in command of HMS *Warspite* at Narvik. Promoted rear admiral in 1942, he commanded the screening force at the Battle of Guadacanal, flying his flag aboard the cruiser HMAS *Australia*. He retired in 1947 and died in 1986 at Bridport.

Drummond worked in commerce between the wars but, although he volunteered for the RNVR in 1939, he was rejected because of his age. He joined the Thames River Service as a seaman, but died in April 1941, as a result of injuries suffered in an accident.

Bourke was promoted to lieutenant-commander, but left the service in 1920 and returned to his pre-war occupation, farming in British Columbia, until forced to retire, because of deteriorating eyesight, in 1931. He became a civil servant and joined the RCNVR during the Second World War. He died in August 1958 at Esquimault.

Lt Harold Auten RNR, English Channel, 30 July 1918, aboard Q ship *Stock Force*.

Lt Harold Auten was one of the longest-serving Q ship personnel, if not the longest. He had a number of different ships, but his VC was won when he commanded the *Stock Force*, a converted collier.

At around 1700 on 30 July 1918, in the English Channel some 25 miles south-west of Start Point, *Stock Force* was torpedoed forward by a U-boat, and was only saved by her 'cargo' of wood. Derricks were blown overboard and the front of the bridge disappeared, Auten being blown under the chart table. Unexploded 12pdr shells from the ship's ammunition store and debris rained down, and seawater thrown up by the explosion soaked everyone on deck. The ship started to settle by the bows. It seemed as if there was good cause to abandon ship, but only the panic party took to the boats. The U-boat eventually surfaced half a mile ahead, and her commander studied the target for the next fifteen minutes. The panic party started to row back in the hope that the U-boat would follow them, as it did, closing to 300yd on the Q ship's port beam. The covers fell away and both 12pdr guns came to bear on the U-boat, opening fire at 1740, the first shot destroying the periscope, and others blowing the conning tower and its occupants into the sea and blasting a hole in the hull. As further shots struck, her bows rose and she slid stern-first beneath the waves.

Stock Force sank at 2125 that night and went down with her white ensign flying. The crew were taken off by a torpedo boat.

Auten was promoted to lieutenant-commander while still in the RNR in 1925 – by which time he was working in the film industry – and commander in 1939. He want back to sea during the Second World War and was engaged in convoy escorts. He died in Pennsylvannia in 1964.

Cdr Daniel Marcus William Beak RNVR, Logeast Wood, France, August/September 1918, with the Royal Naval Division.
In August 1918, the massive Allied offensive against the Hindenberg Line began. Cdr Daniel Beak was in command of Drake Battalion of the Royal Naval Division. Unusually, his VC was not awarded for a single act of valour but for sustained courage over four days in August and, later, for ten days in September.

On 21 August, Beak led his battalion in an attack on Logeast Wood, near Bapaume, capturing four enemy positions under heavy machine-gun fire. Four days later, even though he was wounded with a shell fragment lodged in his skull, he organised the whole of the 63rd Brigade in the absence of its commander and led them under extremely heavy fire to their next objectives. When an attack was held up, he ran forward to lead it, succeeding in breaking up a nest of machine guns and personally bringing back ten prisoners.

Beak's VC was gazetted on 15 November 1918.

After the war, having been discharged from the service, Beak joined the army and became a captain in the Royal Scots Fusiliers. He went to India in 1932, and there he was promoted to major and served with another regiment. He changed again in 1938 when, as a lieutenant-colonel, he commanded the 1st Battalion, South Lancashire Regiment. He later rose to major-general, before retiring from the army in 1945. He died in Swindon in May 1967.

CPO George Prowse RNVR, Pronville, France, September 1918, with the Royal Naval Division.
CPO George Prowse was also serving in Drake Battalion of the Royal Naval Division as it advanced on the Hindenberg Line. Part of the company in which he served had become disorganised under heavy machine-gun fire from a German strongpoint. Prowse collected the men together and led them to take the strongpoint, capturing twenty-three prisoners and five machine guns. Later, he took a patrol forward despite heavy fire from the enemy and took high ground. He also attacked an artillery limber and killed the

three men with it before capturing the limber itself. He also covered the advance of his company with a Lewis gun section, and located two machine guns in a concrete emplacement which were holding up the advance of a battalion to his right, rushing forward with a small party and taking both posts.

Prowse's VC was gazetted on 30 October 1918, but he was already dead, having been killed in action on 27 September during the Battle of Cambrai. He knew that he had been recommended for the VC, as he mentioned this in a letter to his wife. This was the last Victoria Cross to be awarded with the blue ribbon.

APPENDIX IV

MEDALS AND DECORATIONS

Naval personnel were eligible for many of the medals and other awards also available to the army, but they also had their own, peculiar to the Royal Navy.

In both services, the full medal and ribbon were only worn on ceremonial occasions, and smaller versions were available to wear with mess kit. On ordinary uniforms, the everyday practice was to wear ribbons only.

In addition to medals, members of all three services were also eligible for the full range of honours, traditionally awarded on the King's birthday and at the New Year and, in theory, since there were no general elections until after the war in Europe ended, on the dissolution of Parliament. Several of these, including the Order of the Bath and the Order of the British Empire, had a military division, and holders would wear the ribbon of the order with their medal ribbons. Knighthoods were usually reserved for senior officers.

AWARDS FOR GALLANTRY

Victoria Cross: The highest award for the British armed services, open to all services and all ranks. For most of the period under review, the medal ribbon was dark blue for awards to naval personnel and crimson–maroon for members of the army, but the crimson–maroon ribbon was standardised for all services in 1918. Regardless of service, there is a bronze cross depicting a lion standing upon the royal crown, below which a semi-circular scroll carries the inscription 'For Valour' on the obverse, and the date of the act of valour on the reverse. The recipient's details were recorded on the reverse of the suspender clasp.

Albert Medal: Originally awarded for gallantry in saving life at sea, but was later extended to saving life on land as well, and in 1940 was largely replaced by the George Cross. During the period under review, it consisted of dark blue edges and a centre dark-blue strip with two broad white stripes in between. The medal itself was a bronze oval badge with, in the centre, a monogram with the letters 'V' and 'A' upon a dark-blue enamelled background, surrounded by a garter inscribed in raised letters 'For Gallantry in Saving Life at Sea'. The inscription was changed when life was saved on land, and the colours of the enamel and ribbon were crimson for such awards.

Distinguished Service Order: Normally awarded for outstanding command and leadership under fire and available only to officers, but also available to all three services. A red ribbon with dark-blue edges,

Distinguished Service Order (DSO)

Distinguished Flying Cross (DFC)

Distinguished Service Cross (DSC)

Conspicuous Gallantry Medal (CGM)

Distinguished Service Medal (DSM)

Distinguished Flying Medal (DFM)

Distinguished
Conduct Medal
(DCM)

and a gold or silver gilt white enamelled cross with curved arms. The monarch's crown within a laurel wreath is on the obverse, while the reverse has the royal cypher surmounted by a crown. The year of award appears on the reverse of the suspender clasp.

Distinguished Service Cross: Available to RN, Merchant Navy and RAF officers serving with the fleet, for 'meritorious or distinguished services in action'. The ribbon had equal widths of dark blue, white and dark blue, and a silver cross with curved arms. The obverse shows the monarch's cypher surmounted by a royal crown within a circle, while the reverse shows the year of award in the lower arm of the cross.

Distinguished Flying Cross: Instituted on 3 June 1918 for commissioned officers and warrant officers of the newly formed Royal Air Force. The ribbon has violet and white diagonal stripes with a silver cross 'flory', into which feathered wings, an aeroplane propeller and bombs are incorporated on the obverse, with the entwined cypher 'RAF' in the centre. The reverse bears the royal cypher, and the year of award is engraved on the lower arm.

Distinguished Conduct Medal: Available to personnel of the rank of warrant officer and below in all services for 'distinguished conduct in the field', which is stamped on the reverse side. The ribbon has equal widths of crimson, dark blue and crimson, while the round silver medal carries King George V's head.

Conspicuous Gallantry Medal: For Royal Navy and Royal Marines personnel of warrant officer rank and below who 'distinguish themselves by acts of conspicuous gallantry in action with the enemy'. The ribbon was white with narrow blue edges with a round silver medal with the King's head and title on the obverse, and on the reverse, 'For Conspicuous Gallantry' surrounded by a wreath of two laurel branches, surmounted by a crown.

Distinguished Service Medal: For Royal Navy and Royal Marines personnel of warrant officer rank and below who 'show themselves to the fore in action and set an example of bravery and resource under fire'. The ribbon was dark blue with two white central stripes, while the round silver medal showed King George's head on the obverse, and the reverse was similar to the style of the CGM above, but with the words 'For Distinguished Service'.

Distinguished Flying Medal: Also new in 1918, this award was for Royal Navy and Royal Marines personnel of warrant officer rank and below who showed 'valour, courage or devotion to duty performed while flying in active operations against the enemy'. The ribbon had narrow violet and white diagonal stripes, with a silver oval medal carrying King George's head on the obverse, while the reverse showed Athena Nike seated upon an aeroplane with a hawk rising from her hand, and below this the words 'For Courage', as well as the date '1918'.

Mention in Despatches Emblem: Available to all ranks and all services for those mentioned in despatches, but not receiving a higher award. For the Second World War, a bronze oakleaf emblem was worn on the War Medal ribbon at an angle of 60 degrees from the inside edge of the ribbon, or as a smaller emblem worn horizontally when only the medal ribbon was worn.

COMPARISON OF RANKS: ROYAL NAVY AND ARMY

OFFICERS

RN*	Army
Admiral of the Fleet	Field Marshal
Admiral	General
Vice-Admiral	Lieutenant General
Rear Admiral	Major General
Commodore 2nd Class	Brigadier
Captain	Colonel
Commander	Lieutenant-Colonel
Lieutenant-Commander	Major
Lieutenant	Captain
Sub-Lieutenant	First Lieutenant
Temporary Sub-Lieutenant	Second Lieutenant
Midshipman	no equivalent
Warrant Officer	no equivalent
no equivalent	Sergeant Major (RSM and CSM)

* In the Royal Naval Air Service, although the insignia remained the same with the addition of an eagle above the curl (in contrast to the wings for pilots and observers introduced between the wars), the ranks also carried slightly different titles, as follows:

RN	RNAS
Captain	Wing Captain
Commander	Wing Commander
Lieutenant-Commander	Squadron Commander
Lieutenant	Flight Lieutenant
Sub-Lieutenant	Flying Sub-Lieutenant

RATINGS (RN) AND NON-COMMISSIONED RANKS

RN	Army
Chief Petty Officer	Colour Sergeant
Petty Officer	Sergeant
Leading Seaman (Leading Hand)	Corporal
AB – Able Seaman	no equivalent
Ordinary Seaman	Private

RM ranks were similar to those of the Army, but with a senior rank of Commandant General. (*Source:* Imperial War Museum)

APPENDIX VI

MUSEUMS: PORTSMOUTH, GOSPORT, YEOVILTON, CHATHAM

While both the Imperial War Museum and the National Maritime Museum have collections and exhibits relating to the Royal Navy and war at sea, there is no substitute for the museums that are directly linked with the history of the Royal Navy. The Royal Naval Museum at Portsmouth is a 'cover all' museum for the Royal Navy, and also has HMS *Victory* and *Warrior* to give visitors a feel for life aboard a warship in the past. However, those with specialised interests will be better served by visits to the Fleet Air Arm Museum at Yeovilton or the Submarine Museum at Gosport, and for an idea of a working dockyard of the past, a visit to Chatham is a must.

PORTSMOUTH

One of Britain's oldest maritime museums, dating to the founding of a Dockyard Museum in 1911, the Royal Naval Museum is in Portsmouth's Dockyard. It has permanent exhibitions open to the public as well as being home to Nelson's flagship *Victory* and HMS *Warrior*. Visitors can buy tickets to the museum itself or either of the two ships, or the *Mary Rose*, whose salvaged remains are on show. Alternatively, there is a comprehensive ticket that allows visitors

to return over a twelve-month period, so that they can take each of these features in turn – there is a great deal to see in just one day! For further information, visit www.royalnavalmuseum.org.

GOSPORT

Gosport, on the other side of Portsmouth Harbour, hosts the Royal Naval Submarine Museum. In addition to the displays, it is also home to preserved submarines, including HMS *Alliance, Holland 1*, the Royal Navy's first submarine, and a midget submarine. For up-to-date information, visit www.rnsubmus.co.uk.

YEOVILTON

Home to the Fleet Air Arm Museum, which was founded in 1964, Yeovilton has grown from its original collection of just six aircraft to more than forty, representing one of the largest collections devoted to naval aviation in the world, including both world wars and with many of the displays devoted to the Royal Naval Air Service. In addition to the aircraft, a wide range of displays deals with every aspect of naval air power, and includes one on the history of

V/STOL, so vital to modern naval aviation, and there are around 250 models of aircraft and ships.

The museum is based near Ilchester in Somerset, on the B3151, just off the A303, and is situated on land that was part of RNAS Yeovilton. Because the museum is constantly adding to its collection of restored aircraft and displays, and has some on loan to other collections, up-to-date information on the current collection is best found by accessing the museum's website, www.fleetairarm.com.

CHATHAM

Claimed to be the 'most complete dockyard of the age of sail to survive in the world', the former Royal Dockyard at Chatham covers some 80 acres, and has about a hundred buildings and structures. In use as a Royal Dockyard from 1613 to 1984, it is the location of other historic sites, including its defences at the Chatham Lines and Upnor Castle, and HMS *Pembroke*, the Edwardian naval barracks, as well as the Georgian military barracks at Brompton. For up-to-date information, visit www.chdt.org.uk.

CHRONOLOGY

The term 'total war' was an accurate description of the situation faced by the Royal Navy throughout the war years. The importance of maintaining shipping links for the British forces fighting in France, the threat posed by German surface raids not only against merchant shipping but also against coastal towns ranging from Yarmouth to Sunderland, the lurking menace of the German High Seas Fleet, and the feeling of insecurity posed by the port at Rosyth and the anchorage at Scapa Flow all contributed to a high state of alert and much sea time. This was in addition to such enterprises as the Gallipoli campaign and the belated need to convoy merchant shipping in the Atlantic.

1914

1 July: RNAS formed from the Naval Wing, Royal Flying Corps.

4 August: At 0830, Adm Sir John Jellicoe relieves Adm Sir George Callaghan as commander-in-chief of the Grand Fleet at Scapa Flow.

4 August: At 2300, British ultimatum expires, and the United Kingdom and Germany are at war.

The German battlecruiser *Goeben* and light cruiser *Breslau* bombard the harbours of Bone and Philippeville in the French colony of Algeria, before evading the British Mediterranean Fleet and entering the Dardanelles, later transferring to the Turkish navy. On 5 August, the light cruiser *Gloucester* was the first to use wireless interception to detect *Goeben* in Messina.

25 August: Royal Marines land at Ostend, but have to be withdrawn on 31 August.

27 August: First RNAS squadron arrives at Ostend.

28 August: Battle of the Heligoland Bight. Rear Adm Beatty, with his squadron of five battlecruisers supported by light cruisers and a number of destroyers, encounters a German light cruiser squadron and, despite heavy damage to one British cruiser, *Arethusa*, sinks three German light cruisers before the German battlecruisers can intervene.

30 August: Occupation of German colony of Samoa supported by Australian, New Zealand and French warships.

4 September: With naval support, British forces take Dar-es-Salaam.

5 September: *U-21* makes the first successful submarine attack, sinking the light cruiser *Pathfinder* off St Abb's Head.

19 September: Royal Marines land at Dunkirk.

20 September: German cruiser *Königsberg* sinks HMS *Pegasus* in the harbour at Zanzibar.

22 September: *U-9* sinks the British armoured cruisers *Aboukir*, *Cressy* and *Hogue* off the Belgian coast in less than one hour.

27 September: Capture of Duala, Cameroons, supported by five naval vessels.

3 October: First units of the Royal Naval Division arrive at Antwerp.

8 October: RNAS Sopwith Tabloid makes the first destruction of a Zeppelin, *LZ-25*, in her shed at Dusseldorf.

9 October: RNVR AA Corps established to provide air defence, initially of London.

27 October: Dreadnought HMS *Audacious* strikes a mine off Londonderry and sinks. Many of her crew are taken off by lifeboats from the liner *Olympic*.

30 October: AF Lord Fisher of Kilverstone, First Sea Lord 1906–10, recalled to the Admiralty by the First Lord, Winston Churchill.

1 November: Battle of Coronel, in which two elderly British armoured cruisers, *Good Hope* and *Monmouth*, are sunk by two modern German armoured cruisers, *Scharnhorst* and *Gneisenau*.

3 November: First naval bombardment of the Dardanelles by the British and French fleets.

German battlecruisers bombard Great Yarmouth and Gorleston.

9 November: HMAS *Sydney* finds the commerce raider *Emden* in the Cocos Islands and sinks her.

21 November: Three RNAS Avro 504s attack Zeppelin sheds at Friedrichshafen.

24 November: British forces take Basra, supported by British and Indian warships.

26 November: Pre-dreadnought *Bulwark* destroyed by ammunition explosion at Sheerness, killing 746 men from her ship's company of 758.

8 December: Battle of the Falkland Islands. Expecting to find the islands undefended, *Scharnhorst* and *Gneisenau* attack, but the naval force has been reinforced by two battlecruisers, *Invincible* and *Inflexible*, which give chase and sink both German armoured cruisers and two of the three light cruisers.

9 December: Seaplane carrier *Ark Royal* commissioned.

16 December: Hartlepool, Scarborough and Whitby bombarded by German battlecruisers.

21 December: First night bombing raid on Ostend by Wg Cdr Charles Rumney Samson.

25 December: Seven seaplanes flown off from the seaplane carriers *Engadine*, *Riviera* and *Express* to attack the German airship sheds at Cuxhaven in the first bombing raids by shipborne aircraft.

1915

1 January: *U-24* sinks the pre-dreadnought HMS *Formidable* in the English Channel.

Engineer officers allowed to wear the executive curl, but retain purple cloth.

2 January: Bombardment of Dar-es-Salaam by pre-dreadnought battleship *Goliath* and cruiser *Fox*.

4 January: Start of relief operation for Kut-el-Amara in Mesopotamia.

12 January: Capture of Mafia Island, German East Africa.

14 January: German destroyers raid Great Yarmouth.

15 January: RNAS aircraft attack U-boat alongside the mole at Zeebrugge.

23 January: Royal Marines occupy Lemnos.

24 January: Battle of Dogger Bank between opposing battlecruiser forces when Beatty is able to surprise a German raid against trawlers. As the Germans try to escape, the British manage to sink the German armoured cruiser *Blücher* and seriously damage the battlecruiser *Seydlitz*, with damage to other German ships; but the remaining German ships are allowed to escape after the flagship *Lion* is badly damaged and the chain of command falters.

3 February: British, French and Indian ships repulse a Turkish attack on the Suez Canal.

4 February: Drifter *Tarlair* fitted with prototype anti-submarine hydrophones.

16 February: Sloop *Cadmus* lands naval shore party to help contain Indian Army mutiny.

18 February: Germany declares British territorial waters to be an unrestricted war zone. U-boat campaign starts.

19 February: Anglo-French bombardment of the outer forts of the Dardanelles begun.

25 February: Bombardment of Dardanelles forts resumed.

5 March: Bombardment of the Smyrna forts starts, involving three warships, the French seaplane tender *Anne Rickmers* and five minesweepers, one of which was sunk.

7 March: *Winifred* and *Kavirondo* force the German *Mwanza* ashore at the southern end of Lake Victoria.

14 March: *Dresden*, the only German survivor of the Battle of the Falkland Islands, is attacked by the armoured cruiser HMS *Cornwall* and light cruiser *Glasgow* off Chile, and sunk.

15 March: German aircraft attack merchantman *Blonde*, the first to be attacked from the air.

18 March: British and French naval forces enter the Dardanelles after heavy bombardment of the lower forts. One French ship hits a mine and explodes, while HMS *Inflexible* is badly damaged by a mine. The pre-dreadnought battleships *Irresistible* and *Ocean* are sunk by mines, after which the operation is abandoned. First occasion on which two British battleships are lost on the same day.

6 April: False bow waves to be painted on all ships.

9 April: First American-built minelayers ordered.

25 April: Royal Navy provides support for landings by British and Australian troops on the Gallipoli peninsula.

13 May: Pre-dreadnought HMS *Goliath* sunk by Turkish torpedo boat.

17 May: First Sea Lord AF Lord Kilverstone ('Jacky' Fisher) walks out of Admiralty, aged 74.

24 May: Italy joins the war on the side of the Allies against Austria-Hungary.

25 May: *U-21* sinks the pre-dreadnought *Triumph* off Gallipoli.

27 May: *U-21* sinks the pre-dreadnought *Majestic*.

28 May: Adm Sir Henry Jackson succeeds Fisher as First Sea Lord.

June: U-boat campaign spreads to Mediterranean using bases in the Adriatic.

4 June: British forces take Kut-el-Amara in Mesopotamia, aided by thirteen RN and Royal Indian Marine vessels.

23 June: Submarine *C24* being towed submerged by trawler *Taranaki* sinks *U-40*, the first U-boat to be sunk by a decoy ship.

11 July: Two British monitors *Severn* and *Mersey* attack and sink *Königsberg* in the Rufiji river.

1 August: British submarine *E11* raids Constantinople harbour.

6 August: Start of landings at Suvla Bay.

8 August: *E21* penetrates the Dardanelles and sinks the Turkish battleship *Hairedin Barbarossa*.

12 August: Short 184 seaplane from the seaplane carrier *Ben-my-Chree* makes the first successful aerial torpedo attack against a Turkish cargo ship, previously damaged by a submarine, and sinks her in the Dardanelles.

18 September: U-boat campaign in Atlantic suspended, following protests by the United States over the sinking of British ships carrying US nationals, but campaign in the Mediterranean continues.

13 December: First periscope photograph of Constantinople from *E11*.

18 December: Wg Cdr Charles Rumney Samson drops first 500lb bomb on Turkish forces.

19 December: Start of evacuation from Gallipoli.

23 December: Naval operations start on Lake Tanganyika.

26 December: *Mimi* and *Toutou* capture German *Kingani* on Lake Tanganyika.

1916

6 January: Pre-dreadnought battleship *King Edward VII* strikes a mine and sinks west of Cape Wrath.

9 January: British withdrawal from Gallipoli completed.

8 February: British government seeks naval assistance from Japan, resulting in two Japanese destroyer flotillas arriving in the Mediterranean in April.

9 February: Lake steamers *Mimi* and *Toutou* (formerly German *Kingani*) sink German *Hedwig von Wissman* on Lake Tanganyika.

16 February: War Office takes over control of anti-aircraft defences from the Admiralty.

18 February: Conquest of the Cameroons completed.

23 February: Resumption of unlimited U-boat campaign in British waters.

7 March: Second attempt to relieve Kut-el-Amara in Mesopotamia.
  E24, the first British minelaying submarine, lays her first mines in the mouth of the River Elbe.

17 March: Depot ship (ex-cruiser) *Crescent* becomes the first ship to enter the basin at Rosyth.

25 March: Five seaplanes sent from seaplane carrier *Vindex* in unsuccessful attempt to bomb airship shed at Hoyer on the coast of Schleswig-Holstein, but three come down in German territory and their crews are captured.

25 March: HMS *Cleopatra* rams German destroyer *G-194*, cutting her in half.

28 March: Battleship *Zealandia* (formerly *New Zealand*) is first ship to enter dry dock at Rosyth.

1 April: East coast towns attacked by German Zeppelin airships, while *L-15* becomes the first Zeppelin to be brought down by AA fire, landing in the Thames estuary and surrendering to a British warship.

5 April: Final attempt to relieve Kut-el-Amara, using seven river gunboats, ends in failure.

22 April: Grand Fleet makes thrust towards Skagerrak in an attempt to bring High Seas Fleet to battle, but two battlecruisers collide in fog, a battleship collides with a merchantman and, after dark, three destroyers collide.

23 April: German battlecruisers bombard Lowestoft and Yarmouth.

24 April: U-boat campaign again suspended following further US protests.
E22 conducts 'float-off' trials with two Sopwith Schneider seaplanes to see if these can intercept Zeppelins over the North Sea before they can reach the east coast.

24/25 April: German battlecruisers bombard Lowestoft and Great Yarmouth, while the High Seas Fleet is at sea to intervene if British battlecruisers appear.

27 April: Pre-dreadnought battleship HMS *Russell* hits a mine off Malta and sinks.

29 April: Surrender from starvation of British troops at Kut-el-Amara, allowing the armed tug *Samana* also to be captured.

May: *E14* sinks Turkish *Nour-el-Bahr* in Sea of Marmara.

1 May: U-boat campaign extended to western Atlantic.

4 May: Zeppelin *L-7* brought down by light cruisers *Galatea* and *Phaeton* south of the Horn Reefs. *E31* rescues seven survivors and destroys *L-7*.

31 May: Battle of Jutland, with the first use of aerial reconnaissance, by a seaplane flown off the seaplane carrier *Engadine*. British force heavily outnumbers and outguns the Germans, but battle is plagued by poor visibility and poor communications between British scouting forces and the Grand Fleet, while the Admiralty does not pass on information from intercepted signals traffic. In a fast-moving battle, Beatty loses the battlecruisers *Indefatigable*, *Queen Mary* and *Invincible*, and the armoured cruisers *Defence*, *Warrior* and *Black Prince,* plus another five smaller warships (a total of 155,000 tons), and other warships are damaged. The Germans lose eleven warships (a total of 61,000 tons) before managing to regain the safety of their harbours. The Royal Navy lost 6,090 men against 2,550 for the Germans.

5 June: Armoured cruiser *Hampshire* sunk by mine off Orkney, with 643 men lost, including the Secretary of State for War, Lord Kitchener.

17 June: Zeppelin *L-48* shot down, and German naval signal book found in wreckage.

26 July: Turkish destroyer *Yadighiar-i-Milet* damaged by bombing by RNAS aircraft in eastern Mediterranean.

9 August: Submarine *B10* sunk by Austrian aircraft while being repaired at Venice – the first submarine sunk by enemy aircraft.

18/19 August: Scheer takes the High Seas Fleet to sea again, preceded by a reconnaissance force of eight Zeppelins. Submarine *E23* torpedoes the German battleship *Westfalen* 60 miles north of Terschelling, forcing her to return to port. Confusion caused by Zeppelin commander mistaking Harwich light cruisers and destroyers for the Grand Fleet leads Scheer south, away from Jellicoe, who returns to base, losing the light cruiser *Falmouth* as the Grand Fleet crosses the German U-boat line. Tyrwhitt, heading the Harwich flotilla, sees the High Seas Fleet but is unable to attack.

24 September: Zeppelin *L-32* shot down and new German naval signal book salvaged from the wreckage.

26 October: Second German raid on Lowestoft.

26/27 October: German destroyer raid in Straits of Dover, with seven vessels sunk, mainly drifters handling the barrage.

1917

9 January: *U-32* sinks the pre-dreadnought HMS *Cornwallis* 62 miles off Malta.

11 January: Seaplane carrier *Ben-my-Chree* sunk off Kastelorizo by fire from Turkish batteries.

23/24 January: Ships of the Harwich destroyer flotillas engaged with German 6th Destroyer Flotilla off the Schouwen light vessel. Each side loses one ship.

25 January: German destroyers attack Southwold, Suffolk.

29 January: *K13* steam-powered submarine founders during trials in the Gare Loch.

24 February: Reoccupation of Kut-el-Amara, aided by river gunboats.

25 February: German destroyers raid Margate and Westgate.

11 March: British forces reach Baghdad.

16 March: First cutting of a moored mine using a paravane by the minesweeper *Cambria*.

17 March: German destroyers raid Dover Straits, torpedoing one British ship and sinking another.

18 March: German destroyer raid on Ramsgate and Broadstairs.

6 April: United States declares war on Germany.

27 April: German destroyers raid Ramsgate.

4 May: First USN destroyers arrive at Queenstown, Ireland, for convoy escort duties.

10 May: Experimental convoy sails from Gibraltar to the UK.

15 May: Action in the Straits of Otranto when an Allied blockading force is attacked by an Austrian squadron of three light cruisers and two destroyers, which sinks fourteen armed trawlers, a destroyer and two merchantmen before turning back.

17 May: Additional USN destroyers arrive at Queenstown.

20 May: *UB-32* sunk by RNAS Curtiss H12 Large America flying boat in English Channel close to Sunk light vessel, the first U-boat to be sunk by an aeroplane.

24 May: Experimental convoy sails from Newport News to the UK with an armoured cruiser as an escort.

29 May: First air-sea rescue by RNAS flying boat.

30 May: Dummy of HMS *Tiger* sunk by *UB-8* in Aegean.

6 June: First experiments with ASDIC at Harwich.
   Sheerness and nearby naval establishments attacked by German aircraft.

7 June: Flt Sub Lt Reginald Warneford wins the first RNAS VC for shooting down a Zeppelin, *LZ-37*, near Ghent. YES, BUT 1915!

RNAS aircraft destroy *LZ-38* in her shed at Evere, Belgium.

14 June: Convoys receive Admiralty approval and support.

22 June: RNAS observer officers to wear wings instead of the eagle on their sleeves.

2 July: First regular convoy sails from Hampton Roads for UK.

9 July: RNAS aircraft from Mudros bomb *Sultan Selim* and *Midilli* in Constantinople.

Battleship *Vanguard* suffers a magazine explosion at Scapa Flow and sinks, taking the lives of 804 men.

2 August: Sqn Cdr E.H. Dunning makes the first deck-landing on a ship under way, landing aboard *Furious* in a Sopwith Pup. He was drowned in a later attempt when his aircraft went over the side.

21 August: Sopwith Pup landplane flies off cruiser to destroy Zeppelin *L-23* off the Danish coast – the first time this has been achieved.

1 October: Sqn Cdr Rutland makes the first flight from a platform on top of a gun turret in a Sopwith Pup, using B turret aboard the battlecruiser *Repulse*.

2 October: Armoured cruiser *Drake* torpedoed by *U-79* in the North Channel between Ireland and Scotland, and later sinks off Rathlin Island.

17 October: German light cruisers *Brummer* and *Bremse* attack a British convoy running from Bergen, sinking both escorting destroyers and nine of the twelve merchantmen.

17 November: Action off Heligoland Bight after German battleships and light cruisers are deployed to safeguard minesweeping forces, but surprised by British battlecruisers *Courageous*, *Glorious* and *Repulse*. In bad weather, the initial exchange of fire between the British battlecruisers and German light cruisers is inconclusive and the German ships escape in poor visibility as two battleships appear to provide cover.

23 November: Dame Katherine Furse appointed first Director of the WRNS.

26 November: WRNS officially formed.

7 December: Five USN battleships arrive at Scapa Flow to form 6th Battle Squadron, Grand Fleet.

1918

20 January: Turkish battlecruiser *Yavuz Sultan Selim* (ex-*Goeben*) and light cruiser *Midilli* (ex-*Breslau*) enter the Aegean and sink two British monitors. On their return, the *Midilli* strikes a mine and sinks, while the *Yavuz Sultan Selim* runs aground. Despite repeated British aerial attacks, she is refloated on 25 January and returns safely to base.

31 January: Three submarines lost on one day. *E50* mined and lost in the North Sea. *K4* and *K17* both lost in a major fleet exercise off the Isle of May in the Firth of Forth, with the loss of 103 lives.

15 February: German destroyers raid the Folkestone–Gris Nez barrage.

15 March: *Furious* recommissioned with landing-on deck and the first aircraft lifts.

21 March: Destroyer action off Dunkirk, with eleven British ships and four French engaging eighteen German, of which two are sunk.

1 April: Royal Air Force founded, absorbing 55,000 RNAS personnel and 2,500 aircraft.

3 April: Seven British submarines destroyed at Helsingfors (now Helsinki) to avoid capture.

4 April: First successful launch of a two-seat reconnaissance aircraft from a ship when a Sopwith 1½-Strutter flies off a platform on a forward gun turret of HMAS *Australia*.

12 April: Grand Fleet moved from Scapa Flow to Rosyth.

23 April: Attacks on Zeebrugge and Ostend, to close entrances to U-boat and torpedo-boat bases using blockships, enjoy partial success but the entrances are soon reopened.

19 July: Aerial attack on the airship sheds at Tondern with seven aircraft flying from the aircraft carrier *Furious* succeeds in destroying *L-54* and *L-60*. This is the first successful attack by landplanes flying from an aircraft carrier.

8 August: First magnetic mines laid by the Royal Navy off Dunkirk.

14 September: First flush-deck carrier *Argus* commissioned.

1 October: Allied net barrage across Otranto Strait completed.

21 October: U-boats cease commerce raiding.

5 November: Seaplane carrier *Campania* sinks after collision with *Royal Oak* and battlecruiser *Glorious* in Firth of Forth.

8 November: Executive ranks for paymasters, instructors and surgeons, preceded by branch, as in 'surgeon lieutenant'.

9 November
U-50 sinks pre-dreadnought *Britannia* off Cape Trafalgar.

11 November: Armistice ends First World War. Most modern German warships and all U-boats ordered to Scapa Flow, but these are scuttled on 21 June 1919.

BIBLIOGRAPHY

(Published in London unless otherwise stated.)

Akermann, Paul, *Encyclopaedia of British Submarines 1901–1955*, privately published, 1990.

Bell, A.C., *A History of the Blockade of Germany 1914–1918*, HMSO, 1961.

Chesneau, Roger, *Aircraft Carriers of the World, 1914 to the Present*, Arms & Armour, 1992.

Fletcher, Commandant M.H., WRNS, *The WRNS – A History of the Women's Royal Naval Service*, Batsford, 1989.

Gardiner, Robert (ed.), *Conway's All The World's Fighting Ships, 1906–1921*, Conway Maritime Press, 1985.

Hobbs, David, *Aircraft Carriers of the Royal and Commonwealth Navies*, Greenhill, 1996.

Hough, Richard, *The Great War at Sea 1914–1918*, Birlinn, Edinburgh, 2000.

Howarth, Stephen, *The Royal Navy's Reserves in War and Peace 1903–2003*, Pen & Sword/Leo Cooper, Barnsley, 2003.

Jarrett, Dudley, *British Naval Dress*, Dent, 1960.

Keegan, John, *The Price of Admiralty*, Hutchinson, 1988.

King, Brad, *Royal Naval Air Service 1912–1918*, Hikoki, Aldershot, 1997.

Le Fleming, H.M., *Warships of World War I*, Ian Allan, 1970.

Mowthorpe, Ces, *Battlebags*, Sutton, Stroud, 1995.

Preston, Antony, *Aircraft Carriers*, Bison, 1979.

——, *Destroyers*, Hamlyn, 1977.

——, *The History of the Royal Navy in the 20th Century*, Bison, 1987.

Roskill, S.W., *The Naval Air Service*, Vol. 1: 1908–1918, Navy Records Society, Bromley, 1969.

Sainsbury, A.B. and Phillips, F.L., *The Royal Navy Day by Day*, Sutton, Stroud, 2005.

Snelling, Stephen, *VCs of the First World War – The Naval VCs*, Sutton, Stroud, 2002.

Sturtevant, Ray and Page, Gordon, *British Naval Aviation: The Fleet Air Arm, 1917–1990*, Arms & Armour, 1990.

——, *Royal Navy Aircraft Serials and Units 1911–1919*, Air-Britain, Tonbridge, 1992.

Till, Geoffrey, *Air Power and the Royal Navy 1914–1945*, Jane's, 1979.

Thomas, David A., *Battles and Honours of the Royal Navy*, Leo Cooper, Barnsley, 1998.

Thompson, Julian, *The War at Sea 1914–1918*, Sidgwick & Jackson, 2005.

Van der Vat, Dan, *Standard of Power – The Royal Navy in the Twentieth Century*, Hutchinson, 2000.

Wells, John, *The Royal Navy – An Illustrated Social History 1870–1982*, Sutton, Stroud, 1994.

Winton, John, *The Victoria Cross at Sea*, Michael Joseph, 1978.

Wragg, David, *Carrier Combat*, Sutton, Stroud, 1997.

——, *Wings Over the Sea: A History of Naval Aviation*, David & Charles, Newton Abbot and London, 1979.

INDEX

Warship names are only given when these appear in the narrative, rather than duplicating the extensive list of vessels given in Chapter 14. Similarly, Royal Naval Air Service squadrons and naval air stations are dealt with in Chapter 16, with a brief summary of their aircraft and operations. To save space and avoid duplication, details of operations are given in the battle and campaign awards in Appendix II, with additional information in Appendix III on Victoria Cross awards.

Italic numbers denote illustrations.